THE
SADLER'S WELLS BALLET

A History and an Appreciation

A DA CAPO PRESS REPRINT SERIES

The Lyric Stage

GENERAL EDITOR: DALE HARRIS
SARAH LAWRENCE COLLEGE

THE
SADLER'S WELLS BALLET

A History and an Appreciation

by

M A R Y   C L A R K E

WITH FIFTY-FIVE ILLUSTRATIONS

With a new Foreword by the author

DA CAPO PRESS • NEW YORK • 1977

Library of Congress Cataloging in Publication Data

Clarke, Mary, 1923-
  The Sadler's Wells Ballet.

  (The Lyric stage)
  Reprint of the 1955 ed. published by A. and C.
Black, London.
  1. Royal Ballet. I. Title.
GV1786.R6C47 1977 792.8'0941   77-563
ISBN 0-306-70863-9

Published by Da Capo Press, Inc.
A Subsidiary of Plenum Publishing Corporation
227 West 17th Street, New York, N. Y. 10011

FOREWORD TO THE 1977 EDITION

My English publishers, Adam and Charles Black, who originally commissioned this book, have tried several times to persuade me to revise and update it. Pressure of other work at first delayed me but as the years passed I came to believe the task was impossible. So much has happened in the history of our national ballet since 1955 that the additions would have been twice the length of the existing text. Better to let it remain as it is — a period piece.

The story of the growth of the Sadler's Wells Ballet is correct and I would not change my assessment of the characters and the importance of the architects. Only the chapter entitled "The Organisation" is badly out of date and must be read in context.

The granting of a Royal Charter on 31 October 1956 resulted in the change of name to the Royal Ballet and of course the Royal Ballet School. There has been a remarkable and consistent rise in the standards of dancing during the past twenty years and a steady infusion of new choreography, all of it foreseen by the company's founder, the great woman Dame Ninette de Valois.

Dame Ninette has retired, her successor Sir Frederick Ashton CH has retired, but the company under its present director Kenneth MacMillan remains true to the ideals she formulated so many years ago.

Mary Clarke

November, 1976

THE SADLER'S WELLS BALLET

A History and an Appreciation

Jitendra Arya

DAME NINETTE DE VALOIS, D.B.E.

THE
SADLER'S WELLS BALLET

A History and an Appreciation

by

MARY CLARKE

WITH FIFTY-FIVE ILLUSTRATIONS

ADAM AND CHARLES BLACK
LONDON

FIRST PUBLISHED 1955

A. & C. BLACK LIMITED
4, 5 & 6 SOHO SQUARE, LONDON, W.I

MADE AND PRINTED IN GREAT BRITAIN BY
MORRISON AND GIBB LIMITED, LONDON AND EDINBURGH

FOREWORD

THE scope of this book is described in its title. I have attempted to trace the growth and development of the Sadler's Wells Ballet, to assess its achievements and pay tribute to the people who have been responsible for establishing so soundly a British school of ballet. I have used in the sub-title the word "appreciation" because we sometimes forget, when we grumble about a performance, that in continuity, steadfastness of aim and quality of performance the Sadler's Wells Ballet has contributed more than any other company to the pleasure of the London ballet-going public. "Abroad we are a novelty, at home we are a habit," said Ninette de Valois once in a curtain speech. This book is the result of an attempt not to take the Sadler's Wells organisation for granted but to discover what we owe to it and what we may expect from it in the future.

I should perhaps emphasise that the book is primarily concerned with the Sadler's Wells Ballet. The activities of the Sadler's Wells Theatre Ballet are briefly recorded in Appendix B, but no list of this company's productions is given. A detailed one exists in *The Ballet Annual No. 9*, and the company may, in any case, one day deserve a book to itself.

I have received help and advice from many busy people who have spared precious time to answer questions and untangle problems. To all of them I am grateful, but I must take responsibility myself for opinions expressed and conclusions reached.

Dame Ninette de Valois has been unfailingly kind and patient, and never once said to me that there were far too many books about ballet already. Mr. Philip Richardson placed the complete file of *The Dancing Times* at my disposal and thus provided me with my most valuable source material. Mr. Arnold Haskell has offered suggestions and encouragement throughout and Miss Sheila McCarthy (Mrs. Arthur Picton) gave up an entire week-end to talking about the early years of the company. Miss Evelyn Williams talked endearingly about Lilian Baylis. Miss Margot Fonteyn gave me permission to quote from an unpublished letter and Mr. Michael Ayrton allowed me to quote from an unpublished essay he had written on Constant Lambert. Dr. Geoffrey Keynes lent me much interesting material about *Job*, including the original designs and figures made for a toy theatre. Miss Celia Sparger devoted much time to explaining to me one of the most fascinating jobs in the entire organisation, that of physiotherapist at the Sadler's Wells School.

My principal sources are listed in the form of a bibliography. I must acknowledge, however, a special debt to Miss P. W. Manchester's book, *Vic-Wells: A Ballet Progress*, the first detailed account of the company to be published. (I was continually frustrated in my search for information about the earliest performances by the response, "But everything I can remember is in Bill Manchester's book.") In addition, Miss Manchester generously read the manuscript of the present volume and offered much advice.

Many other people have provided information or lent material. Mr. Cyril Beaumont allowed me to consult the Ballet Diaries of the late Lionel Bradley, which are now in the collection of the London Archives of the Dance, and the officials of the Vic-Wells Association placed their valuable collection at my service. Miss Beatrice Appleyard, Mr. Alan Carter, Mr. Anatole Chujoy, Mr. Ivor Guest, Mr. Gordon Hamilton, Miss Molly Lake, Miss Joan Lawson, Mrs. Janet Leeper, Miss Sylvia Lockwood, Mr. W. Beaumont Morris, Canon C. B. Mortlock, Miss Trude Michel, Mr. Peter Revitt, Miss Peggy van Praagh, Mr. Franklin White, Mr. G. B. L. Wilson and Mr. Michael Wood have all given me assistance, and Miss Joan Kelley undertook the formidable task of compiling the Index. Finally, I must thank my publishers, A. & C. Black, whose encouragement has been equalled only by their patience.

M. C.

London,
April 1955.

CONTENTS

PART I

A NATIONAL BALLET

PART II

THE CHRYSALIS YEARS

PART III

THE YEARS IN ISLINGTON

PART IV
THE WAR YEARS

PART V
THE ROYAL OPERA HOUSE, COVENT GARDEN

ILLUSTRATIONS

PART I

A NATIONAL BALLET

CHAPTER I

THE ARCHITECTS

A⊤ the beginning of 1931, when the new theatre of Sadler's Wells in Islington was opened, a small group of dancers appeared on the programmes and was described as "The Vic-Sadler's Wells Opera Ballet." The company consisted of six girls and their teacher, who was also ballerina and director of the company, and called herself Ninette de Valois.

To-day the company is known as the Sadler's Wells Ballet. It dances at the Royal Opera House, Covent Garden, for the greater part of the year as a national company and is large enough to require its own train, "the Ballet Special," when it tours the United States. There is a soundly established sister company at Sadler's Wells Theatre and a fully educational and partly residential school doing invaluable work in the background.

All this has been accomplished within the short space of some twenty-five years, and has been accomplished so completely that few people now stop to wonder how it all came about. Why was it that this company prospered and progressed so steadily for a quarter of a century while other troupes, which began with far greater artistic and financial resources, languished, divided or disintegrated? What was the secret? What was the magic formula?

The answer is simple but unromantic. Luck has played a part and general circumstances have sometimes favoured the company, but the only secret formula of success is that throughout its twenty-five years the Sadler's Wells Ballet has been run well in every department by people who understood their job, were patiently willing to work for the future as much as for the present, and were selflessly devoted to the work they had undertaken.

The loyal and gifted team has throughout been directed by a woman of genius who knew in the beginning what the ultimate goal must be and, even more important, knew how to get there. She was helped in particular by two colleagues, Constant Lambert and Frederick Ashton, who must rank with her as architects of the

3

Sadler's Wells Ballet, but none of their plans could have succeeded without the loyal support of the dancers and theatre staff who remained steadfastly with the company, several of them for the greater part of the twenty-five years. Ursula Moreton, Ailne Phillips, Joy Newton, Harold Turner, Pamela May, Michael Somes, Julia Farron and Leslie Edwards are only some of the dancers who have given long service in various capacities. Margot Fonteyn has devoted her entire dancing career to Sadler's Wells and Robert Helpmann gave them the whole of his. Innumerable others have given ten or fifteen or more years of their working lives to help build the present organisation.

This long and loyal service has not been given because the ballet offered safe and comfortable employment. Only in recent years has it been able to provide more than a modest living, and no one is ever likely to make a fortune in the business. It is doubtful whether the original small group in 1931 had any illusions about being pioneers of English Ballet. They probably stayed because they enjoyed the work, despite the difficulties, stringencies and daily crises. It was an enterprise that was exciting in its early days and it became even more exciting by the mid-'thirties, when the possibilities for development were apparent to everyone. By then loyalties were truly won and the people who had murmured during the first hard years, "Well, once things are fairly straight I *will* escape and take an easier job," found that they were tied by the heartstrings and had neither wish nor power to leave.

Lilian Baylis believed in the plan from the beginning and gave practical demonstration of her faith by providing a theatre and backing—both moral and financial. Among the dancers, however, probably only one knew how much work, and how much glory, lay ahead, and that was the young Director of the company, Ninette de Valois.

Ninette de Valois

"It is the belief of the present Director, that if the ballet at Sadler's Wells does not survive many a Director, then it will have failed utterly in the eyes of the first dancer to hold that post." So said Ninette de Valois to the editor of *The Dancing Times* when her company was first established in 1932. It was an abrupt, rather dictatorial disclaimer of personal achievement which was to be echoed years later when she brought her company back from their first triumphant tour of America. The audience that night at Covent Garden had cheered all the dancers and began to clamour for the Director, who sat well back in her box determined not to take a call. Finally she was induced to go on to the stage and arrived—furious. "Ladies and gentlemen," she snapped, "it takes more than one to make a ballet company," and with that she rang down the curtain.

This has been her conviction throughout the life of her company and it is a genuine one. She is perfectly aware of all that she has accomplished, has faith in her methods and enjoys her present position but her work has never been to enhance her own reputation. She has worked for nearly thirty years for English Ballet and not for Ninette de Valois.

Edris Stannus began dancing as a child because her mother (who decided her stage name should be Ninette de Valois) wished it and not because she had any great enthusiasm herself. She played the piano and had two happy years studying painting at an art school before she began to give her whole time to ballet. Her principal teachers were Espinosa and later Cecchetti, and both have influenced her views on the teaching of classical ballet. She did not take her dancing too seriously but was always being described in provincial Press notices as a budding Pavlova. (One paper became quite ecstatic about "this bright, bonnie girl with any amount of character in the piquant features that gleam with intelligence, with radiant inspiration, beneath a tossing tangle of thick brown hair.") In 1914 she auditioned for the Lyceum pantomime, with a number pinned on her tunic, and was so successful that she remained principal dancer in the annual pantomime there until 1919. In 1919 she danced in the Italian Opera Season at Covent Garden, and afterwards she appeared in revues with great success as a soubrette dancer. She organised and toured with a small ballet company on the old Gulliver circuit, automatically taking charge of the group and showing then a natural bent for administration. She was a good dancer and a lively companion (Margaret Craske, who was in the touring company, remembers her simply as being "loads of fun"), with no very strong ambitions or even ideas about the future.

Then in 1923 she joined the Russian Ballet of Serge Diaghileff, learned much about the working of a first-class ballet company, and realised how she might employ her taste for organisation rather than actual dancing. She left Diaghileff after two years and became for a while a rather earnest visionary—serious, hard-working, difficult. "As serious as God and as touchy as Hell," said one of her colleagues. Nevertheless she soon made an impression in this new world she had set out to conquer, and towards the end of 1930, a twenty-seven-year-old Arnold Haskell was writing that Ninette de Valois had "fought valiantly for English dancing in so short a time and with such quiet determination that her record amazes me."

The need to fight every step of the way in the earliest days of British ballet may have caused Ninette de Valois to adopt a somewhat strict and governessy air in public, but during rehearsals her natural gaiety would break out and her dancers adored her. It was her personality and her example alone which persuaded people in the early 'thirties that something would eventually grow out of the Vic-Sadler's Wells Opera Ballet. Now that many of her ambitions are realised and her ideals accepted, she is more relaxed and reflective. (One would say "mellow," but that the word cannot encompass her Irish temperament with its sudden storms, enkindling laughter and blazing enthusiasms.) Yet fundamentally her character has changed little, and the gifts which enabled her to carry through the great project of establishing a ballet tradition in a country where none existed before have remained as fresh and genuine as when she first went to see Lilian Baylis in 1926.

She has always possessed a gift for lucid and convincing argument and can talk her way into, and out of, anything. In the early days she had to do a great deal of talking—mostly of the battling kind, trying to secure rehearsal time and rehearsal space for her dancers, musicians for her orchestra and materials for her wardrobe. The habit is now ingrained. She never loses an opportunity of stating her case and is never too busy to answer a criticism, explain and justify a course of conduct, or correct a misapprehension. She always seems to know which way public opinion is blowing and after ten minutes of her easy, reasonable discourse, any lecture audience is usually convinced of her fundamental wisdom and ready to go out and die for Sadler's Wells.

With her associates the spell does not always work quite so quickly, but her own sincere conviction that the other point of view is "nonsense, darling" usually enables her to win the day. Fair-minded and willing to listen to argument, Ninette de Valois is nevertheless almost unshakeable in her conviction that her own point of view is the right one. "And she nearly always is right," her opponents admit reluctantly; "*damned* right."

Her disarming frankness in conversation has helped her through many a problem. A dancer going to ask for a rise may be refused but may be given such a detailed account of the company's problems and finances that he comes away feeling honoured by "Madam's" confidence in him and the original purpose of his visit is forgotten.

As is often the case with quick and rapid talkers, Ninette de Valois forgets many things she says and frequently changes her mind, announcing each decision with such finality that until people know her well they are disconcerted by the subsequent *volte-face*. When this happens on questions of repertoire there are sometimes tears and complaints that "Madam promised," but if she sometimes raises false hopes, de Valois never wavers in her long-term loyalty to her artists. Dancers who have given good service are never cast aside but are found useful jobs within the organisation or recommended for the important positions abroad which are increasingly offered to graduates of Sadler's Wells.

"Madam's rages" are feared by the younger dancers, but they soon come to understand that these storms evaporate as rapidly as they explode. The only really black days are those when she is suffering from one of her bad migraines, looks terrifyingly ill and yet refuses to go home and rest. Then people tread quietly and refrain from argument. For Ninette de Valois is by no means a robust person and has suffered much ill-health. Compensation has been granted her, however, in that she is able to accomplish prodigious quantities of work when feeling well. She will rapidly grasp the essentials of a lengthy argument or financial complication at committee meetings and she is usually ready to move on to the next item before most of her colleagues have understood the one under discussion. Her aptitude for figures has astounded many eminent financiers, and Chairmen regularly describe her as an ideal committee woman. She could have had a brilliant Parliamentary career if her mother had not made her into a dancer.

Women who achieve much in public life are often suspected of being hard, humourless and rather heartless, but reputations of this kind are usually false. Many dancers have found in Ninette de Valois their warmest friend in adversity, and her Irish charm will quickly subjugate the sourest critic or most frightened new student at the School. She goes off into gales of laughter at the recollection of a ludicrous incident or just a mildly funny story and loves laughter for its own sake. Many of her favourite stories are against herself. When Robert Helpmann used to give imitations of "Madam in a rage" at company parties, no one laughed more helplessly than Madam. She quotes with glee a letter she received early in the war which told her frankly it was time she "got out" and ended "hoping this finds you in the same frame of mind as it leaves the writer, yours truly, well wisher." Her favourite audition story is of the furious mother of a rejected (and quite unsuitable) child who rounded on her in a fury and demanded, "Who are YOU, Madam, to say my child has no talent." [1]

The stories of her far-sightedness are as numerous as the stories about Lilian Baylis and her appeals for money. "Madam doesn't always notice us," complain some dancers; "she is always looking at the pupils in the School and thinking 'there will be a good crop ready in five years' time'." Arnold Haskell has told how she visited him at his Air Raid Wardens' Post in Bournemouth in 1941 and, ignoring national disasters and threats of invasion, proceeded to outline her plans for the enlarged School at the end of the war. On a more recent occasion he suspected she wasn't listening to what he was saying, and then discovered she had been turning over in her mind the sort of mattresses that should be ordered when the School became a residential establishment.

Her vision is so extraordinary and the future is so clear in her own mind that she sometimes neglects to explain her plans fully to the people who are to carry them out. She may, for instance, decide a dancer has an important future as a teacher or choreographer and cherish her towards that end, but it seldom occurs to

[1] One of the few incidents she did not find amusing occurred during the war when she registered in Leeds with the 1898 group for National Service. The clerk wrote her down as Mrs. Arthur Connell—no responsibilities. The dancers thought it was very funny indeed, but Madam considered it an example of lamentable inefficiency.

her to tell the dancer in question what she has in mind, and years of heartbreak may result.

Her work as administrator and educationalist has recently over-shadowed Ninette de Valois' gift for choreography. The revolutionary, *avant-garde* works of the late 'twenties and early 'thirties are mostly forgotten and her reputation as a choreographer rests on the later, larger productions which have become a permanent part of the English repertoire. Much of her daily work is tiring and worrying and it is not conducive to creative thought. "Never start a ballet company, my dear," she will sometimes say when she is very tired; "you always have to be one jump ahead of them." Yet there are many sides of her personality which have not yet found expression. Her great love of simple beauty of movement, so apparent in her classroom *enchaînements* and, above all, in the free movement which she teaches in the *plastique* class at the School, has yet to be revealed in her choreography—although there are glimpses of these qualities in the passages for the Children of God in *Job*.

Long experience, a quick brain, and more than a fair share of intuition have equipped Ninette de Valois so well to carry out her responsibilities, that it is hardly surprising she should find it difficult to delegate real responsibility. Nevertheless she has retained the loyal and efficient service of colleagues who are by no means servile yes-men. They are all prepared to argue on matters of policy in their separate departments, and equally prepared to ask and accept advice.

No other individual in the Sadler's Wells organisation, however, has an overall grasp of both broad policy and departmental details to equal that of de Valois, and consequently heads are sometimes shaken and anxieties voiced about the future. Had the Sadler's Wells Ballet been designed to display the talents or promote the personal glory of Ninette de Valois, there might be ground for anxiety, but she has built a ballet "to survive many a Director," and it is not conceivable that she will neglect to make provision for its wise direction in the future.

Frederick Ashton

Frederick Ashton and Ninette de Valois have, perhaps, only one characteristic in common, but fortunately it is the one of major

importance to Sadler's Wells: they both have, and have had for
some thirty years, complete faith in English Ballet.

Ashton had an exotic childhood in beautiful Peru, followed by
a few unhappy years at Dover College, and he came to dancing
comparatively late. While Ninette de Valois was dancing *The
Dying Swan* on the end of every pier in England ("with full lime-
light effect," as one paper reported), he was dreaming of Pavlova,
whom he had first seen in Peru. He was obsessed with a passion
for the dance, above all for the purely classical ballet, but could
find no outlet for his ambitions. In 1924 he took some private
lessons with Leonide Massine, and when Massine left London he
advised the young Ashton to go to Marie Rambert for further
instruction. Marie Rambert's genius for discovering talent was as
then virtually untested, but she at once realised that this boy was
no ordinary dancer and she nurtured and developed the artist.
Working with Rambert's dancers he met Sophie Fedorovitch and
created his first ballet for the stage. He arranged ballets for Karsavina and Lopokova, who danced as guests for Rambert, and he
came into contact with the legendary world of the Russian Ballet.
In the late 'twenties he joined Ida Rubinstein's company and with
her toured the capitals of Europe for a year, assimilating knowledge, drinking in beauty wherever he went, and learning his craft
(like de Valois) by working in a large company under two great
choreographers, Nijinska and Massine.

Ashton returned to London in time to participate in the first
Camargo Society programmes, and for that Society and for the
Ballet Club he made a number of beautiful, charming, elegant,
rather heartless works. He earned a precarious living to begin with
(he received five shillings a performance for dancing in *The Jew in
the Bush* at the Old Vic in 1931) but gradually he began to make a
reputation as an English choreographer of importance. When he
accepted Lilian Baylis' modest offer of a permanent place in the
Vic-Wells Ballet, as dancer and resident choreographer, in 1935
he knew that this was the best place in which to develop his craft,
and his long friendship with both Lambert and de Valois must
have influenced his decision. Having made the offer, Baylis and
de Valois gave Ashton a free hand and allowed him to produce a
rapid succession of new ballets for them. Markova had left and the
full-length classics were temporarily out of the repertoire, so his

Angus McBean

FREDERICK ASHTON, C.B.E.

CONSTANT LAMBERT

a drawing by Michael Ayrton

responsibility was considerable. "He might have wrecked us," Ninette de Valois wrote later, "but in fact he made us."

Ashton has made steady and continual progress as an artist ever since. His work has become richer in invention and deeper in feeling, while his taste remains exquisite. His knowledge of music and art increases all the time. He has been fortunate in his friends and collaborators, who have helped him and encouraged him loyally. During most of his career with Sadler's Wells he had Constant Lambert to assist him musically, Sophie Fedorovitch to design his ballets and Margot Fonteyn to interpret them. The company love him and cherish his ballets, for he has great natural charm and can be both amusing and witty. Sometimes he will sink into black depths of despair when inspiration seems to have fled, his mind is blank concerning his next ballet, and hundreds of brilliant and promising young choreographers—each with fifteen masterpieces planned and ready for production—seem to be springing up all around him. He tends to be waspish, difficult and rather petulant when put out or worried about a new production, but at other times, when satisfied with his work, he can assume an Olympian and rather grand detachment and remains undismayed (although a little hurt) when critics and commentators make unkind remarks.

Frederick Ashton is, above all things else, an artist. He is the complete choreographer in the same way that Fonteyn is the complete ballerina. He takes an active part in the daily running of the Sadler's Wells Ballet but has no real taste or flair for administration. His real work, the work which no one else can do, is to produce beautiful ballets. He has contributed more than thirty to the Sadler's Wells repertoire already and the world is all before him.

Constant Lambert

"I do not believe that any ballet company can have roots or a policy of lasting value, or hold the prolonged interest of the public, if it lacks first-class musical leadership," wrote Ninette de Valois in a tribute to Constant Lambert, and in that sentence she summarises the contribution that he made to the organisation from its first performance in 1931, until his death in August 1951. He not only guided the musical policy of the company but at the same time maintained excellent day-to-day performances from the orchestra. Complaints of inadequate musical accompaniment were never levelled against the Sadler's Wells Ballet while Lambert was in command. He preserved the same standards whether working with a tiny orchestra at Sadler's Wells, playing one of two pianos during the war-time tours, or marshalling the resources of a great orchestra at Covent Garden.

Constant Lambert composed ballets and arranged and selected the music for them as well as directing operations from the orchestra pit, but his influence extended beyond the purely musical side. His rich personality, his erudition on all manner of subjects and his magnificent *visual* as well as musical taste (rare quality in musicians) enabled him to advise and help on almost every problem that arose.

Lambert was the son of an Australian painter, George Washington Lambert, and the brother of a distinguished sculptor, so that his early environment was artistic as well as musical. From Christ's Hospital he went to the Royal College of Music, where Vaughan Williams first discovered his exceptional gifts. While still a student, he was commissioned by Diaghileff to compose *Roméo et Juliette*, and although the music is not remembered (it has never been published), the violent demonstration in Paris at the first performance of the ballet resulted in widespread publicity for all who were concerned with it. *Roméo et Juliette* brought Lambert into contact with the world of ballet and the artistic entourage of Diaghileff (which comprised most of the major talents of the time) and doubtless influenced the direction of his subsequent career.

After *Roméo et Juliette* life must have seemed a little dull. Lambert earned his living in London by playing the piano at schools of dancing (a terrible drudgery of Schubert duets which he never forgot), wrote film criticism and sometimes served behind the counter of the Holborn bookshop over which he lodged. By the time he was twenty-five, however, he was back in the world of ballet and confidently taking charge of orchestral matters for the Camargo Society. On 5th May 1931 he steered the Old Vic orchestra through its first complete performance of ballet. His first big success as a conductor came with the production of *Job* by the Camargo Society.

Lambert was among the first to champion English dancers and choreographers, and he recognised the possibilities of the Vic-Wells Ballet long before the majority of ballet critics were aware of its formation. "Of the many efforts which are being made in this country to preserve the art of ballet," he wrote in 1932, "that of the Old Vic rests, to my mind, on the soundest basis and is the most likely to succeed." When Lilian Baylis offered him a permanent job with the Vic-Wells Ballet for the season 1932–33 he consequently accepted and threw in his lot with Ninette de Valois and her dancers, tickled by the idea that just as ballet had been swallowed up a century ago by the fashion for opera, so might ballet at Sadler's Wells, at first by means of the opera, win its way back into favour in London.

Lambert was a man of great culture and great zest for living, a full-blooded, sometimes Rabelaisian character, who complemented admirably the more gentle Ashton and the more formal de Valois. He had the sort of rich and fruity voice that is made for good conversation. He was a brilliant broadcaster and a perfect orator for such entertainments as *Façade* or *A Wedding Bouquet*. His sense of humour was enormous and ranged from the most delicate, deadly shafts of wit to splendid absurdity on a Gargantuan scale.

Michael Ayrton has described a famous railway journey on which he and Lambert became involved in an argument about the relative merits of cats and fish and their representation in Oriental art. They began to draw to illustrate their argument until all available paper had been used up. "The argument was not exhausted. As dusk fell, Constant inscribed in pencil above the carriage door a small goldfish seen head on. Gradually fish of many varieties, and cats posed in numerous ways, came to decorate the available wall space. Night came on and we worked like the Cro-Magnon man in total darkness. Occasionally, by the light of matches, we inspected our work. Small cats appeared riding large fish. Small fish were revealed inside large cats. Fish bit cats. Cats sat on fish. In due time, only the ceiling remained virgin, and it was not without difficulty, for we were both heavily built, that we climbed each into a separate luggage rack to continue, like twin Michaelangelos to design upon the vault."

Lambert had no patience with pretentiousness, affectations or plain stupidity. He greatly disliked theatrical conductors, feeling that their own "theatricality" prevented them from "sinking their personality into the ultimate and esoteric collaboration which alone produces a moving experience on the stage. 'Theatricality' in fact is the deadly enemy of good theatre." With conceited dancers he had equally little patience. "Tell that young man to stop talking about Beethoven's symphonies," he once commanded. "Tell him to try and keep time when he is dancing."

The work which Constant Lambert did for Sadler's Wells was deeply appreciated by critics and audiences, and although it left him little time for composition his reputation was by no means insular. When he appeared at the conductor's desk for the first performance by the Sadler's Wells Ballet in America the New York audience welcomed him with a spontaneous ovation, and both George Balanchine and Lincoln Kirstein thought he was the real hero of the evening.

His knowledge and advice was so freely available to all the artists of Sadler's Wells that they relied heavily on his judgments and his tastes are strongly reflected in the muscial repertoire. He had great enthusiasm for "light" music and the work of composers such as Chabrier, Meyerbeer and Auber, whose compositions are so admirably suited to the ballet theatre, and he was a great champion of English composers like Purcell and William Boyce. For Stravinsky, Hindemith and Schönberg he had less enthusiasm.

Lambert did not force his opinions on his collaborators, however. "The longer I work in ballet," he said in a broadcast discussion in 1948, "the more convinced I am that the ballets which endure are those in which no one collaborator can say, 'This is my ballet.' Nightly quarrels round the supper table are far more fruitful in the long run than polite letters from a distance."

In conducting, too, he did not impose any inflexible rules, but when asked the favourite question, "Do the dancers follow the conductor or does the conductor follow the dancer?" he would usually reply that in classical ballets the customer, i.e. the dancer, is always right, whereas, in modern ballet the dancer's task is usually to follow the conductor's interpretation of the score. Ideally, however, the question would not arise. "A conductor and a dancer who have worked together for years, have such a sense of intimate collaboration that neither stops to analyse who is leading the other at a given moment."

Few of Lambert's compositions remain in the ballet repertoire to-day. *Rio Grande* and part of *Horoscope* are still popular in the concert hall, but *Pomona* would probably have dated by now. *Tiresias*, his last composition, has its admirers, but it seems likely that Lambert will be remembered as a composer chiefly for his compositions outside ballet, such as the *Dirge from Cymbeline* and the beautiful *Summer's Last Will and Testament*. This masque for orchestra, chorus and baritone was adapted from the poem of Thomas Nashe, and Dr. Colles has written that it reflects "the strange mixture of ribaldry and tenderness, mirth and satire which belonged to Nashe's unique personality." No small part of its perfections may, perhaps, be attributed to the fact that these characteristics also belonged to the character of the composer. There has been no personality comparable to Constant Lambert attached to the Sadler's Wells Ballet since his death, and although it continues to profit from his work, his loss becomes more apparent and more grievous as time passes.

CHAPTER II

THE ORGANISATION

THE Sadler's Wells organisation to-day consists of a major company of about 75 dancers at the Royal Opera House, Covent Garden, a company of 35–40 dancers at Sadler's Wells Theatre, and a School which can deal with some 250 pupils (not all of them full-time). Each branch has its own dance staff and is a fairly self-contained unit, but there is constant interchange of teachers and no rigid line of demarcation between departments. Dame Ninette de Valois is Director of all three branches and is ultimately responsible for all their policies.

The financial affairs of the two ballet companies are linked, not to each other, but to the opera companies which co-inhabit the theatres in which they perform. It is therefore difficult to separate their results from the overall results of the two theatres. The Sadler's Wells Ballet at Covent Garden shares with the opera company the Arts Council grant to the Royal Opera House, which was £240,000 in 1953–54, and was renewed for the same amount in 1954–55. The Sadler's Wells Foundation received £100,000 from the Arts Council in 1953–54, towards the operating costs of the opera and ballet companies at Sadler's Wells and the Sadler's Wells School. The Royal Opera House, which gets full benefit from the work that is being done at the School, has, over the years, gradually increased its contribution towards the expenses.

These Arts Council grants are high but necessary. In its Ninth Annual Report, for 1953–54, the Council stated categorically: "If half a million pounds of the public money now invested annually, by the Arts Council and Local Authorities, in opera, ballet, theatre and music were withdrawn, nearly all the national institutions of music and drama in this country would have to close down. Covent Garden, Sadler's Wells and the Old Vic would be 'dark.' . . . The arts are attracting far bigger audiences in Britain than ever before, yet they cannot catch up with their rising costs of production and performance."

In other words, it is no longer an economic proposition to run opera and ballet seasons in London throughout the year at present prices of admission. Before the war short seasons at Covent Garden were heavily subscribed in advance by private patrons. The prices charged were high and the ballet companies used to make money as a rule, but seasons of Grand Opera, which were vastly more expensive to put on, nearly always lost money, and more than one company of promoters went bankrupt. During the months between these seasons the theatre was used for a variety of purposes and could be hired by anyone able to afford the rent.

When Covent Garden was reopened in 1946, however, it was under the direction of a Trust whose avowed policy was to establish there a national lyric theatre presenting opera and ballet in repertory throughout the greater part of the year and, with varying degrees of success, this has been done. Admission prices have been increased gradually, but for ballet they are still only a small percentage above the pre-war figures and have not risen to the same degree as wages and almost all commodities. Prices of opera seats are considerably below the pre-war average. During the Russian Ballet seasons at Covent Garden immediately before the war a good stall cost 15s. and a seat in the Grand Tier was also 15s., while the gallery cost 2s. For first nights these prices might be increased by 50 per cent. To-day these seats are priced at £1, £1. 2s. and 4s. respectively. If the Arts Council grant was withdrawn, either the prices of all seats would have to be doubled or drastic new policies would have to be introduced in order to keep the theatre open.

Whether prices should be raised to meet at least part of the deficit, and whether the grant to Covent Garden should come from general Arts Council funds or be made a separate responsibility like the Tate and National Galleries, are matters of opinion and part of the whole problem of public responsibility for the arts.

The Opera House is leased by the ground landlords, Covent Garden Properties Limited, to the Ministry of Works, which in turn leases it to The Royal Opera House, Covent Garden Limited. The ground landlords are responsible for the main structure of the building, and the Ministry of Works for internal maintenance and repair, responsibilities which it in turn passes on to the sub-tenant. Although in some respects it is an expensive building to maintain, the proportion of the Arts Council grant which is spent on the

B

Opera House itself is small. By far the largest portion of the annual expenditure at Covent Garden is on salaries for the opera and ballet artists, including contract payments to visiting companies. In 1953–54 these totalled £211,400. The orchestra cost £85,600, stage wages and performance expenses £92,860, front of house wages and expenses (including publicity and administration) £75,870, and new productions £84,970. Rent, rates and maintenance were only £49,650.

It is important to remember, when discussing the present cost to the country of Covent Garden, that the Sadler's Wells Ballet went there in 1946 in a very successful financial condition. Its wartime earnings had paid off much of the 1939 building debt on Sadler's Wells Theatre and it was also able to pay for the school buildings in Colet Gardens. There was money over to help launch the Sadler's Wells Theatre Ballet. From 31st December 1945, however, the company's earnings have gone into the coffers of the Royal Opera House and are linked to the fortunes of the opera company at that theatre—which lost a vast amount of money on its early seasons and is never likely to make any.

After the departure of the ballet, Sadler's Wells Theatre struggled to build up another company and to enlarge and maintain the School, but by the end of four years found itself in a precarious financial position with nearly all its reserve of £75,000 depleted. The matter was raised in public, some changes took place in the apportionment of grants and Covent Garden increased its contribution to the School. Changes in business policy at Sadler's Wells helped to improve the situation gradually but there can be no doubt that of the four companies operating from the two theatres it is the Sadler's Wells Ballet which is the one big money-maker. It has played in this respect an important part in making possible the establishment of a resident opera company at Covent Garden. In 1953–54, the Arts Council Report admitted, "Covent Garden would have been faced with a serious deficit had the Sadler's Wells Ballet Company not brought home a timely profit from its triumphant tour of North America."

The American tours have indeed brought in large quantities of money but against these earnings must be offset the wear and tear which costumes and scenery (and sometimes dancers) suffer from the continual travelling and all the loading and unloading. An arduous American tour can cost the company many thousands of pounds in physical depreciation, and the psychological aftermath of the 1950–51 tour was serious and prolonged.

Touring brings rewards as well, however, and few members of the companies would wish to forgo their overseas seasons. It is right that a national company of such dimensions should be seen in the great opera houses of the world, and it is also desirable that the Sadler's Wells Ballet should visit occasionally those cities in Great Britain which possess theatres large enough to accommodate a full repertoire, representative of the company. The Sadler's Wells Theatre Ballet, smaller and more adaptable, tours more easily and carries a heavier burden of keeping the name and achievements of Sadler's Wells before the public in the provinces of this country and in the smaller theatres on the Continent. The recent tour of South Africa made by this company was the first to be under-taken by a Sadler's Wells troupe and it achieved remarkable success.

The Sadler's Wells Ballet dances at the Royal Opera House, Covent Garden, for a large proportion of the year, sharing per-formances equally with the opera company. The opera and ballet companies are in no sense Government controlled and are free to manage their own artistic policies, although they do, of course, have to keep the Arts Council informed and satisfied about expendi-ture—a duty made easier by the fact that both bodies have the same finance officer. The Sadler's Wells Ballet, as in 1931, is still directed by Ninette de Valois. Frederick Ashton is her Associate Director[1] and Robert Irving is Musical Director.[2] An honorary Board of Advisors, appointed by the Royal Opera House, Covent Garden Limited, is available for consultation. The membership of this Board, at the time of its inception in 1951, was Ninette de Valois, Frederick Ashton, Arthur Bliss, Humphrey Searle, John Piper, Mifanwy Piper and Sophie Fedorovitch. In 1955 it consisted of Professor William Coldstream, the Pipers, Searle and Sacheverell Sitwell.

The orchestra is the Covent Garden Orchestra. During combined seasons of opera and ballet this body of musicians is capable of first-class playing, but when the opera company goes on tour it has first call on the musicians and so many replacements are brought

[1] Since May 1952.   [2] Since December 1949.

in at Covent Garden that the quality of the orchestra changes very considerably.

The size and expense of opera house productions have imposed a fairly conservative policy on the ballet at Covent Garden, so that the importance of the second company, where experimental work can be undertaken less expensively in a more intimate theatre, is increasingly apparent. Nevertheless, both companies are intended as creative organisations, offering opportunities to composers, choreographers, designers and dancers on two different levels of production. Training throughout the organisation is directed towards the aim of a company that can work for any choreographer and is capable of any style of dancing. A completely expressive instrument with a sound technical foundation is the ideal, and it is one that is still only partly realised. The communication of passionate enjoyment in dancing, which flows so warmly from Russian dancers, is something almost unknown at Sadler's Wells.

Comparisons between ballet companies are usually futile: too many things are unequal before the comparison begins. The Sadler's Wells Ballet to-day, for example, has a reputation that can only be compared with that of Diaghileff's Russian Ballet, yet how different have been the policies and the results. Diaghileff revolutionised the whole art of ballet, and English ballet has followed acquiescently the principles of ballet-making which he and his choreographers evolved. Diaghileff was not working for a long-term future, however. Present beauties were his constant preoccupation, and to help him in the creation of ballets he turned to all the greatest painters, musicians and dancers of his day. While he ruled his kingdom of ballet he was an absolute monarch, and if a dancer or choreographer left him to work elsewhere it was regarded as an act of *lèse-majesté*, but he was not interested in any future company that might exist after his own departure. Had he not died in 1929, he might well have abandoned ballet for other interests and left his dancers as leaderless as they, in fact, became.

Through his activities, however, ballet influenced all the arts (and even fashions) for twenty years.

Sadler's Wells is an empire, built more soundly on a foundation that will withstand many changes in the monarchy, but its influence outside ballet is less great. It has always been up to date with artistic taste and achievement, but never ahead, and the only revolution in public taste for which it has been responsible is that it has made ballet a popular experience and a household word. At the same time, it has never flirted with novelty for its own sake, as Diaghileff did occasionally in the 'twenties, and the record of past commissions is an impressive one. Composers who have written music for the Sadler's Wells Ballet include Vaughan Williams, William Walton, Arthur Bliss, Alan Rawsthorne, Lord Berners, Lennox Berkeley, Gavin Gordon, Malcolm Arnold, Arthur Oldham, Denis ApIvor and Constant Lambert. Graham Sutherland, John Piper, Rex Whistler, Leslie Hurry, Sophie Fedorovitch, Edward Burra, Antoni Clavé, Osbert Lancaster, Oliver Messel, Eugène Berman, Derain, Bérard, Cecil Beaton, William Chappell, McKnight Kauffer, Robert MacBryde, Robert Colquhoun, and Isabel Lambert have decorated their ballets. The Sadler's Wells Ballet may not have "discovered" many of these artists but in many cases it employed them before they were widely known, and has put the whole theatre in its debt by first encouraging men like Hurry, Piper and Osbert Lancaster to work for the stage.

The ballets of Robert Helpmann, particularly *Hamlet* and *Miracle in the Gorbals,* may be said to have had a strong influence on the production of drama, and Mr. Hurok is emphatic that the American tours of the Sadler's Wells Ballet have changed the entire box-office situation in respect of dance attractions throughout the United States.

This record, in the space of twenty-five years, is not inconsiderable, but it has not bred in the directors of the company any sense of complacency. There are still weaknesses which need to be overcome and new problems which have to be faced. There are, for instance, very few artists in the company capable of playing character parts with proper authority. Make-up is not a strong point at Sadler's Wells and young dancers are usually so lightly built that it is difficult for them to be convincing in middle-aged or elderly rôles. Gradually, however, a beginning is being made in persuading dancers who have left the permanent company to return as guest artists for these parts, and the great success of Pamela May and Harold Turner in mime rôles may encourage more dancers to follow them. Mimes and character dancers are insufficiently honoured in England to-day; for years they have been dismissed with a shrug of contempt while interest centred on the purely classical dancer. There are signs, however, that their vital importance in a large company is beginning to be appreciated again (as it was in the days of Diaghileff and de Basil) and the example of the Royal Danish Ballet has helped to bring the lesson home.

The standard of male dancing in England is improving all the time and there have never been so many promising, sturdy boys as there are in the School to-day. No answer has as yet been found, however, to the problem of displaying to full advantage the talents of the men once they join the ballet companies, particularly the Covent Garden company. A basis of classical ballets may be excellent training for the female dancers, but it is a less rewarding occupation for the men, and unfortunately there is little modern choreography in the repertoire which shows them to advantage. There is a great wastage of talent in this respect and to see the men all working together in a company class is a revelation of ability seldom suspected in the theatre.

The Sadler's Wells Ballet has had a faithful audience from the very beginning, an audience which has erred rather on the side of over-enthusiasm than inadequacy of numbers. (As early as 1931 the critic in the *Referee* was describing the behaviour of the Sadler's Wells audience as "like the enthusiasm of a crowd at a football match—cheering on the local team, win or lose.") The move to Covent Garden widened the audience to a general theatrical public rather than a faithful band of "regulars," and exhibitions of extreme partiality are now less common. There is seldom need for concern about attendances, for the company has filled the opera house to an average of 90 per cent. of capacity on ballet nights ever since 1946, but there is a new problem of maintaining a spirit of interest and adventure between dancers and audiences throughout a long season. "Abroad we are a novelty; at home we are a habit," said Ninette de Valois once in a curtain speech, and habit, alas, breeds boredom and audiences "applauding mildly in musquash" (Richard Buckle's phrase), while dancers give lackadaisical performances. Sadler's Wells has managed to maintain interest to an extraordinary degree by variations in cast, by allowing opportunities to young dancers at *matinées,* frequent new productions and programme building which spaces the classics evenly among modern all-dancing ballets. But it is no easy task.

A large company cannot give great opportunities to all the dancers all the time, particularly when much of the repertoire consists of the classical ballets in which there are only one or two *dancing* rôles of importance. There are usually a few artists who feel aggrieved, ill-treated and misunderstood, but this is true of any ballet company anywhere and placidly contented dancers are not likely to be very good artists. There is strict discipline within the Sadler's Wells Ballet under the totalitarian rule of Dame Ninette, and although dancers occasionally ask for rôles, they only get them if Madam and her staff are satisfied that they have the ability.

Company class every morning is compulsory and this is usually followed by rehearsals which continue well into the afternoon. Costume fittings, photo calls, sometimes visits to a masseur, all have to be fitted in afterwards and the dancer is expected to be back in the theatre at least an hour before the performance at night. During performances Dame Ninette or her assistant, Ailne Phillips, together with the ballet master Harijs Plucis, keep a watchful eye on things from the staff box, paying strict attention to actual execution of steps and seldom being bluffed by theatrical effectiveness alone—although theatrical presentation is a quality to be encouraged as well.

There is no way known to any director of any ballet company of keeping every dancer satisfied all the time. English girls are easier to manage than other nationalities (a fact recognised by foreign employers from Pavlova to Bluebell), but even English girls have ambitions and temperaments and they also have mothers or husbands who hold prejudiced opinions of their abilities. Only a firm discipline can hold a company together over a long period of time, and although they grumble and chatter away rebelliously at times, the dancers, in the long run, submit to the discipline because they know it is ultimately for their own good.

Much freedom is allowed the dancers for outside activities, pro-viding these do not interfere with the work of the Sadler's Wells Ballet, to which their first duty is owed. Leave of absence for several weeks in the year is granted to the principals to enable them to accept engagements as guest artists or to do film or stage work. Margot Fonteyn receives invitations from all over the world, and has danced in Norway, Paris, Copenhagen, Milan, Belgrade and

Granada with particular success. Beryl Grey has visited Sweden and Finland, Violetta Elvin has had triumphs in Milan and in France, while some of the dancers from the Dominions have combined visits to their families with performances throughout their own countries; for example, Nadia Nerina and Alexis Rassine in South Africa, and Rowena Jackson and Bryan Ashbridge in New Zealand. Choreographers are similarly given leave to make ballets for other companies; for example, Frederick Ashton has worked in New York and Copenhagen and John Cranko in Australia and Paris. The artists return invigorated by their new experience and encouraged by the success which seems to attend Sadler's Wells dancers wherever they go.

Over the years the company has had remarkably little "temperament trouble." (Claude Newman walked out of one of the first company classes when he thought he had been wrongfully accused of tripping someone. Consternation reigned for several minutes—he was then the only male dancer—but he was prevailed upon to return and has remained with Sadler's Wells as dancer, mime and teacher ever since.) The smooth running has been largely due to the fact that control has always remained in the right hands and no individual dancers have ever been able to impose their personalities at the expense of the whole. Markova in the early 'thirties, Helpmann during the war, and Fonteyn to-day have won personal reputations that have almost, but never quite, overshadowed the company. The particular fortune of Sadler's Wells has been that all three artists had true humility in the theatre and never sought to abuse their positions.

The Sadler's Wells Ballet to-day is in the position of a great ballerina who, after years of endeavour, has reached the very pinnacle of fame—and is faced with the difficult, anxious task of remaining there. The danger, as Constant Lambert foresaw long ago, is that "we may eventually finish up with a superb body of executants living artistically speaking in the past," and there is a body of opinion which believes this situation has already been reached at Covent Garden. But in the world of the theatre nothing remains the same. After great periods of advance there must be a pause for consolidation, and after the pause there will either be further advance or gradual slipping back. Had the Sadler's Wells Ballet no other resources than the company at Covent Garden we might expect a period of decline to set in, but there is a lifeline leading from the School through the Sadler's Wells Theatre Ballet, and it is on the quality of the sustenance that comes through this lifeline in the form of new, young talent that the future of the major company will depend. Ninette de Valois foresaw the situation as long ago as 1938: "For it is the next generation of directors, choreographers and dancers that may rear its head in some assurance," she wrote in her introduction to *The Vic-Wells Ballet*. "They will know of the past pioneer work, but they will, in their security, knowledge and favourable circumstances, no doubt rebel and decide to encourage an evolution from what will be, at that time, an accepted standard."

PART II

THE CHRYSALIS YEARS

CHAPTER III

THE CHRYSALIS YEARS 1926–1931

THE story of the Sadler's Wells Ballet really began early in 1926, when Ninette de Valois opened her Academy of Choreographic Art in London and looked around for a repertory theatre that might be willing to house and employ a small group of dancers from which might evolve in time a permanent British ballet company. She had the whole scheme quite clearly worked out in her own mind and for the next five years all her energies, thoughts and actions were directed towards her goal. The work that was done during these five years and the experience that was gained are of importance in tracing the development of the company. The theory behind the running of a ballet company had been learned by de Valois during the two years she was with Diaghileff; between 1926 and 1931 she served her practical apprenticeship as producer, choreographer, teacher and administrator.

The Background

It is difficult to realise to-day how enormous was the task that de Valois set herself. She intended to build up a national ballet in a country that had no native tradition of classical dancing whatever. There had always been a public for good dancing, and there had always been excellent English dancers, but for a variety of reasons no native school had developed and no permanent company had been established. At various periods since the sixteenth century, however, it had seemed as if we might have been on the verge of establishing something in the nature of a national ballet in England.

The elaborate Masques of the Tudor and Stuart courts had, for example, developed by the early seventeenth century into not only fantastic spectacles but genuinely integrated works, presented with a taste and magnificence that was probably not to be equalled by English artists in the theatre for another three hundred years. But the Masque was a hothouse flower and in the frigid air of the Civil War period and the subsequent Protectorate it quickly withered

and died and never succeeded in making the transition from the
court to the public theatre. After the Restoration the Court itself
gave no lead to the dancers and there was no positive effort to
establish anything like the state ballets of France, Russia or Denmark.

By the end of the reign of Queen Anne, however, theatrical
dancing was once more an important feature in London, and John
Weaver, the dancing master from Shrewsbury, was producing at
Drury Lane his "dramatic entertainments of dancing" which
anticipated the *ballets d'action* of Noverre. Weaver not only made
these practical experiments in the theatre but published the first
English attempt at a history of dancing (in 1712) and also detailed
descriptions of some of his own productions and a collection of
Anatomical and Mechanical Lectures upon Dancing. His contemporary,
John Rich, first brought Marie Sallé to London to dance at Lincoln's
Inn Fields, and it was in London, in 1734, that she made her great
costume innovation by dancing *Pigmalion* in draperies instead of
the usual formal pannier. Noverre himself worked in London, and
in his 1781 company at the King's Theatre was an English male
dancer, Simon Slingsby, who was famous on both sides of the
Channel, and talented enough to give the great Vestris cause for
discomfort and jealousy.

The vogue for ballet grew and rival managers—among them
Mr. O'Reilly and Mr. Taylor, who were to be immortalised by
Ninette de Valois in *The Prospect Before Us*—competed both for
theatres and for the services of highly skilled dancers and choreographers from France. During the period of the Napoleonic wars it
became increasingly difficult to maintain the supply of French
artists, and names like Miss Cranfield and Miss Twamley appear
among the dancers, while an English choreographer, James d'Egville,
achieved considerable success with his productions. Had the war
with France lasted a few years longer it is very possible that an
English school of dancing might have developed, but with the
coming of peace, the English dancers were submerged in the great
influx of foreign dancers who came pouring back to London. Most
of the great names of continental ballet through the next hundred
years can be found on the playbills of the London theatres.[1]

[1] Curiously, Marie-Anne de Cupis de Camargo, whose name is now associated
with so much pioneer work in the English Ballet renaissance of our time, seems
to have been almost the only dancer of note who did *not* visit London.

The golden age of ballet in London in the eighteen-thirties and eighteen-forties rested entirely at the fashionable theatres on the vogue for the foreign ballerina—above all on the great galaxy of Taglioni, Elssler, Grisi, Cerrito and Grahn—and those English dancers who succeeded in finding favour usually disguised themselves under a foreign name. Just as Hilda Munnings became Lydia Sokolova and Patrick Healey Kay became Anton Dolin, so, in the days of the Romantic Ballet, did James Sullivan disguise himself as James Silvain, while plain Mister Charles Edward Stacey took the stage as Monsieur Charles. One English dancer gave promise of achieving fame under her own name, but poor Clara Webster died at the age of twenty-three from burns received on the stage.

While the foreign visitors held sway at the Italian Opera in front of the wealthy and fashionable audience, the English dancers found livings at smaller theatres and provincial houses. Christmas was their great season, for then pantomimes gave abundant employment both to the women, who played Columbine and took up wands and wings as fairies, and to the men who played clowns and Harlequins and built up another tradition which we have subsequently lost—that of brilliant, and essentially English, character dancing.

The Romantic Ballet, a fashionable and never a popular entertainment, faded like one of its own phantoms as the fashionable world turned its attention to the opera. In the second half of the nineteenth century the French dancers went home, and in England ballet moved to the music hall, where it remained quite happily, enjoying a quarter-century of fantastic popularity at the Empire and the Alhambra and filling a place in the entertainment world roughly comparable to that provided by the ice shows of to-day. The one legacy English ballet has to thank the Empire and the Alhambra for is that they made an ordinary, popular audience familiar with good dancers, and the widespread popularity of artists such as Adeline Genée, Lydia Kyasht and Phyllis Bedells was no small help when those ladies came to lend their support and enthusiasm to various movements important in the development of ballet in England.

The Influence of Diaghileff

The arrival of Diaghileff's *Ballets Russes* at Covent Garden in 1911 profoundly and completely altered all former ideas about the art of ballet. It cannot be over-stressed that the Diaghileff Ballet was all-important in shaping our modern conception of what might be achieved by true collaboration of the arts of music, painting and dancing, and without the example of that greatest of all companies, ballet would probably never have risen above the level of a music-hall entertainment in this country. It would certainly not have developed along its present lines.

London was immensely responsive to the Russian Ballet from the very first season, although it could not be said to have had a widely "popular" appeal, and it was not very successful on those occasions when it toured the provinces. In London, however, at the height of the fashionable season, it attracted an audience of exceptional artistic and intellectual quality and lastingly influenced all musicians, artists, poets, writers and dancers who came into contact with it. Marie Rambert, Ninette de Valois, Constant Lambert, Ursula Moreton, Anton Dolin and Alicia Markova all worked with and learned from Diaghileff, and Diaghileff himself went twice to see Frederick Ashton's first ballet. "He formed the tastes of our generation," wrote Lydia Lopokova when he died.

The advent of Diaghileff did not, however, change very rapidly the prospects for the average well-trained English dancer. In the first quarter of this century the chances of earning a living as a ballet dancer were virtually limited to appearing in music halls, variety houses and revues with perhaps an annual engagement in that standby for hard-up dancers, the Christmas pantomime. In addition there was the rare chance that an exceptional dancer might by accepted by Pavlova for her *corps de ballet* (in its later years her company was almost entirely English) and a very few dancers were accepted by Diaghileff, although never more than about half a dozen in the whole life of his company.

The early career of Ninette de Valois in the commercial theatre is typical of the average English dancer in the early nineteen-twenties. The average dancers, however, stayed in that *milieu*, and only the ones with exceptional intelligence or ability went any farther. It was by no means the general rule for an English-trained ballet dancer to be impressed by or enthusiastic about the Diaghileff Ballet, particularly as it was in the 'twenties, its most esoteric period. The average English dancer might enjoy and accept the romantic ballets such as *Les Sylphides* or *Carnaval*, with their familiar music, but the more aggressively modern work of Massine and Nijinska, Balanchine and Lifar was beyond their comprehension.

De Valois, however, had the intelligence to see that the Diaghileff Ballet was setting the standard for the ballet of the future and she realised that the only way in which she could begin to understand the organisation and working of that company was to join it. She had eleven years of theatrical experience behind her, but she knew that as far as the Diaghileff Ballet was concerned she was only at the apprenticeship stage, and in 1923 she joined "unconditionally the *corps de ballet* . . . to acquire certain essential knowledge which previous stage experience had not provided." Inside the company she soon progressed to important solo rôles and, in an atmosphere of hard work and complete dedication, she began to understand the way a ballet company operated and to appreciate the strange amalgam of the arts that is ballet. Her own book, *Invitation to the Ballet*, gives a detailed account of her years with Diaghileff and she has elsewhere[1] given an amusing instance of how her artistic education was furthered. "It was during the production of *Zéphire et Flore* at Monte Carlo. One day in the rehearsal room we had a dress parade of the costumes. Diaghileff and Braque the designer were both present. The nine muses were very depressed, our costumes seemed dull and incomplete, and Diaghileff, overhearing our grumblings, told us to 'stop wondering whether the costumes suited us, but to consider instead whether we suited the costumes.' He went on to tell us that the costumes had been designed to fit the ballet and the scene and not, as we imagined, for each individual dancer. The next morning I went into the theatre to see the backcloth for the ballet. It was then I understood. In this simple cloth lay the key to everything that one could not find an explanation for in the costumes. My mind could put them together there and then, and I stood as entranced as if the whole ballet had been paraded for my special benefit."

The association with Diaghileff might have yielded far less had Ninette de Valois not possessed such an extraordinary alertness of mind and strength of intellect. In 1925 she knew she was ready to leave Diaghileff although she was obviously destined for further promotion. Arnold Haskell thought she was mad, but de Valois

[1] *The Dancing Times*, April 1933.

C

was not particularly interested in dancing the leading rôles that would have been offered to her. She knew that she wanted to have a company of her own and she had a shrewd notion of how to go about organising one.

Towards a British Ballet

Ninette de Valois was not, of course, alone in her desire to establish a British ballet company. The entire dancing profession was thinking in that direction in the nineteen-twenties and Philip Richardson through *The Dancing Times* was lending strong encouragement and support. The desire to establish *something* was widespread, and little bursts and shoots of activity and experiment were going on all over the place. Some of them were of high quality, some came no nearer the art of ballet than a knowledge of the five positions. As far back as 1915, for instance, a Manchester teacher, Alfred Haines, had formed "The Haines English Ballet," which toured for many years and appeared at the larger London variety houses as well as in the provinces (it was with this company that Harold Turner made his first appearance in 1927). A platform for English dancers had been provided by *The Dancing Times* at the annual Sunshine *Matinées*, in aid of the Sunshine Homes for Blind Babies, which it had been running since 1919. These *matinées* were designed to show the best talent available in England and also some distinguished foreign artists. All the dancers gave their services and in time the performances became virtually "all-British" entertainments. In 1925 the artists appearing included Phyllis Bedells, Ruth French, Anton Dolin, Ninette de Valois, Ursula Moreton, Molly Lake, Margaret Craske and a young pupil of the Princess Seraphine Astafieva named Alicia Marks.

Astafieva was but one of the distinguished teachers who settled in London and imparted to her pupils a true understanding and appreciation of classical ballet. Nicholas Legat and Enrico Cecchetti were to leave their mark on English ballet, and as early as 1922, Cyril Beaumont founded the Cecchetti Society to perpetuate the teaching of the Maestro. Marie Rambert, Ninette de Valois, Margaret Craske, Derra de Moroda, Jane Forestier and Molly Lake were on the committee of this Society. Among other English teachers of note were Grace Cone, Phyllis Bedells and Ruth French, who were all producing excellent dancers.

Another active spirit was Edouard Espinosa, head of a great dancing family, a vigorous teacher and prime mover in the efforts that were being made to improve standards of teaching throughout the country. As early as 1916 Espinosa had been so horrified by some examples of bad teaching he had seen, that he appealed to Philip Richardson to publish in *The Dancing Times* a syllabus setting forth what every teacher ought to know, and demanding that some competent tribunal should examine the qualifications of individual teachers. The proposal aroused interest, but there was little contact among members of the profession at that time, and nothing came of the scheme until after the end of the first world war. Then Espinosa and Richardson tried again. *The Dancing Times* organised the first of what became known as Dancers' Circle Dinners in order to promote friendship among the leading teachers and give them an opportunity to know one another. Madame Adeline Genée was invited to take the Chair and in order that the Continental Schools might be represented, Madame Karsavina (Russia) and Madame Cormani (Italy) were also invited. Phyllis Bedells accepted an invitation to represent the British teachers. The same guests were invited to a second dinner at which it was hoped to consolidate the preliminary discussions, and at this second dinner the formation of an examining body was approved by the hundred teachers present. The title was to be "The Association of Teachers of Operatic Dancing of Great Britain" and Madame Genée, Madame Karsavina, Madame Cormani and Miss Bedells, together with Espinosa, were appointed to the Committee, with Richardson as Honorary Secretary. It was this body, which, under the presidency of Dame Adeline Genée, was to develop into the Royal Academy of Dancing and grow steadily in strength and importance. To-day it is presided over by Miss Margot Fonteyn.

Improved teaching meant a larger supply of talented dancers, and many were the attempts to use these dancers in productions which might be described as British ballets. Anton Dolin in the middle 'twenties was dancing at the Coliseum with various partners —Phyllis Bedells, Nemchinova, de Valois, Anna Ludmila—and he was anxious to recruit a small company to use in his performances. When he opened the Dolin-Bruce School of Dancing off Leicester

Square in October 1925, the *Evening News* reported the event under the hopeful headline : "The Nucleus of the British Ballet." Dolin was quoted as saying that he hoped to establish a company that might eventually tour the world, and he envisaged ballets which might portray "the teeming life of the Old Kent Road, as a ballet theme no less enthralling than *Petrouchka*."

Flora Fairbairn, who gave some classes at the Old Vic in 1924 (usually in the small gap at the back of the Circle), had advocated a British ballet company in the *Old Vic Magazine* that year and she collaborated with Cyril Beaumont in the formation of a small company called the Cremorne Company (irreverent dancers called it "the Cream Horn"). This was a purely private enterprise and drew its dancers from several sources, although many were students from Miss Fairbairn's Mayfair School. A performance was given at the Scala Theatre in March 1926, but the company had no resources for establishing itself on a permanent basis, and it disintegrated after accomplishing the two usual results of such ventures: it provided much valuable experience and it lost money.

An infinitely less ambitious undertaking but one which foreshadowed much exciting and beautiful work in English ballet was the production at the Lyric Theatre, Hammersmith, in the revue *Riverside Nights* of a small ballet by Frederick Ashton called "A Tragedy of Fashion, or The Scarlet Scissors." On the night of 15th June 1926 this first collaboration between Ashton the choreographer and Sophie Fedorovitch the designer was seen, with Marie Rambert herself among the dancers. The importance of the occasion was at once apparent, and among the first to congratulate Ashton after the performance was Ninette de Valois. From this production developed the first small ballets of Ashton, and the little seasons arranged by Marie Rambert at the Lyric and Arts theatres, culminating in the formation of the Ballet Club which presented its first programme on 16th February 1931, in Rambert's Ladbroke Road studio (it did not become the Mercury Theatre until 1933).

The success of the Rambert performances rested initially on the presence of Ashton, a gifted choreographer, and the taste and judgment of Marie Rambert. Companies recruited from dancing schools tended to give performances that resembled dancing school displays unless there was a creative artist to exploit them. De Valois had learned from Diaghileff the vital importance of the choreographer's rôle and experience at home in London strengthened her ambition, which was not to train Kensington children to perform at dancing displays, but to train artists and servants of the theatre, who would be capable of understanding and interpreting choreography in its highest forms. She persuaded her stepfather to finance for her a school which she opened at 6A Roland Houses, Roland Gardens, South Kensington, early in March 1926. In the course of her search for a suitable name for the School, she consulted Cyril Beaumont and explained to him that she wanted the emphasis to be on choreography. He considered and then suggested she should call it "The Academy of Choreographic Art."—and by that somewhat pompous but really quite explicit title the school was known.

The Academy of Choreographic Art

Advertisements were duly issued and Ninette de Valois wrote an article for The Dancing Times on "The Future of Ballet," in which she declared: "The true aim of modern ballet is a serious practical effort to extend the authentic methods of the classical ballet. It is to forward and expand the possibilities of the art of dancing in harmony with the other arts of the theatre. . . . There is no question that the teachings of the Classic School are the sure and only foundation—limitless in its adaptability, it consequently proves its power to meet the varied requirements of the theatre."

The Academy provided not only ballet classes but courses in décor and costume designing (conducted by Vladimir and Elizabeth Polunin, "artist-painters to the Diaghileff Russian Ballet"), and boasted a music library, a reading library and a theatre art section. At the head of the announcements about the school, beneath the title, ran the statement, "Principal—Ninette de Valois." She was not quite twenty-eight years old.

A small group of students were soon hard at work. Ursula Moreton was assistant teacher to "the Prin," as the students called Miss de Valois, and Molly Lake was also one of her chief helpers. The pleasant studio had grey painted walls and pale blue linoleum and the girls wore plum-coloured tunics, the material for which had to be bought at Messrs. Barkers in Kensington. The dancers (or more usually their mothers) had to ask for a certain Mr. Finch, who could always produce the right shade of material for the

Academy tunics at once. In addition to the daily ballet class, the students were introduced to Dalcroze eurhythmics and a class remembered with special affection was de Valois' own "composition class," for which the dancers wore soft shoes and performed lovely soft plastic movements, full of contrasts and clear lines. (It survives at the Sadler's Well School to-day but is called "plastique.")

Frederick Ashton was among the first to take lessons at the Academy and Molly Lake remembers him as "always arranging things, even then." If he didn't know how to describe the steps he wanted he got the dancers to perform them and then fitted them together in a fashion that pleased him. Ashton's own strongest memory of the Roland Gardens studio is of de Valois banging a hole in her new linoleum with the stick she used to make the dancers keep time. Her classes were not easy; prepared herself to give every ounce of energy to her work, she expected others to be willing to work just as hard. Other dancers who enrolled quite early at the Academy were Beatrice Appleyard, Freda Bamford, Joy Newton and Rosalind Patrick, who was later to become an actress as Rosalind Iden and is now Mrs. Donald Wolfit.

Having established her school, Ninette de Valois began to look around to find a theatre in which she could begin to work out her ideas. She had come to the conclusion that the only place in which an English ballet might be born and nurtured was within a repertory theatre. Anything self-supporting and existing independently would at that time have been utterly impossible. There were some good dancers available, but virtually no choreographers, no real public interest and no money whatsoever. Even if an enormous subsidy had been forthcoming, it is doubtful whether with the material then available anything of value could have been accomplished. Ninette de Valois decided that the thing for her to do was to attach her little group of dancers to a repertory theatre, where they might work in the dramatic productions, gain theatre experience and then perhaps gradually develop a life of their own as a resident ballet company. She began to look around for a theatre that might receive her ideas sympathetically.

First she wrote to Barry Jackson at the Birmingham Repertory Theatre, and would have been quite prepared to emigrate to Birmingham if he had been willing to make the experiment.

Barry Jackson, however, was not prepared to risk such a fantastically ambitious long-term plan, and although he was sympathetic he could do nothing for her.

Lilian Baylis, of the Old Vic and Sadler's Wells

It was on the suggestion of a friendly music critic that de Valois addressed her next letter to Lilian Baylis at the Old Vic Theatre in the Waterloo Road, on the unfashionable South Bank of the Thames. The Old Vic at that time was the nearest thing to a people's theatre that London has ever had. Shakespeare and opera were given there at very low admission prices and for quite ridiculously small production costs, yet the standards of performance were remarkable and the choice of plays and operas adventurous.

The letter from Ninette de Valois duly arrived and Evelyn Williams, who was secretary to Miss Baylis at the time, distinctly remembers opening it and thinking, "Well, with writing like that and a name like that she shouldn't waste much of our time." But Lilian Baylis was interested and wanted to see the writer of the letter, so an appointment was made for an afternoon in the early summer of 1926. Ninette de Valois arrived in a big floppy hat and immediately started to explain just what she wanted to do and how she proposed to set about doing it. She made it perfectly clear that, however successful the long-term project might prove to be, the running of such a ballet company would never be a money-making concern.

Nevertheless Lilian Baylis was still interested. She liked de Valois' face, liked her personality and liked the practical approach which took account of the financial implications and did not require her, then, to put up any capital. Also she was badly in need of someone to train and look after the movement of her dramatic students and to arrange dances in some of the plays. (By a strange coincidence this work had been done many years previously at the Old Vic by Mrs. Wordsworth, the well-known teacher of dancing, who had in fact taught Ninette de Valois as a child.) It was arranged that Miss Baylis should visit the Academy of Choreographic Art with her producer (Andrew Leigh), and after she had satisfied herself that de Valois was a competent teacher she made her an offer. "£1 a week, dear, for the teaching; £2 for arranging a short dance per show (when required), and £3 if there's more than one dance to do." "I took it on," said Ninette de Valois, "and for four years earned on an average about £7 a month." But she had a foot in the door and she knew that it was now up to her to justify the Lady's faith and to equip herself and her little group of students for the day when Sadler's Wells Theatre would be rebuilt and her real dream of a permanent ballet company in London might begin to be realised.

The offer from Lilian Baylis seems meagre indeed—and how different from the offer which was to come from Covent Garden just twenty years later—but it was as much as she was able to do at the time, and both she and Ninette de Valois knew that things could grow from the humblest beginnings. Perhaps this long-term patience, this ability to plan for the future and to accept the necessity of learning to walk before running was attempted, was the essential bond of sympathy between Lilian Baylis and Ninette de Valois. Lilian Baylis had wanted to have a ballet company long before she met Ninette de Valois—she used to buttonhole Philip Richardson occasionally and demand, "*When* are we going to have a British Ballet?"—but she knew that little could be done until she had a second theatre and she had not until then come across anyone to whom she felt the job of establishing a ballet company might be entrusted. She was not exactly a balletomane—she had no time for that—and she had quite probably never heard of de Valois professionally when she engaged her. She had, however, been the first teacher of dancing on the Rand in her South African days and had passionately loved her life out there, teaching the wives, mistresses and daughters of South African millionaires to dance. (Mark Twain went to one of her classes and she tried to teach him the Lancers.) This made it easy for her to understand and sympathise with a woman who wanted to devote her life to forming a company of dancers, and together they laid their plans. British Ballet had found its champion and the promise of a home in which to grow up, and all the promises made at those early interviews were subsequently fulfilled. "She never wavered or went back on any of the important plans laid down in theory," wrote Ninette de Valois when Lilian Baylis died. "Indeed she ruthlessly championed my cause throughout those trying four and a half years of waiting for better opportunities."

When the plan for the establishment of a third company was announced to the staff of the Old Vic, however, they took a rather different view of the enterprise. They considered the whole thing a great nuisance and maintained that there simply wasn't *room* for another company at the Vic as it was in the nineteen-twenties. Already the Shakespeare and Opera companies "fought for the one stage, the one set of dressing-rooms, the scenery, the costumes, the services of the staff. On opera nights Miss Baylis' office was used by the leading women as a dressing-room; coffee and buns were served to the chorus from the cubbyhole which the secretary shared with the treasurer, the Press representative, the producer and any-one else who wanted a parking-place. One washed in cold water from a tap in the prompt corner, taking care only to use it when a noisy battle or chorus was in progress on the stage." [1] Only two years had passed since the Old Vic had managed to get Morley College moved to other premises (Emma Cons, Miss Baylis' aunt and predecessor as Manager of the Old Vic, had allowed this evening school to grow up in what should have been the scene dock and dressing-rooms of the theatre), and now there was a plan to bring *dancers* into the desperately overcrowded, under-equipped building. It is not difficult to understand the lack of enthusiasm shown by the theatre staff at the Old Vic.

Nevertheless, there was the long-term possibility of the acquisition and rebuilding of Sadler's Wells Theatre in Islington. Lilian Baylis had long known that she must have another theatre if her dream of a permanent opera company was not to be submerged by the ever-increasing success of the Shakespeare company, and the actress Estelle Stead had many years ago suggested to her that the derelict theatre of Sadler's Wells might offer a solution. It was the late Sir Reginald Rowe, however, who carried through the actual resolution to acquire this theatre and rebuild it in its present form. Rowe became a Governor of the Old Vic about 1920 and had given invaluable assistance in settling a builders' strike which had threatened the very fabric of the Old Vic theatre during the reconstruction of the stage in 1923. He had always been passion-ately interested in the theatre and gradually came to devote more and more of his time and energies to the Old Vic. When he

[1] Evelyn M. Williams, "I knew Lilian Baylis," *Woman's Hour*, B.B.C. Light Programme, Monday, 6th December 1948.

showed Lilian Baylis the dilapidated building out at Islington (it had just been rejected as a site for a pickle factory) she must have been filled with foreboding, but she was never one to baulk at difficulties, and once convinced that this might indeed prove the best choice for her second theatre, she took the plan to her big, indomitable heart and worked unceasingly to realise the dream.

The Old Vic was still in debt on its own reconstruction (demanded by the L.C.C., which could turn a blind eye no longer on the overcrowding), and it was felt that the Vic could not itself make any appeal for the rebuilding of Sadler's Wells. It signified formally that it would willingly help, although not conduct, the scheme and would take over the theatre when it was eventually reclaimed. The organisation of the appeal was to be managed by Reginald Rowe, who undertook full responsibility for raising the necessary money and in fact succeeded in carrying the whole crazy-seeming scheme through. The Sadler's Wells Fund was inaugurated by an appeal in the Press signed by the Duke of Devonshire, as Chairman of the Committee of the Fund, on the 30th March 1925, and for the next six years Reginald Rowe worked unceasingly to bring the plan to fruition. A memorial plaque on the staircase at Sadler's Wells to-day commemorates his work for the theatre. This does not mean, however, that Lilian Baylis sat back and let him get on with the work alone. She expended unlimited energy on the great task she had set herself; no journey was too far, no task too burdensome if it might result in further contributions to the rebuilding fund.

While these great efforts towards the new theatre were being made, Ninette de Valois was also preparing herself for the opportunities that would come with its reopening. The immediate business in hand, namely the training of drama students at the Old Vic, she enjoyed immensely. Among her pupils were Elizabeth Allen, Heather Angel and Esmond Knight, whom she remembers with affection as "a born dancer, with a lovely natural jump." The Old Vic could not afford to employ professional dancers for the opera ballets but entrusted these interludes to non-professionals, often office workers, who attended classes at the Vic and had a flair for graceful movement. They paid about 1s. 6d. a lesson and devoted most of their spare time to rehearsing or to the actual performances, simply for love and in admiration of the work that was being done at the Old Vic. There could be no question of arranging complicated opera ballets for these dancers, but de Valois sent one of her pupils, Rosalind Patrick, along to help them and to give classes, and Rosalind Patrick was responsible for most of the opera ballets during the next few years at the Old Vic.

The Festival Theatre, Cambridge

Opportunities at the Vic being, at least temporarily, limited Ninette de Valois needed to find outlets for her creative abilities elsewhere. At much the same time that she was having her first discussions in the Waterloo Road her cousin, Terence Gray, was launching an experimental theatre in Cambridge. Terence Gray was then about thirty years of age, a clever young bearded Irishman of considerable wealth who had a bad stutter and drove about Cambridge in an electric motor-car. He was also something of an Egyptologist. He was not a professional man of the theatre but a tremendous theorist and he poured out his ideas during the next few years in four books and a monthly theatre magazine. He took over a disused theatre on the unfashionable outskirts of Cambridge, named it the Festival Theatre and reconstructed it as an art theatre from which he intended "to attack the realistic tradition of acting and production." In the best art theatre traditions, the Festival had a good restaurant, an excellent cellar, a special box for latecomers and a ban on paper-wrapped confectionery. The programmes were printed on black paper with the typically Irish instruction, "To read this programme in the dark, hold it up to the light."

The theatre had no proscenium, a stage on several levels with numerous outlets and a curved auditorium which met the forestage at each side. There was a built-in cyclorama, props and scenery were abolished, and much importance was given to lighting. The only thing which Gray seems to have overlooked was the provision of accommodation for an orchestra in those productions for which music was a necessity. The musicians were eventually placed in a small area at the front of the stalls at the foot of one of the staircases leading from the forestage to the auditorium. This was not an ideal arrangement as the staircase was frequently used for rapid exits and many a short-sighted dancer would bring her exit to an ignominious conclusion by colliding violently with the conductor.

It was, above all, a producer's theatre and all attention was concentrated on the broad sweep of the production and the richness and variety of the lighting. (The lighting equipment was designed by Gray's partner in founding the Festival Theatre, Harold Ridge, who later designed the lighting system for the Shakespeare Memorial Theatre at Stratford-on-Avon.) Gray initially supervised the productions himself, appointing a team to carry out the work on each play, for example, a producer, a choreographer, a designer and sometimes a musician. Ninette de Valois was engaged as resident choreographer at the Festival, a task which began with the arrangement of choruses in Greek dramas and later included the production of small ballets and dance plays which were performed by students from her Academy of Choreographic Art.

The opening production at the Festival of the Oresteiad Trilogy of Æschylus was a triumph alike for Gray's theories, Herbert Prentice's production and Ninette de Valois' choreography. It was the first assignment of such a nature that she had ever tackled and she had the advantage of working in a theatre which allowed an extraordinary amount of freedom and "elbow room." She could bring her Chorus of Furies, for instance, rushing through the audience and up the steps to the forestage. Norman Marshall, who made his name as a producer at the Festival Theatre, has described her handling of the choruses as having "the beauty of strength and power, and although so uncompromisingly modernistic in manner they reproduced with perfect faithfulness the essential ritualistic quality of the Greek drama." This production of the *Orestia* in October 1926, marks the emergence of de Valois the serious choreographer, and was a presage of what was to be achieved later in *Job*. The little numbers arranged in her early days as a soubrette dancer had been left far behind and the extraordinary reach and grasp of her intellect was becoming apparent. She was passionately interested in the advanced and experimental theatre at that time, a rebel and a modernist, very much aware of how much she had yet to learn and with an air of such intellectual seriousness that an American once approached her in Cambridge and said, "Excuse me, but I guess you can tell me the way to Girton."

Norman Marshall has described the years at the Festival Theatre in his book, *The Other Theatre*, and gives a vivid picture of the young de Valois whom he remembers as being " rather like a young schoolmistress who made a point of dressing neatly and sensibly to set the girls a good example. At rehearsals her way of dashing about the stage . . . scolding, goading and exhorting, was so reminicent of a hockey practice that the company nicknamed her 'The Games Mistress.' One of the actors who had a habit of getting out of position remarked that at any moment he expected her to blow a whistle, admonish him for being offside again, and send him off the field. . . . She always appeared to be in a hurry, as if she had already made up her mind about all the work she had to do in the future and had no time to waste."

In fact de Valois probably had very little time to waste, for in addition to work at the Festival, she arranged the dances at the Old Vic for *The Tempest* and *A Midsummer Night's Dream* that autumn and continued to conduct her School in London. She showed very early her extraordinary ability to perform efficiently and at the same time half a dozen tasks that would be full-time commitments for ordinary mortals. Consequently she remembers those Cambridge years mainly as a succession of journeys across the fens in milk-trains, running at all imaginable and unimaginable hours of the day and night. She was still liable in 1926 to receive telegrams from Diaghileff saying, "Come at once dance Les Biches Turin," and she was also arranging ballets for Anton Dolin at the Coliseum and even danced an apache number with him in "Traffic in Souls" in the revue *White Birds* in 1927.

During the winter of 1927 the Academy of Choreographic Art had been responsible for the choreographic work in some half-dozen plays at the Old Vic and the same number in Cambridge. In addition, Ninette de Valois was working on an ambitious new ballet to music by Arthur Bliss which was first produced at her London studio on 22nd January 1928. This was *Rout*, an attempt to portray in a dance built up of groupings and what was then called "futuristic" movement, frequently of a contrapuntal nature, the revolt of modern youth against the conventions of the older generation. The ballet was based on a poem by Ernst Toller, recited by Rosalind Patrick (and later by Vivenne Bennett), and the dancing began before the recitation was completed, without other accompaniment. It then continued to the Bliss music. The work was arranged entirely for female dancers who wore Greek tunics, tights and soft shoes. The composer, Arthur Bliss, and Dr. Malcolm

Sargent played the pianos for this performance and Mrs. Lovat Fraser sang the voice part. *Rout* was received with great solemnity and respect by everyone who saw it and it became a staple item in the early repertoire of the Academy of Choreographic Art, being danced in Cambridge and Dublin as well as in London.

Ninette de Valois remained responsible for choreography at the Festival Theatre until 1931, when she was succeeded by Hedley Briggs. The opportunities offered by the association were of great value, for she learned there an enormous amount about the modern theatre, the various styles and methods of production and the part that could be played by lighting.

Her young students enjoyed the trips to Cambridge for rather different reasons. They were all very young at the time, most of the girls being between fourteen and eighteen years of age, and in Cambridge they lived in digs and felt like real professionals, eating all their meals in the excellent grill-room at the theatre alongside the resident repertory company which included, during Gray's tenancy, Maurice Evans, Margaret Rawlings, Hedley Briggs, Robert Morley, Vivienne Bennett, Gabriel Toyne and Flora Robson. The dancers usually appeared in small ballets or *divertissements* which preceded the plays but they were sometimes employed for dances in the plays as well.

The Festival Theatre passed out of Terence Gray's hands in 1933, and became a fairly conventional repertory theatre for a while but later fell derelict. Gray himself became a wine-grower in France until the war, when he returned to his native Ireland where he now breeds race-horses.

The Abbey Theatre, Dublin

At the beginning of 1928 another repertory theatre called in Ninette de Valois when at the suggestion of W. B. Yeats, who had seen her work in Cambridge, the Directors of the Abbey Theatre in Dublin invited her to establish and direct a school of ballet to be attached to that theatre. The Abbey Theatre building owed its existence to the generosity of Miss Horniman (afterwards of the Gaiety Theatre, Manchester) who in 1904 bought the Mechanics Theatre and the old Dublin Morgue, knocked them into one building, equipped it as a theatre and handed it over to the Irish National

Theatre players in admiration of their work. It was situated on the north bank of the Liffey, Dublin's unfashionable equivalent to the south bank of the Thames, and Ninette's mother inquired plaintively why her daughter *always* had to go and work in theatres on "the wrong side of the river." The Abbey Theatre seated some 550 and had a tiny stage; in the foyer was a peat fire which contributed an aroma but little warmth to the inside of the auditorium. But it had been the centre of Irish theatrical experiment and achievement throughout a most fruitful period.

After the war and the troubles in Ireland, the Free State Government gave this little theatre, then in a precarious financial state, an annual subsidy; in the first year £800 and in subsequent years £1,000. As a result of this subsidy the Directors were able to alter part of the building and establish there a school of acting and a school of ballet. Naturally her other commitments prevented Ninette de Valois from devoting much time to the school herself, but she organised it and started it and then left Sara Patrick in Dublin to take charge, visiting the school herself for a fortnight during each season and staging several ballets and plays for them.

The school was housed in the upper rooms over the Peacock Theatre, a tiny theatre adjoining the Abbey and consisting of part of the old Mechanics' Institute which was used for experimental work and amateur performances. Students joining the ballet school, if under fourteen, paid £12 a year in fees; if over fourteen, £14 a year. At the end of a three-year training, if they proved satisfactory, no more fees were claimed and it was estimated that even during training the students could reduce their fees by at least 50 per cent. from the payments they received while performing. The Abbey Theatre can, therefore, probably claim to be the first theatre in the British Isles to have housed a state-aided ballet school.

The first performances for the students had to be simple *divertissements* and little ballets, and a few students from the Academy of Choreographic Art were usually brought over to help. The most important productions with which de Valois was concerned were W. B. Yeats' "Plays for Dancers," which were written for performance with musicians, screens and masked players. In 1929 she was responsible for *Fighting the Waves,* a version of Yeats' play, *The Only Jealousy of Emer,* which had been arranged to include many dancers. The play was based on the old Irish legend of

Cuchulain and told how after his death his wife Emer and his mistress Eithne Inguba met beside his seemingly bewitched body to draw back his soul from the Sidhe. The dancers of the Abbey School formed the waves and Ninette de Valois danced at their head. The music was written by George Antheil, a friend of Ezra Pound, who had spent part of the winter with Yeats at Rapallo.

The most popular of Yeats' dance plays was *The King of the Great Clock Tower*, which was produced in Dublin on 30th July 1934, with the great Irish actor F. J. McCormick as the King and Ninette de Valois as the Queen. Yeats had a very high opinion of de Valois' art, and he particularly wanted her for this play, but it was the last in which she appeared, for by this time her responsibilities in London had increased so greatly that she was forced to sever her connection with the Abbey. During the six years much experience had been gained, however, and several genuinely Irish ballets produced, such as *Fedelma*, a mime ballet based on the Irish legend of "The King of the Land of Mist," which had music specially composed by William Alwyn. Among the dancers who worked at the Abbey were Toni Repetto, Nesta Brooking, and Jill Gregory, who came over to join the Vic-Wells Ballet in 1933 and is now ballet mistress of the company at Covent Garden. The Abbey Theatre closed the ballet school soon after de Valois' resignation, but it was carried on privately by one of the original pupils and in this guise it is still in existence.

Ballets for the Repertory Theatre

From the beginning Ninette de Valois had been of the opinion that a British ballet company would have to be built very slowly and gradually. She thought that those responsible for launching such a company must first prove their worth to the repertory theatre movement before expecting any financial assistance. Any large expenditure on British ballet at that time would have been unwarranted, because the dancers were simply not ready for any grand enterprises, and a few inevitable failures might have snuffed out completely the flame of the candle. "I am not with the crowd that says, 'English dancers only want a chance,' " she wrote in 1928, "—they still want a lot more knowledge as well, especially about dancing in the theatre."

At the beginning of the 1928–29 season at the Old Vic, de Valois became responsible for the opera ballets as well as the dances in the plays, and her dancers from the Academy of Choreographic Art took part in the Old Vic productions. In order to show the sort of work her students were capable of and had been doing in Cambridge and Dublin, she took the Court Theatre in Sloane Square and presented there, in November 1928, three performances of "ballets suitable for the Little Theatre movement." Among her dancers were Ursula Moreton, Molly Lake, Sheila McCarthy, Rosalind Patrick, Joy Newton, Freda Bamford, Stanley Judson and Hedley Briggs.

The programme included a slight but charming *Scène Venitienne* danced to music by Respighi, several short numbers and *divertissements*—among which Hedley Briggs' *Nobodye's Jigge,* to music by Richard Farnaby from the Fitzwilliam Virginal Book, was especially successful—a classical *Scène de Ballet* to music of Gluck, and a revival of *Rout.* The most unusual work was *The Scorpions of Ysit,* which was based on a dance drama by Terence Gray, with music by Elsie Hamilton "composed in the modes of ancient Egypt." The attempt on the part of the singer to reproduce Oriental intoning seems to have disturbed some of the audience and more than one critic found the story unintelligible, but the choreography for the seven scorpions was thought clever and Ursula Moreton received praise for the moving sincerity of her mime as the mother. All the costumes and *décor* were designed by the staff or students of the Academy of Choreographic Art. The music, under the direction of Norman Franklin, was arranged for string quartet, harp and two pianos.

The performances lost £200 but they earned de Valois an astonishingly good and perceptive crop of Press notices. The *Morning Post* declared that "everybody on the stage showed a sense of style and often very considerable technical ability. . . . Indeed, intelligence and imagination in every detail were keynotes of the whole *matinée,* which showed once more that, given the opportunity, we could produce a very good Ballet in England." "The great merit of the programme," said *The Times,* "was its variety," and "behind everything was an idea." The enthusiasm of Philip Page led him into an amazingly accurate prophecy: "There is in existence, though it is not widely known, an Academy of

D

Choreographic Art," he wrote. "Not yet can it tack the word 'Royal' in front of its name, but after its activities at the Royal Court Theatre yesterday it is obvious that this must come in time. . . ." The warmest tribute, however, came from Francis Toye in his B.B.C. Lecture on "Music in the Theatre," broadcast on 5th December 1928: "Some people who call themselves the Academy of Choreographic Art gave a *matinée* of little ballets last week at the Court Theatre. In this connection there are two things that I could wish, firstly, that they would change their preposterous title, and secondly, that I had more time to talk about their *matinée*, which was extremely interesting, and in many ways very original. . . . We have heard a great deal lately about schemes for starting English ballet and so on, and I must say that enterprises like this one are most encouraging in that respect."

Less than a month later, on 13th December, the first ballet was given at the Old Vic, when Ninette de Valois produced Mozart's *Les Petits Riens* as a curtain-raiser to the Christmas production of *Hansel and Gretel*. The ballet had a Watteau setting and de Valois herself appeared as Rosalind, a pastoral coquette, while Ursula Moreton "was charming as the slighted nymph who devises an ingenious retaliation upon the maid who had beguiled her lover from her." Stanley Judson and Hedley Briggs were the cavaliers, and pupils from the Academy danced in the ensemble. The orchestra was conducted by Charles Corri, who was then resident opera conductor at the Vic, and whose wife Martha Mayall had been "ballerina" with the Carl Rosa Opera and later ballet mistress for the operas at the Old Vic.

Five months later another small ballet was produced to precede *Rigoletto*. This was *The Picnic* (later known as *The Faun*), to music by Vaughan Williams. The choreography was by Ninette de Valois and the costumes by Hedley Briggs. The *corps de ballet* was drawn from the Old Vic Opera Ballet and the Academy of Choreographic Art, and Harold Turner appeared in the leading part of "a satyr," by permission of Marie Rambert, whose pupil he was at that time. Ursula Moreton, Molly Lake and Stanley Judson had the other solo parts. The story concerned a party of villagers who quarrel on a midnight picnic party and thus disturb the woodland folk, who take their revenge by appearing as strange phantoms and terrifying the mortals.

Summing up on the achievements of the season, the Annual Report of the Old Vic Theatre for 1928–29 said: "Perhaps its most far-reaching and important events were concerned with the Old Vic's first tentative efforts at founding a school of English Ballet. Such a development of the operatic side of the work has always been an ideal that the Manager has set in front of her; and in the indomitable hands of Ninette de Valois this ideal has been translated into an achievement. By their appreciation and support the audience have not only justified the extra trouble and expense involved by this new departure but have made a considerable development of the scheme possible in the coming seasons, preparations for which developments are now in train."

The success of the two previous ventures persuaded Lilian Baylis to allot a slightly larger share of the programme to the ballet the following Christmas. On 17th December 1929 a short *divertissement* and the ballet *Hommage aux Belles Viennoises* were presented in front of *Hansel and Gretel* with a cast that included Ninette de Valois, Ursula Moreton and Frederick Ashton. This little ballet, danced to a set of waltzes and mazurkas by Schubert, was a favourite from the beginning, and even when the complete ballet was no longer given, one number in it survived as a *divertissement* for many years in the Vic-Wells repertoire. This was a dance for two girls and a man, based on a Tyrolean Schuhplatteln, and was originally performed by Freda Bamford, Frederick Ashton and Sheila McCarthy—who learned the man's steps as well as her own and estimated that by the time she left the Vic-Wells Ballet she had taught the dance to some seventeen different male partners.

Soon afterwards Ninette de Valois organised another programme, which was presented at the Lyric Theatre, Hammersmith, by the Academy of Choreographic Art in conjunction with the Festival Theatre, Cambridge, on 28th March 1930. This *matinée* illustrated the work she had been doing at the Festival, Abbey and Old Vic Theatres. Unfortunately, she tore a leg muscle at the dress rehearsal and was only able to appear in *Fighting the Waves*. Sheila McCarthy replaced her in *Les Petits Riens* and Ursula Moreton in *The Picnic*. The programme was made up with a play by Gordon Bottomley, *So Fair a Satrap*, which represented the Cambridge contribution.

In December 1930, the Christmas production of *Hansel and Gretel* at the Old Vic was preceded by a *Suite of Dances* to music of Bach, arranged by Goossens, in which Harold Turner danced. These light-weight, unpretentious dancing ballets won the warm hearts of the Old Vic audience very easily, and Lilian Baylis began to think seriously about the part that the ballet company might play when she had the new theatre in Islington ready.

Sadler's Wells

By 1930, of course, rebuilding of the derelict theatre of Sadler's Wells was well away. The rebuilding fund, after five years' unmitigated effort, had reached some £70,000 and the theatre was to be ready for use by the beginning of 1931. Ninette de Valois went with Lilian Baylis to look at the theatre in its rough, unfinished state. From the gallery it was a vast expanse of white, without paint, upholstery or seats. Both women were quiet and preoccupied —struck by the grandeur of the building and aware of all that it was going to mean to them in the future.

Practical discussions were going on about the financial implications of establishing a permanent ballet company, and Ninette de Valois called on Reginald Rowe armed with the balance-sheet for the year's working at the Academy of Choreographic Art. She had proof that her school was a paying proposition and she offered to hand it over to Sadler's Wells as a going concern in return for the establishment of an opera ballet and a training school within the walls of the new theatre.

She explained that ballet on a proper scale needed a large theatre and an orchestra; it also required within the walls of the theatre a properly organised school—and a theatre training school for English classical dancers was the crying need of English ballet at that time. With a repertory organisation such as the Old Vic and Sadler's Wells a school and company could be run in conjunction on an economic basis not practicable in a private venture. Profits from the school would help to offset the cost of dancers' salaries and the dancers could be used in a variety of ways in the two theatres.

Reginald Rowe inspected the balance-sheet of the Academy of Choreographic Art and realised that the school was indeed making enough money to pay for the modest company envisaged. As there was no financial risk or capital outlay involved, it was

not difficult to persuade the Governors to accept the plan, and it was decided that the Vic-Sadler's Wells Opera Ballet should commence by engaging six salaried dancers with Ninette de Valois as "*prima ballerina*, director and principal choreographist." For opera ballets needing more dancers, senior students from the school would be used and for special ballets to be given before the shorter operas the theatre would engage the necessary male dancers from outside. At the beginning of the 1931 season the company would make a start by providing the opera ballets needed in the repertoire and would perform the five special ballets, which were already mounted and dressed, as curtain-raisers to short operas. It was envisaged, however, that as the venture grew the permanent company would be strengthened, male dancers would be added, and a special ballet performance for "the whole evening" once a week would be instituted, with works mounted by other choreographers. The season at the Vic and Wells was to be for nine continuous months from September to May each year—a guarantee of employment almost unknown to English dancers at that time. The big Sadler's Wells Room was to be given over to the ballet and the school was to remain permanently at Sadler's Wells, although the company would play at either the Vic or Wells, as the opera and Shakespeare companies were to play alternate fortnights at each theatre.

Her plan approved and accepted by the Governors of the Old Vic and Sadler's Wells, Ninette de Valois called a meeting of her students and their parents and explained what was going to happen. Ursula Moreton, Freda Bamford, Sheila McCarthy, Joy Newton, Beatrice Appleyard and Nadina Newhouse became the first salaried members of the company.

The move to Sadler's Wells meant, however, that de Valois had to close down her studio in Roland Gardens, and on the page announcing the opening of "The Sadler's Wells Theatre School of Ballet," she inserted an advertisement in *The Dancing Times* proclaiming that this "fully equipped studio" was TO LET. The twin advertisements illustrate the biggest milestone of de Valois' career; they also record the anxiety of a young teacher—for having handed over her school and her income, she was left with a studio on her hands and commitments for several years' rent. Fortunately, a tenant for 6A Roland Houses was very quickly found.

CHAPTER IV

THE CAMARGO SOCIETY

CHANCE and coincidence seem to conspire in the theatre to throw up strangely significant simultaneous happenings. The year 1926, for instance, had been momentous for the three chief architects of the Sadler's Wells Ballet: in that year de Valois had first made contact with Lilian Baylis, Ashton had created his first ballet and Constant Lambert's first ballet, *Roméo et Juliette*, had been presented by Diaghileff. The year 1930 was another such *annus mirabilis*, for it saw the announcements of the establishment of a permanent ballet at Sadler's Wells and the formation of the Ballet Club, and it witnessed the first performance staged by the Camargo Society, which was to be of infinite value and importance in publicising and encouraging these twin nurseries of English ballet.

The Camargo Society actually dates from the autumn of 1929, for it was then that Philip Richardson invited Arnold Haskell to lunch with him to discuss some means whereby a society for the production of ballet in England might be formed. Diaghileff had died in Venice the previous August, leaving no will, let alone any administration capable of continuing his company, and his impresario in England, Eric Wolheim, had made it clear that the Diaghileff *Ballets Russes* could not go on in the form in which it had been known for the past twenty years.

Something would be needed to fill the void, and both Richardson and Haskell believed that there was sufficient talent available in England to produce not a substitute for the Diaghileff Ballet but something interesting and important in its own right. In their preliminary talk, over an excellent luncheon in a restaurant named Chez Taglioni, they decided it would be a good idea if a society could be formed somewhat on the lines of the Stage Society for the production of ballets three or four times a year. They subsequently invited some twenty-five dancers, musicians and artists to an informal dinner at the Moulin d'Or in Romilly Street, and at this dinner Ninette de Valois, Mrs. Lovat Fraser and Edwin Evans were invited to draw up a tentative scheme for further discussion. After a couple more dinners the name "Camargo" had been decided upon, committees had been elected, Mr. Montagu-Nathan had been designated secretary, and a general plan of campaign worked out ready for presentation to the public at an inaugural dinner which was held at the Hotel Métropole on Sunday, 16th February 1930, with Madame Adeline Genée in the chair.

The General Committee of the Camargo Society was as follows: Lydia Lopokova, Choreographic Director; Arnold L. Haskell, Art Director; Edwin Evans, Chairman and Musical Director; Alfred Tysser, Treasurer; Marie Rambert, Phyllis Bedells and P. J. S. Richardson. On advisory committees were Grace Cone, Ninette de Valois, Tamara Karsavina, Penelope Spencer, Anton Dolin and Stephen Thomas, and supporters who lent their names to the enterprise were: *Dancing*—Seraphine Astafieva, Margaret Craske, Margaret Einert, Ruth French, Anna Ludmila, Tilly Losch, Alicia Markova, Marie Rambert, Errol Addison, Frederick Ashton. *Décor*—Grace Lovat Fraser, Paul Nash, George Sheringham. *Music*—Arnold Bax, Lennox Berkeley, Lord Berners, Arthur Bliss, Herbert Howells, Gustav Holst, Constant Lambert, Malcolm Sargent, R. Vaughan Williams. It was an amazing showing.

The inaugural dinner was an unqualified success; all the leading dancers in England attended and many prominent musicians. It is interesting to note that George Balanchine and Boris Kochno were among those present. Sir Herbert Morgan proposed the toast of The Camargo Society, the witty and corpulent Edwin Evans replied (declaring that he was willing to do anything for the Society short of dancing for it), and Lydia Lopokova proposed the toast of The Guests.

The aims of the Society were stated to be the production of original and classic ballets before a subscription audience at a West End theatre four times a year on Sunday evenings and Monday afternoons. For these productions the collaboration of eminent composers, painters and choreographers would be invited and the best dancing talent would be engaged. It was stressed that the Society was not formed to take the place of Diaghileff or to carry on the Diaghileff Ballet but to make the next phase as interesting as possible. The Society was to be entirely for the production of "ballet" without any qualifying adjective, whether national or æsthetic. Subscribers paid three guineas or two guineas a year, depending on the seat required, and for an extra guinea could reserve the same seat for the entire season. A one guinea membership was available for students. A competent, even if small, orchestra was considered a necessity despite the extra expense that it involved, and supporters were invited to make special donations in addition to their yearly subscription if they could afford to do so.

The enormous executive of advisory committees was soon whittled down to a smaller group who actually did the work, and the first programme was given at the Cambridge Theatre on 19th October 1930. It opened with a revival by Madame Genée of the ballet from *Robert the Devil* and concluded with a set of *Variations and Coda* to Glinka music, arranged by Nicholas Legat, in which the entire company appeared and a *pas de deux* was danced by Ninette de Valois and Anton Dolin. The two principal novelties were *Danse Sacrée et Danse Profane* (Debussy) with choreography by Ninette de Valois, and masks and costumes by Hedley Briggs, danced by members of the Academy of Choreographic Art, and the production of Constant Lambert's ballet *Pomona*, for which Frederick Ashton created the choreography and Vanessa Bell designed scenery and costumes.[1] In this ballet, the outstanding creation of the evening, the American ballerina Anna Ludmila appeared as Pomona, while Anton Dolin was Vertumnus. The entire programme was conducted by Constant Lambert.

The Cambridge Theatre was filled by a distinguished audience who were enthusiastic about what they saw. Lydia Lopokova described it as "a thrilling occasion," and one member of the audience was so convinced that it was an historic occasion that she bought six copies of the programme. The Press was also enthusiastic and encouraging, Ashton's choreography for *Pomona* earning especially high praise. It proved emphatically, said one critic, "that that hitherto mythical personage, a British choreographist of the first rank, is amongst us."

Subsequent programmes were given in February, April and July 1931, and among the ballets produced were *Cephalus and Procris,* music by Grétry, choreography by Ninette de Valois, costumes by William Chappell, in which Harold Turner, Alicia Markova and

---

[1] Augustus John had originally agreed to design the ballet, but he was out of the country at the time of the production.

Prudence Hyman had the leading rôles; *Capriol Suite*, which had been first given by the Marie Rambert Dancers at Hammersmith in February 1930; Ninette de Valois' ballet *Rout*, strengthened by the inclusion of five male dancers (one was Frederick Ashton); *La Création du Monde* (Milhaud), a Negro conception of the creation as it might have been acted in one of their ceremonies, with choreography by Ninette de Valois; *Façade*; *The Jackdaw and the Pigeons*— performed by the Vic-Wells Ballet, "by kind permission of Miss Lilian Baylis"; and finally *Job*. It was, as Edwin Evans said, a stupendous effort and it left the Society "breathless and cashless."

It had succeeded, however, in shattering the myth of inferiority which had clung to the idea of an English ballet, and it had proved not only that dancers, composers and designers were available in England but that it was possible to have native choreographers of importance as well. From the beginning the Sunday-night performances drew audiences which were large and enthusiastic and at the same time knowledgeable and influential in all the arts. The Press paid close attention to what was going on, praising the actual achievements and keeping in front of the public the future hopes for a British ballet company. *Pomona*, *Capriol Suite* and *Façade* were all immediately popular and *Job* made a particularly deep impression on all the critics. Richard Capell in the *Daily Mail* said, "The whole representation had a beauty both strange and dignified—more, one would say that at times sublimity was attained." *The Times* found it "that rare thing, a completely satisfying synthesis of the Arts." Arnold Haskell placed it with Ashton's *Mercury* as one of the finest works seen for a long time and suggested that de Valois' future as a choreographer might lie in the large spectacular ballet: "Her smaller works, such as *Cephalus and Procris*, strike me as somewhat finicky in detail, but in the heroic she is almost without rival."

The Camargo Society was doing invaluable service, but the executive committee had no easy task for they were, after all, "a management without a company" and every participant in every programme had to be recruited individually. The dancers received a flat rate of £1 a performance and the orchestra was paid £100. It had been estimated at the beginning that some six or seven hundred subscribers would suffice to guarantee modest productions but, in fact, the membership never quite attained the figure that was considered "safe" in the early estimates. On the other hand, theatrical expenses showed their historic tendency to work out at considerably more than was budgeted for as an outside estimate. The orchestra was a continual worry, for only one full orchestral rehearsal could be afforded before each programme, and the success of *Job* might well have been jeopardised had not Gustav Holst come to the rescue and personally (though secretly) financed one extra rehearsal because he had learned that Lambert was worried as to whether the orchestra's performance would be "all right on the night."

Nevertheless, the value of the work that was being accomplished was so self-evident, and the enthusiasm and devotion of the executive committee was so strong, that the Society not only embarked on another season but began to make plans for a summer season at the Savoy Theatre, to be open to the general public. At the end of the first season J. M. Keynes (later Lord Keynes) had taken over the duties of Honorary Treasurer and sat on the executive committee with Lydia Lopokova, Edwin Evans, Constant Lambert, Marie Rambert and Ninette de Valois. Sufficient influential patrons were found to act as guarantors for the Savoy season, and an ambitious programme was devised for the four weeks from 6th June to 2nd July 1932.

Olga Spessiva (Spessivtseva) was invited to come from Paris to dance *Giselle* and *Le Lac des Cygnes*, and the other principal dancers were Ninette de Valois, Alicia Markova, Lydia Lopokova, Phyllis Bedells and Anton Dolin. Dancers from the Vic-Wells Ballet and the Ballet Club included Ursula Moreton, Rupert Doone, Stanley Judson, Pearl Argyle, Frederick Ashton, William Chappell and Walter Gore. The orchestra was conducted by Sir Thomas Beecham and Constant Lambert; Ninette de Valois was Ballet Mistress; and special curtains by McKnight Kauffer, William Roberts and Walter Sickert were used as visual accompaniment to the musical interludes.

The repertory of ballets available to the Camargo Society by this time included *Job, High Yellow, The Origin of Design, Fête Polonaise, The Lord of Burleigh, Rio Grande, Ballade, Façade, The Enchanted Grove, Mars and Venus, Cephalus and Procris, Le Spectre de la Rose, Regatta, Pomona* and *L'Après-midi d'un Faune*. Sergueeff's revival of *Giselle* with Spessiva, Anton Dolin and Ruth French (as Queen of the Wilis) was the most important new production undertaken during the season, and Spessiva's performances in this and in

Le Lac des Cygnes (Act II) made a deep impression on the young English dancers who took part in the season as well as upon the audiences.

Among other ballets, Sir Thomas Beecham conducted his own arrangement of Handel's music for Ninette de Valois' ballet *The Origin of Design*, and musically this was one of the most pleasing works in the repertoire. Sir Thomas also made a profound and lasting impression with the speed at which he insisted on taking the *pas de quatre* in *Le Lac des Cygnes*, and it seems only fair that history should also record the names of the four dancers who managed to keep up with him; they were Sheila McCarthy, Nadina Newhouse, Ailne Phillips and Kathleen Crofton.

Another problem the dancers had to contend with was the shortage of washing facilities in the Savoy Theatre at that time, and as they were all covered with black wash at each performance of *Création du Monde* this was a major difficulty. Finally the dancers involved were given a suite, entirely covered with dust sheets, in the Savoy Hotel, and amazed diners used to see a troupe of jet black girls, wearing dressing-gowns and carrying towels and sponge bags, scuttling through the main door and across the vestibule of the hotel to the stairs.

These minor tribulations excepted, however, the season was a decided success. It had been the first serious British attempt to produce ballet in the West End and it attracted an appreciative public. The Press was excellent and, as C. B. Mortlock said in the *Daily Telegraph*, "it made artistic history." It did not, however, make money, for the expenses were heavy, and the Society entered its next season in a precarious financial condition.

It was then that J. M. Keynes came to the rescue and secured for Camargo an invitation to present two gala performances of ballet at the Royal Opera House, Covent Garden, on Tuesday, 27th June, and Thursday, 29th June 1933, by arrangement with the Government Hospitality Fund, in honour of the World Economic Conference which was then being held in London. The Queen and other members of the Royal Family attended the first performance, the Prime Minister and members of the Cabinet the second. On both occasions the Opera House was filled to capacity, and as a result the Camargo Society was able to clear all its outstanding debts and found itself with a small balance in the bank.

The first two acts of *Coppélia* were given, with Lydia Lopokova, Stanley Judson and Hedley Briggs as the three principals, and with Ninette de Valois, Ursula Moreton and Frederick Ashton leading the character dances, and the second act of *Le Lac des Cygnes*, with Alicia Markova and Anton Dolin. In addition, Dolin performed a character dance to music by Moskowski. Several other dancers appeared with the Vic-Wells Ballet for the occasion, notably Frederick Ashton and Frederic Franklin.

It is revealing to note the growth and progress of the Vic-Wells Ballet through the Camargo programmes. Originally a few dancers are listed as appearing "by permission of Miss Lilian Baylis." By July 1931 *The Jackdaw and the Pigeons* is performed by "The Vic-Wells Ballet by kind permission of Miss Lilian Baylis." The four-week season at the Savoy is presented by "The Camargo Society in conjunction with the Vic-Wells Ballet and the Ballet Club." By the time of the Covent Garden galas in 1933 the Vic-Wells Ballet is able to provide the major ballets, *Coppélia* and *Le Lac des Cygnes* (although strengthened by guest artists), and Ninette de Valois is described somewhat quaintly in the programme as "mistress over the ballet."

The Camargo Society had, of course, to rely to a large extent on the dancers of the Vic-Wells Ballet and the Ballet Club for its productions, but it was able to offer them West End presentation that they could never have achieved themselves, and it financed productions on a scale that neither company's exchequer could contemplate. The co-operation was close and all three organisations benefited: ballets first produced at the Camargo Society were later "by arrangement" taken into the Vic-Wells repertory, and ballets produced at the Vic and Wells or the Ballet Club were given a shop window in Camargo programmes.

By the autumn of 1933, in fact, the Society had so completely done what it set out to do that there was practically nothing left for it to do. It had kept the idea of English ballet constantly in the minds of the public and of musicians, artists and dancers, and it had helped in building a repertoire for the permanently established ballet company at Sadler's Wells. When it was no longer financially practicable to continue the quarterly Sunday night performances the Committee decided that it would be more sensible to put all the ballet eggs in one basket and suggested that it should use its resources to offer from time to time to produce, at its own expense, a ballet for Sadler's Wells. As a start, the cash in hand was donated to the Vic-Wells Ballet. The production of Ashton's *Apparitions* in 1936 was made possible by the Camargo Society and was its last gesture for English ballet.

A large debt of gratitude is due to all its supporters and to the artists who gave their services so willingly for a cause in which they had such faith. When the Russian Ballet returned in full force in 1933 the Vic-Wells Ballet had established itself securely enough to withstand the impact. Without the assistance of the Camargo Society it is very doubtful whether this would have been possible, and the Russian "invasion"—which in fact acted as a stimulus and incentive—might have submerged English ballet in the same way as did the French invasion a century before.

PART III

THE YEARS IN ISLINGTON

CHAPTER V

THE BEGINNING

THE Vic-Wells Ballet was named heir to the Camargo Society
because it was the only permanently established ballet company
operating in a theatre large enough to stage the more ambitious
Camargo Society productions. The Ballet Club had played, and
was to continue to play, a vital part as an artistic fertilising agent,
but it was not in a position to offer performances regularly to the
general public in a full-sized theatre. Ninette de Valois, on the
other hand, had the advantages of a permanent home for her
company inside the theatre of Sadler's Wells and the moral support
of Lilian Baylis.

Sadler's Wells Theatre in Rosebery Avenue, Islington, was
reopened on Twelfth Night, 1931, in the midst of the Depression,
on a night of fog and hard frost. The appropriate Shakespeare play
was given, with a cast typical of the Old Vic at that time: it included
John Gielgud, Ralph Richardson, George Howe, Leslie French
and Dorothy Green. Before the play, however, there was an
opening ceremony with an equally distinguished cast. On the stage
were Lilian Baylis, Sir Johnston Forbes-Robertson and Dame
Madge Kendal, plus the mayors of the seven boroughs which had
contributed to the rebuilding fund. The staircases on each side of
the stage were occupied by the opera company, and the proceedings
began with the singing of the National Anthem at its unfamiliar
full length, the first verse being sung by Joan Cross, who commanded the O.P. staircase, the second by Constance Willis, who
commanded the other staircase, and the third by the entire audience.

The Mayor of Finsbury then gave the new theatre his municipal
blessing, Sir Johnston Forbes-Robertson recalled personal memories
of Samuel Phelps, his teacher, and Dame Madge Kendal, another
Phelps pupil, added her blessing. A telegram from the Prince of
Wales, "our chief subscriber," was read and a statement on the
financial situation made. The theatre had cost some £85,000,
towards which £70,000 had been raised (it was said that thousands

E

of sixpences had been subscribed and thousands of shillings as well as the larger offerings), but a debt of £21,000 remained, while the Old Vic itself faced a rebuilding debt of another £7,000. The Trust Deed was held by a committee under the Charity Commissioners so that the theatre could be run without payment of rent and the prices of admission kept low enough to attract the working people of North London. Seats were advertised at prices from 6d. to 5s. 9d., which were much the same as those asked at the Old Vic.

Lilian Baylis, who could rock the foundations of the Old Vic in storming over the price of one costume, accepted this heavy indebtedness philosophically and surveyed her new theatre with pleasure: 1,648 seats, all tip-ups, and an uninterrupted view of the stage from all of them. Over the proscenium was a plaque depicting a scene from *A Midsummer Night's Dream* (which still stands witness to the original plan to take Shakespeare to North London) and above it the arms of the Borough of Finsbury. "Woman's Life Dream Realised," said the *Daily Express* next day, but the papers made no special clamour about the advent of the new theatre. Amy Johnson was flying to China, the Marx Brothers were in London for the first time, Sophie Tucker was at the Palladium and the new Kingsway Tunnel was on the point of opening. A rather bare, new theatre out at Islington, with an austere grey curtain and no carpets on the floor, had little claim to publicity. As for the newly formed little ballet company, no popular paper showed the slightest awareness of its existence.

"The Vic-Sadler's Wells Opera Ballet" had actually given its first performance just before Sadler's Wells was reopened. In December 1930 the dancers went down to Bournemouth to give a few performances at the Pavilion before "a large and appreciative audience." Augmented by Harold Turner and Hedley Briggs as guest artists, they performed *The Faun,* a programme of *divertissements,* and the Bach-Goossens *Suite de Danses.* There were the usual mishaps; some costumes were left behind and Freda Bamford sprained an ankle, but the experience was valuable and the *Bournemouth Echo* said "the grouping and tableaux were models of perfection."

Back in London the dancers concentrated on opera ballets. They had taken over completely from the former amateur dancers, and

SADLER'S WELLS THEATRE

Lilian Baylis (*extreme right*) inspecting the ruins of Sadler's Wells before her new theatre was built. Standing on the 'stage' are Matheson Lang, Edith Evans and Balliol Holloway; (*below*) Mrs. Matheson Lang, Sir Arthur Pinero and Squire Bancroft

THE OLD VIC WARDROBE

Lilian Baylis (*centre*) inspecting the costumes for a new production

Beatrice Appleyard, Joy Newton, Anton Dolin, Ninette de Valois,
Ursula Moreton and Alicia Markova at rehearsal

BRITISH BALLET IN DENMARK
A curtain call at the Royal Theatre, Copenhagen
Left to Right: Harold Turner, Phyllis Bedells, Ninette de Valois, Adeline
Genée, Anton Dolin, Alicia Markova, Ruth French, Stanley Judson

as there were only six of them and they appeared in every opera, the task was somewhat complicated. Opera and drama were then playing alternate fortnights at the Old Vic and Sadler's Wells, so that although the ballet school and all the rehearsals were held at the Wells, on alternate fortnights the dancers had stage calls and performances at the Vic. Rehearsing was continual, because if the girls were not actually dancing they were appearing as pages, train-bearers, bodies in sacks in *Rigoletto* or bewitched princes in *Lohengrin*. They spent their spare time travelling on the 67 bus, under-dressed in practice clothes, always having left something vital in the wrong theatre. Nevertheless, they were able to present in the next few months two sets of *divertissements* (in which Claude Newman appeared "by kind permission of C. B. Cochran"), one preceding *Tosca* and the other preceding *Il Trovatore*, the full ballets in *Carmen, Aïda* and *Faust* (for which Frederick Ashton was engaged to partner Ninette de Valois), and the incidental dances in *Il Trovatore, The Lily of Killarney* and *The Magic Flute*.

By the spring Lilian Baylis decided they might risk a complete evening of ballet, and this was planned to take place at the Old Vic on 5th May. The profits from the school were earmarked for the development of the ballet, and from the beginning the school had prospered. Classes for office workers, which were held at the Old Vic, also brought in a little money. Every penny went straight into the ballet, however, and Ninette de Valois supported herself chiefly by giving classes to children of the wealthy and fashionable at Heathfield in her spare time.

The important point about the foundation of the Vic-Wells Ballet was that it had to be entirely self-supporting; it received no grant, donations or financial support from the day it started and had to be prepared to pay its own way and justify its existence in the theatre.

The "first full evening of ballet" was planned with some care to include several established favourites and a new creation, *The Jackdaw and the Pigeons*. Anton Dolin appeared as guest artist and Constant Lambert was invited to conduct. The presence of Anton Dolin lent considerable lustre to the performance, and his contribution during the early years of the company was of immense value, although he was never for any length of time a regular member of the company. The faithful Old Vic audience could be counted on to support any venture which Lilian Baylis commended to them, but Dolin was able to attract the ballet audience, and it was the combination of these two elements which provided the public support without which all the dreams of Baylis and de Valois could have come to nothing.

The programme for 5th May 1931 was as follows: *Les Petits Riens, Danse Sacrée et Danse Profane, Hommage aux Belles Viennoises, The Jackdaw and the Pigeons, Scène de Ballet* from *Faust,* Bach *Suite of Dances, Spanish Dance* (by Dolin) and *The Faun.* The Old Vic was completely sold out and many people were turned away. The programme was long but the audience loved it, and the new ballet, *The Jackdaw and the Pigeons,* was well received, although the more sophisticated members of the audience found this bird ballet, based on Aesop's fable, rather tiresome and silly: "stale prancings and pantomimic trivialities" was one unkind comment. Ursula Moreton, Sheila McCarthy and Stanley Judson all distinguished themselves in the course of the evening, and Dolin earned special praise for his strength and elegance in the Bach Suite. Leslie French, then appearing with the Shakespeare company, also contributed his services and appeared in *The Faun* with Ursula Moreton.

The success was so positive that it was decided to repeat the programme at Sadler's Wells on 15th and 21st May. Lambert once again consented to conduct, at a greatly reduced fee, and Dolin was so enthusiastic about the whole venture that he asked and obtained permission from Jack Buchanan to appear again at Sadler's Wells in the first evening of the ballet there. On 21st May *Cephalus and Procris* (produced for the Camargo Society the previous January) was given for the first time at Sadler's Wells and Lydia Lopokova appeared in it as guest artist, at her own special request, thus lending the considerable *cachet* of her name and reputation.

With a generosity typical of all her work in the theatre, Lopokova asked only out-of-pocket expenses for her performances at the Wells and then suggested that the money be divided among the young members of the ballet company who appeared with her. Not to be outdone in generosity, the young dancers promptly handed over the sum to the Fund for the repayment of the building debts on the theatre.

The management were surprised at the success of the three ballet performances. In the Annual Report for 1930–31 they recorded that it had been "astonishingly satisfactory to discover so large

OLD VIC & SADLER'S WELLS

Founded by
EMMA CONS IN 1880

RE-OPENED 1931

Lessee and Manager - - LILIAN BAYLIS, C.H., M.A., Oxon. (Hon.)

The Vic-Wells Ballet

(Under the Direction of NINETTE DE VALOIS)

Saturday, October 24th, at 2.15 prompt

~~AT THE OLD VIC~~

OWING TO GREAT SUCCESS
REPETITION OF

JOB

A MASQUE FOR DANCING
by GEOFFREY KEYNES.

Music by VAUGHAN WILLIAMS.
Choreography by NINETTE DE VALOIS.

ANTON DOLIN

By kind permission of JACK BUCHANAN and R. H GILLESPIE

AS

SATAN

SADLER'S WELLS.   **Nov. 6th at 7.45**

THE OLD VIC.   **Nov. 13th at 7.45 Nov. 14th at 2.30**

DIDO AND AENEAS (*Purcell*)

1st Production by Vic-Wells Company
FOLLOWED BY

CEPHALUS AND PROCRIS

A Ballet in 2 scenes with music by GRETY

On November. 6th, special appearance of

LYDIA LOPOKOVA

AS

PROCRIS

Musical Director   –   –   **CONSTANT LAMBERT**

OLD VIC PRICES.—Reserved Seats: Stalls and Circle, 5/-; Side Circle, 2/4; Pit, 3/6, 2/4. Unreserved Seats: 5d. to 3/6. Box Office open 10 a.m. to 10 p.m. 'Phones: Hop 3424 and 3425 (2 lines) *Underground*: Waterloo, Lambeth North. *Buses*: 1, 33, 48, 67, 68, 69, 169. *Tram* · 68.

SADLER'S WELLS PRICES.—Reserved Seats: Stalls and Circle, 5/9, 3/6 and 2/4. Circle and Pit, 2/4. Amphitheatre, 1/10 and 1/3. Unreserved Seats: Pit, 1/10 and 1/3. Gallery, 10d. and 6d. Box Office Open Daily, 10 a.m. to 10 p.m. 'Phone: Clerkenwell 1121 and 1122. *Underground*: Farringdon Road Station *Tube*. The Angel *'Buses* 19, 38, 63, 67, 161, 175. *Trams*: 35, 51, 53, 75, 79, 81.

WILLIAMS & STRAHAN, LTD., Printers, London, S.E.1.

and enthusiastic a public eagerly waiting for the presentation of this difficult and eclectic form of art, which has not hitherto been treated seriously in London unless it hailed from a foreign country." Lilian Baylis consequently felt she might risk a performance of ballet once a fortnight throughout the 1931–32 season, which would run from September to May, and engaged Constant Lambert as conductor and Musical Director.

The 1931–32 season opened at the Old Vic on 22nd September and this first full season was fittingly introduced by a performance of *Job*, which the Camargo Society lent to the company and for which Vaughan Williams asked only a nominal fee. Dolin repeated his magnificent performance as Satan and the impact of the ballet was instantaneous. The first slight programmes may not have seemed very important, but a work like *Job* at once revealed the power and the creative force of de Valois as a choreographer and the possibilities for serious English ballet.

Job was not only a *succès d'estime* but a popular success as well, and the Vic and Wells were crowded whenever it was given. It has remained in the repertoire of the Sadler's Wells Ballet ever since and now occupies a very special place in the traditions of the company and in the affections of everyone who has been associated with Sadler's Wells.

This "Masque for Dancing" had been invented by Dr. Geoffrey Keynes some years previously. An ardent balletomane and a great authority on the work of William Blake, he had felt that Blake's *Illustrations of the Book of Job*, first published as a series of twenty-one engravings in 1825, unconsciously provided settings which could easily be translated on the stage, while there were "innumerable suggestions in his figures for attitudes and groupings, which cried out for their conversion by a choreographer into actuality and movement." He prepared a detailed scenario for a stage production and persuaded his sister-in-law Gwendolen Raverat (*née* Darwin) to design backcloths based on Blake's drawings and to colour small cut-out figures to represent the leading characters in the main scenes and groupings. These designs were prepared for a toy theatre, and when the cardboard figures were assembled they illustrated very exactly the main climaxes of the action as they were eventually to appear in the ballet. Dr. Keynes had completed his scheme for the ballet by 1927 and had persuaded Ralph Vaughan

Williams (a cousin of the Darwins) to compose the music. He sent a French translation of the scenario to Diaghileff, who was at that time the only person in a position to produce such a ballet, but the subject did not appeal to Diaghileff and he rejected it as too English and too old-fashioned. Dr. Keynes can probably take credit, however, for having sown a seed in the great man's mind which was later to bear fruit in the production of *Le Fils Prodigue*.

With the formation of the Camargo Society, Dr. Keynes saw another chance of having *Job* produced, and he invited Lilian Baylis and Ninette de Valois to come and see the models and the toy theatre. They were at once interested and it was agreed that de Valois should undertake the production, following the scenario of Dr. Keynes and using Mrs. Raverat's designs. Dr. Vaughan Williams had stipulated that there should be no *pointe* work (which he detested) and that *Job* should not be described as a ballet, so the description "a Masque for Dancing" was adopted. De Valois made a very careful study of the Blake engravings and began to plan her production, while Mrs. Raverat set to work painting scenery at the Old Vic. The production was to be presented by the Camargo Society at its fourth programme and Geoffrey Keynes undertook to finance it, being assisted by several friends, in particular by his brother Maynard and Sir Thomas Dunhill.[1] Constant Lambert rescored the music for a much smaller orchestra and *Job* was produced for the first time at the Cambridge Theatre on 5th and 6th July 1931.

Job won much esteem for both the Camargo Society and the Vic-Wells Ballet. With *Job*, Edwin Evans used to say, Camargo stepped on the map of Europe. Karsavina said, "The dignity of the greatest tragedy of all ages is nowhere impaired by a mere dance for the dance's sake, and yet this production fully answers the qualification of ballet. The quality of mime in *Job* is that of the flowing pattern of a well-conceived dance." Perhaps Lydia Lopokova, at first not very enthusiastic but greatly impressed after seeing it performed at Oxford during the Ninth Annual Festival of the International Society for Contemporary Music, put her finger

---

[1] One benefactor was later taken to a performance by Geoffrey Keynes and his wife. The eminent man sat solemnly through the opening ballet, which happened to be *The Jackdaw and the Pigeons*, and at the end said politely to Keynes, "Yes, old boy, very interesting. But tell me, which one was Job?"

on the most important achievement when she wrote to Geoffrey Keynes: "My chief pleasure was that it differed from the Russian ballet tradition, the most important merit of *Job.*" Ashley Dukes, writing in the American *Theatre Arts Monthly* about the English theatre in general, said *Job* was by far the most satisfying achievement of the English theatre that season, representing "the impressive silence in the midst of unimpressive talk."

Job owed no small part of its success to the performance of Anton Dolin as Satan, Blakish and devilish, yet superbly arrogant and physically magnificent in a way that none of his successors have been able to equal, although all of them (and Robert Helpman in particular) have given striking and valid interpretations. At the time of the first Vic-Wells performances Dolin was still appearing in *Stand Up and Sing*, but Jack Buchanan (to whom all honour) gave him permission to dance at the Vic, and his performance was a major feature of the success of the ballet—although the timing was so close that he had to take his last curtain half-dressed in evening clothes, with a taxi waiting at the stage door to whisk him back to the Hippodrome. Lilian Baylis wrote him her thanks: "Ellen Terry was one of the first great players who gave such practical help to the Old Vic, and you are the first great dancer, and I shall pray and remember you always with very great affection."

The opening night of the ballet season at the Old Vic included, in addition to *Job*, a new light ballet by Frederick Ashton called *Regatta*. This was danced to bright, hornpipey music by Gavin Gordon and was set "on board the steam yacht *Old Vic*, off Cowes." Stanley Judson appeared as a Cabin Boy, Freda Bamford, Sheila McCarthy and Joy Newton as "Yachting Girls," Walter Gore and William Chappell as "Two Young Men" and Ninette de Valois was the glamorous Foreign Visitor. *The Times* described the ballet as "true-blue British romps and nautical humour" and it was much to the taste of the audience. The ballet is interesting now as marking the first creations for the company of Gavin Gordon and Frederick Ashton—although the subject seems anything but typical of Ashton's usual taste.

The next ballet to be added to the repertory, on 23rd November, was de Valois' *Fête Polonaise*, "lent" by the Camargo Society but with new costumes and *décor* by O. P. Smyth, who was then in charge of scene-painting at the Old Vic. The ballet, to music by

THE OLD VIC

FOUNDED BY EMMA CONS IN 1880.

Lessee and Manager - - LILIAN BAYLIS, C.H., M.A., Oxon. (Hon.)

Wednesday, December 16th, 1931, at 7.45.

The Vic-Wells Ballet

(Under the direction of NINETTE DE VALOIS)

THE JEW IN THE BUSH

(First Performance)

Music by GORDON JACOB.

Choreography by NINETTE DE VALOIS.

Costumes and Decorations by BERNARD GUEST.

STANLEY JUDSON   FRED ASHTON.   FREDA BAMFORD.

MARIE NIELSON   URSULA MORETON.   TRAVIS KEMP.

FÊTE POLONAISE

(*Glinka*)

Special Appearance of

PHYLLIS BEDELLS

URSULA MORETON.   STANLEY JUDSON.   MARIE NIELSON

Other BALLETS include :

REGATTA   (*Gavin Gordon*)

NINETTE DE VALOIS   WALTER GORE   WILLIAM CHAPPELL

STANLEY JUDSON   SHEILA McCARTHY   FREDA BAMFORD   JOY NEWTON

SUITE OF DANCES (*Bach Goossens*)

MARIE NIELSON   STANLEY JUDSON   SHEILA McCARTHY

BEATRICE APPLEYARD   CLAUDE NEWMAN

THE FAUN (*Vaughan Williams*)

URSULA MORETON   STANLEY JUDSON

Musical Director - - CONSTANT LAMBERT

HOLIDAY PROGRAMME

At Vic and Wells will include revival of " The Taming of the Shrew," " A Midsummer Night's Dream," " Henry V " and " Hansel and Gretel." **SYBIL THORNDIKE** will appear as the Citizen's Wife in " The Knight of the Burning Pestle

PRICES —Reserved Seats : Stalls and Front Circle, 5/6 ; Pit Stalls and Circle, 3/6 ; Pit Stalls and Side Circle. 2/6. Unreserved Seats, 6d.

WILLIAMS & STRAHAN, LTD., Printers, London, S.E.1.

Glinka, was an unpretentious suite of dances of no special importance choreographically but attractive, light and well danced, and
on three occasions there was the additional attraction of Phyllis
Bedells appearing as guest artist. Despite the unsophisticated
costumes, "run up" in the Old Vic wardrobe, the ballet remained
popular for several years, and when the Camargo Society was dis-
solved the company acquired the pretty Edmund Dulac costumes
and scenery which enhanced it considerably. The ballet was revived
at the New Theatre in 1941 but was then danced in front of Chappell's setting for the third act of *Coppélia*, and although it was
danced much better than in the early days both the company and
the audience had outgrown it and it did not last for very long in
the repertoire.

Frequent new productions were very necessary in those early
days to hold the interest of the audience, and Ninette de Valois had
to arrange most of them herself. On 16th December 1931 she
presented at the Old Vic *The Jew in the Bush*, with music by Gordon
Jacob (who conducted some performances) and costumes and
decorations by Bernard Guest. Frederick Ashton appeared in this
ballet as the Jew and had a great success in a grotesque character
part. The ballet was given at Christmas with *Hansel and Gretel*, and
it also preceded Donizetti's *Daughter of the Regiment* on several
occasions.

On 30th January 1932 a special *matinée* was given at Sadler's
Wells when Alicia Markova appeared with the company for the
first time. The programme was notable for containing the first
performances by the Vic-Wells Ballet of two works by Arthur
Bliss, *Rout*, revived by Ninette de Valois, and a short new ballet,
Narcissus and Echo, in which Markova made her début before the
Sadler's Wells audience. This little ballet was arranged by de Valois
to a transcription of Bliss's "Rhapsody for Strings and Two Voices"
and had costumes by William Chappell. Markova also appeared
in *Cephalus and Procris*, and the bill was made up with *Regatta* and
Suite of Dances.

Markova subsequently appeared at other performances, and on
the strength of the public interest aroused, a brief "season" of ballet
at the Old Vic and Sadler's Wells was planned for the following
March with Markova and Dolin as principals. The billing for the
season is interesting: Dolin's name, twice as large as the others,

SADLER'S WELLS

Lessee and Manager - - LILIAN BAYLIS, C.H., M.A., Oxon. (Hon.)

The Vic-Wells Ballet

(Under the direction of NINETTE DE VALOIS)

AT

SADLER'S WELLS

Saturday, January 30th, 1932, at 2.30

Special appearance of

ALICIA MARKOVA

ROUT (*Arthur Bliss*)

(1st performance)

Choreography by NINETTE DE VALOIS.

NARCISSE and ECHO

(*Arthur Bliss*)
(1st performance)

Choreography by NINETTE DE VALOIS

Costumes by WILLIAM CHAPPELL

ALICIA MARKOVA

URSULA MORETON   MARIE NIELSON

STANLEY JUDSON

CEPHALUS and PROCRIS

(*Gretry*)
(By arrangement with Camargo Society)

ALICIA MARKOVA   STANLEY JUDSON   JOY NEWTON

REGATTA (*Gavin Gordon*

NINETTE DE VALOIS   STANLEY JUDSON   TRAVERS KEMP
KIT LAWRENCE   SHEILA McCARTHY   FREDA BAMFORD
JOY NEWTON

SUITE OF DANCES

(*Bach—Goossens*)

MARIE NIELSON   STANLEY JUDSON   URSULA MORETON
TRAVERS KEMP   BEATRICE APPLEYARD   SHEILA McCARTHY
· FREDA BAMFORD

Musical Director - - CONSTANT LAMBERT

SADLER'S WELLS PRICES.—Reserved Seats : Stalls and Front Circle, 6/-; Pit Stalls and Circle, 3/6 and 2/6; Amphitheatre, 1/6 and 1/3.   Unreserved Seats Pit, 1/6 and 1/3; Gallery, 9d. and 6d.

WILLIAMS & STRAHAN, LTD., Printers London, S.E.1.

heads the poster, with Alicia Markova and Ninette de Valois placed equal below.

By this time the permanent company numbered twelve, Marie Nielson and Ailne Phillips being among the latest recruits. For the special season of eleven performances (five at the Vic and six at the Wells) the company was enlarged still further and six male dancers were engaged on a six-weeks' contract for the occasion: among them was Antony Tudor, who appeared by permission of Marie Rambert. A repertoire of sixteen ballets could be announced, including five new productions, and Ninette de Valois, Frederick Ashton and Rupert Doone were listed as choreographers.

The "season" opened at the Old Vic on 4th March 1932 with the first Wells production of a Fokine ballet, *Le Spectre de la Rose*, and a new ballet *Italian Suite*, for which de Valois and Dolin collaborated in the arrangement of the dances. *Le Spectre de la Rose* was danced by Dolin and Ninette de Valois, neither of them particularly well suited by style and temperament to the romanticism of the ballet. They were, however, capable of presenting Fokine's choreography faithfully and well, and for some reason ballets which serve to show off the talents of star dancers are always popular with the public.

Italian Suite was danced to music of Lalo in costumes by Phyllis Dolton. An opening *Prelude* was followed by a *Pas de Quatre* for Marie Nielson, Ailne Phillips, Stanley Judson and Travis Kemp, then Anton Dolin performed a *Serenade* of his own arrangement, followed by a *Pas de Deux* (to music by Cottrau) for himself and de Valois, and the final *Ensemble* was arranged by de Valois.

Les Sylphides followed on 8th March with a *corps de ballet* of sixteen dancers. Markova danced the *Mazurka* and the *Valse pas de deux* with Dolin, Sheila McCarthy danced the first *Valse* and Ursula Moreton the *Prelude*. The Fokine choreography was used but the setting was a severe one of painted trees and curtains, and in such a setting it was not easy to capture the elusive mood of the ballet. It was not until Arnold Haskell intervened in 1937 that the Vic-Wells were able to use Benois' original setting for the ballet. Nevertheless, *Les Sylphides* plays an important part in the repertoire; to the audience it typifies the popular conception of "ballet," and for the dancers it is an invaluable experience in stage deportment, an ideal training-ground for the *corps de ballet*. It is also one of the

OLD VIC & SADLER'S WELLS THEATRES

Lessee and Manager - - - LILIAN BAYLIS, C.H., M.A., Oxon. (Hon.)

PRELIMINARY NOTICE.

SADLER'S WELLS.

OLD VIC.

Friday, March 4th, at 8 p.m.
Saturday, March 5th, at 2.30 p.m.
Monday, March 21st, at 8 p.m.
Tuesday, March 22nd, at 8 p.m.
Wednesday, March 23rd, at 8 p.m.

Season Commencing

Friday, March 4th, 1932.

Monday, March 7th, at 8 p.m.
Tuesday, March 8th, at 8 p.m.
Friday, March 11th, at 8 p.m.
Monday, March 14th
Wed., Mar. 16th, at 2.30 p.m.
Saturday, March 19th. at 8 p.m

The Vic-Wells Ballet
(Under the direction of NINETTE DE VALOIS)
WITH
ANTON DOLIN
ALICIA MARKOVA   NINETTE DE VALOIS

URSULA MORETON	STANLEY JUDSON	MARIE NEILSON
SHEILA McCARTHY	KEITH LESTER	AILNE PHILLIPS
FREDA BAMFORD	TRAVIS KEMP	Beatrice APPLEYARD
JOY NEWTON	ANTONY TUDOR	Nadina NEWHOUSE

(By Permission of MARIE RAMBERT).
and Company.

The following ballets will be given during the season :—

• Job - - - - - -	Vaughan Williams
Spectre De La Rose (1st Perf.) - - - -	Weber
Nursery Suite (1st Perf.) - - - -	Elgar
Les Sylphides (1st Perf.) - • • • -	Chopin
Italian Suite (1st Perf) - - -	
The Enchanted Grove (1st Perf.) - - -	Ravel
• Cephalus and Procris - - - - -	Gretry
Fete Polonaise - - - -	Glinka
The Jackdaw and the Pigeons - -	Hugh Bradford
Regatta - - - - -	Gavin Gordon
Hommage Aux Belles Viennoises - -	Schubert
Suite of Dances - - - - -	J. S. Bach
"Scene De Ballet" from "Faust" - - -	Gounod
Narcissus and Echo • • - -	Arthur Bliss
Rout• • • • • •	Arthur Bliss

There will be further additions to the above list.

Choreographers ...	NINETTE DE VALOIS, FREDERICK ASHTON RUPERT DOONE
Musical Director - - -	CONSTANT LAMBERT

* These ballets are given by arrangement with THE CAMARGO SOCIETY.

most perfect choreographic compositions ever made, a small miracle of movement and design.

Rupert Doone's ballet, *The Enchanted Grove*, had been first produced by the Camargo Society. It had a baroque setting by Duncan Grant and concerned a Court entertainment interrupted by the arrival of a Japanese Courtesan (Ninette de Valois), her attendants and admirers. The Courtesan entered on a Horse (M. Lindsay, F. Pulvermacher) which *The Times* described as "a Ming version of the Griffiths' Brothers famous steed." The music was a transcription by the composer of Ravel's *Le Tombeau de Couperin*. The house was sold out for the first performance and the audience was enthusiastic. At least one critic thought the ballet "a delightful, if inconsequent, piece," but more people agreed with P. W. Manchester's verdict that it was "a ghastly bit of Rococo Chinoiserie" and it was soon dropped from the repertoire.

The fifth new production in this short season was *Nursery Suite*, which was given for the first time at Sadler's Wells on 19th March. The choreography was by Ninette de Valois and *décor* and dresses by Nancy Allen, one of the younger members of the scene-painting staff at the theatre. As Sir Edward Elgar had originally composed the *Nursery Suite* for the two princesses, Her Royal Highness the Duchess of York came to see the first performance, and as Queen and Queen Mother she has followed the fortunes of the company with interest and sympathy ever since. Sir Edward Elgar was also present at the *première* and was delighted with the ballet, especially commending Dolin's performance as Georgie Porgie.

The publicity afforded by this production gave Lilian Baylis much satisfaction, and altogether the little season of ballet had been very well received. It had demonstrated that more frequent performances might be given in future if the steady progress could be maintained, and Markova had completely won the hearts of the Vic-Wells audiences. Arnold Haskell, a severe critic in those early days, had noted with awe that there had been a full house on a Monday night and he wrote: "The whole company is now working together as an ensemble. This was especially noticeable in the beautiful *Danse Sacrée et Danse Profane*, which were perfectly interpreted."

The company returned to its usual modest proportions for the remaining two months of the regular season, but had the satisfaction

THE FIRST PROJECT FOR *JOB*

Gwen Raverat's toy theatre figures made to illustrate a scene from Geoffrey
Keynes' ballet, and (*below*) the Blake design upon which the group is based.
"So the Lord blessed the latter end of Job more than the beginning."

Blake's drawing of the Three Comforters, whose arm movements are closely reproduced in de Valois' choreography for *Job*. *Below:* Stanley Judson as Elihu against the Blake-inspired *décor*

J. W. Debenham

of knowing that in a year of bad fortune at the two theatres the ballet had been almost uniformly successful and self-supporting. It had by this time become evident that there was a much bigger public for opera in Islington than there was for Shakespeare, and in December 1931 it had been decided to give two weeks of opera at the Wells to one at the Old Vic. This greatly reduced the loss on both theatres and in some weeks eliminated it altogether. It was the beginning of the gradual realisation that it would eventually prove more practicable to separate the companies and lodge the opera and ballet permanently in Islington, leaving the Shakespeare company in possession in the Waterloo Road, where it was always more successful.

Sadler's Wells had shown a serious deficit on the first year's workings, and although the second year showed better results, the theatre was to be a continual source of anxiety for several years to come. The heavy cost of the orchestra was one of the worst anxieties,[1] for expenses were highest for the opera and opera nights were by no means always sold out. (Sir Hugh Walpole claimed to have once found himself all alone in the six-shilling stalls at a performance of *Il Trovatore*.) The ballet fared better, as it could manage with a smaller orchestra, and it consistently drew good houses. It was decided, consequently, to increase the number of ballet performances to two a week during the 1932–33 season and to give week-day *matinées* for the first time. The whole company was given a year's contract and Markova and Dolin were engaged for the first three months, Markova at a fee of five guineas a performance. Lilian Baylis hoped that she would "do lots of well-paid work, but . . . manage to come to us between the good engagements," and she also added a reminder that any opportunity that might be afforded to Markova to advertise the Vic and the Wells in the course of these good engagements should not be neglected.

Summer Interlude

Between the close of the 1931–32 season and the implementation of the ambitious plans for the subsequent season, the dancers of the Vic-Wells Ballet participated in two ventures of considerable

[1] Lilian Baylis used to have nightmares about it and wake up screaming, "The orchestra!"

importance in the history of English ballet. From 6th June to 2nd July they took part in the Camargo Society's season of ballet at the Savoy Theatre and learned much from the experience of dancing every night for four weeks before a sophisticated and critical West End audience. In September they made their first trip abroad on an expedition to Denmark, which was organised by the Association of Teachers of Operatic Dancing of Great Britain (now the R.A.D.) at the instigation of Madame Adeline Genée.

This visit of a British Ballet to Copenhagen was made under the auspices of the Anglo-Danish Society and coincided with the British Trades and Arts Exhibition in that city. It was not strictly a Vic-Wells undertaking, but that company provided the *corps de ballet* and most of the repertoire. The group was strengthened by guest artists and young scholars from the R.A.D., among them Felicity Gray and a talented fourteen-year-old named Doris May, who was to join the Vic-Wells school the following year and eventually to change her name to Pamela. [1]

Two full programmes of British ballet were given at the Royal Theatre in Kongens Nytorv and two mixed programmes. On the King of Denmark's birthday the British Ballet shared a Gala Performance with the Royal Danish Ballet. Geoffrey Toye and Constant Lambert were the conductors and Stephen Thomas acted as Stage Director. The principal dancers were Phyllis Bedells, Ninette de Valois, Ruth French, Alicia Markova, Ursula Moreton, Stanley Judson, Harold Turner and Anton Dolin. The ballets presented were *Job, Les Sylphides, The Lord of Burleigh, Création du Monde, Regatta, Fête Polonaise, Hommage aux Belles Viennoises* and a *Divertissement*. At the last performance Adeline Genée herself appeared with Dolin in her dance scena, *The Love Song*.

One Danish newspaper caused something of a flurry in advance by expressing alarm at the prospect of a visit from a British ballet troupe: "Let's hope there are plenty of Russians. British people dance well and their step dancers are marvellous, but British ballet—I know of nothing more horrible." In the event the Danes seem

[1] In actual fact the choice of name was made for her. After weeks of indecision, Doris decided that she would call herself Angela May and went to Miss de Valois to announce this great decision, only to be told cheerfully, "It's too late now, dear. The programmes have been printed and you are down as Pamela."

to have enjoyed the lighter ballets and *divertissements* but to have been somewhat puzzled by *Création du Monde* and utterly mystified, although respectful, about *Job*. "To fully understand the text, one must preferably have the Bible at hand," said one newspaper. Svend Kragh-Jacobsen, however, to-day Denmark's foremost critic and historian of the dance, recognised in *Job* and *The Lord of Burleigh* the talents of two gifted choreographers and made many journeys to London in subsequent years to follow their progress. Another reaction, which illustrates just how new a venture British ballet was at this time, was expressed by a British journalist who had gone to Copenhagen for the Exhibition. "It is a remarkable thing," he said, "that we have to come all the way to Copenhagen to have brought home to us that we have such good dancers in England." Lilian Baylis later commented on another aspect: "We seem to have been too modest as a nation and we assumed our ballet was in the rear and not in the van of the movement. In Denmark, *Job* was considered more modern than anything seen in Denmark before."

All the critics seem to have been impressed by the individual dancers, however, and Anton Dolin was paid the rare compliment of being compared to Hans Beck, the great Danish ballet master, pupil of Bournonville himself. Turner, Markova, de Valois, Ruth French and Phyllis Bedells all won praise but, secure in the possession of a long native tradition of ballet, the Danes seemed to have great difficulty in understanding why some of the dancers called themselves by Russian names.

The English dancers all enjoyed the visit immensely and were delighted by the friendliness and hospitality of their Danish hosts. The company were met on their arrival at Copenhagen by Madame Genée and several members of the Danish Ballet (who gave them an enormous breakfast), and their stay included all the traditional Danish entertainments, notably a trip to Elsinore (where the dancers bought a picture postcard of Hamlet's reputed grave and all autographed it before sending it to Lilian Baylis), and a tour of the Tuborg brewery where, to their great disgust, the fifteen-year-olds were given only fruit cordial for refreshment.

Philip Richardson of *The Dancing Times* accompanied the party, and as they seemed to be one man short he appeared for the first time on any stage as "Job's Spiritual Self," being prompted in

F

whispers by the dancers and acquitting himself with so much distinction that he has ever since refused to appear in another ballet, preferring to rest on his laurels and feeling, anyway, that to appear in any other part would be something of an anti-climax. "The rôle of the Godhead, remarkably enough, was entrusted to an editor," said one of his notices. There were parties at the Adlon after the performances at night, and so much warm hospitality in private homes that Stanley Judson came home and wrote an article for the *Old Vic and Sadler's Wells Magazine* on, "What the Danish Girl can Teach Ours."

Much excitement was caused on the day of the King's birthday Gala Performance by police fears of a big socialist demonstration. Elaborate precautions were taken and every dancer was issued with a special card to admit her to the theatre. Constant Lambert was told that a police official would be sitting immediately behind him, in the front row of the stalls, and if trouble started he was to take instructions from this official. But, to the secret disappointment of the dancers, nothing whatever happened and the performance passed off without incident.

The crossings, however, were rough as only that North Sea passage can be, and the dancers were all horribly ill. An additional complication was provided by the fact that as Wendy Toye was only fourteen her mother travelled with her, and the railway officials immediately assumed that Mrs. Toye must be the wife of Geoffrey Toye (in fact they were not related) and assigned them a double cabin. This arrangement was duly rectified, but no one told the steward, who appeared the next morning with tea for two. He eyed the unslept-in bunk, looked at Major Toye and said, "What's happened to the lady?" Being by this time thoroughly tired of the whole joke, the conductor replied briefly, "I've chucked her through the porthole."

CHAPTER VI

ALICIA MARKOVA—CLASSICAL BALLERINA

1932–1933

ON account of the Danish expedition the 1932–33 season of ballet did not open at Sadler's Wells until 5th October. Antony Tudor, Claude Newman, Travis Kemp, Guy Massey and Toni Repetto were by now all permanent members of the company, and the situation in regard to male dancers was vastly eased. It was even possible to give *Job* with the same set of Sons for several performances in succession instead of having to rely on the help of any dancers appearing in West End shows, who might be able to fit in an odd performance at the Vic or Wells between the acts. At the time of the first ballet performance at the Vic, for instance, Stanley Judson had been appearing at the Plaza doing three shows a day, and Dolin was dancing at the Hippodrome. One night in December 1931 it seemed as if *Job* could not possibly go on, because nearly all the seven Sons had taken jobs in Cochran's *La Belle Hélène* and were wanted for rehearsal in Manchester at 10 a.m. the following morning. The dancers, however, offered to appear at the performance and travel overnight to Manchester, where they all showed up at their rehearsal on the stroke of ten o'clock, despite a virtually sleepless night. This is but one example of the help that was given so generously during the early days of the Vic-Wells Ballet.

(Lilian Baylis, as usual, had a practical solution for overcoming the shortage of male dancers which she realised was hampering the work of her ballet company. She was watching a rehearsal of *Job* from the stalls of the Old Vic one day, and at the conclusion turned to Sheila McCarthy, who was with her, and said, "Now dear, I want all you girls to marry all those boys and breed me a nice strong race of male dancers.")

On the opening night of the 1932–33 season the Vic-Wells Ballet was seen for the first time in *Le Lac des Cygnes*, a production of the second act reconstructed by Markova and Dolin, who danced the leading rôles. The performance seems to have been promising rather than good in itself; it was a very unpretentious production and relied for its success on the dancing of Markova and Dolin. For the first time the Wells had a truly classical ballerina, and Ninette de Valois must at once have recognised that if she could secure Markova as a permanent member of her company for the whole of the next season she would be able to present some of the great classical ballets. For the moment, however, Markova was making only occasional appearances, and it was important to maintain public interest with new productions and give the young dancers as much experience in a variety of rôles as was possible.

The first new ballet of the season was by Ninette de Valois, a cheerful piece of nonsense about customs officials called *Douanes*. The music was written by Geoffrey Toye and Hedley Briggs designed the costumes. The ballet was an immediate success with the audience and provided a piquant character part for de Valois as the Tight Rope Dancer, while Dolin's gift for comedy was given full rein in the character of a Cook's Man (later taken over by Stanley Judson). Antony Tudor had a small part as a Passport Officer.

On 17th October the Vic-Wells company presented Frederick Ashton's ballet, *The Lord of Burleigh,* which had been made originally for the Camargo Society. The scenario was by the music critic Edwin Evans, who also selected and arranged the Mendelssohn music, most apt to the sentiment of the ballet, which was orchestrated by Gordon Jacob. Costumes and *décor* were by George Sheringham. The idea was a delightful one. The characters from various Tennyson poems are introduced to each other, for instance Lady Clara Vere de Vere, the Lord of Burleigh, Katie Willows, Mariana and Edward Gray. "Surely every human feeling demands that they should be brought together and find mutual solace in that emotion which, we are told, is akin to love. Of the other characters, some are paired, some left unattached—for, in the realm of poetry, as of the ballet, there are inevitably more women than men, yet none of them 'superfluous.' "

In the theatre, however, the ballet seemed slightly to misfire. It had its devotees but never a large public. This may have been partly due to the fact that Edwin Evans and Ashton never really had sufficient opportunity to discuss the scenario and what had been

THE LORD OF BURLEIGH

Anton Dolin and Beatrice Appleyard

THE SCORPIONS OF YSIT

Beatrice Appleyard (*centre*) as the Goddess Ysit with the two Marsh Women, Ursula Moreton (*left*) and Phyllis Worthington, and the seven scorpions: (*left to right*) Sheila McCarthy, Nadina Newhouse, Molly Brown, Freda Bamford, Joy Newton, Peggy Mellis, Joan Day

J. W. Debenham

LYDIA LOPOKOVA
in *Coppélia*

Anthony

MARKOVA and **HELPMANN**
in *Le Lac des Cygnes*

J. W. Debenham

CARNAVAL

Alicia Markova and Stanislas Idzikowski as Columbine and Harlequin,
with (*left to right*) Ailne Phillips, Joy Newton, Nadina Newhouse, and
Elizabeth Miller

intended as a narrative became more of a *divertissement*. The first performance at the Wells had Alicia Markova as Katie Willows and Dolin in his original rôle of the Lord of Burleigh, a part which required both a brilliant dancer and a good mime.

Another Camargo Society production, *The Origin of Design*, was revived by the Vic-Wells Ballet on 7th November. De Valois revised her choreography slightly, but despite the beautiful Handel-Beecham music the ballet was not a popular success. *Scorpions of Ysit*, produced on 15th November, enjoyed a longer life. This was a revised version of the ballet produced at the Royal Court Theatre in 1928, and had new music by Gavin Gordon and new costumes by Sophie Fedorovitch (her first work for the Wells). The story concerned the Egyptian Goddess Ysit who walks abroad accompanied by her seven Scorpions: Tefen, Befen, Mestet, Mestetef, Petet, Thetet and Maatet. Weary, she wishes to rest and sends Tefen to knock on the door of the hut of the first Marsh Woman, but the woman, frightened by the scorpions, shuts the door in the Goddess's face. The walk is resumed and Tefen knocks on the door of the second hut where the second Marsh Woman overcomes her fear and lets the Goddess in. The scorpions, left alone, plan to avenge themselves on the first Marsh Woman, and Tefen enters the hut and stings her baby to death. When the Goddess returns, however, she realises what has happened and restores the child to life before resuming her walk, surrounded by her scorpions.

In its new guise the ballet proved more comprehensible and was well received, although the grotesque treatment of the scorpions—effective enough when isolated from the more realistic movements for the humans—provoked so much laughter that it detracted from the moving lament for her child as danced by Ursula Moreton, the Marsh Woman. De Valois had meant the scorpions to be funny, and there was always much laughter during rehearsals, but audiences were never absolutely certain in those days that it was seemly to laugh at a ballet, and when the choreographer invited her family to see a rehearsal the work was received in solemn silence. Beatrice Appleyard had a personal success as the Goddess Ysit, beautiful and impassive, in a striking head-dress of black velvet sewn with large golden curtain rings.

During his stay with the Vic-Wells Ballet Anton Dolin was allowed to give the first performance of his solo to Ravel's *Bolero* on 6th December. He stated explicitly in the programme that he did not intend the dance to be authentically Spanish: "It is a personal interpretation of the music—an improvisation of the moment." As such it was highly successful with the public and has continued to be so until this day. Dolin has danced it all over the world, on stage and television, but few people remember that it had its origin at Sadler's Wells. Ninette de Valois, in any case, always disapproved of it and thought it "music hall."

Dolin also appeared that season in his original rôle of Vertumnus in Constant Lambert's ballet *Pomona*, which was staged at Sadler's Wells, by arrangement with the Camargo Society, on 17th January 1933. The ballet was revised considerably for this new production and it was the company's first attempt at a smart, sophisticated Ashton ballet. They tried it just a little too soon. Dolin was excellent as Vertumnus, of course, but the part did not suit Stanley Judson so well when he took over. Helpmann managed to bring it back to life the following season and Beatrice Appleyard was a beautiful Pomona, but the company as a whole did not really make a success of the ballet until a much later revival with Pearl Argyle and then Margot Fonteyn as Pomona. It was good experience for the dancers, however, and probably good for the audience, too, as it pointed unmistakably the direction which Ashton's choreography was likely to take. The costumes and *décor* were by Vanessa Bell, and the inclusion of *Pomona* in the repertoire undoubtedly attracted a smart and *avant-garde* audience to the Wells whenever it was given.

The problem of attracting a stalls audience to Sadler's Wells was being gradually overcome by the good work of the Sadler's Wells Circle, founded by Lady Ottoline and Mr. Philip Morrell in 1931, with a chief objective of filling the more expensive seats at the theatre (stalls prices then ranged from five shillings to seven shillings and sixpence). This group was responsible for altering the curtain time to a later hour and it made contributions towards the cost of new productions. Ninette de Valois' next ballet, *The Birthday of Oberon*, was assisted in this way, for it was an ambitious undertaking and the company's first attempt at a choral ballet. The work was based on Purcell's *Faery Queene*, which had long been a favourite with Constant Lambert. Naturally the complete opera could not be attempted, so Lambert concentrated on the Masque of the Seasons from the fourth act, interpolating certain other music from the opera, and making it into a comparatively self-sufficient *divertissement*. John Armstrong was invited to design both costumes and scenery, and Lilian Baylis spent a happy time scouring the bargain basements with him in order to buy materials for some forty-eight chorus dresses. (A visit to the sales was one of Lilian Baylis's favourite occupations, and it was always difficult to stop her buying materials which might be cheap but were unlikely ever to be used. On this occasion she chose to go off on her bargain hunt immediately after Ursula Moreton's wedding.)

The ballet was presented on 7th February and used about thirty dancers in addition to the large chorus. An introductory song was followed by a series of simple rural dances and then the more technical Dance of the Seasons, ending with a formal tableau. Hermione Darnborough (now Mrs. Muir Mattheson) had her first big personal success in the variation arranged for her as Summer. Beatrice Appleyard appeared as Spring, Ursula Moreton as Autumn and Freda Bamford as Winter. The ballet received an exceptionally good Press and was much praised by a small section of the audience, but it never became popular and did not survive for very long. It was probably attempted before the company had adequate resources —both financial and artistic—to do justice to such a project.

The time was now approaching for the first big production of a classical ballet by the Vic-Wells. The help and willing co-operation given by Lydia Lopokova had been of much assistance already to the company and she now suggested that Nicolai Sergueeff, who had reproduced *Giselle* for the Camargo Society the previous summer, should be invited to produce *Coppélia* at Sadler's Wells.

Sergueeff had been Régisseur at the Imperial Theatres in St. Petersburg from 1904 until 1917, and had devoted much labour to writing down in a form of stenoscript the choreography and production details of the great ballets in the repertoire of the Imperial Russian Ballet. He had left Russia in 1918 and was called in by Diaghileff to reconstruct *The Sleeping Princess* for the 1921 production at the Alhambra. He spoke little French and less English, but Lopokova translated letters and acted as interpreter at rehearsals. She also consented to dance Swanilda at the first two performances and suggested that the artist Edwin Callighan, a big shaggy Irishman, might design the costumes. Only the first two acts of the ballet were given, the last act *divertissement*, which has nothing to do with the story, being omitted. Stanley Judson appeared as Franz and Hedley Briggs as Dr. Coppelius. Geoffrey Toye persuaded Constant Lambert to let him conduct the ballet, declaring it to be his favourite work in the world. The Wells was crowded for the first performance and the ballet has retained its popularity, in a variety of different productions, ever since. Lydia Lopokova made her two appearances as Swanilda and then Ninette de Valois took over. The precise and sparkling choreography and the gaiety of Swanilda suited de Valois admirably and she was the first of a long line of delightful English ballerinas to dance the part at Sadler's Wells.

At this time, however, the little company was hard pressed to fill all the parts in the ballet. The six friends of Swanilda also had to appear in the character dances in the first act and had about eight bars of music in which to change from *pointe* shoes to character shoes. Knotted ribbons obstinately refused to come untied, and eventually the girls kept scissors in the wings and cut through the ribbons every night, taking care to conceal this wanton extravagance from the eyes of Lilian Baylis.

An event of great importance to the ballet occurred during the rehearsals for *Coppélia*. A young man named Robert Helpmann arrived from Australia with an introduction to Ninette de Valois and an earnest desire to renew his studies as a dancer, which had begun under Novikoff with Pavlova's company in Australia, but had been interrupted by a subsequent career in musical comedy. He arrived wrapped in a large overcoat, and when he entered the Wells room in the middle of a class Ninette de Valois felt that something quite important had happened. "The entrance was discreet and well-timed: I thought—personality; he was polite but quite self-assured, so I decided, unselfconscious; an odd resemblance to Leslie Henson made me hope for humour, and a thoughtfulness about the face in repose was reminiscent of Massine. This unknown young man impressed me with a strange sense of power; here, possibly, was an artist of infinite range. . . ." She took him on for the *corps de ballet*, as his early training and his theatre experience indicated that he would be able to make himself useful, and announced that she thought she could "do something with that face" —a famous remark which Helpmann has since admitted was uttered in by no means flattering tones.

Robert Helpmann accordingly danced in the *corps de ballet* in *Coppélia* and made an impression very rapidly, both by his performance and by the extraordinary amount of brilliantine he used on his hair. Without question he had a face and a personality that were made for the theatre, and when visitors inquired who the newcomer was, Ninette de Valois told them confidently, "That is my next leading male dancer." His name was on the bills by the beginning of the next season, and on the opening night he was to be entrusted with the part of Satan in *Job*, the most important rôle for a man in the entire repertory.

1933–1934

The season 1933–34 opened at Sadler's Wells on 26th September with exciting prospects. Alicia Markova had signed a contract for the entire season, choosing to devote herself for a salary of £10 a week to a repertory ballet company that was prepared to offer her the famous rôles in the classical repertoire on which a ballerina's reputation must rest.

Markova had had the good fortune of being taken into the Diaghileff company at a very early age (where she was put into the care of Ninette de Valois), and by the age of seventeen she had worked under many great choreographers and teachers and understood the hard work and discipline that were essential for a career in ballet. After the death of Diaghileff she had known a period of great unhappiness and anxiety when it seemed as if all her early good fortune had deserted her, but an invitation from Frederick Ashton to appear in one of his ballets restored her confidence and introduced her, through the Ballet Club and the Camargo Society, to the exciting possibilities for English ballet. Now Ninette de Valois, through Lilian Baylis, was able to offer her a position as ballerina of the rapidly developing company at Sadler's Wells and to promise her the opportunity of dancing in such ballets as *Giselle*, *Casse Noisette* and *Le Lac des Cygnes* as they were gradually added to the repertory. For two full seasons Markova was to be the wonderful jewel of the Vic-Wells Ballet, but for the first three months of the 1933–34 season they could also boast the presence of Stanislas Idzikowski, one of Diaghileff's greatest male dancers. Fokine's *Carnaval* was produced for him, and the *Blue Bird pas de deux* was added to the repertory—the first little bit of *The Sleeping Beauty* to be performed by the Vic-Wells Ballet. In addition Idzikowski appeared in *Le Spectre de la Rose* with Markova, the *pas de trois* from *Le Lac des Cygnes* (with Markova and de Valois) and created the leading male rôle in Ashton's *Les Rendezvous*.

The opening night programme was a remarkable one. After *Les Sylphides*, Markova and Idzikowski danced *Le Spectre de la Rose* and then followed a new de Valois ballet, *The Wise and Foolish Virgins*. Markova and Idzikowski then danced the *Blue Bird pas de deux* and the evening ended with *Job*, in which Robert Helpmann danced Satan for the first time.

The Wise and Foolish Virgins had an almost identical story to that used by Ashton many years later for his ballet *The Wise Virgins*. The music was by Kurt Atterberg and *décor* and costumes by William Chappell. The Wise and Foolish Virgins await the entrance of the Bride and when she enters they dance, but the Wise Virgins first take care to extinguish their lamps. At the end of the dance they fall asleep and the Bride dreams of the Bridegroom. Preparations are made for the reception of the Bridegroom who enters accompanied by a Musician; after a general dance there is a procession into the Banqueting Hall, but the Foolish Virgins, whose lamps have burned out, are denied admittance and are driven away by two angels. Both music and choreography were judged by *The Times* critic to be "ingenious rather than right or inevitable. . . . The essential simplicity has been missed." Another critic rather rudely compared the Virgins' lamps to raspberry sundaes and everyone was at pains to point out how much better as a ballet was *Job*. Markova had a certain success as the Bride, but the ballet did not survive for very long.

At the end of October *La Création du Monde* was taken into the Vic-Wells repertoire. Ninette de Valois considered at that time that it was without any doubt her best dance work, as she did not think *Job* was pure ballet but "a simple and sincere dramatic production based on the art of the theatre in general." *La Création du Monde*, which had been produced for the Camargo Society's third programme on 26th April 1931, utilised a subject which had been treated in 1923 by Jean Borlin for the Ballet Suédois and the Milhaud score which had been composed for that production, but de Valois created entirely new choreography.

The creation was portrayed as it might have been acted by Negroes in one of their ceremonies. A trinity of heathen gods evoke from Chaos first the trees and plants, then the lower animals and finally Man and Woman. The rôles of Man and Woman, created by Leslie French and Ursula Moreton, were first performed at the Old Vic by Antony Tudor and Ursula Moreton. The ballet was exceedingly well thought of, and it has long been a matter of regret that it has been allowed to disappear from the repertory. Cyril Beaumont wrote of it: "It is a work of originality and is much more than the stringing together of a series of movements to fit a given rhythm. It is a successful attempt to use the dance as an art-form to convey the impression of a primitive people seeking to express a lofty aim." P. W. Manchester, in her book *Vic-Wells: a Ballet Progress*, said, "The surge and stress and agonies of evolution were excitingly realised, and the moment when Man, with his Woman, first stood on his feet to face the new world was a heart-stopping experience."

The dancers were masked and blackened [1] and were not recognisable as popular personalities, which may have reduced the box-office appeal of the ballet, and unfortunately it never achieved sufficient popularity to hold a place in the repertoire. When it was revived in 1935 the Negro conception was abandoned and Man and Woman were white people, but even so the ballet was not given many performances and by the time the appreciative minority began to suggest its revival everyone had forgotten the choreography.

Idzikowski's brilliant performance as Harlequin was the *raison d'être* of the revival of *Carnaval*, but was almost the only commendable thing about it. Like other Fokine ballets, it seemed to elude the dancers at Sadler's Wells, although it was staged with care by Madame Evina and the original choreography was preserved. Technical competence is only a minor factor in the successful recreation of a Fokine ballet, style and sensitivity being of major importance, and it was not until 1954 that the company was fully to succeed in one of his ballets—in the magnificent revival of *Firebird*. *Carnaval* is, in any case, the most elusive of them all, and only the Royal Danish Ballet might be able to capture now its delicacy and period charm. The first Wells production was hampered by an outdoor setting, instead of the usual Bakst indoor

---

[1] "Those poor de Valois girls. Whatever will they be asked to do next?" was the comment of one elderly female spectator.

scene with its little sofas, and the costumes were only the roughest approximation of the original designs. Markova, moreover, was not happily cast as Columbine and, apart from Idzikowski, none of the dancers added very much to their reputations.

In December Frederick Ashton began work on *Les Rendezvous*, for which Constant Lambert had arranged a confection of Auber music and William Chappell designed a simple set and delightful costumes—which he has not equalled in all the half-dozen versions he has since designed. It was Ashton's first important creation for the Vic-Wells repertoire, and he chose to produce the sort of ballet he could do best—dancing for dancing's own sake. "It has no serious portent at all," he said; "it is simply a vehicle for the exquisite dancing of Idzikowski and Markova." It was also a piece of first-rate craftsmanship, beautifully constructed, concise, witty and admirably planned. Markova's speed, delicacy and elegance were perfectly exploited and Idzikowski soared and bounded about the stage while Ninette de Valois, Robert Helpmann and Stanley Judson made a great success of the merry little *pas de trois*. Twenty years later, *Les Rendezvous* is still in the repertoire of the Sadler's Wells Theatre Ballet and is a prime favourite, fresh and gay as ever, although less attractively decorated.

Idzikowski left the company on the termination of his contract, saying farewell at the Old Vic on Boxing Night in *Le Spectre de la Rose* and *Carnaval*, and from then until the end of the following season Markova reigned supreme. Work was already in progress on the first major classical production in which she was to appear, and *Giselle* was ready for presentation at the Old Vic by 1st January 1934.

It was a night of thick fog, but although people were arriving all through the first ballet (a revival of *Pomona*) the theatre was completely filled before the curtain rose on *Giselle* and excitement and expectation were intense. The ballet had been produced by M. Sergueeff, who had also staged the Camargo Society's production at the Savoy Theatre the previous year, in which many of the Vic-Wells dancers had appeared. *Décor* and costumes were by William Chappell. By great good fortune Anton Dolin was able to appear as Albrecht, and thus the Vic-Wells Ballet was able to show *Giselle* for the first time with two dancers of the very first quality in the leading rôles. (Unhappily Dolin succumbed to

GISELLE

Alicia Markova and Anton Dolin   Margot Fonteyn and Robert Helpmann

THE RAKE'S PROGRESS

gastric influenza before the second performance, and his place was taken at twenty-four hours' notice by Stanley Judson.) Hermione Darnborough was Myrtha, the Queen of the Wilis, and Robert Helpmann managed to make quite a lot of the subsidiary part of Hilarion. It was, however, Markova's performance which dominated the ballet, and Dolin was the first to pay tribute: "Markova's performance in *Giselle* has proved her, at the early age of twenty-three, worthy to rank with all the great artistes. She has done something she will find it difficult to surpass." She has, since then, developed her performance so beautifully and become so much identified with the ballet that she has established herself as the outstanding Giselle of her generation. Twenty years afterwards she can now fill the greatest theatres of London, Paris or New York as guest artist in this ballet with any company with which she chooses to appear, but it was the Vic-Wells Ballet which gave Markova her first opportunity to dance her greatest rôle.

At the end of 1933 a very valuable legacy had come to the Vic-Wells Ballet when the Camargo Society declared that it would renounce all rights in *Job* and would waive all fees for performances already given that season. At a Dancers' Circle Dinner held in January 1934, Maynard Keynes publicly announced that the Society would in future devote its entire resources to helping the Vic-Wells Ballet. The company were not only freed from the small performance fees they had previously paid but were also presented with the scenery and costumes of a number of ballets.

While her husband, as Treasurer of the Camargo Society, was making these important arrangements, Lydia Lopokova was also giving valuable assistance. Sergueeff was busy rehearsing *Casse Noisette* for the Vic-Wells company, and Lopokova was constantly present to translate, interpret and demonstrate. She would play all the parts at once—Drosselmeyer taking snuff, a naughty child refusing to greet the guests, and Clara's simple delight in her doll. In the course of these rehearsals Sergueeff one day noticed Elsa Lanchester, then a member of the Old Vic Shakespeare Company, rehearsing for Ariel in *The Tempest*. He liked the way she moved and decided she would do a better Danse Arabe in *Casse Noisette* than any of the dancers. He rushed upstairs to the office, where he cried excitedly, "Dramateek lady! dramateek lady!" and gesticulated wildly. When the management realised what he was getting at they quailed from the task of explaining to Sergueeff that Elsa Lanchester belonged to the drama and not the ballet company, and instead asked her what she thought about the suggestion. She gladly agreed to perform the Danse Arabe, and in the event stole practically all the notices and publicity about the production.

Casse Noisette was given on 30th January at Sadler's Wells. It was a large production, with some forty performers, and the company was augmented by The Lord Mayor's Boy Players,[1] who appeared in the battle of the toy soldiers and mice. They filled this function admirably on the whole, although there were occasional mishaps when a shoe or some attachment of a costume would be left on the stage after the fray, and during rehearsals an occasional lost boy would be found backstage who explained his presence with the cheerful announcement, "I'm a mouse."

The ballet was decorated by Hedley Briggs on a very modest budget, and its success was mainly due to the sparkling, delicious Tchaikovsky music and to Markova's performance as the Sugar Plum Fairy, exquisite in its crisp yet delicate virtuosity. Stanley Judson was her Cavalier and one critic said Robert Helpmann "was conspicuous in the Chinese Dance." *Casse Noisette* filled the theatre (despite the counter-attraction of the first Ballets Jooss season at the Gaiety Theatre), and it seems to be a ballet with a perennial popular appeal. The music and the fairy story, so suitable for children, will always attract the "general" audience, and a good Sugar Plum Fairy will always draw the balletomanes. Its success at Sadler's Wells, however, has always been in spite of the appearance of the ballet, and it has never emerged as the delightful fairy-tale it ought to be. Given beautiful *décor* of the Benois quality and a careful production, with full attention to all the mime and character parts as well as fine dancing, it could be worthy of an opera house repertoire.

The revivals of *Giselle* and *Casse Noisette* delighted most of the Vic-Wells audience, but inevitably one section began to clamour for new ballets. Unless new productions were given almost every month at this time attendances began to drop, and this had to be

[1] The Lord Mayor's Boy Players had been founded in 1929 at the suggestion of King George V. Beautifully trained singers who appeared in several productions at the Old Vic, they were a kind of revival of the Boy Players of Shakespeare's time and wore a scarlet Elizabethan costume.

avoided at all costs if the company was to continue. Frequent new productions meant a heavy schedule of work for the company, and above all for Ninette de Valois, who had to produce most of the new ballets herself. Frederick Ashton had gone off to New York to produce the Gertrude Stein-Virgil Thomson opera *Four Saints in Three Acts* for "The Friends and Enemies of Modern Music," and until he returned and joined the Vic-Wells Ballet as a permanent member, the additions to the repertoire consisted of classical revivals and de Valois ballets.

Her next production, on 3rd April, was *The Haunted Ballroom*, designed very much to exploit the strong dramatic gifts of Robert Helpmann. The ghost story (based on Edgar Allen Poe) was very suitable for translation into a ballet, and Motley designed an eerie ballroom setting which faded to show a night sky, powdered with stars, when the ghosts appeared. Geoffrey Toye composed music that was theatrically romantic and contained a waltz which was later to become a best-seller (and the backbone of the B.B.C. Light Programme). There was a brief prologue which introduced the characters and established the atmosphere of the ballet, a major scene in which the Master of Treginnis is forced to dance to his death by a company of phantoms, and a final epilogue when his body is found and his heir realises that the same fate will one day overtake him. The ballet has been criticised for mixing *pointe* work (for the three women characters) with freer movements for the ghosts, but in the theatre the result is effective and it helps to distinguish the three particular phantoms from the mass of grey shapes. The dance for the Master of Treginnis is not remarkable, but was probably never intended to stand out too much from the general pattern of movement. Helpmann was more than capable of covering up this weakness in any case, and he carried the ballet to triumphant success. Alicia Markova, Ursula Moreton and Beatrice Appleyard were charming and elegant as the three female characters who were named after them. Markova's brilliant *chaîné* turns in the second scene might well have bewitched any sleepwalker, and in the diaphanous costume she seemed almost transparent as she skimmed and floated about the stage. The small part of the young Treginnis was mimed by Freda Bamford at the first performance and later by a young dancer named Margot Fontes, who was thought to be quite promising. The effective little part of the Strange Player was created by William Chappell.

The applause at the end of the first performance was almost hysterical and it was obvious that de Valois had produced a winner. Although *The Haunted Ballroom* achieved such an instantaneous and continuing public success, however, it did not have a good Press and has never met with much favour from the critics. *The Times* called it an "unsatisfactory ballet because mime and dancing are not fused," and Arnold Haskell complained that it was an " overlong and diffuse attempt to tell a Poe-German film melo-drama," representing "that confused thinking against which Fokine fought."

The important and ambitious season came to an end on 24th April. Markova was securely established as a true ballerina and was worshipped by her audience. Robert Helpmann had progressed unquestionably to the head of the company and was, in fact, the first major artist to be developed from within its ranks. A sound basis of classical productions had been added to the repertoire, and two new ballets had been presented which seemed assured of a long life (and are, in fact, still alive to-day). Attendances had been good throughout the season, but money was still tight, and Lilian Baylis continued to appeal for financial support at every possible opportunity. (She had a happy knack of knowing how to reach the heart of any particular audience. When addressing the guests at a Dancers' Circle Dinner, for instance, she would appeal for money "particularly on account of the great expenses entailed in maintaining an orchestra *worthy of the dancers.*") Nevertheless, there had been a handsome legacy from the Camargo Society and its wholehearted support had turned in the direction of the Vic-Wells Ballet all the goodwill and assistance of England's most influential balletomanes. A typically practical expression of good-will was made by Maynard Keynes that very April when he brought an international congress of some 800 economists to see the Vic-Wells Ballet.

At the end of the season Stanley Judson and Travis Kemp sailed for a tour in South Africa with the Levitoff Ballet, headed by Vera Nemchinova and Anatole Oboukhoff, and neither of them returned to the company. Markova decided to return for another year—despite tempting New York offers—and prevailed upon Lilian

Baylis to raise her salary to £15 a week "with an additional fiver to cover extra performances," *i.e.* the one Saturday *matinée* given each month. During the summer months she did a music-hall tour with Dolin which helped supplement her modest salary as well as being an unusual and interesting experience. Ruth French was engaged for the 1934-35 season to share with Ninette de Valois some of the heavier technical rôles. Freda Bamford decided to leave, but Ursula Moreton, Beatrice Appleyard, Hermione Darnborough, Ailne Phillips and Sheila McCarthy remained with the company, and Walter Gore, Claude Newman, William Chappell and Rollo Gamble were the other soloists.

1934-35

The season 1934-35 opened at Sadler's Wells on 2nd October and all performances up to 15th December were at Sadler's Wells. On the opening night Ruth French made her début with the company in *Fête Polonaise*, and at the next performance Helpmann appeared as Albrecht in *Giselle* for the first time. The company was dancing well and was seen to have established a definite personality. It might not be as brilliant and as exciting as Colonel de Basil's Russian Ballet which had had such successes at the Alhambra during the summer, but it had something very positive of its own to offer, and was not just something with which to make do during the winter while waiting for the Russians to return next summer.

A new ballet was produced on 9th October, *The Jar*, with choreography by Ninette de Valois and music by Casella. The ballet was based on a story by Luigi Pirandello, which had been used previously by Jean Borlin for the Ballet Suédois, about the adventures of a highly prized jar in a Sicilian village and the plight of a tinker who mends it from the inside and then cannot get out because of his humped back. The *corps de ballet* walked away with most of the notices, although Helpmann enjoyed himself as the infuriated farmer who owned the jar, and Walter Gore had one interesting dance as the Tinker. Beatrice Appleyard looked delightful as the farmer's daughter but had very little to do. The choreography, according to Cyril Beaumont, was modern in spirit, including many interesting movements and groups, and sometimes reminiscent in manner of Nijinska's work, for which de Valois always had a great

G

admiration. The ballet was gaily and attractively decorated by William Chappell in bright colours and was a useful "opener" for some time.

The next classical production was the most ambitious to date, no less than the four-act full-length version of *Le Lac des Cygnes*. Ninette de Valois and Evelyn Williams had flown to Paris during the summer to consult Sergueeff about it, and although language again presented difficulties, Sergueeff had become very excited about the swan patterns, waving his arms and explaining rapidly, "Zig-zag, zig-zag," and seemed to be in favour of such a revival. It was agreed that the ballet should be ready by the end of November. The first performance was made the occasion of a big charity gala in aid of Queen Charlotte's Hospital, which benefited to the extent of over £1,000.

Since that date the company has frequently launched a new ballet or a new production with a gala performance, and the policy has been markedly successful. In the early years they were sometimes criticised for devoting the increased takings to a charitable cause instead of putting the money towards their own humble exchequer, but at that time it was more important to widen the audience and attract people to the ballet than to pocket the few extra pounds. Goodwill engendered by these gala performances and the wide publicity given to them in the Press helped keep the more expensive seats filled throughout the season. It was not until much later when the company was soundly established and had no need to worry about attendances that the proceeds from gala performances could be devoted to its own charitable or educational projects, such as the Ballet Benevolent Fund and the Sadler's Wells School.

The production of *Le Lac des Cygnes* was decorated by Hugh Stevenson, a young designer recommended to Ninette de Valois by Marie Rambert, for whom he had designed several ballets. He was faced with the formidable task of creating three different settings and a large number of costumes on a very limited budget, and although the need for economy prevented him from designing as beautiful a production as he would have desired, he understood the spirit and the requirements of the ballet and succeeded remarkably well. Inevitably some costumes lacked an appropriate richness in execution and the wigs were uniformly hideous, but the main requirements of the ballet were fulfilled and Markova looked the ballerina she was in both the simple white *tutu* of Odette and the golden tutu decorated with red-gold sequins which she wore as Odile. Her performance was, of course, the focal point of the production and it won wholehearted approval. As Cyril Beaumont described it: "Markova, the first English dancer to attempt the exhausting rôle of Odette-Odile, with all the traditions that a host of *ballerine*—Legnani, Pavlova,[1] Karsavina, Spessivtzeva, Nemchinova, to mention but a few—have contributed to it, achieves a distinct success."

Robert Helpmann partnered Markova and achieved an independent success with his mime and dancing as the Prince Siegfried. The gap between Markova and the other dancers of the company was noticeably wide, but Elizabeth Miller and Doris May attracted attention in the *pas de trois* in which they appeared with Walter Gore. Ursula Moreton and Walter Gore led the Czardas with style, and among the peasants the dark little Margot Fonteyn stood out in particular. The regular audience began to "keep an eye" on her. Constant Lambert extracted the full beauties from Tchaikovsky's score and the familiar music no doubt helped in the ballet's success. As in all the Vic-Wells productions, the company was excellently rehearsed and the staging smooth and easy. If there was nothing of greatness apart from Markova's performance it was a creditable achievement within the limits of the resources available, and de Valois was always conscious of the fact that productions of the classical ballets which must, choreographically, be the foundation of her company's repertoire could always be improved, enlarged and better dressed as time passed and fortune favoured the company. The mounting of *Casse Noisette, Giselle, Coppélia* and *Le Lac des Cygnes* was described by Arnold Haskell as being of first-class artistic importance which would bring its reward in an increase of dancing power, and the merit of these faithful revivals was underlined the following year by some decidedly inferior classical productions shown in London by the Lithuanian Ballet.

The custom of presenting a short ballet as a curtain-raiser before the Christmas production of *Hansel and Gretel* was again observed in 1934, and in that year the choreography was entrusted to Sara Patrick. She produced a suite of dances based on the *Uncle Remus*

---

[1] The big brilliants used in the crown which Markova wore as the Swan Queen were the actual ones used by Pavlova herself.

stories, the first performance being given at the Old Vic on 19th December. Hugh Stevenson was once again invited to design the costumes and *décor*, and the music was by Gordon Jacob. Claude Newman appeared as Mr. Bear, Frank Staff as Brer Rabbit, Sheila McCarthy had a lively solo as Mrs. Buzzard and Margot Fonteyn appeared as one of the six little rabbits. *Uncle Remus* did not meet with favour from either the dancers or the public and was not taken into the regular ballet repertoire.

On 26th March the Vic-Wells Ballet added another Camargo Society production to their repertoire. This was Constant Lambert's ballet *Rio Grande*, with choreography by Frederick Ashton, and costumes and scenery by Edward Burra. (The Camargo Society had called the ballet *A Day in a Southern Port*, but at the Wells Lambert's original title for the music was used.) The production was not intended to be a literal interpretation of the words of Sacheverell Sitwell's poem; as a programme note explained, "the theme is suggested by the music." Angus Morrison was the solo pianist, Valetta Jacopi sang the alto solo and members of the Vic-Wells Opera Company made up the chorus. The rather exotic little ballet was of no great importance and some people disliked it intensely, but once again it provided a touch of sophistication in the repertory and is remembered now as being the ballet in which Margot Fonteyn, aged fifteen years and ten months, played her first important rôle at Sadler's Wells. She appeared as the Creole Girl (created by Markova), dancing with William Chappell and winning from that moment his admiration and devotion which culminated in his book about her, published in 1951: "Made up the colour of a dark golden peach grown on some Southern shore, she glowed like a Mediterranean day and her wide radiant smile would have warmed a continent." *The Dancing Times* called her performance "the most notable event of the past few weeks" and said that the further opportunities, which were soon to be given to her, would be watched with interest.

By this time de Valois knew that Markova would be leaving the company before very long, and she knew that in future she would have to rely on the talent within her company, the young artists who had been gradually emerging throughout the season. Elizabeth Miller, Pamela May and Margot Fonteyn were all gifted dancers and interesting personalities, and she had faith in their ability. At the same time she was anxious that others should recognise the native talent within the company, and she lost no opportunity of declaring her confidence in her young dancers.

Markova's departure had been foreshadowed at a Dancers' Circle Dinner held in her honour in February. "I shall always be most grateful to Miss Lilian Baylis and Miss Ninette de Valois for helping me, through the Vic-Wells Ballet, in this country," she said, "but I feel the time has come for me to take my art out into the world." She did, at that time, still think it might be possible for her to return for one more season, but obviously she would not remain in Islington indefinitely.

While Markova was dancing ballerina rôles at Sadler's Wells her sister, Doris Barry, was appearing as a soubrette at the Windmill Theatre, and one evening she took Vivian Van Damm, the general manager of the Windmill, to Sadler's Wells to see Alicia dance. It was his first experience of ballet and Markova's dancing made a profound impression. The next day he called Doris into his office and inquired whether her sister would like to have her own company. Van Damm had the financial support of Mrs. Laura Henderson, owner of the Windmill Theatre and a remarkable figure in London theatre business. Mrs. Henderson was the widow of a wealthy jute merchant, a plump little woman, less than five feet tall, with spectacles and a pretty grey-white wig and the vitality of a whirlwind. She was interested in Van Damm's proposal to take a British ballet company on tour throughout the country and, with certain stipulations, agreed to put up a considerable amount of money.

After some discussion and an interview with Lilian Baylis it was agreed that Mrs. Henderson should provide independent financial backing for a tour of the Vic-Wells Ballet, beginning with two or three weeks in London and followed by several weeks in the provinces. Markova was to be the "star" of the company and was to appear in one new ballet, and *Giselle* was to be redressed, Mrs. Henderson undertaking to meet the expense of these new productions. Markova became a Director of Vivian Van Damm Productions Ltd. (a syndicate with Mrs. Henderson and Vivian Van Damm as the other directors) and signed a year's contract to appear at the head of their ballet company. It was hoped originally that Helpmann would sign a similar contract and co-star with her, but he was already committed to appear in the revue *Stop Press* at the Adelphi Theatre and could not accept any such offer. Van Damm naturally felt he must have a male dancer of repute to replace Helpmann, and as Dolin happened to be free he was the obvious choice. He signed a year's contract with Van Damm, and both he and Markova were guaranteed salaries which were vastly higher than they could earn at Sadler's Wells (and roughly five times the size of the salary which was then being drawn by the Director of the Vic-Wells Ballet). Vivian Van Damm Productions Ltd. were to present a two-week ballet season at Sadler's Wells Theatre after the conclusion of the normal opera and ballet season, and would then present the company for one week at the Shaftesbury Theatre in order to show them to a West End audience. Afterwards there would be a provincial tour.

Helpmann went into his revue when the regular season ended, and for the first week of the special season at Sadler's Wells Harold Turner, who had recently joined the company as a leading soloist, was billed with Markova as principal dancer, Dolin joining at the beginning of the second week. The Sadler's Wells audience welcomed the prospect of seeing ballet every night for two whole weeks and the management hoped that the season would afford visitors to London for the Jubilee of King George V an opportunity of seeing the work of an English ballet company.

The season was launched on 20th May with the new ballet which Mrs. Henderson had stipulated, and which happened to be *The Rake's Progress*. The scenario for this ballet and the music had been written by Gavin Gordon, who first offered it to Frederick Ashton, but Ashton was not attracted by the subject which he felt was "not for him." However, it appealed to Ninette de Valois and she decided to produce it. The ballet was first scheduled for April, but had to be postponed as in February de Valois fell ill and had to undergo an operation (it was performed by Dr. Geoffrey Keynes). She conducted a certain amount of business from her bed, planned the production, inspected designs and issued instructions, but naturally could not do any work on the actual choreography until she was back in the theatre. Despite these handicaps, however, and despite the fact that she must have known her company was approaching a turning point in its career, she created a ballet that was not only good but was to become a cornerstone of the English ballet repertoire.

Based on the series of paintings by William Hogarth (housed in the Sir John Soane Museum in Lincoln's Inn Fields), the ballet was a superb piece of theatrecraft and, like *Job,* it was of a strongly native inspiration and owed nothing to the style of the Russian Ballet. The subject contained little prettiness but gave much scope for robust humour and strong characterisation, while Gavin Gordon's music was brilliant theatrical stuff, helping the action, adding to the humour, carrying the whole tragic story to its relentless end. Rex Whistler was an ideal choice for the designer. He had worked for the Camargo Society and had some experience of the West End theatre, but it was above all his feeling for the eighteenth century that made him the right, indeed the only, designer for *The Rake's Progress.* He was an artist who could re-create period without ever turning it, by a touch of personal comment, into *pastiche,* and his designs reproduced both the squalor and the elegance of eighteenth-century London. His original drop curtain for the ballet was one of the finest pieces of draughtsmanship ever seen in the theatre. (Professor Henry Tonks, who had taught Whistler at the Slade School, once told Sir Osbert Sitwell that "during the entire course of a lifetime he had only met two or three people who were natural draughtsmen, and that Rex was one of them.")

The three collaborators achieved a magnificent unity of style, and their reward has been the progress of the ballet itself, which has developed from a successful novelty into a classic of British choreography.

On the opening night it was Harold Turner's performance in the two contrasting rôles of the elegant Dancing Master and the demented Man with a Rope which received the ovation. Walter Gore did not then make a great deal of the part of the Rake, although when he returned as guest artist to play it again at Sadler's Wells Theatre in 1952 he gave an unforgettable performance. Markova, too, was not ideally cast as the Young Girl, a part obviously intended for a *demi-caractère* dancer rather than a strictly classical ballerina. In the smaller parts several dancers of the first cast left their mark for ever on the rôles they created, particularly in the blowsy, rowdy second scene: Ursula Moreton as the Dancer, Sheila McCarthy as the Woman with the Corsets, Joy Newton as the seedy, bedraggled ballad singer and Jill Gregory as the little coloured servant (for some reason no longer coloured) have never been excelled.

The following Monday Anton Dolin returned to the company to dance in the redressed *Giselle* with Markova, and was given a warm welcome. The season ended with a performance of *Le Lac des Cygnes*, Markova's last at Sadler's Wells Theatre.[1] It was an occasion of much hysteria and lamentation from the audience. Markova has always had a legion of passionate admirers, and that night feeling ran so strongly that many of them were declaring they would never have reason to go to Sadler's Wells again. For two years Markova had so dominated the young company that such "fans" had tended to overlook the amount of progress that was being made among the young dancers. Consequently, they found a future without Markova almost unimaginable. For the first time in her life she made a speech from the stage, saying simply, "Thank you all, from the bottom of my heart," and afterwards she had to hire three taxis to take home the flowers that had been sent to her.

There was still an opportunity for Londoners to see Markova with the Vic-Wells Ballet, however, during the one-week season at the now vanished Shaftesbury Theatre, which began on 3rd June with *The Jar* and *Giselle*. The season was well received and a varied programme of classic and modern ballets was presented. The provincial tour started with visits to Blackpool and Bournemouth and after a holiday in July was resumed in August—Glasgow, Edinburgh, Manchester, Birmingham and Leeds all being visited for one week. A full orchestra went with the company, in charge of Constant Lambert, and they were welcomed everywhere.

During this tour the arrangements for the forthcoming 1935–36 season had, of course, to be settled. Helpmann was under contract to return to Sadler's Wells, and Markova and Dolin were under contract to Vivian van Damm. It was obvious that no merger could take place as the policies of a repertory company and a commercial company headed by two famous stars were bound to be irreconcilable. Markova and Dolin consequently left the Wells to form their own company, which was to do much valuable pioneer

---

[1] A young man who was to play a big part in the future history of the company had a small part that evening: Michael Somes appeared very solemnly as the "Usher" in the ballroom scene.

work in showing British ballet to provincial and West End audiences,[1] and the Vic-Wells Ballet had to learn to stand on its own feet.

Markova's departure came at the logical time and her decision was without doubt the right one, both with regard to her own future career and from the point of view of the Vic-Wells Ballet, but the departure of another dancer during the 1934–35 season has ever since been the subject of much bitter controversy. Antony Tudor left the company after a brief and not particularly remarkable sojourn with them in order that he might devote himself to choreography elsewhere. He had produced ballets of unmistakeable promise for Marie Rambert before he joined the Wells in 1933, and during the time he was with them he repeatedly asked to be allowed to create a ballet, returning for a second season only because he believed he was at last to be given an opportunity. The tightness of money and the risk of failure were the reasons de Valois gave for postponing such a production, and the only choreography Tudor did for the Wells was in the operas *Carmen* and *Faust*. Discouraged by the lack of opportunity to create ballets (he was never very interested in appearing as a dancer), Tudor determined to leave. De Valois suggested he should join the Russian Ballet of Colonel de Basil for a couple of years in order to gain experience of a large organisation (as she herself had done under Diaghileff), and promised to take him back into her company and give him opportunities as a choreographer later on when she could afford to do so. Tudor, however, preferred to go on creating ballets for the Ballet Club, and for them he made *The Descent of Hebe, Jardin aux Lilas, Dark Elegies* and *Judgment of Paris*, before leaving to found the London Ballet in 1938. The following year he received an invitation to join the newly formed American Ballet Theater, and for this company he created *Pillar of Fire, Romeo and Juliet, Dim Lustre* and *Undertow*, winning international recognition and a place among the great choreographers of his generation.

All this glory might have accrued to the Vic-Wells Ballet had he remained and been given his head. Whether he would have developed so strong and individual a style within that organisation

[1] Mrs. Henderson lost some £30,000 on the enterprise and must often have remembered Lilian Baylis' words at their first business interview: "You will do much good for British Ballet—but you will lose a fortune."

it is impossible to say. Whether he should have been invited to work with them in the late 'thirties when *Jardin aux Lilas* had shown his full mastery is a matter of opinion. At the time he left in 1935 de Valois could afford only one choreographer in the company in addition to herself and she chose Frederick Ashton, a choreographer of more experience and renown than Tudor, and an artist whose work was in very strong contrast to her own ballets. Like Diaghileff, from whom she learned her job, Ninette de Valois has never sought for numerous choreographers. One at a time, in addition to her own increasingly infrequent productions, has been the general rule, and one of the worst moments of her life was when she heard it boasted during the war that in one year sixty new ballets had been produced in London: "I think this was dreadful. It was more than the number of solo dancers. I think a company should never have more than two or three choreographers. In all his twenty-five years Diaghileff only produced four choreographers. Standard is the most important thing."

The choice of Ashton as resident choreographer was more than justified over the years, for he served the company surpassingly well, and it was not until he left them for war service that another choreographer, Helpmann, was launched. Nowadays, with less financial anxiety, de Valois has tried only two other English choreographers at Covent Garden, Andrée Howard and John Cranko, although out at Sadler's Wells Theatre, with the smaller company and, more particularly, with the experimental Choreographers' Group, she is willing to let the young aspiring choreographer try his hand. She has pursued this course steadfastly and with determination, despite occasional protests and criticisms, because she believes it is the right one. Frank Staff, Walter Gore and, above all, Antony Tudor left the Wells and produced their ballets for Marie Rambert. One may regret the loss of their talents, but at the same time one has to recognise that the de Valois policy has not been unsuccessful.

The summer tour of 1935 ended at the Grand Theatre, in Leeds, on Saturday, 7th September. The performance marked the farewell of Markova and Dolin and the end of the first period in the history of the Vic-Wells Ballet. With help from established artists, the quality of their performances and the attraction of their names, the basic spadework had been done. The ballet had established itself and was accepted as part of the theatre's policy at Sadler's

Wells. The financial position had been steadily strengthened, the company was permanent and increasing in size every year, and adequate orchestra rehearsals had been fought for and secured. The needs of the ballet for more rehearsal rooms were recognised by the Governors of Sadler's Wells and were henceforth taken into account when plans were made for future enlargements and improvements.

The first two years had been the hardest from every point of view, financial, emotional and physical. For two years the dancers had worked on a concrete floor in the rehearsal room because the expenditure of the hundred pounds necessary to instal a wooden floor could not be approved by the finance committee. Only dancers can appreciate the full horror of this situation. It was painful even to go on *pointe*, a fall could mean serious injury and everyone suffered from perpetual sore toes. Eventually the wooden floor was installed, but working conditions were anything but ideal. The company might be housed permanently in a theatre, but it had to share that theatre with the opera company and also with the ballet school. Only one good rehearsal room was available by 1935, and the ballet company had the use of the stage for *two hours a week*—provided opera rehearsals allowed it! The infrequency of the ballet performances doubled the amount of rehearsing, and the requirements of the school and the office workers' classes (essential for training future dancers and for bringing in a steady income) monopolised the rehearsal room for some forty-eight hours each week. This left about two and a half hours each day for ballet company rehearsals. In addition, a small room was available for rehearsing principals, but this room was likely to be demanded at any time for board meetings of directors or producers. Evening rehearsals were impossible, because then the rehearsal room had to do duty as a coffee room for the audience before and during the performance. The dancers numbered twenty-five at this time, extras being drawn from the school, as now, to supplement the larger productions. At least five new productions were considered essential every season and opera ballets had to be provided in addition. The amount of work which was accomplished within the cramped quarters was astonishing and wonderful testimony to the devotion of the artists and the continual vitality and inspiration of Ninette de Valois.

Despite hard work and sore toes, it was a happy company. The dancers were all young and idealistic, hope was high and endeavour strong, and they were all genuinely interested in and anxious for each other's success. They accepted the difficult conditions cheerfully, took their careers so seriously that they would rather have died than miss a performance, and even managed to make a joke of the mice. (The mice had always infested the Old Vic and they lost no time in moving to the new theatre of Sadler's Wells. They had a special passion for ballet shoes, finding the glue particularly succulent, and would hide in dressing-rooms, jump out of practice clothes, and even get into baskets of costumes. During one summer holiday they devoured all the masks used in the ballet *Job* and were a serious problem to the management. Joy Newton for years treasured a letter she received from Lilian Baylis, politely turning down her request for an increase in salary and concluding with a postscript: "Do try and do something about the mice in the dressing-rooms, dear.")

Ninette de Valois faced the next phase in her company's progress with considerable confidence. She knew her dancers had both the talent and the singleness of purpose to succeed, but the dancers themselves were not quite so certain about the future. Margot Fonteyn, for instance, had by then danced several small solos and had made an impression on the audience, while the critics would often single her out to mention her sincerity, her feeling and the gentle charm of her dancing; but she was as yet quite unaware of what the future might hold for her. "Isn't it terrible about Markova leaving?" she wrote to a friend that summer. "I cannot think what will happen next season without her; we shall all have to work very hard, but even hard work can't make a Prima Ballerina if there isn't one."

CHAPTER VII

FREDERICK ASHTON AND THE BUILDING OF A NATIVE REPERTOIRE

1935–36

THE period from September 1935 up to the outbreak of war in September 1939 was one of rich artistic activity at Sadler's Wells, and no small part of the credit for the rapid flowering of the young company was due to Frederick Ashton. He joined the Vic-Wells Ballet at the beginning of the 1935–36 season as dancer and choreographer, and was invited to produce at least three new ballets during that first season. Over the next four years he created a series of varied and beautiful ballets which raised the prestige of the company enormously, helped to develop and display the talents of the dancers and attracted artists and musicians of international reputation to work with the company. He also brought with him his own fashionable audience which had applauded his smart and elegant little ballets at the Ballet Club and found his bigger productions at Sadler's Wells equally delightful.

Performances of ballet were to be almost entirely at Sadler's Wells Theatre in future. The cost of frequent exchange between the two theatres had proved prohibitive both on account of the destruction of stage properties involved and the heavy expense of cartage. Once again in 1934–35 the success of the ballet season had exceeded that of the opera, and for the first time there was a net surplus on the year's working at Sadler's Wells. The Annual Report noted with satisfaction that "the year's work has led to the discovery of several very promising young dancers, who will get bigger chances in the near future of displaying their talents." A concession of great importance had been won for the two theatres that year when, following representations made on their behalf, the Commissioners of Customs and Excise adopted a new interpretation of a section of the Act governing Entertainment Duty and granted exemption from this heavy duty to the Old Vic and

Sadler's Wells. The new ruling applied to any concern which did not work for profit and provided performances "whose purpose is partly educational" and the Vic-Wells organisation thus conferred an important benefit on drama and music in Great Britain—a benefit which was to be exploited in a variety of different ways and in curious circumstances in later years, but which has remained of fundamental importance to the whole financial structure of the serious repertory theatre.

To the great joy of Constant Lambert the orchestra was enlarged for the 1935–36 season, and it was at last possible to use the full score of *Job* instead of the condensed version. Performances were to be given twice a week (every Tuesday evening and alternate Friday evenings and Saturday *matinées*). Ursula Moreton and Ailne Phillips took charge of the theatre school and the company classes were taken by Margaret Craske and Madame Anna Pruzina, a Russian who had worked in conjunction with Novikoff and who inspired her pupils to greater efforts by exclaiming continually, "Ze 'igher eet goes, ze better eet is." Pearl Argyle, a Ballet Club dancer of great beauty and exquisite sensibility, who had also appeared with *Les Ballets 1933* and in West End productions, joined the company as a leading dancer, and another acquisition was Mary Honer, a brilliant technician who had appeared in musicals and cabaret. Robert Helpmann and Harold Turner led the male dancers and Ruth French returned as an occasional guest artist. The policy of the Director remained unchanged: "The guarding of the classical tradition, the encouragement of the modern and, above all, the fostering of native talent, choreographically, musically and pictorially."

The season opened on Friday, 27th September, with a programme that indicated neatly the talents upon which the season was to depend. An Ashton ballet, *Les Rendezvous*, opened the programme and was danced by Harold Turner and Margot Fonteyn, who inherited the central rôle originally made for Markova. This was followed by de Valois' ballet, *The Rake's Progress*, now danced by Robert Helpmann and Elizabeth Miller. The final ballet was Fokine's *Carnaval*, with a setting and costumes at least approximating those of Bakst and with Pearl Argyle as Columbine, Mary Honer as Papillon, Helpmann as Harlequin and Ashton as Pierrot. The opening night clashed with a *première* by the Woizikowski

Company at the Coliseum and Sadler's Wells was not full, although there was a good audience. The evening was, however, remarkably successful. The company was dancing admirably together, thanks largely to the benefit of daily performances during the preceding tour, and was seen to be a group of young artists all at a rather similar stage of development with much to give at the moment and promising even more in the future.

Fonteyn, following Markova in one of her most individual rôles, revealed a different but delightful quality, and Elizabeth Miller in *The Rake's Progress* succeeded at once in a rôle that had never suited Markova anyway. The critics suddenly woke up to the fact that the Vic-Wells Ballet was indeed a ballet company and not just a background for Markova, and the performances of this season first won the company the wholehearted enthusiasm and support of Arnold Haskell. He headed his review of the opening night: "Dazzling new star of the Future: Auspicious opening to the Season." *The Observer* noted that the company had lost Markova but gained Pearl Argyle, "and it has produced from its ranks a budding ballerina, who looks like blooming with the best. Margot Fonteyn, a sixteen-year-old, already displays the poise, the spirit and the promise of a star."

Ashton was planning to produce Stravinsky's *Baiser de la Fée* in November, but in the meantime he supervised a revival of *Façade* for the company, adding one new number and dancing himself the central character of the Dago. The ballet had been made originally for the Camargo Society in 1931 and had then been acquired by Marie Rambert for the Ballet Club, the choreographer receiving the munificent sum of £5 for his work. John Armstrong designed some new costumes for the enlarged version at the Wells, but his original setting (the one with a cow on the end of a pier) was used.

The music for the ballet derived from William Walton's orchestral suite of the same name, which was an elaborated version of several of the numbers originally written to be rendered in conjunction with Edith Sitwell's poems and constituting with them an "entertainment" for speaking voice and six instruments. This "entertainment" had been devised by the Sitwells and Walton together and had first been given at the Sitwells' house in Chelsea in January 1922. The title came from a private family joke, a "bad painter" having said of Edith Sitwell, "Very clever, no doubt—but what is she but a Façade!" This had delighted the Sitwells enormously and they seized on it as a perfect title for their entertainment.[1]

When Ashton came to make a ballet from the music he aimed simply at creating a *divertissement* to the music itself and made no attempt to interpret the poems. By the time the ballet was produced in 1931 the storms of ridicule about *Façade* that once raged in the popular Press had died down and, ironically, Walton's music has by now probably become the most popular suite by a contemporary composer of the front rank. "As a musical joker he is a jewel of the first water," wrote Ernest Newman after hearing *Façade*, and it was this quality in the music which appealed to Ashton and delighted the sophisticated Camargo Society and Ballet Club audiences. When it came into the Sadler's Wells repertoire a larger, more heterogeneous audience enjoyed it just as much and it has been in the repertoire ever since the first performance on 8th October 1935, apparently increasing in popularity all the time, still drawing loud laughs in all the obvious places and being a smash hit during the first Sadler's Wells American tour in 1949.

For the first performance the company was able to offer an admirable cast. Helpmann danced the Scotch Rhapsody with Mary Honer and Elizabeth Miller; Fonteyn once again inherited a part from Markova but made a success of the Polka nevertheless; Turner and Chappell danced the Popular Song and Molly Brown was the Débutante. The new Country Dance had Pearl Argyle as A Maiden, Richard Ellis as A Yokel and Helpmann as The Squire, hilarious in a deerstalker. Pearl Argyle also appeared with Ashton in the Tarantella Finale, although this change of partners was later abandoned and the Débutante danced the Tarantella as well as the preceding Tango.

On 29th October a re-dressed version of *Douanes* was given its first performance. Sophie Fedorovitch certainly gave the ballet more style and elegance than it had originally had, but the choreography was seen to be wearing rather thin. Ninette de Valois repeated her lively performance as the Tight-Rope Walker, Helpmann was the Cook's Man, Ashton a Passport Officer and Turner an Eccentric Passenger. The first performance was conducted by the composer, Geoffrey Toye.

[1] The strange history of this entertainment has been fully recounted in Sir Osbert Sitwell's *Laughter in the Next Room.*

Anthony

POMONA

Pearl Argyle and Robert Helpmann

Left: Robert Helpmann, June Brae, Frederick Ashton and Joan Sheldon in the Fox-trot from *Façade*. *Right:* Margot Fonteyn and William Chappell in *Rio Grande*. *Below:* Frederick Ashton, Lord Berners and Constant Lambert planning a ballet

The increasing importance of the Vic-Wells Ballet as an artistic endeavour to be proud of was demonstrated in November when a visiting deputation of foreign music critics, forty representatives from some twenty different countries, went to the Wells, at the suggestion of Edwin Evans, to see *The Rake's Progress, Façade, Blue Bird* and *Job*. Lord Tyrrell, Chairman of the British Council at the time, wrote after their visit: "The foreign music critics were enchanted by their visit to Sadler's Wells and are loud in their praises of the artistic standard set by your performance."

Baiser de la Fée, Ashton's first major production since joining the company, was ready for presentation by 26th November. He had been delighted with the material he found available to work with at Sadler's Wells, and from the beginning found inspiration in Margot Fonteyn. Pearl Argyle and Harold Turner he had known at the Ballet Club, and he was well satisfied with the cast he assembled for the ballet. "I could not have a better or more efficient company of artists than the ballet company this season with which to interpret my choreographic conceptions," he wrote in the *Old Vic and Sadler's Wells Magazine*.

The allegorical ballet in four tableaux by Igor Stravinsky had been "inspired by the Muse of Tchaikovsky" and Ashton intended similarly to use the classical basis of dancing with his own individual interpretation, "by taking the necessary liberties for the construction of a choreographic spectacle emanating directly from the character and style of the music—which in no way will be a realistic treatment." Sophie Fedorovitch, as was her wont, concentrated the essentials of decoration into a synthesis of simplicity, grandeur and beauty. The ballet opened with a prologue, "The Lullaby of the Tempest," in which Ursula Moreton made one of her brief and telling appearances as the Mother. The backcloth for this scene was formed of gradually darkening semicircles of dark red, like "an angry rainbow." The second scene of a village festival was less successful (Ashton was not yet altogether happy when working with a large group of dancers), but the third scene in which the Young Bride loses her Bridegroom to the Fairy was one of Ashton's lyrical masterpieces and contained for Fonteyn and Turner the first of the long series of exquisite *pas de deux* he was to make for Fonteyn over the years. In her first important creation Fonteyn justified all the confidence of de Valois; the quality of a ballerina was apparent,

H

the gifts that must come from within and can be developed but never imposed by the most careful teaching. Pearl Argyle in a greenish-grey and white costume and a strange and beautiful make-up was at her best as the Fairy, her cold classicism being magically used by Ashton. "The first important romantic ballet to be produced by a British company," wrote Arnold Haskell.

Fonteyn's real trial as a potential ballerina came just before Christmas when she danced the Swan Queen Odette in *Le Lac des Cygnes* for the first time. The full four-act production was given, with Helpmann as the Prince, but the rôle of Odile was danced by Ruth French as the double assignment would obviously have been too much for the immature Fonteyn. Ruth French, a brilliant technician, had been dancing many of the more exacting classical rôles that season, for instance in *Casse Noisette* (with Turner), and the "peasant" *pas de deux* in *Giselle*. She gave valuable assistance on many occasions when the Wells were short of dancers, but never stayed long enough to assume a real place in the company. On this occasion interest was inevitably directed towards Fonteyn, and her performance was received with delight—all the more genuine in that it was recognised by the critics that she had still far to go and they were more than content to wait. "She suggests the true spirit of the dance in an altogether exceptional way," wrote Francis Toye. "Of all English dancers I have seen I consider her easily the best." "She is young," said *The Observer*, "but her youth need be held neither for nor against her. She has technique, feeling, style, and it is on these that she passed the test with honours." Arnold Haskell's enthusiasm was now truly roused: "Margot Fonteyn in the famous rôle gave a truly great performance. No other word will do. She has fully earned that rare title 'ballerina,' and time will certainly give her authority and full mastery of detail."

A revival of *Nursery Suite* was also shown that December, and it had a particular interest as it was performed entirely by young students holding Vic-Wells scholarships. These scholarships were the outcome of a scheme (originally proposed by the Misses Cone) which the Governors had approved some eighteen months previously to establish a link between the leading dancing schools and the Vic-Wells Ballet. Certain schools were invited by the Governors of the Vic-Wells Company to give a scholarship, value £10 a year for two years, such scholarships to be competed for only by the pupils of the school offering them who were over twelve and under fifteen years of age. The successful candidates were to be given five hours' special tuition each week, approximately from the beginning of April to the end of July, in practical stage work, by the Ballet Mistress of the Vic-Wells Ballet, in addition to the lessons they continued to take at their own schools. From time to time these students might be used in ballets in which children were required, and in fact they were soon appearing in *Casse Noisette*, with a special programme note which listed their names and the schools from which they came. *Nursery Suite* was revived especially for these young dancers, with somewhat altered choreography and re-dressed by William Chappell for the occasion. The youngsters acquitted themselves very well, and Julia Farron, who held the Cone School scholarship, first attracted attention at this performance.

Soon after Christmas Ninette de Valois produced a new ballet, a charming *pastiche* of French eighteenth-century mannerisms, in its way as much an animation of paintings as *The Rake's Progress* or *Job*. *The Gods go a'Begging* drew its inspiration from the style and spirit of Watteau's paintings and was an entirely delightful ballet. Hugh Stevenson's soft pastoral setting and simple costumes blended admirably with the Handel music, and Pearl Argyle and William Chappell were ideally cast as the immortals who visit the earth disguised as a Shepherd and a Serving Maid. Ailne Phillips and Mary Honer were the two pert little serving maids, and Ursula Moreton and Robert Helpmann led the more formal dances with elegance. Comparisons with the Russian Ballet had inevitably been made throughout the life of the Vic-Wells Ballet and usually the English company had suffered, but now the tide was beginning to turn, and many people said openly that the de Valois version of *The Gods go a'Begging* was a more complete and unified work of art than the Lichine version presented by de Basil.

At the end of January the company travelled to Cambridge to dance the opening performance at the new Arts Theatre, which was being launched by Lydia Lopokova and Maynard Keynes. It was an opportunity for the ballet to show its gratitude for all the help they had in the past received from "the King and Queen of Cambridge," and in honour of the occasion *Siesta*, the new Ashton *pas de deux*, was given as an overture and companion to

Façade. The programme was made up with *Les Rendezvous* and *The Rake's Progress*. The company had a tremendous welcome in Cambridge (where it has ever since had a faithful public) from an audience representative of both town and gown. *Siesta* had been shown first at Sadler's Wells Theatre on 24th January 1936, having been postponed from 21st January on account of the death of His Majesty King George the Fifth. It was danced by Pearl Argyle and Robert Helpmann, Pearl Argyle's dress being designed and made by Matilda Etches. Haskell described it as a "study of dalliance between naps on a hot summer day. In form it is a *chic* and ingenious trifle from a high-class revue, or a sonnet by a poet of the decadent school." It was only a butterfly creation, however, and soon disappeared.

Very different was Ashton's next ballet, *Apparitions,* which received its first performance on 11th February 1936. The ballet had been devised by Constant Lambert on a romantic theme, similar to the programme of Berlioz' "Symphonie Fantastique," of a poet's dreams under the influence of laudanum. He selected the music from the piano compositions of Liszt (the centenary of whose birth was that year being celebrated), and the action of the ballet was worked out in close consultation with Ashton. They were anxious that the designer should be Cecil Beaton (who had worked with Ashton on a ballet "The First Shoot" in the Cochran revue *Follow the Sun*), and as he was interested in the proposition, Lilian Baylis made a formal offer. She explained that money was still very short and she could not afford large fees, but was willing to pay £50 to Beaton if he would design the ballet. Like so many other artists who worked for the Vic and the Wells, Beaton was more interested in the opportunity than the money and he accepted the offer.

He designed a wonderful Gothic romantic setting for the poet's study and, as expensive settings for each separate scene could not be contemplated, he improvised brilliantly with white flats and evocative shadows and threw all the colour into his costumes. The monks' purple robes and the flaming scarlet costumes of the orgy scene required no special skill in cutting and making, but the ballroom costumes were more subtle in design and would have lost all their richness and beauty unless made by an expert. Beaton consequently handed over his £50 to the incomparable Madame Karinska and entrusted her with the task of executing his designs for the ball dresses. As is her custom, she delivered the dresses at the very last moment, but every one was a masterpiece. Beaton and Karinska was a combination undreamed of before in the history of the Vic-Wells Ballet, and their united talents gave the ballet a luxurious beauty surpassing any other work in the repertory. *Apparitions* was further aided by a grant from the Camargo Society, which handed over the remaining balance of its funds towards the cost of this production.

Lambert described the first night as "the biggest success we have ever had at the Wells," and for a company at that precise point of development *Apparitions* was a perfect ballet. It had all the soul-sick romanticism beloved of the young, and in the small theatre it had heartbreaking beauty and earnestness which disappeared when it was later danced by older, more conscious artists, at Covent Garden. Choreographically the ballroom scene was, and is, a masterpiece, and the *Galop* is one of the most exciting passages in all ballet, but after that superb example of tragic gaiety the ballet falls away badly, and only the white-faced impassioned mime of Helpmann held it together. Fonteyn, young, gentle and lovely as the Woman in Ball Dress, showed a new grasp of the character, which she sustained beautifully and almost unconsciously throughout the ballet. How moving was her sorrowful entry in the epilogue when she motioned the cloaked figures to bear away the dead body of the poet. Lambert's choice of music was a major factor in the success of the ballet, for he had an extraordinary sense of theatrical effectiveness and he spent much time working with Gordon Jacob on the orchestration.

The last new ballet of a busy season was *Barabau*, produced by Ninette de Valois on 17th April. Balanchine had made the first version of this work for Diaghileff, and it had received its first performance in London on 11th December 1925 at the London Coliseum. De Valois used the words and music by Rieti but devised new choreography, and new designs were provided by Edward Burra. The ballet was based on an old Italian nursery rhyme:

> *Barabau, Barabau, why did you die?*
> *You'd wine in your cellar, your bread was not dry,*
> *And salad you grew in your garden near by:*
> *Barabau, Barabau, why did you die?*

In the Diaghileff version Serge Lifar had appeared as the comic sergeant in charge of the soldiers and Woizikowski had been Barabau. At Sadler's Wells, Harold Turner played the part of Barabau, a greedy, cunning peasant, Frederick Ashton had a certain amount of fun with the Sergeant, and Ninette de Valois waved a bottle of chianti with charm and vigour as the peasant woman. Sixteen women and ten men from the opera company lent their services, and all the dancers gave spirited performances. All the material seemed to be there for a vigorous burlesque ballet in de Valois' most exuberant vein, but in fact it did not quite come off. The faithful Wells audience gave it a rapturous reception on the first night and it earned a few good notices. As with most ballets, there were some people who liked it very much, and de Valois herself believed in it sufficiently to revive it again in 1939, but the war seemed to kill it for ever. The original production was assisted by the Sadler's Wells Society, which contributed £120 towards expenses.

The season at Sadler's Wells ended on 15th May with a programme consisting of the two new successes *The Gods go a'Begging* and *Apparitions,* the *Blue Bird pas de deux* and *Façade.* At the beginning of June the company visited Cambridge and played to capacity audiences for eight performances. After a holiday, they reassembled in mid-July and then made a provincial tour of six weeks, visiting Birmingham, Manchester, Nottingham, Edinburgh, Glasgow and Newcastle-upon-Tyne.

Mathilde Kschessinska, who had come to London to dance with the de Basil company at Covent Garden and was receiving a vast amount of publicity, gave a special lesson to the company just before they began their tour, as an expression of goodwill and encouragement to the company's newly launched Five-Year Plan. Kschessinska, most celebrated of the Imperial Russian ballerinas and even to-day a vigorous teacher and legendary figure in Paris, was full of enthusiasm for the English dancers. "Judging by the girls who come to me for teaching, you will soon have an absolutely first-class national ballet," she said. Also, "I find English girls amazingly gifted for the dance (*douées pour la danse*)."

The Five-Year Plan

The Five-Year Plan for the Vic-Wells Ballet had been inaugurated by Arnold Haskell and some influential well-wishers to build up some kind of subsidy which could be used to consolidate and extend the good work which had already been accomplished. So long as the company operated on a shoestring budget there was a constant threat that the artists might be forced by economic necessity to leave the Wells for more remunerative work in the commercial theatre. It must be remembered that actors went to the Old Vic for only one or two seasons, as a rule, whereas it was essential for the ballet company to retain the same dancers over a long period of years if anything in the nature of a native style or tradition was to be built up.

The Five-Year Plan hoped to raise by donations a capital sum of £25,000 to be invested as a reserve, the income to be devoted to clearly defined objects. "No form of investment will pay quicker or more substantial artistic dividends," wrote Arnold Haskell in a pamphlet announcing the plan. An Executive Committee was set up consisting of The Lady Brocket (Chairman), The Lady Burghley, The Lady Anne Rhys, The Lady Mary Manningham-Buller, Lady Penny, The Hon. Edward Astley, Miss Lilian Baylis, The Hon. Eveleigh Leigh, Miss Ninette de Valois, Arnold L. Haskell, Captain R. H. C. Jenkinson. The objects of the plan were as follows:

Academic

1. To provide periodical engagement of special teachers for various subjects outside the scope of the regular teaching staff.
2. To provide grants for special study to members of the ballet endowed with outstanding ability.
3. In order to secure talent for the ballet, to grant a limited number of scholarships giving free tuition to selected children, with an option on their services on the completion of their training, first as apprentices and afterwards as salaried artists. In this connection to arrange through the Board of Education for the general education of such pupils to take place in the school.

Production

1. To give financial assistance to defray the initial cost of mounting and producing traditional ballets.

2. To give the same assistance should circumstances merit to new works.

3. For the purpose of record to pay for the filming of important ballets and studio photographs of essential groupings.

Benefits

To enable grants to be made to members of the ballet on their retirement in special cases and where meritorious services have been rendered.

To make any gift which would materially benefit the welfare and health of the members of the ballet and in consequence raise the standard of their performance.

Salaries comparable to those paid in the commercial theatre were not, of course, envisaged, but it was hoped that the guarantee of permanent employment and long-term contracts would provide sufficient compensation to the dancers.

The publicity given to this Five-Year Plan, resulted in some expressions of fear from dancing schools that the Sadler's Wells School might become a kind of menace to their continuing livelihood, and Ninette de Valois was at pains to explain the real facts through the columns of *The Dancing Times*. She pointed out that the School attached to Sadler's Wells Theatre, was a school devoted to producing young artists for the Vic-Wells Ballet, or any other repertory ballet company in existence that might apply to the School.

Examinations, commercial engagements, film work or the other activities undertaken by most schools for their students did not then and do not now concern the Sadler's Wells School. There was no agency attached to the theatre, the number of students was strictly limited and certain students were continually being advised that they were not in fact suitable for the highly specialised career of a repertory ballet dancer. Talent suitable for such a career was naturally scarce, and only a certain number of the Wells' own pupils could hope ultimately to get into the company. Other teachers were asked to sacrifice perhaps one student from time to time with the special talent needed for repertory ballet, and hand such a dancer over to the Wells for specialised training in a specialised environment within the walls of the theatre. The money asked for under the Five-Year Plan would bring no individual financial gain since it would all go back into the work of the ballet at Sadler's Wells. Phyllis Bedells was among the influential teachers who immediately and warmly supported the plan, and the Royal Academy of Dancing sent a donation of one hundred pounds as soon as the scheme was announced as "a mark of appreciation of the work the Vic-Wells Ballet has done during the past few years."

Donations began to come in and the scheme began to function at once. At a Dancers' Circle Dinner to Lilian Baylis in April 1937, Arnold Haskell was able to announce that some famous *décors* had been bought and many of the company were being sent to Paris for special lessons. "The scheme is to buy for the School and the ballet anything that may be of permanent value," he said, "lessons from great teachers, historic *décors* or editions of music, also to benefit not only the dancer but the painter and the musician by educating him in a medium that can carry the message of British art throughout the world. . . . It is like buying a masterpiece for the nation, but a masterpiece that you can watch growing and that will bring employment and prestige." The scheme continued to operate until CEMA and the Arts Council during the war gradually took over the functions of private patrons of the arts and provided the kind of subsidy which the Five-Year Plan sought to build up. The "Benefits" section now works independently as the Sadler's Wells Ballet Benevolent Fund and remains dependent on contributions from private individuals to carry on its important work.

1936–37

The 1936–37 season at Sadler's Wells opened on 22nd September with *Baiser de la Fée*, the third act of *Casse Noisette*, the *Aurora pas de deux* from the last act of *The Sleeping Princess* and *Façade*. The de Basil dancers were still in England and most of them attended the opening. Alexandra Danilova was among them and, as always, had plenty of intelligent comments to make. She liked June Brae—"*Elle a des mains personnelles,*" and after watching Fonteyn dance the *Aurora pas de deux* with Helpmann she said sagely, "*Si elle ne soit pas 'spoilt' elle va être une grande danseuse.*" And at the end of the evening: "What I particularly like is that *la petite Margot* has not so far been given the best parts in all the ballets. . . . It seems to me that the Sadler's Wells company has all the future before it."

Performances that season were on Tuesday evenings and alternate Friday nights and Saturday afternoons. Ruth French and Pearl Argyle had left and also Beatrice Appleyard, one of the original members of the company, who joined the Markova-Dolin Ballet. Although she never returned to the Vic-Wells company she remained in close touch and in 1951 went out to Turkey to take charge of the national ballet school there which had been started by Ninette de Valois in 1947. She is now married and running her own school in Turkey.

The group of artists who remained and now headed the company were an exceptionally well-balanced and complementary group. Working in a *milieu* ideally suitable for their own development, they found in each other sympathetic colleagues, each able to contribute something to the work that was being done. The wisdom and experience of Ursula Moreton, Joy Newton and Sheila McCarthy were there for important character parts, and de Valois herself, although she danced less and less often, contributed an adult sophistication and intelligence. In Margot Fonteyn there was a budding ballerina of present delight and infinite future promise, while Elizabeth Miller, Pamela May and now June Brae were all delightful artists of very different individual styles. Robert Helpmann was developing all the time as a dancer and an actor of power and variety, Ashton contributed occasional performances of great sensitivity and artistry while Harold Turner had an utterly different, vigorous, engaging manner and brilliant technique which delighted the gallery. Among the women, Mary Honer matched the technical brilliance of Turner and although she was at first accused of musical comedy mannerisms she had a refreshingly forthright approach which was perhaps a good antidote to too much "interpretation." William Chappell, a limited dancer, was so good in the parts that really suited him that they have ever since been associated with his name: the Strange Player in *The Haunted Ballroom*, the Shepherd in *The Gods go a'Begging* and above all the Rake's friend in *The Rake's Progress*, "a study in sinister silliness." Alan Carter and Michael Somes were just beginning to be noticed in the *corps de ballet*.

These were the dancers who during the next three years were to be responsible for shaping the real character of the Vic-Wells

Ballet and bringing it to a remarkable level of artistic achievement. Accidents of time and place bring certain artists together at formative periods in their artistic lives with results that might otherwise never happen. Had Constant Lambert not joined the Vic-Wells Ballet as Musical Director in the beginning the whole history of the company might have been different, and had Ashton and de Valois not had this particular group of gifted dancers to work with they might never have built a repertoire of such merit in so short a time. Ashton in particular found in Fonteyn a ballerina ideally suited to the interpretation of his ideas—poetic, immature and lovely—and had she not been there he might neither have worked so well nor stayed so long. The season 1936–37 was to be momentous for both of them, but for de Valois the choreographer, as distinct from de Valois the guiding spirit of the company, it did not begin too well. Her new ballet *Prometheus* was produced at Sadler's Wells on 13th October and enjoyed only a very temporary success while it remained a novelty.

The first version of this Beethoven ballet had been given at the Burg Theatre in Vienna in 1801 with choreography by the great Viganò. A few descriptions of this version, although no actual choreography, have survived. In 1929 Balanchine had intended to revive it at the Paris Opéra, but was prevented from doing so by illness, and Lifar instead produced the ballet and danced the name part in Paris and also, in a curtailed version, at the Savoy Theatre in London in 1933. De Valois had done the chorus work in a production of *Prometheus* at the Festival Theatre in Cambridge and this may have aroused her interest in the subject. For the Wells production the music was arranged by Constant Lambert to fit the modified version of the story which was to be used for the ballet, and John Banting, who had been responsible for *Pomona*, designed the costumes and scenery. The ballet attempted to treat the story in semi-serious fashion, the music being too obviously lighthearted for an heroic spectacle (although it hardly justified the extreme frivolity of the costumes).

Prometheus returns from Heaven with fire and instead of being acclaimed as a hero is only saved from mob violence by his wife. In the second scene Prometheus is shown as a moody family man with his wife and six children, saved from complete boredom by the advances of the Other Woman who has gained the torch and tries to use it to win his affection. Prometheus, however, seizes the torch and thrusts aside the Other Woman who, in a fury, tells his wife he is unfaithful. The wife believes the charge and summons the citizens to destroy him, but he calls the Spirits of Fire to his aid and once more ascends to the mountain top. Helpmann and Turner shared the rôle of Prometheus and neither of them made anything very memorable of the character, who was anyway allowed no memorable characteristics by the choreographer. Ninette de Valois herself appeared as the wife, and June Brae made her first big impression at Sadler's Wells as the Other Woman, in a fantastically silly bell-shaped hoop skirt.

June Brae had first attracted attention in *The Rape of the Lock* at the Ballet Club and subsequently danced in many ballets for Madame Rambert. Her first important part at the Wells was as the Fairy in *Baiser de la Fée*, and soon afterwards she danced the solo Waltz in *Les Sylphides* and Chiarina in *Carnaval*. She was to have an even greater opportunity in Frederick Ashton's next ballet.

Nocturne was given a gala *première* on 10th November in aid of Queen Charlotte's Hospital, but mindful of their regular audience, the management increased the prices of only half the seats in the theatre, the other half remaining at their normal rate, so that on this particular evening it was possible to pay anything from sixpence to three guineas for admittance.

The theme of *Nocturne* had been originally suggested by Edward Sackville West when Ashton had been staying at Knole. The music chosen was by Delius, *Paris—the Song of a Great City*, and against the background of an evening's revelry in a great city a little human tragedy was played out. Sophie Fedorovitch designed one of her lovely, unobtrusive settings, just a low balustrade against a night sky with white pillars on each side on which were pasted advertisements for a ball. A simple flower girl falls in love with a handsome roué, momentarily neglected by his rich beauty, and is caught up for a while in the gaiety of the dancers until the young man is forced to choose between his partners and unhesitatingly departs with the Rich Girl, leaving the flower-seller heartbroken and inconsolable. An elderly spectator tries in vain to comfort her and then walks away to watch with resignation the dawn of a new day over the great city.

It was a ballet of the 'nineties in mood and setting, exquisitely interpreted by a charming, disinterested Helpmann, the warm and radiant June Brae, and Fonteyn, vulnerable and pathetic, as the flower girl. Ashton, the aloof observer, suggested infinite compassion with a minimum of gesture. The company of Edwardian beauties and elegant young men were admirably contrasted with the grotesque and brilliant figures of the masquers, in black and yellow costumes obviously inspired by the drawings of Callot. The Delius music was used with such sensitivity and understanding by Ashton that it proved an ideal partner to the choreography, and must be one of the most successful uses of existing music in all ballet.

Nocturne found immediate favour with both the sixpenny and the three guinea seatholders and remained in the Wells repertoire fairly consistently thereafter. When new costumes and décor were made for the Princes Theatre, slight amendments were introduced which did not improve the look of the ballet and les affiches disappeared from the pillars. At Covent Garden the ballet never made its full effect, possibly because the characterisation was too muted and understated to project into the vast auditorium, although the patterns of the dances and the rich masses of colour in the women's costumes continued to give pleasure. Helpmann and Ashton, Brae and Fonteyn remained the ideal interpreters. Michael Somes could never look sufficiently heartless, Pauline Clayden had the poignancy but not the smooth flow of movement, and in subsequent casts Pamela May as the Rich Girl was the only one to capture the original spirit of the ballet.

The day after the Nocturne première the Vic-Wells Ballet made their first appearance on television, on 11th November 1936. They danced excerpts from Job and the experience was not particularly rewarding. The fragments of the ballet could give viewers no idea of its real nature and the dancers were almost overcome by the heat. They rehearsed and gave two performances on the same day under terrific lights and by the end of the evening the temperature of the steps leading up to Heaven rose so much that the unfortunate barefooted angels ascending and descending thought they must be heading for the other place. Technicians promised that sessions would be shorter in future. Further television performances were given subsequently of Façade, Casse Noisette (Act III) and Les Patineurs, and in March 1937 the B.B.C. made a film consisting of episodes from the final section of *Façade* for use as part of an exhibition film to be lent to television-set dealers.

Lilian Baylis was interested in the new medium and grateful for the fees paid by the B.B.C. (the first few appearances brought in £460), but she was unimpressed by the actual results as shown on the television screen. After her first visit to Broadcasting House she turned away from the small screen in disgust. "*That's* no good" she snorted. "*Much* too small. Those girls will never get married like that." Nevertheless both the company and the B.B.C. persevered in numerous attempts and experiments to present ballet in an acceptable form on the television screen, and if none of the girls have actually married as a result of these appearances, they have certainly in recent years added greatly to their fame and reputations.

The Christmas holiday season was appropriately chosen for the first performances of *Casse Noisette* in new costumes and settings designed by Mstislav Dobujinsky, a Russian artist who had been among those invited by Diaghileff to contribute to *Mir Iskousstva*. He was a designer with a special affection for "the haunting beauty of Tsarist St. Petersburg," and should have been an ideal choice. The Christmas party of Act I was indeed delightful, but the Kingdom of Sweets was far less successful in both colour and design. Dobujinsky is, in fact, one of the most erratic designers who have ever worked for ballet; on the one hand there is his magnificent *Ballet Imperial* setting for the Ballet Russe de Monte Carlo, on the other his *Raymonda* for the Lithuanian Ballet. The charming *Papillons* and the pretty set for the first scene of Ballet Theatre's *Mam'zelle Angot* must be offset against the sugary confections of *The Fairy Doll* (for Pavlova), and the sickly backcloth for *Casse Noisette* at the Wells. If the ballet was no better off decoratively, however, its popularity did not decrease. On this occasion Margot Fonteyn and Robert Helpmann danced the *pas de deux,* and if no one at the Wells has ever surpassed Markova's crystalline perfection, at the same time no one has ever really failed. In Dobujinsky's pink and white costume and pretty silver coronet Fonteyn was delightful. Jean Bedells was the new Clara (her predecessor, Julia Farron, had grown up into a Mirliton) and June Vincent was Franz. The Lord Mayor's Boy Players once again obliged as mice.

On 19th January Fonteyn crossed another brook in her journey towards the ultimate goal of the *prima ballerina's* crown. She danced the name part in *Giselle* on that night for the first time and was again partnered by Helpmann, with whom she was to enjoy so triumphant a progress over the next ten years. Markova and Dolin, then dancing at the London Hippodrome in pantomime, came on to the Wells as soon as their act finished and arrived at about 10 p.m., just in time for the mad scene. It was a performance of promise rather than complete achievement, as all first per-formances in all great rôles must be. The shy, trusting village girl came easily to Fonteyn, but the mad scene succeeded chiefly because of the pathos of extreme youth (she was only seventeen) rather than on account of conscious artistry. In the second act she was still a little hesitant, although her dancing had a natural beauty of style and phrasing. Pamela May was well cast as the Queen of the Wilis, cold and imperious with a clean, purely classical line. All three young artists were to build and develop their performances in these famous rôles until they were worthy to take their places among the great interpreters of Giselle, of Albrecht and of Myrtha.

Barely had the excitement over Fonteyn's Giselle subsided than Ashton was ready with a new ballet, which was to prove one of the most popular, and indeed one of the best, the company has ever had. *Les Patineurs* was introduced on 16th February to a first-night audience that doted on it from the moment the curtain rose and acclaimed it with something little short of rapture. Once again Constant Lambert had found some little-known theatre music, this time by Meyerbeer, ideally suitable for dancing, and with the simple device of pretending that everyone was on skates, Ashton was able to weld an infectious concoction of lyric and virtuoso dances into a geniune ballet.

It was the first Wells ballet to exploit both the technical brilliance and cheerful personality of Harold Turner and by this time the company could pit against his brilliance the almost equal virtuosity of Mary Honer and Elizabeth Miller as the two girls in blue. Fonteyn and Helpmann, a little aloof and more poised than the other skaters, were the couple in white, and June Brae and Pamela May frothily feminine in the *pas des patineuses*. It was suddenly brought home to everyone that there were a number of really good dancers in the *corps de ballet,* and Michael Somes, in particular, astonished by his elevation in the *pas de huit*. William Chappell's pretty costumes and Christmas card setting were entirely right for

the Victorian tunefulness of the Meyerbeer music. The audience
took the ballet to its heart at once and it has retained its popularity
ever since. To-day, with all the resources that the company can
command, it is still not over-easy to cast successfully and it is a
lasting tribute to the high level the company had reached by the
beginning of 1937. Turner, in fact, took the ballet so much in his
stride that he thought nothing of tossing off a performance of
Harlequin in *Carnaval* as the opening ballet to precede the *première*
of *Les Patineurs*.

Les Patineurs might very easily have had a different history. It
was originally Ninette de Valois who intended to use the music,
but she could find in it no stimulus to her imagination and made
little progress. Ashton heard the music being played on the piano
at rehearsals and longed to use it for a ballet. Consequently when
de Valois asked him if he would care to take over the production
he accepted with delight and received as great an opportunity as
he had previously given her when he turned down Gavin Gordon's
suggestion about *The Rake's Progress*.

It might well have been expected that the season would end in
anti-climax after such a record of successes, but these were vintage
years and by the end of April Ashton produced another winner,
this time a ballet unlike anything the Wells had attempted before
(or since) and comparable in Ashton's own experience only to
Four Saints in Three Acts.

A Wedding Bouquet was the idea of Lord Berners, who wanted
Frederick Ashton to make a ballet pantomime out of one of
Gertrude Stein's plays and who both wrote the music and designed the *décor* and costumes. The name of the play was *They
must be Wedded to Their Wife*, but this was thought too long for
advertising and was changed to *A Wedding Bouquet*. Lord Berners
went to visit Gertrude Stein in Bilignin and she liked the idea and
he found in her house a carpet which gave him the pattern for the
backcloth for the ballet. Gertrude Stein had seen the carpet in the
house of Sherwood Anderson's brother-in-law in America: "They
had a rug there made by an old woman in Virginia we liked so
much and Sherwood said he would send us one and he did. I think
it was the same one and we have it in Bilignin and everybody,
especially French people, admire it every time they see it, the pale
colours are so American and the river and the house and the simple

CHECKMATE

June Brae as the Black Queen with Harold Turner as the Red Knight

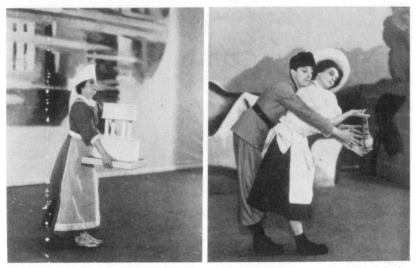

NINETTE DE VALOIS

Left: in *A Wedding Bouquet*. *Right:* with Frederick Ashton in *Barabau*

A WEDDING BOUQUET

Robert Helpmann, Mary Honer and Margot Fonteyn

harmony of it." Gertrude Stein's little Mexican dog Pepe was to be in the ballet and Alice B. Toklas wanted him to be "a little one on wires little like the real Pepe, but they said no, it had to be a little girl," although, everyone admitted that "even the littlest little girl is going to be a very large little Mexican."

Afterwards Gertrude Stein and Alice B. Toklas went to England and Gertrude Stein lectured at Oxford and Cambridge and stayed with Lord Berners, because she had been told that his house was "the only house in England where the corridors where the halls are warm." They met Frederick Ashton and were told that the ballet was making progress and was all very sad and everybody had to laugh and Gertrude Stein thought that was very nice. She also thought it was very nice that Constant Lambert had had the idea of putting in the programme the description of the characters as she had made them in the play "like they used to do in melodrama, the first I ever wrote was that, *Snatched From Death or The Sundered Sisters.*"

The ballet was first spoken of as a choral ballet and the opera chorus did sing or chant the words at the early performance, but it was all entirely unlike any other choral ballet before or since. The words explained the action, introduced the characters, made utterly irrelevant comments, worked themselves into a frenzied rhythmical accompaniment or injected an occasional apt phrase that devastated dancers and audience alike. Not all of the words have ever been really intelligible but gradually the audience got to know certain phrases by heart and the ballet has a devoted public, although inevitably it has always been a rather special one and to this day there are people who detest the whole affair, don't "understand" it, and think it an absurd waste of time and talent.

The original cast of the ballet was a perfect one to exploit its lightheartedness and sophistication and nearly every performance was a collector's piece: Ninette de Valois, prim and fussy as Webster the maid, June Brae beautifully, helplessly tipsy as Josephine who may not attend a wedding, Harold Turner as Paul, "pleasant, vivacious and quarrelsome," William Chappell as that unexplained elder brother John "who regrets the illness of his father," Pamela May as the difficult Violet for ever in pursuit of the timid Ernest (Claude Newman), Elizabeth Miller the faintly neat Therese, Michael Somes as Guy, "unknown" and free to soar about the

I

stage in wonderful, effortless jumps, Leslie Edwards as the obsequious Arthur, and Molly Brown and Jill Gregory as those ridiculous bridesmaids. Julia Farron, the littlest little girl, delighted everyone as Pepe, the dog which aspires to be a ballerina, and Mary Honer's gift for rather inane comedy was for the first time given scope as the Bride. She simpered and blushed and giggled her way through the ballet and danced magnificently in the curious nocturnal *pas de deux* with the Bridegroom.

Robert Helpmann, until *A Wedding Bouquet*, had no special reputation as a comedian, and had in fact been getting into rather a groove of romantic and/or classical parts which exploited the mood of "bewitched weariness" which became him so well. *A Wedding Bouquet* gave him a refreshing and rewarding change and established him overnight as a comic actor of the first quality.

Margot Fonteyn as the forlorn Julia went through the ballet in a haze of distracted love for the bridegroom that was just a little too realistic to be comfortable; she later broadened the performance and transferred it from the realm of tragedy to tragi-comedy yet managed to convey at the same time the rather undeveloped intellect of Julia. Such a character can belong only to provincial France and is at times disquieting to an English audience, but Fonteyn saved the ballet from becoming just a romp and preserved the special flavour of "bitterness" for the final curtain.

Gertrude Stein was delighted with the whole affair. "English dancers, when they dance, dance with freshness and agility and they know what drama is, it all went so very well, each time a musician does something with the words it makes it do what they never did do; this time it made them do as if the last word had heard the next word and the next word had heard not the last word but the next word. After all, why not." The *première* on 27th April was an important social occasion and the gossip writers paid as much attention to the Countess of Asquith, Elsa Lanchester, C. B. Cochran, Sir Thomas Beecham and other personalities in the audience as they did to the actual performance. At the end Gertrude Stein took a curtain call with Lord Berners and Frederick Ashton and went on to the stage "where I never had been with everything in front all dark and we bowing and all of them coming and going and bowing," and the reception was tremendous.

Afterwards at a party everyone made a great fuss of the author and she noted with endearing honesty: "I always do like to be a lion, I like it again and again, and it is a peaceful thing to be one succeeding."

The season ended in May, a brief visit being made to Bournemouth for one week just before the last performances in London. The successes of the new ballets had been reflected in the box-office receipts and both the opera and the drama had also had a good year. For the first time in their histories, in fact, the Old Vic and Sadler's Wells could each show a profit and were left with a respectable balance of working capital with which to start the new season. A considerable amount of debt was repaid and Sadler's Wells was able to purchase out of revenue three small houses in Arlington Street at the back of the theatre, needed for future expansion. The increase in box-office receipts as compared with the previous season was greater than between any two successive seasons before. At the end of May the ballet company was to go to Cambridge to dance at the Arts Theatre for a week, but everyone was already preoccupied with preparations for the forthcoming visit to Paris in the middle of June for which Ninette de Valois was creating a new ballet. "You won't see the stage staff as usual," said Lilian Baylis on the last night of the season, "they're packing up. You can hear them at it."

The Vic-Wells Ballet had been invited by the British Council to appear for the period 15th to 26th June, in connection with the Paris International Exhibition, as representatives of British artistic achievement. The honour was considerable, but unfortunately the British Council did not follow up the invitation with anything like an adequate advance publicity campaign. It was hardly surprising that few Parisians knew anything about the visit until it was almost over. There was a very brilliant opening night attended by the President of the French Republic and Mme. Lebrun, Sir Eric and Lady Phipps, and all society, but the people who might really have helped the season were curiously neglected. Les Archives Internationales de la Danse, for instance, then an influential body, were not officially invited; the principal dancers of the Opéra had to pay full prices and important critics were turned away from the box office. The box office maintained a polite fiction that seats were unprocurable and one distinguished patron in consequence accepted a *strapontin* seat and arrived at the theatre to find no one at all in the seats surrounding her.

Le Théâtre des Champs-Élysées was only about half filled for the early part of the visit, but audiences improved towards the end of the week and those people who did find their way seemed genuinely enthusiastic while the supporters who had followed the company across the Channel cheered loyally from the gallery. There were no posters to be seen in Paris advertising the season and it was a long time before the dancers eventually came across a small bill announcing "Le Vic-Wells Ballet du Sadler's Wells Théâtre de Londres." They stood in front of it in the street and cheered.

The ballets taken were *Pomona, Apparitions, Nocturne, Les Patineurs, Aurora pas de deux, Façade, Pas de Trois* from *Le Lac des Cygnes, The Rake's Progress* (*La Vie du Débauché*), and in addition the first performance was given of *Échec et Mat,* subsequently better known as *Checkmate.*

This work, in one scene with a prologue, had been suggested to Ninette de Valois by the composer Arthur Bliss, an old friend with whom she had worked before. He was responsible for the book of the ballet and the music and by a happy inspiration the poster artist E. McKnight Kauffer was invited to design the scenery and costumes. A brief prologue before a drop curtain showed Love and Death sitting at a chessboard; Love backs the Red Knight to win, Death the Black Queen. The curtain then rose on a chessboard setting with an angry-coloured backcloth, and here the figures played out their game as a strong human drama rather than an authentic game of chess. The ballet was undeniably impressive and London music critics writing home from Paris were enthusiastic. Richard Capell was full of praise for the ballet and concluded: "The Islington ballet gave a faultless performance. . . . If this had been Russian ballet all Paris would surely have flocked to the show."

So much of *Checkmate* is so good that its weaknesses are perhaps the more apparent. The major fault, as Haskell was quick to point out, was in the timing. "Each climax, well planned when it comes, is over-long delayed with an enormous loss of effect and the spectator becomes irritated at moments." Nevertheless the final climax is intensely dramatic and moving, the music pounding relentlessly on towards the destruction of the Red King, and it brings the ballet to a fine conclusion. De Valois had an admirable cast for the first performances. June Brae, who created the Black Queen, suggested not only the evil single-mindedness of the character but also the warmth and fascination so essential to explain the subjugation of the Red Knight. Harold Turner was a strong and handsome Red Knight (strength is essential here or there is no tragedy), and Pamela May gave real tenderness to the Red Queen. In the small but vital part of the Red King, Robert Helpmann gave a tremendous performance of nervous terror that has never been approached by any of his successors. As long as he played it the fate of the Red King was the focal point of the ballet, but it has since become a mere adjunct to the rest of the action.

Such reviews as got into the Paris papers were admiring and respectful, and the dancers were too busy enjoying Paris to worry very much about the lack of public clamour. Many of them studied with the leading Paris teachers and although the stay could not be long they profited greatly from the experience. The company were deeply touched by the voluntary appearance of Nicolai Sergueeff at all their performances, quiet and watchful in the prompt corner. He was to come to London for the 1937–38 season as ballet master, and Henry Robinson, the stage manager, made a firm resolve that this time he really would teach him English. (He did make a little progress, but to the end of his life Sergueeff's prowess in the English language was strictly limited.)

The company went on holiday after the Paris visit, although some of the dancers stayed on to work in the Paris studios. They reassembled for a provincial tour in August and early September, for which Pearl Argyle rejoined them, her name going at the head of the bills with Helpmann's, while Fonteyn and Turner came below.

1937–1938

The new season at Sadler's Wells opened quietly but with an air of confidence. *Checkmate* was introduced to the London audience on 5th October, and received much praise and publicity. It drew such large houses to begin with that when the composer paid a surprise visit he was forced to watch from the wings as there simply was not a seat in the house. The Duke and Duchess of Kent and Arturo Toscanini visited the ballet and Toscanini was much impressed by *Checkmate*, which he described as one of the outstanding stage-works of the day.

Some money from the Ballet Fund had been used to buy the original Benois setting for *Les Sylphides* (following the Benois exhibition at Tooths), largely through the good offices of Arnold Haskell, and this immeasurably improved the appearance of the ballet. Two other works were re-dressed in the autumn of 1937: *The Lord of Burleigh* by Derek Hill, and *Les Rendezvous* by William Chappell. Neither were improvements, although the white costumes with pink and blue ribbons devised for *Les Rendezvous* by Chappell were at any rate innocuous compared with some of the other versions he designed later.

De Valois' great ambition of producing that season a full-length version of *The Sleeping Princess*, under Sergueeff's direction, had to be postponed, however, because it was found that Sadler's Wells simply was not large enough to accommodate it. It was less a matter of stage space or the number of dancers available than shortage of dressing-rooms, shortage of wardrobe space for the vast number of costumes, and shortage of space for the scenery. The building was due for enlargement, and it was obvious that *The Sleeping Princess* must be put off until that enlargement had taken place. Lilian Baylis shared Ninette de Valois' bitter disappointment, but at a business interview at the Old Vic in the middle of November the two women accepted the necessity for postponement philosophically and began to revise their plans, looking forward with confidence to a time when they would eventually be able to bring the ballet into the Sadler's Wells repertory. Two days after this interview, on 25th November 1937, Lilian Baylis died.

The blow was sudden and deep. At each of her theatres, staff and artists were temporarily stunned, bewildered and uncertain about what was to happen now that The Lady, whose personality and dogged determination had built up from nothing, a national drama, opera and ballet, was no longer with them. It was imperative, however, that her work should go on as she would herself have wished, and immediately a new licence was applied for in the name of Bruce Worsley for the two theatres, while responsibilities in the various departments were apportioned to the people best capable of carrying on with the work in hand.

The ballet company, on 26th November, danced *Carnaval*, *Baiser de la Fée* and *Job*, and before the performance of *Job*, Ninette de Valois in a short and moving speech, spoke to the audience of Lilian Baylis. After *Job* the curtain did not rise again and the audience stood for a moment in tribute to the woman who had given London a permanent ballet company, and accommodation for a theatre school of ballet. In a deeply appreciative memoir which she wrote later for *The Dancing Times*, Ninette de Valois stressed the fact that the work which Lilian Baylis did was impersonal, built for the generations to come. "The work has not been thought out just for the present, but for those days, months and years that go to make the future. In brief, through the courage of one being, there has been planted for you in the middle of London a true heritage. It is your duty to protect this gift—and see that it lives and expands."

At the beginning of each season it had been Lilian Baylis' custom to make a round of every dressing-room at each of her theatres, presenting the artists with a sprig of heather. That autumn, for the first time, she had brought rosemary. "But she need not have made this change," wrote Ninette de Valois, "for it is impossible that the English Ballet could ever forget."

The only fitting memorial that could be raised to Lilian Baylis was the completion of her work. The Completion Fund for the two theatres had been her constant care, and with the approval of the Governors of the Old Vic and Sadler's Wells a communication was now issued, signed by Lord Lytton and Sir Reginald Rowe and also by Lord Hambleden, President of the Sadler's Wells Society, and Sir Edward Marsh, Chairman of the Vic-Wells Completion Fund. The appeal for the Completion Fund had originally been for £30,000, of which £15,000 was to clear the two theatres of debt and £15,000 was for additions to Sadler's Wells. This programme was, however, based on minimum requirements, and by the end of 1937 it was calculated that a further £10,000 would be needed for rebuilding at Sadler's Wells. Of the £40,000 thus required, a little over £10,000 had been subscribed, leaving nearly £30,000 to be collected. Subscriptions were asked for specifically as a tribute to the memory of Lilian Baylis, and it was proposed that the large building to be added to Sadler's Wells should be named The Lilian Baylis Memorial. A dinner was arranged at the Mansion House by the Lord Mayor of London, and the Duke of Kent made a moving speech in which he declared the Old Vic and Sadler's Wells had "created the nearest thing to national drama, national opera and national ballet that we yet possess in this country." A collection at the dinner raised no less than £5,124.

Among the most urgent requirements were a new scene dock, a new wardrobe room, new sewing-rooms, and rehearsal rooms for both the opera and the ballet, the very accommodation, in fact, which would make possible a production of *The Sleeping Princess* and the proper development of the opera and ballet companies.

One of the last instances of Lilian Baylis' unerring judgment where people were concerned was her promise to Robert Helpmann that he should play Oberon at the Old Vic when *A Midsummer Night's Dream* was produced in the winter of 1937. He had asked her for an increase in salary, and when she explained that this would not immediately be possible he countered with a request to be allowed to act. One can imagine her quizzical look, and her quick memory of his achievements as an actor within the ballet. She said yes. He studied under Beatrice Wilson and made a very positive success, playing opposite Vivien Leigh's Titania in that enchanting Guthrie-Mendelssohn-Messel production which has set a standard for our generation.

It was during Helpmann's absence that Frederick Ashton's next ballet *Horoscope* was produced, on 27th January 1938, and in it another male dancer made his name at Sadler's Wells. Michael Somes had been attracting attention for a considerable time in small parts, and his remarkable elevation in *Les Patineurs* had placed him in a special category among the dancers of the *corps de ballet*. *Horoscope* gave him a major creation, and an opportunity of dancing with Fonteyn and Pamela May in one of Ashton's loveliest ballets. Once again it was a genuine and close collaboration on which Ashton worked with two of his closest friends and colleagues—Constant Lambert composed the music and Sophie Fedorovitch designed costumes and setting.

The book of *Horoscope* was by Lambert and was very simple, concerning the influence of the signs of the zodiac on two young lovers. The young man's life is ruled by the Sun in Leo, the Moon in Gemini; the young woman's by the Sun in Virgo, the Moon in Gemini. The contrasting forces of Leo and Virgo, the one strong and energetic, the other timid and sensitive, struggle to keep the man and woman apart, but their common sign, the Gemini, brings them together, and through the influence of the Moon they are finally united.

Lambert's score was probably his finest for any ballet, concentrated yet ideally arranged for the development of the action, exciting in rhythm and beautiful in melody. Sophie Fedorovitch also excelled herself, and her work on *Horoscope* was admirably described by Cyril Beaumont (in an article in *The Studio* for April 1939): "The blue drop-curtain, decorated with a formalised presentation of the signs of the zodiac in white, makes an excellent introduction to that astrological ballet. The settings themselves, a suggestion of grey skies relieved with isolated banks of clouds, provide a characteristic background against which she sets her costumes, in the main delicately tinted."

The choreography was Ashton at his most felicitous and also his most moving; instead of being just smart or beguiling he was beginning to look into the heart of things and he had a company who could interpret his ideas most beautifully. Michael Somes naturally attracted most attention as the Young Man, but Fonteyn, warm and feminine, danced with triumphant assurance. Pamela May as the Moon was, by intentional contrast, cool and remote, subordinating all emotion to the clean lines of the dancing. Richard Ellis and Alan Carter were admirably paired as the Gemini, and Elizabeth Miller led the fiery followers of Leo.

The ballet, deservedly, had an ovation and something like twenty curtain calls. "With *Horoscope*," wrote a delighted Haskell in the *Daily Telegraph* next morning, "ballet, now truly indigenous in England, reaches a splendid maturity." It was one of the most complete and entirely satisfying productions in the history of the Vic-Wells Ballet but, alas, it was to have but a short life. Less than two years after its creation it fell victim to the German invaders in Holland and has never since been performed. Not only were the costumes and settings lost but also the entire orchestral score, the only copy of the music in existence. A concert suite had been recorded and this, with some photographs, is all that survives. It is possible, however, that the gods loved *Horoscope*: it never suffered from indifferent casting or too frequent performance, and it lives in the memory in the full beauty of its youth.

The postponement of *The Sleeping Princess* had left the company without a new ballet for the spring, so as a sort of substitute Ninette de Valois decided to produce *Le Roi Nu*, a ballet based on the Hans Andersen story of "The Emperor's New Clothes." The attractive music by Jean Françaix had been composed for a version of the ballet which Serge Lifar had undertaken some two years previously and the Lifar scenario was followed fairly closely. Hedley Briggs matched the music with a nice confection of pink and white *décor* and some attractive costumes. *Le Roi Nu* had a certain mild interest and Ashton, Chappell and Newman enjoyed themselves in fantastic make-up as the three tailors, but Helpmann had an impossible part as the Emperor and although Pearl Argyle (and later Pamela May) looked amazingly lovely as the Empress there was little dramatic need for her presence, which had to be justified by the introduction of a Lover and consequently a *pas de deux*. The climax of the story, unfortunately, was the death of the ballet because the Emperor obviously could not be shown naked, and the various alternatives (first a shirt, then a brief pair of drawers) were so inept that they made nonsense of the child's exclamation, "But he is wearing nothing at all"—delivered with much conviction if little truth by a very small Margaret Dale.

On 10th May a Gala Performance in the presence of Her Majesty Queen Elizabeth was arranged in aid of the Lilian Baylis Memorial Extension to the theatre and also for the Vic-Wells Ballet Fund. *Horoscope*, *Checkmate* and *Les Patineurs* were given, and for the occasion Ashton put together a short ballet to Lennox Berkeley music called *The Judgment of Paris*. Pearl Argyle, an obvious choice for Venus, looked lovelier than ever in a beautiful Chappell costume and, in fact, the whole ballet looked handsome and photographed wonderfully. A page of pictures in *The Bystander* survives, but no one seems to remember very much else about it.

The season ended earlier than usual because the builders were anxious to get on with work on the extensions; £21,000 had already been collected for the Completion Fund and no time was lost in putting the work in hand. The company went off on tour very happily, for Sadler's Wells was already given over to incessant hammerings during the day. Chaos reigned backstage as electricians and stage staff were bundled into dressing-rooms so that a start could be made on the alterations which it was hoped to complete by the beginning of the next season. Housebreakers were busy demolishing the old houses in Arlington Street at the back of the theatre and everyone began to dream of proper wardrobe space and an end of the unsatisfactory system of bunching costumes into one of the largest dressing-rooms or stacking them in baskets under the stage, where they provided a happy foraging ground for the Islington mice.

While this vital work went on, the ballet visited Oxford and Bournemouth and then, after a summer holiday, set off on another short tour which took them to Dublin and to Cardiff for the first time. Despite the international crisis, business was good and the tour was an unprecedented success. These summer tours took place at a time of year unfavourable to theatre business in general, and in the early years visits had been mostly confined to summer resorts or university towns. As they reached farther afield, however, they maintained their ability to pay their way, although large profits were quite out of the question if a full-scale company and a full orchestra were to be toured. Once again, the tours were evidence of the long-term outlook which governed all the activities of the ballet company at Sadler's Wells. Ninette de Valois herself listed the factors which made touring worth while and stressed the following points:

1. It gives at least two months' extra work to some eighty artists.
2. It keeps a large repertoire of ballets in active rehearsal and succeeds in giving the artists as many performances in four weeks as Sadler's Wells can offer them in sixteen. It must be remembered that on tour we give eight performances per week and when in London only two.
3. It greatly increases both the popularity and reputation of our work, thus both directly and indirectly enlarging the size of our audience for the future.

The vital importance of touring a good orchestra was never questioned; apart from maintaining the general artistic standard of the performances, it was in itself an attraction in towns where the audience was, inevitably, more interested in music than ballet.

The Munich crisis diverted the activities of every available work-man to more urgent tasks in August 1938, and the alterations at Sadler's Wells were not completed by September, so the ballet and opera appeared at Streatham Hill and Golders Green for two weeks at each theatre, alternating opera and ballet. The ballet returned home to Sadler's Wells on 18th October and was given a tumultuous welcome. No small part of the happiness that evening was due to the presence of Ninette de Valois in the theatre, fit again after a recent illness, and full of plans for *The Sleeping Princess*, which was at last definitely scheduled for February 1939, made possible by the extensions to the building.

A new scene dock, adjoining the tiny one that already existed in Arlington Street, had been installed, with a paint frame and racks so that scenery could be made at Sadler's Wells and not transported every time from the Old Vic. The wardrobe room beneath it, fitted with great presses, would obviously be of inestimable benefit for storing ballet dresses, and a new ballet rehearsal room and ballet offices on the Rosebery Avenue side of the theatre were well under way. New dressing-rooms[1] and shower-baths brought joy to the company, and on the stage the extra fourteen feet in depth and eleven feet added to the wings made the large-scale productions much more comfortable. Apart from the immediate improvement in working conditions there was also the nice thought that the improvements would save at least £2,000 a year on cartage expenses from storage points outside.

The first new ballet of the season was *Harlequin in the Street*, produced on 10th November. Ashton had originally made this ballet for the Arts Theatre in Cambridge and, with customary generosity, Maynard Keynes presented the Derain *décors* and costumes to the Vic-Wells Ballet when it was decided to revive it in London. The happy link with ballet history, through Keynes and Lopokova to Derain, designer of *La Boutique Fantasque*, intro-duced a delightful French *décor* to the Wells repertoire. The street scene was Derain at his best, and the cheerful green and white stripes of Harlequin's costume—extending from his cap to his shoes —remain a happy memory, together with June Brae's lovely gown of grey with its green edging and salmon-coloured decorations.

---

[1] Some of the old dressing-rooms were so small that each artist in turn had to go out into the passage to put on his costume.

The original Cambridge production, some two or three years previously, had been a brief comedy of about ten minutes' duration, but Ashton expanded it to more than twice this length for London and added some more music by Couperin. The ballet was an amusing little comedy of manners, well explained by its title. Perhaps it never rose above the level of pleasantness, but it had warm admirers who still regret its disappearance from the repertoire. (The *décor* alone would justify revival, but during the difficult days of the war it was painted over and used for another ballet.) In 1938 interest was centred on the performance of young Alan Carter as Harlequin, a tall boy of great promise with a lively, impish face. His dances of elevation and brilliant *batterie* were well contrasted with the formal *terre à terre* dancing of La Superbe and Monseigneur (June Brae and Michael Somes), and the ebullient character dancing of the Bread Boy (Frank Staff at his best) and the Birdcatcher (Richard Ellis).

On 15th November, only five days after the *première* of *Harlequin in the Street,* came the important evening on which Fonteyn danced for the first time the double rôle of Odette-Odile in *Le Lac des Cygnes.* For some time she had been dancing Odette, but two-thirds of the rôle was new to her and she had never before attempted anything so arduous: it was to be a foretaste of her staying power and ability to dominate a large production which would be so necessary in *The Sleeping Princess.* She came safely through the ordeal, although the performance was but a tentative outline of the deeply moving interpretation she gives to-day and which, indeed, seems to increase in richness with every performance. But she had without doubt won her title of *prima ballerina,* English born and reared within an English ballet company, and one wonders if she remembered that night the misgivings she had felt as to whether the company could provide a replacement for Markova, for "even hard work can't make a *prima ballerina* if there isn't one."

That there was indeed a *prima ballerina* was confirmed by Fonteyn's performance in *The Sleeping Princess,* which was first presented at Sadler's Wells on 2nd February 1939, at a Gala Performance in aid of the Housing Centre and graced by the presence of Her Majesty Queen Mary. The capacity audience cheered the performance enthusiastically, but the event was perhaps more important as a presage of future triumphs than entirely satisfactory in itself. The ballet had been mounted by an English company and choreographically it was there intact as far as all the important numbers were concerned. It came far nearer the original than the Diaghileff 1921 production at the Alhambra (in which Ninette de Valois, Ursula Moreton and Sergueeff had all appeared), many numbers being included which had not been seen since St. Petersburg days. (Sergueeff had himself been in the original St. Petersburg production as a child and had appeared as one of the rats in the Prologue and in the Grande Valse in Act I.)

The magnificent Tchaikovsky score was one of the chief joys of the production. As there was at the time only one copy of the full score in London (and an incorrect copy at that) it had meant a great deal of hard work for Constant Lambert, but he was himself entranced by the abundance of delightful melodies and he laboured to rectify errors so that the movements should be accurate and more complete—apart from the traditional cuts—than in any performance given previously in England. Music and choreography were thus faithfully presented, but decoratively the production was depressing in both colour and design.

Nadia Benois, the designer, had of course been faced with no enviable task. Her problem, artistically, was "to give a picture of Perrault's fairy tale 'La Belle au bois dormant,' seen through the prism of Tchaikovsky's music or, in other words, as Princess Aurora falls asleep in the sixteenth century and wakes up again in the seventeenth, to show the poetical aspect of those two epochs seen through the emotional eye of Russia's nineteenth century." In practical terms this meant some 200 costumes and four sets on a very limited budget, because large capital investment in new productions simply was not possible at Sadler's Wells and there was then no Arts Council to come to the rescue. A lighthearted ballet such as *Coppélia* could be made gaily pretty at small expense, but *The Sleeping Princess* had been planned in the first place to exploit all the opulence of the Imperial Russian theatres in a fabulous epoch. It was not a ballet that could be treated in a cheap and cheerful fashion, and shoestring pretensions to grandeur are usually an embarrassing failure. The costumes for the ensemble dances were the least successful and showed an extraordinary addiction to dull mauve and grey tones, but many of the classical *tutus* for the fairies and all those for Aurora were attractive. Carabosse, the

King and Queen and the courtiers fared less well, and more than any other Wells production this *Sleeping Princess* suffered from truly hideous wigs. Helpmann as Prince Florimund was afflicted with a blond page-boy affair that flapped as he danced, and it is still a matter of surprise that the combined wig and headdress for the Blue Bird did not lead to mass resignations among the male dancers forced to wear it.

Despite these inadequacies, however, the ballet represented a genuine triumph of rehearsing and organisation, and when a rather tired Ninette de Valois thanked the first-night audience for its enthusiasm she paid special tribute to the people backstage and in the orchestra as well as to the seventy dancers for the way they had worked on the production. (She took no credit herself but an indication of her labours was contained in her concluding remark that she would now like to emulate Aurora and go to sleep for one hundred years.)

The ballet was from the very beginning a decided popular success and its popularity has never waned. All the early perform- ances were of course danced by Fonteyn and Helpmann, and other dancers who rose to the demands of the exacting choreography (exacting in style rather than actual technical difficulty) were June Brae as the Lilac Fairy, Elizabeth Miller as the Fairy of the Song Birds, Julia Farron, neat and charming in the "finger" variation, and Turner and Honer in the Blue Bird *pas de deux*. Ursula Moreton worked her usual miracle by making the little Cinderella *pas de deux* in the last act interesting, and Pamela May had beautiful classical style and brilliance as the Diamond Fairy in the *pas de quatre*, danced to what is now generally known as the Florestan music.

The ballet was given twelve times before the end of the season, a total surpassed over the season only by *Checkmate*, *Harlequin in the Street* and *Façade*, which were each given thirteen times at Sadler's Wells between October and May. This was the more remarkable as *The Sleeping Princess* constituted a full evening's programme and performances were still only at the rate of two a week, but on the other hand the ballet had received a tremendous amount of publicity. The excitements of the inaugural gala per- formance were followed by the honour of an invitation to appear at a Command Performance at Covent Garden on 22nd March in honour of the visit of the President of the French Republic and

Madame Lebrun. The Sadler's Wells Ballet performed Act I (The Spell) and Act III (The Wedding)[1] of *The Sleeping Princess* with the London Philharmonic Orchestra, Constant Lambert conducting. Between the two acts Sir Thomas Beecham conducted the orchestra in a performance of Debussy's *Iberia*. A description of the scene in the opera house was broadcast and the next day's papers reported the occasion at length.

After the Command Performance Lord Clarendon wrote to Bruce Worsley, as Manager of the Old Vic and Sadler's Wells: "By command of the King, I write to convey to you and Miss de Valois and all members of the Sadler's Wells Ballet, His Majesty's deep appreciation of the excellent performance that was given at Covent Garden on Wednesday evening. Such perfect artistry could not fail to make a profound impression on all who had the good fortune to see it, and I am to convey to you His Majesty's sincere thanks."

Subsequently two television performances were given of the ballet in virtually the same form as at the Command Performance.

Another tribute paid to the widespread popularity of the ballet was less formal. Herbert Farjeon's *Little Revue* at the Little Theatre contained a wild burlesque called "The Creaking Princess," in which Hermione Baddeley and Cyril Ritchard, as Mme. Allova and Harold Helpmeet, performed an astonishing *pas de deux* in costumes all too reminiscent of those worn at Sadler's Wells.

Whether the distractions of *The Sleeping Princess* had proved too much for the company, or whether Ashton was suffering from understandable reaction after his long series of successes, the next new ballet, produced on 27th April, was a complete failure. The usual way of the Wells audience with an indifferent ballet was to cheer it loudly on the opening night and then gradually lose interest, but the gallery openly disapproved of *Cupid and Psyche* at its first performance, and booed it loudly. (The gallery by the late 'thirties was a vociferous body with strong partisan tendencies; there were even occasions when rival factions would hang banners over the edge of the amphitheatre proclaiming their respective loves, Helpmann and Turner.)

[1] The last act was slightly rearranged so that it included the fairy variations from the Prologue but omitted the *pas de quatre* for the fairies Diamond, Gold, Silver and Sapphire.

HOROSCOPE

Pamela May as the Moon with Alan Carter and Richard Ellis as the Gemini

THE SLEEPING PRINCESS

Margot Fonteyn as the Princess Aurora in the Vision Scene of the
first production of this ballet by Sadler's Wells

Cupid and Psyche was an attempt to treat a rather sad little story in an ultra-smart and witty fashion. The music by Lord Berners was light enough and Sir Francis Rose designed shiny, bright sets and costumes, but Ashton seemed quite unable to weld his ingredients into an interesting choreographic design. It was as if someone had said, "Wouldn't it be fun to show Venus as a rather shop-soiled floozie, to have Cupid fly away on a wire at the end, and to have two figures placed at the head of the steps on each side of the stage declaiming the story before each scene"—and then the joke went rather stale before it even got on to the stage. As in *Le Roi Nu,* the story posed one insoluble difficulty and no one was ever able to think of a way of indicating that Cupid was in fact invisible to Psyche. The pity was that Julia Farron and Frank Staff, who had the leading rôles, were each at a vulnerable stage in their career, and the failure of the ballet probably wounded them more deeply than it would have wounded more experienced artists. It was given only three times.

The season ended on 18th May with a performance of *The Sleeping Princess*. Once again the financial results had been satisfactory, despite the cost of the new productions, and attendances had been excellent. The management thought the time had come to increase ballet performances to three a week, and proposed to do this at the beginning of the next season, in September 1939. The new ballet rehearsal room, with a specially constructed floor of rubber and composition, was at last ready and two immense new dressing-rooms had been brought into use. A new production of *Coppélia* was planned for October. The company meanwhile went off to dance in Cambridge, Oxford and Bournemouth, and after their holiday reassembled for a northern tour. They went first to Manchester, then to Liverpool and then to the Royal Court Theatre, Leeds,[1] where they gave their last performance on Saturday, 2nd September. The next day war was declared and the company disbanded. The years of steady, gradual development in Islington were at an end and a new phase of the company's history was beginning.

[1] By strange coincidence the first phase in the company's history had also ended in Leeds, for it was in that city that Markova made her last appearance with them in 1935.

K

PART IV

THE WAR YEARS

CHAPTER VIII

BALLET IN WARTIME

THE declaration of war on 3rd September 1939 resulted in the immediate closing of all the London theatres as a precautionary measure, and any thought of opening the ballet season at Sadler's Wells on 18th September, as intended, had to be abandoned. It was decided to reopen the school as usual, however, and the students reassembled towards the end of the month. The company re-formed in Cardiff instead of London on 18th September, and started off on a provincial tour with a small but representative repertoire and an accompaniment of two pianos.

This tour was very much in the nature of an experiment. No one knew at that time whether there would be any support for theatrical performances, and it was impossible to foresee how much or how quickly wartime stringencies would affect transport. The whole company gladly agreed to work on a strictly co-operative basis. Each dancer received a basic minimum salary considerably below the peacetime level, but when the takings in any one week warranted it, the difference, or a proportion of the difference, between the basic and the peacetime salary was added. It was expected that by this arrangement a living wage could be earned by every dancer, and in lucky weeks there might be an odd pound or so as a bonus. All the principal dancers and the *corps de ballet* took part in the tour. Elizabeth Miller had married and left the company; Frank Staff and John Nicholson also resigned. Among the newcomers were Leo Young and John Field. Constant Lambert and Hilda Gaunt, the company's beloved and invaluable rehearsal pianist, played the pianos.

In each town six evening performances and three *matinées* were given, and the repertoire included *Les Sylphides, Harlequin in the Street, Checkmate, The Gods go a'Begging, The Rake's Progress, Les Patineurs, Horoscope* and *Façade*. The tour opened on 2nd October in Leicester, and the company then visited Leeds, Birmingham,

Southsea, Brighton, Cambridge and Nottingham. From the beginning they were successful. Every week the dancers received something above the basic salary, and for several weeks—notably at Birmingham, Brighton and Cambridge—they drew a full peacetime salary. At Cambridge the returns exceeded even their pre-war record.

By this time London had recovered from the first shock of the war and life was returning to something like its normal character. There had been no signs of enemy aircraft over the capital and theatres were gradually reopening. The ballet, together with the opera, returned to Sadler's Wells on 26th December 1939, with full orchestra, for a trial period of one month. A guarantee against loss was given by the Vic-Wells Ballet Fund and during the next few difficult years the Fund frequently performed this service.

The London audience was obviously delighted to have the company back and the gallery was as full as ever, but the stalls and circle showed many empty seats, and it was only during the final week of the season (it was extended until 27th January), when the success of *Dante Sonata* caused a last-minute scramble for seats, that the more expensive parts of the theatre were full. In her customary last-night-of-the-season speech Ninette de Valois expressed appreciation for the final crowded houses but pointed out plainly that these could not retrospectively fill empty seats—an echo of Lilian Baylis who used to scold her Old Vic audiences on last nights with the exhortation, "We must have better Monday nights, you bounders!"

Ashton's *Dante Sonata*, created in those early months of the war when emotions were disturbed and all human values seemed to be called in question, was so completely a product of the time that it could hardly fail to have a profoundly moving effect upon anyone who saw it. It was a barefoot composition with a simple basic theme of the unending struggle between the forces of light and the forces of darkness. Unlike the general run of good-versus-evil ballets (and there have been dozens and dozens by different, mostly indifferent, choreographers), *Dante Sonata* allowed no final victory; both sides had their momentary triumphs and their moments of shame, despair and disaster. The whole ballet was charged with such a fierce emotional intensity that it left both dancers and audience exhausted at the end of its brief duration. The turgid music—Liszt's sonata "*après une lecture de Dante*"—was exactly right for such a ballet, and once again Ashton had ideal collaborators. The simple abstract design of Sophie Fedorovitch for the backcloth and her costumes —white draperies for the Children of Light and black and grey entwined with snakes for the Children of Darkness—contributed to the meaning of the ballet without in any way interfering with the design of the choreography. Imaginative lighting also made a very positive contribution.

Constant Lambert later described in a broadcast the way in which he and Ashton worked together on the creation of the ballet: "The general lay-out, by which I mean not the dancing as such but the association of various characters with various themes and the general dramatic sequence, was then established mutually by Ashton and myself. I played the piano at almost all the rehearsals while the choreography was being created, so that when it came finally to orchestrating the ballet, I had the whole stage picture in my mind. I am certain that, apart from whether people like *Dante Sonata* or not, it has a visual-cum-musical unity which could only have been achieved by this form of collaboration."

The dancers caught and reflected the emotional tension to an amazing degree: Fonteyn and Somes, Children of Light tortured by the evil of the world, had moments of great beauty, and one brief, heart-stopping moment of ecstasy when they ran towards a shaft of golden light, their bodies seeming to cry aloud, "The sun, the sun!" Helpmann and June Brae led the writhing, dæmonic Children of Darkness and gave their very unattractiveness an unhealthy beauty and fascination. Most remarkable of all, however, was Pamela May's performance as one of the Children of Light when, in two brief solo passages, with quick broken steps and an anguished tossing of her head, she danced some terrible unexplained grief.

In some ways *Dante Sonata* was the most personal of all Ashton's ballets, and it became personally associated with all the people who helped in its creation. With different casting it never made anything like the same impact, and it belonged so much to its time and period that in later years and on wider stages its original truth disappeared. In those early years of the war, however, it had a very real depth and meaning, and the memory of its significance at that time does not grow less with the passage of years.

The London season ended with a performance of *The Sleeping Princess*. This ballet, the largest of the company's productions, was the first to show the effects of war and the disappearance of male dancers which was later to be such a serious problem. Already the Lord Mayor's Boy Players had been evacuated from London, so the pages had to be played by young girls from the ballet school. The flower waltz at the beginning of Act I was reduced from twelve couples to ten, and on one occasion Robert Helpmann had to go on as the fourth prince in the Rose Adagio and then change himself into Prince Florimund. Bluebeard and Prince Hohlicke disappeared from the fairy-tale characters in the last act and Prince Hohlicke has never been restored.

Another provincial tour with two pianos followed until the end of March, and at its conclusion Harold Turner left the company to join the newly formed Arts Theatre Ballet. The Vic-Wells Ballet returned to Sadler's Wells on 1st April and opened with *Le Lac des Cygnes*. A new de Valois ballet, a comedy, was promised for later in the season, for the company expected to be in London throughout most of the summer of 1940 with the exception of a five-week tour to Holland, Belgium and France in May and June. The season started well. Attendances were better and the full-length classics in particular attracted almost full houses. Alan Carter had taken over many of Turner's rôles, notably the Blue Skater in *Les Patineurs*, and when he fell ill there was some hasty reshuffling of parts. Helpmann showed his amazing capacity for "getting away with" almost any kind of part by taking on the Blue Skater at very short notice and making a success of it through sheer stagecraft and presentation.

On 15th April the new production of *Coppélia*, enlarged to include the third act (orchestrated by Gordon Jacob) and with new settings and costumes by William Chappell, was given its first performance. The choreography was credited to Petipa and Cecchetti, reconstructed by Nicolai Sergueeff from his notation of the original, but the choreography of the Hymen *pas de deux*, the male variation and the *finale* in Act III were arranged by Sergueeff himself. Chappell's gay toy-town setting for the first act established the young and cheerful atmosphere of the production, and the company extracted a lot of fun from the ballet. Swanilda was one of Mary Honer's most delightful performances at Sadler's Wells; she had a very strong technique and exactly the right soubrette manner for the part. Helpmann managed to make quite a character of Franz, and Pamela May gave a very lovely performance of the purely classical "Dawn" variation—one of the most difficult of all solos, in which the ballerina comes on to the stage cold and has to make something of a variation which has no real climax or conclusion.

On 24th April another ballet by Ashton was ready. This was *The Wise Virgins*, which was danced to an arrangement of some choral preludes by J. S. Bach, orchestrated by William Walton. Ashton had long wanted to use some Bach music for a ballet and had a special affection for the lovely melody of "Sheep may safely graze." When he came to plan his ballet he determined to make the Bride the central figure, and to present the story as a morality at the end of which the wise virgins would enter with the Bride and Bridegroom and all the Host of Heaven to the marriage celebrations, while the foolish virgins would be shut outside.

The ballet was unlike any other work of Ashton's. It had a deep-felt serenity and a mood of acceptance which may have been made possible by the release of emotion in *Dante Sonata* only a few months previously. The choreography, alternately flowing with a simple grace and then building up into tableaux as splendid as baroque sculpture, was beautifully attuned to the glorious music and the designs of Rex Whistler.

The setting for *The Wise Virgins* was in fact the most magnificent *décor* that Rex Whistler ever produced and the costumes were almost equally beautiful. The setting showed a giant baroque doorway, supported by huge winged figures of angels on each side, set in a wall of long, pink fluted bricks. The doors themselves were heavy and golden, studded with giant nails. The foreground consisted of a pillar on each side of the stage decorated with sculptured groups of cherubs, and this design was echoed in the groups of four dancers who represented cherubs and wore pink tights and black velvet jerkins. A lovely drop-curtain for the ballet had a central motif of a smoking lamp, and above this, where the smoke thinned, cherubs supported a scroll on which was written the parable of the wise and foolish virgins.

The performance of Margot Fonteyn as the Bride, wrapt in wonder and quiet happiness, was the focal point of the ballet, but the whole production had a strangely peaceful and satisfying completeness.

The importance of "cultural propaganda" to the neutral countries began to be canvassed very widely in the spring of 1940, and the Sadler's Wells Ballet undertook to visit Holland, Belgium and France. (On the very day they were due to leave Holland a German ballet company was advertised to arrive.) They left for Holland at the beginning of May, and on Monday, 6th May, gave their first performance at the Royal Theatre in The Hague. Their success was instantaneous and overwhelming and the Press the next day was full of admiration for the artistic achievement of the company, which had obviously come as a complete surprise to the Dutch, who had no idea that work of such quality was being done in the English ballet theatre.

On the Tuesday afternoon the company went by motor bus to Hengelo, which was only some eight kilometres from the German border. The amount of military activity everywhere was very obvious throughout the journey, and some feelings of disquiet were aroused by the spectacle of barbed wire fencing, heavily guarded and partly blocked bridges and the great number of troops. By the time the company reached Hengelo they learned that all leave had been cancelled and all trains had been commandeered by the Government. But the performance was given, the theatre was full and the audience enthusiastic.

The night was spent in Hengelo and the next morning the dancers left for Eindhoven which, to everyone's relief, was farther from the German border. There they danced in the Philips' Theatre in the midst of the great Philips' factory, and after the performance returned to The Hague. The next day they went to Arnhem and gave a performance there, leaving the town in buses for The Hague at about 1 a.m. on the morning of Friday 10th May. Two hours later Holland was invaded by the Germans, and in another two hours' time German troops had occupied Arnhem. The ballet reached The Hague at 3 a.m. and by 3.30 there were fierce air battles taking place overhead and showers of leaflets came tumbling down informing the Dutch people that the Germans were there to "protect" them from an English invasion.

Then followed four days of uncertainty, anxiety and forced inactivity for the dancers while they waited for arrangements to be completed for their evacuation. For Ninette de Valois it must have been four days of almost unbearable responsibility, but her courage and good humour never flagged. Her powers of argument were such that grim army officers who came to inform her that there simply were no buses in Holland, finished up by sending along enough transport for the whole company within half an hour. Eventually staff, dancers and musicians were bundled into buses, leaving behind all their scenery, costumes, music and all personal belongings except for the little they could carry or wear. (Some people are said to have worn three suits and Ninette de Valois wore Frederick Ashton's dinner jacket over her own clothes, as he was fiercely determined it should not fall into German hands.)

After a nightmare journey of some nine hours they arrived at Velsen, where they had to spend another day in a pension commandeered by the military for troops and refugees. Late at night they at last got through to the harbour of Ijmuiden and were conducted to the cargo boat which was to take them back to England. A kindly sailor stood by the gangway calling out, "Vic-Wells Ballet this way," and as she passed him Ninette de Valois must have sighed a little, wondering why on earth she ever started such an enterprise. "You 'aven't 'arf done it now, mum," was the sailor's comment.

Weary, bedraggled and hungry, the ballet company settled down in the hold of the cargo boat. By then even the wit and gaiety of Ashton and Helpmann, which had done so much to keep spirits lively during the journey, were being quenched by sheer fatigue and lack of food, for money ran out very early on the trip and for the last two days there had been very little to eat. The crossing itself was appalling and lasted more than twenty hours, but eventually, at about three o'clock in the morning on Tuesday, 14th May, the dancers were safely home in London. They had left behind them the scenery, costumes and music of *The Rake's Progress, Checkmate, Dante Sonata, Horoscope, Façade* and *Les Patineurs*, and some of these ballets were not restored to the repertoire for many years, while the loss of the *Horoscope* music has ever since prevented its revival. But the precious human life-blood of the company was unharmed, and it was typical that Ninette de Valois in writing about the Holland visit should express no grief or despondency about their own losses but only admiration for the calmness, efficiency and courage of the Dutch people "under circumstances that do not bear thinking about."

Despite the disaster in Holland, however, the company was able to open a London season at Sadler's Wells by 4th June. The programme consisted of *Les Sylphides, Dante Sonata* and *The Wise Virgins.* The Benois set for *Les Sylphides* had not been taken to Holland and was unharmed. The simple setting and costumes for *Dante Sonata* could be quickly renewed, and the Ballet Fund once again stepped into the breach with a grant towards replacements. *Dante Sonata* was danced to the Columbia recording of the music, made by Louis Kentner with the Sadler's Wells Orchestra under Lambert, until the lost orchestral score and parts could be renewed. The full-length classics were intact as they had not been taken on tour, but *The Sleeping Princess* was showing more signs of the call-up—the waltz dwindled to eight couples and by August was omitted altogether.

The company danced right through the summer of 1940, when disaster after disaster befell the Allied armies. The audience was rather less brave than the dancers, and attendances would drop off at times of particularly bad news—Norway, Dunkirk, the capitulation of France—but then they would rally again, and the quality of performances never faltered.

On 4th July Ninette de Valois produced a new work, a hilarious comedy character ballet which was just what was needed to ease the tension of the time. *The Prospect Before Us* had a highly complicated scenario based on episodes from John Ebers' *Seven Years of the King's Theatre.* It treated the whole eighteenth-century ballet world in a spirit of burlesque and irreverence akin to the Rowlandson drawings which inspired the *décor* and costumes by Roger Furse. The music used was by William Boyce, arranged by Constant Lambert, who had edited the Boyce sonatas and returned them to circulation some ten years previously. (Several sections were familiar to the ballet audience as they had been used by first Ashton (1930) and then Frank Staff (1938) for *The Tartans.*)

The drop curtain of "The Burning of the King's Theatre" was such a lusty piece of Rowlandson characterisation that it always caused a buzz of comment and delight when it appeared, and the settings, one back-stage, one on-stage, were lively and interesting. The costumes were mostly based on ballet designs of the period and were a nice mixture of elegant eighteenth-century costume for the men and Greek draperies for the women, while the Cupid costume of pale blue smothered in pink roses was a period confection that might have come straight from the archives of the Paris Opéra.

The story concerned the rivalries of two London theatre managers in 1789 and their efforts to secure the most celebrated dancers for their own particular theatre, a rivalry made more furious by the conflagrations which razed each theatre in turn. Clear narrative was hardly possible, yet the sequence of events was neatly worked out, and individual scenes had enormous wit and fun. Broad humour engulfed the ballet every time Robert Helpmann (as Mr. O'Reilly, Manager of the Pantheon) stepped on the stage, and his irrepressible clowning dominated the whole work, culminating in an utterly drink-sodden dance at the end which, by some miracle, remained just as funny no matter how many times it was seen. His performance has now entered ballet history (although Stanley Holden was a brilliant successor in a later production), and it was so hugely enjoyable that one almost forgave the over-playing in some scenes which robbed the other dancing of its full effect.

Like all de Valois ballets, *The Prospect Before Us* called for first-rate characterisation in every tiny part. Unforgettable are Pamela May's style and elegance as the haughty Mademoiselle Théodore, the bored conceit of Alan Carter and John Hart as Didelot and Vestris, Mary Honer's blowsy good humour as a Street Dancer, and Margaret Dale's devastating coyness as Cupid. Michael Somes, Richard Ellis and Leslie Edwards, with strange make-up and enormous feet, looked like a trio of Doctor Johnsons and, as Mr. Taylor's Lawyers, performed a dance of solemn deliberation that was as clever a parody of legal niceties as anything W. S. Gilbert ever wrote.

Façade came back into the repertory on 23rd July, in a still further enlarged version and with entirely new *décor* and costumes by John Armstrong to replace those lost in Holland. The ballet had always been rather broader in its humour at Sadler's Wells than at the Ballet Club, and this re-dressing and expansion broadened and indeed coarsened it still further. The new backdrop showed a full-bosomed woman standing at the window of a doubtful-looking residence,[1] while a pair of lengthy and capacious bloomers fluttered

----

[1] Miss P. W. Manchester tells me that this lady is a feature of the wallpaper design in a New York drug store. Whether the wallpaper inspired John Armstrong or whether it is a tribute to the popularity of the ballet, we have been unable to discover.

on a washing line outside. When the curtain rose Ashton was already on stage, and his Latin American prowlings distracted considerably from the Scotch Rhapsody, but his *Noche Espagnole* which followed was a very wicked and very funny parody of Dolin's *Bolero*. The new Foxtrot was performed in nineteen-twentyish "mad gay" costumes to the music Walton had written as a setting for "Old Sir Faulk." The waltz dancers were now dressed in long muslin skirts decorated with wide sashes, while the black gloves, which had formerly given such emphasis to the arm movements, were replaced by white ones. In this guise *Façade* has remained immensely popular ever since. It still gets laughs in all the obvious places, and it can be guaranteed to win over any audience sceptical or prejudiced in advance about "ballet." Yet the change in spirit has always been regretted by those who knew the ballet in its youth and there is much sad shaking of greying heads when it is given. The late Lionel Bradley disliked the new version so much that he could seldom be prevailed upon to remain in the theatre when it was being given.

The next revival was de Valois' *Barabau,* which was expected to emerge as a thoroughly topical satirical picture of Dictators and Blackshirts, but despite good performances by Ashton, Helpmann and Molly Brown, it fell rather flat and was soon abandoned.

By the end of the season male dancers were beginning to disappear rapidly. William Chappell was in the Army, Richard Ellis and Stanley Hall with the Navy, and Leo Young[1] and Paul Reymond had joined the R.A.F. The Spanish dance and the Czardas had been dropped from the third act of *Le Lac des Cygnes*, and the *pas de trois* had been moved into the ballroom to make up for their absence. At one stage Joan Ross had to be disguised as "J. Ross" and go on as the Beast with Beauty in *The Sleeping Princess*—but this was as near as the company ever came to playing rôles *en travesti*.

The long summer season came to an end on 6th September. The theatre was three-quarters full, although by then air-raid

---

[1] Leo Young was the company's first war casualty. He died in hospital on 22nd November 1941, aged twenty-seven, some eighteen months after enlisting. An Australian, he had joined the Vic-Wells Ballet in August 1939 and volunteered for the R.A.F. after the 1940 experiences in Holland. He fell ill soon afterwards, and the last months of his life were spent in hospital.

warnings were increasingly frequent and there was an "alert" between two scenes in *The Prospect Before Us*. The company intended to return to Sadler's Wells after a three-week break, but on the following evening, 7th September, the bombing of London was suddenly intensified and a week later Sadler's Wells Theatre was commandeered as a rest centre for air-raid victims. Instead of returning to London the ballet consequently went off on an ENSA tour of garrison theatres, followed by a provincial tour, and then spent a short period of rest and rehearsal at Dartington Hall in Devon.

Administration of the Old Vic and Sadler's Wells companies from London soon proved to be impossible. Communications were thoroughly unreliable, not to say chaotic, and if the work of the drama, opera and ballet companies was to continue it was obvious that they would have to set up wartime headquarters outside London. In mid-November the offices of both theatres were transferred to Burnley in Lancashire, where, thanks to the generosity of Jess Linscott, its managing director, the Victoria Theatre became their headquarters for the next two years.

This move was of considerable importance for all three companies, because for the first time it gave them a national as distinct from a metropolitan character. Instead of performing for the greater part of the year before their own devoted London audience in their own theatre, they were suddenly transplanted to the heart of the country and had to stand on their own feet as part of the general theatrical life of Great Britain. In many respects this did all three companies a world of good. The ballet in particular, which was becoming a rather precious organisation supported by a faithful but limited public, was sent out to conquer a vast new audience. It was an audience of ordinary theatregoers and in many cases, such as when the company danced in Garrison Theatres on makeshift stages, an audience which might well have been actively hostile to ballet.[1]

It was their success in winning popularity with such a widely varied assortment of spectators that really established their right to be considered a national ballet company. It transformed them

---

[1] Some spectators, of course, remained hostile. After one Garrison Theatre performance, a soldier was heard to say, "Ee, fancy paying toopence fer thart. A'd rather spend anoother 'apenny and 'ave a stamp to write 'ome."

from a group of young artists working in a secluded and special atmosphere into a thoroughly professional and amazingly adaptable company, led by two artists, Fonteyn and Helpmann, of quite exceptional quality.

The New Theatre, St. Martin's Lane

London, before very long, began to get used to the bombing and to want as many of the ordinary amenities of living, including theatres, as possible, and it was a London theatre manager, Mr. (now Sir) Bronson Albery, who made it possible for the Sadler's Wells Ballet to return to the capital. The generous terms which he offered enabled the three Old Vic and Sadler's Wells companies to make use of the New Theatre in St. Martin's Lane for London seasons, and the ballet appeared there for the first time on 14th January 1941.

The New Theatre, a small and cosy building, upholstered in traditional red and gold, was considerably smaller than either the Old Vic or Sadler's Wells, and it is astonishing to go there to-day and reflect that all the full-length classical productions in the ballet repertoire were, during the war years, shown on its comparatively tiny stage. The size of the theatre had some advantages, however, for it meant that the financial risk was less great and the depleted condition of the company was less apparent than it would have been on a larger stage. Most of the ballets looked well there, and as the amount of good male dancing was bound to decline on account of the call-up, the smaller amount of dancing space was less of a handicap than it might have been. Prices of seats were slightly higher than at Sadler's Wells and ranged from about 1s. to 11s.

The first New Theatre season was nevertheless considered highly venturesome. Performances were given daily at 2.30 p.m. and twice a week at 4.30 p.m., despite protests from working members of the audience who were thus only able to attend on Saturdays. Tyrone Guthrie, then Administrator of the Old Vic and Sadler's Wells, would not risk an orchestra, so two pianos were used. Constant Lambert and Hilda Gaunt played frequently, Angus Morrison played for occasional performances, and later Mary and Geraldine Peppin and Marjorie Reed. While the music was thus

Right: Robert Helpmann as Dr. Coppelius

Anthony

Below:

THE PROSPECT BEFORE US

Pamela May, Frederick Ashton and Ursula Moreton

Anthony

Serge Lido

Above: In Paris with ENSA. Robert Helpmann, Margot Fonteyn, and Pamela May in a café on the Champs-Élyseés

Right: Robert Helpmann and Constant Lambert discussing a score between performances

J. W. Debenham

limited it was not thought advisable to attempt the full-length classical ballets, and these were consequently presented in *divertissement* form. *The Wise Virgins* had to be given without the drop curtain and setting as they would not fit the stage, and it was danced instead in front of simple gauzes. Now that both orchestra and chorus were missing Constant Lambert moved into a box for *A Wedding Bouquet* and declaimed the words himself, with enormous relish and occasional personal interpolations (on one occasion he remarked reprovingly, "Webster! your boots are squeaking.").

There was, however, no resting on the old repertoire and existing reputation. New productions were rightly considered vital for the company's well-being, and on 27th January the first performance was given of Frederick Ashton's ballet *The Wanderer*, which had been rehearsed at Dartington and composed in little more than ten days. This choreographic fantasy in four scenes was danced to the "Wanderer Fantasie" of Schubert, music which was admirably suitable for the two-piano accompaniment now forced on the company. For the scenery and costumes Ashton turned to the distinguished painter Graham Sutherland, whose first work for the theatre this was. The four movements were simply named after the music: *Allegro con fuoco*, *Adagio*, *Presto* and *Finale-Allegro*.

The Wanderer (Helpmann) was no nineteenth-century traveller but, as Lambert explained in his programme note, "a mental and emotional traveller who belongs to all time." His reactions to worldly success, love, compassion, doubts and despairs were suggested and "in the fourth movement he summons up all the elements of his life and conquers both the external and internal worlds by a supreme effort of will." The strong rhythms, sweet melodies and vigorous forward progression of the music made it well suited to the theatre. The dancing was exciting and original and richly varied in style and mood. Helpmann, as the somewhat neurotic and introspective central character, was on stage throughout and it was the intensity of his performance that held the ballet together and made it something more than an abstract choreographic fantasy. Fonteyn suggested the glitter of the world in some brilliant virtuoso passages, and there was an unforgettably lovely *pas de deux* for Pamela May and Michael Somes. The slow second movement, with its strange figures clad in dull greens and browns, made use of heavy, lunging *terre à terre* movement which suggested the oppressive weight of

L

mental torment. The dancers moved in wide circles and made beautiful floor patterns which echoed the sweeping curves and circles of Sutherland's backdrop for this scene. The backdrops were in fact wonderful paintings which made fine settings for the dancers, but Sutherland's costumes were less successful and only in the case of the vegetable, earthy colours for the *corps de ballet* in the *adagio* section did they have real affinity with the *décor*.

The Wanderer, like all other adventurous works of art, suffered some cheap sneers and mockery from people who had no idea what Ashton was getting at and no intention of trying to find out. It succeeded with all lovers of fine dancing, however, and always received magnificent performances. It also won some very devoted admirers, chief among them being Beryl de Zoete, who wrote of a subsequent revival: "There is no ballet in which the texture of dance and music is more closely related, nor which more nearly realises the kind of correspondence imagined by Dalcroze. Ashton's fine sense of form here imposes itself on material as romantic and turbulent as in *Dante Sonata*, but with a subtler and firmer control of his medium; and the significance of his abstract choreography was so sensitively rendered in the medium of line and colour by Graham Sutherland that there are moments in which the dance groups seem to take mobile form from within the canvas. . . . *The Wanderer* is the finest example of what I would call Ashton's architectural imagination, in which he surpasses every English choreographer."

After another provincial and ENSA tour the company returned to the New Theatre on 18th May for six weeks, the longer hours of daylight permitting later performances, and immediately attendances improved. *Fête Polonaise* was revived for this season (it required only four men) but it proved rather weak tea after the heady wine of the more recent ballets and was not helped by being danced in front of the setting for *Coppélia*, Act III. More successful was Ninette de Valois' new ballet which was presented on 28th May.

De Valois had originally planned to produce *Orpheus and Eurydice* at Sadler's Wells the previous autumn, using both the opera and ballet companies in a full production of Gluck's opera, and Sophie Fedorovitch had completed designs for this production. With Sadler's Wells closed, however, and the opera and ballet companies touring independently, such a project would obviously not be possible for years to come, and de Valois therefore decided to produce *Orpheus* as a ballet, retaining certain recitatives and arias which would be sung as accompaniment to appropriate action on the stage. As Edwin Evans put it, "the ballet overflowed into the opera."

The story of the opera was followed quite closely but the ballet reverted to the tragic ending. There were some beautiful passages, notably the dancing of the Blessed Spirits and Eurydice in the Elysian Fields. The return to earth was suggested by the cheerful dancing of children and peasants, and in this section Margaret Dale, John Hart, Julia Farron and June Brae were all delightful. The arias, sung by Nancy Evans and Ceinwen Rowlands, were beautiful in themselves but tended to slow down the action too much, and the choreography devised to parallel them was rather conventional. Helpmann, in a bright tan body make-up and white tunic, was not a very convincing Orpheus, and Fonteyn, though dainty and musical as Amor, had no very great opportunities. The outstanding performance in the ballet was that given by Pamela May as Eurydice, beautiful in her lime-coloured draperies and deeply moving in her anguish and pleading. The ballet had the usual rapturous reception, but Herbert Farjeon in the *Tatler* said he would "bet anybody a fiver that the Wells won't be doing it in 1945" and he was right. (After the first performance Gordon Anthony gave a party in his studio which was decorated to look like the Tomb of Eurydice, a long glass table, headed with white lilies and floodlit gauze, representing the tomb. Food rationing was getting severe by then and one gossip writer described the food on this table as having "a quite abstract, visual beauty.")

The Conscription of Male Dancers

By the end of this season the call-up had practically done its worst. Leslie Edwards made his last appearance on 18th June in *A Wedding Bouquet* (as the ubiquitous Arthur) and took a special curtain afterwards. On the last night of the season, 21st June, Ashton had to replace Edwards in *Dante Sonata*, and this also marked his own last appearance as a permanent member of the company before going into the Royal Air Force (although he was given leave to appear during the London summer season). It was the last performance of Michael Somes, and Alan Carter was leaving too. All the pre-war male soloists had now been removed, with the exception of Helpmann, who was granted exemption as he was rated the "key member" of the company.

There was a great deal of discussion about the problem in the national Press, Bernard Shaw writing at considerable length to the *Daily Telegraph*, and many other distinguished people also asking for the exemption of dancers on the ground that their special talent were more valuable to the community while they remained in their own jobs. Nicolas Bentley remarked that anyway they were "so few as to be almost negligible," and Sir Osbert Sitwell said roundly, "if we are, as we claim, a civilised nation, we must protect the arts." Arnold Haskell put forward a sensible suggestion that the word "exemption" should be modified to "postponement" until an overwhelming emergency occurred.

Ninette de Valois, however, never asked for exemption although she had to watch her first vintage of male dancers leaving her one by one. She maintained that the military requirements of the nation must come first, and she felt that her dancers had no greater claim than many other artists or young men at a crucial stage in their professional studies. She did not believe that military service inevitably ruined a dancer, and the dancers demonstrated the truth of this by making straight for the theatre whenever they were on leave, exchanging their army boots for ballet slippers, and giving astonishingly good performances. (Michael Somes, in particular, once astonished everyone by doing an excellent Blue Bird and Carabosse at the same performance of *The Sleeping Princess* when on forty-eight hours' leave, although he had never appeared as Carabosse in his life before.)

Throughout the war, by contrivance and careful choosing of her repertoire, Ninette de Valois managed to carry on and present acceptable performances, and she received magnificent support from the few men who did remain out of uniform. Robert Helpmann, in particular, gave unsparingly of his talents and energies, and was very largely responsible for the immense popularity which the ballet won during the war years.

The May-June season had been very successful, and seemed to warrant the engagement of an orchestra for the next London season. As the Ballet Fund was prepared to underwrite the financial risk the administration was prepared to agree. The season which started at the New Theatre on 21st July was in fact so remarkably successful that the box-office value of an orchestra was proved for all time, and the company never again reverted to two pianos for their major seasons. The company gained a useful character dancer in Gordon Hamilton, an Australian who had been dancing with the Anglo-Polish Ballet under the name Alexander Walewski.

The restoration of the orchestra made the full-length classics possible again, and *Coppélia*, *Le Lac des Cygnes* and *Giselle* were at once restored to the repertoire. They attracted a steady public, and the company tended to concentrate on them during the war years as they were an excellent training ground for the dancers, an education in classicism for the audience, and they required few men with strong technical ability. Nevertheless it was sometimes difficult to find enough male soloists. John Hart at this time had to dance leading rôles in nearly every ballet, and when he was not actually dancing was kept busy learning yet another rôle.

The depleted company was, of course, giving vastly more performances now than had been the case at Sadler's Wells, where they had shared the theatre with the opera company. For example, between 26th December 1939 and 6th September 1940, when performances were still at the Wells, the ballet had given seventy-eight performances in twenty-four weeks, whereas between January and August 1941 they gave 110 performances in only thirteen weeks in London. *Les Sylphides* was the most frequently performed ballet (on the two counts of intrinsic excellence and a cast requiring only one man), but the classics gradually occupied a larger section of the repertoire until in some seasons they would fill half the number of performances.

One crumb of comfort thrown by authority to the ballet world that summer was an official announcement by the Industries and Manufactures Department of the Board of Trade that clothing coupons need not be surrendered for ballet shoes, which would be exempt under the Consumer Rationing Order, 1941, provided "they are shoes with blocked or unblocked toes, made expressly for dancing with the sole ending at least one inch from the tip of the toe, and at least half an inch from the tip of the heel."

For a short London season in September-October *The Sleeping Princess* was restored to the repertoire. Evening performances were put back to 5.30 p.m. and only given four days a week with *matinées* every day except Monday. Attendances once again dropped below capacity because the working population, who formed the back-bone of the regular audience, simply could not get to the theatre in time. *The Sleeping Princess* maintained its popularity, although it had been still further cut down by this time. There were no musicians by the lake in the Vision Scene, no pages to carry Aurora's bridal train (so she didn't wear it) and no male courtiers. The waltz, however, was restored, rearranged for twelve girls instead of the original twelve couples, and the boys have never made their way back into it. Fonteyn's Aurora seemed to grow in sureness and radiance at every performance, and Helpmann took over Carabosse in addition to Prince Florimund and enjoyed himself hugely in a grotesque make-up. During this season he also made his first appear-ance as Dr. Coppelius, and his whimsical and highly comic old gentleman was such a success that this conception of the part in-fluenced the whole temper of the ballet *Coppélia* for a decade to come.

The season ended on 25th October with a performance of *The Sleeping Princess* at 6 p.m., just one hour after the curtain had come down on the *matinée* performance of the same ballet which had also been danced by Fonteyn. The evening was a tragic one for Pamela May who was that night dancing the Lilac Fairy. She injured her knee during the Prologue variation and had to be helped from the stage. She limped back for one further episode but was in obvious pain, and when she again retired, Mary Honer, on stage as the Violet Fairy, stepped forward and completed the ballet for her. In the last act Mary Honer appeared as the Lilac Fairy in the *entrée*, then changed and danced the Blue Bird *pas de deux*, and Julia Farron returned as the Lilac Fairy in the apotheosis. Thus in one performance the Lilac Fairy had been impersonated by three different dancers and the whole shuffling of parts managed with such composure that strangers in the audience may never have noticed the substitutions.

Pamela May, however, did not dance again for over a year and was sorely missed from the company. She had developed into a classical dancer of quite exceptional quality and style, and *The Dancing Times* always maintained that her arabesque was the most beautiful in English ballet. She was sometimes described as "a dancer's dancer" because she did not then always establish the immediate warm contact with an audience such as June Brae, for example, achieved the moment she came on stage; but for the discriminating her performances were always rewarding.

CHAPTER IX

THE DRAMATIC BALLETS OF ROBERT HELPMANN

IN August 1941 Frederick Ashton was claimed by the Royal Air
Force and the Sadler's Wells Ballet lost their resident choreographer. Ninette de Valois was faced with a prospect of seeing his
ballets decline gradually in performance, for he had always made
full use of the strength of the company as it was when he created
any particular ballet, and it was becoming increasingly difficult to
cast such ballets adequately. *Les Patineurs* once had four changes of
cast in five months and fell into a very unsatisfactory condition,
and it was inevitable that others would suffer in the same way.
The modern repertoire, therefore, seemed likely to change in character during Ashton's absence, and it became imperative for de
Valois to find another choreographer to take his place.

The choice, for a variety of reasons, fell on Robert Helpmann.
His popularity at that time was such that had he produced a
thoroughly mediocre work his public would probably have supported it to the extent of paying for the production—and this was
a factor which could not be overlooked. Helpmann, it is true, had
no great experience of producing ballets, but he had years of
theatre knowledge, an extraordinarily strong dramatic sense,
musical sensitivity and an alert and lively brain. As an experienced
man of the theatre and leading dancer in the company, he could
be counted on to get the best out of the dancers, the music and the
lighting under the awkward conditions of rehearsing on tour and
in theatres where the stage might be only available for odd half-
hours at a time.

"Comus"

Helpmann had always been more interested in the dramatic and
theatrical aspects of ballet than in the pure abstract technique of
classical dancing, and this personal enthusiasm naturally influenced
the nature of his choreography. For his first production he turned
to Milton's *Comus*, following the action of the Masque very closely

and retaining two of the speeches which he spoke himself. Constant Lambert undertook to select and orchestrate some music written by Henry Purcell for various operas and plays, and Oliver Messel was invited to design the settings and costumes. The ballet was presented at the New Theatre on 14th January 1942, and was received with rapture. Over the next six months it was to be performed no less than fifty-nine times in London alone, and from the box-office point of view Helpmann the choreographer was an immediate success.

His production of *Comus* was styled "a masque," and it was in fact in the nature of a mimed play with incidental dances. Helpmann, as Comus, spoke Milton's verse with impeccable audibility but with the slightly over-deliberate enunciation which marred his acting at one time. Fonteyn was the lost and frightened Lady, John Hart and David Paltenghi her stalwart brothers, Margaret Dale the Attendant Spirit, and Moyra Fraser had her first important creation as the water goddess Sabrina. Messel's settings were beautiful, but his costumes did not completely solve the problem of suggesting the period and at the same time being suitable for ballet. There was nothing strikingly original in the dances, but Helpmann showed a thoroughly professional grasp of theatre production, and he told his story clearly and effectively. *Comus* was an interesting and promising début and it had an excellent Press.

The Ballet Boom

Performances were at the rate of nine a week during this Christmas season, and also during the three-week season which took place at the New Theatre during March. The ballet was attracting larger and larger audiences, and the wartime boom was beginning to get under way. Instead of just managing to break even, the Sadler's Wells Ballet began to make money, and in some subsequent years the profits were to be as high as £15,000. "Commercialism!" shrieked Bloomsbury at once, and the more fiercely intellectual critics began to proclaim "the war must not be made an excuse for a lowering in the standard of British Ballet." Quite how they expected standards *not* to be lowered in wartime was never fully explained. The argument and the battle went on for the duration. Without doubt artistic standards slipped a little and departures from original long-term policies were forced on de Valois, but she had to keep her company going somehow, and she had to adopt the policies which would best maintain it under desperately difficult conditions.

War was, in fact, the only excuse she ever *did* offer for short-comings in the company and looking back at those difficult, yet financially prosperous, years she now considers the war the only major setback the ballet ever suffered. At the time, her viewpoint was rather different from that of her critics. They disapproved of the immediate present, comparing it to the lovely past when they, a perceptive and appreciative audience, shared in the building of a new artistic enterprise in England. Ninette de Valois, however, was as usual looking *forward*, perhaps ten years ahead, to a time when the uncomfortable present would have been weathered and she could proceed with her real work. Star billing of Fonteyn and Helpmann, nine performances a week, programmes that perhaps erred on the side of popularity, were conditions that were forced on the company by circumstances outside their control; but they were to bring benefits later—primarily in the shape of a public large enough to maintain long seasons in London when the company achieved its goal of appearing at Covent Garden.

The most serious aspect of the boom that developed during the war was that a vast new audience grew up without having any idea of what good male dancing could and should be.

Every effort was made by Ninette de Valois to have the male rôles adequately rendered, although it must have been heart-breaking to see boys continually drafted into the Services just as they were beginning to lose their classroom coltishness and develop some stage sense. She continually appealed to teachers through-out the country to help her maintain the supply by sending any promising boys to the Wells school. "Do not hesitate about letting me know of a promising male dancer," she said. "At sixteen he may be vital to the continuance of British Ballet, at seventeen it may be too late." The Wells organisation, of course, had special facilities for high-speed training and, although in principle de Valois detested such forcing of youthful talent, she had to accept it on account of "the letters marked 'O.H.M.S.' in the theatre letter rack."

The Sadler's Wells Ballet School offered scholarships to boys in their mid-teens, and was prepared to grant maintenance fees during the completion of their training in London. The School was now once again housed at Sadler's Wells Theatre. Ursula Moreton had left London to be with her husband, so Ailne Phillips came back to take over the administration of the School, a task she performed almost singlehanded for the remainder of the war. Ninette de Valois still found time to teach there occasionally, however, and Nicolai Sergueeff was also on the staff. (He and Madame Sergueeff had lost their home quite early in the air raids and had arrived at Sadler's Wells among the other bombed-out families beautifully organised, with their belongings neatly packed into bundles and properly arranged for living in a rest centre. When admiration for their orderliness was expressed, they explained simply that they were, of course, "used to being refugees.")

Camping out in theatres was a not infrequent experience during the war years, for accommodation was always difficult on tour, particularly if a company arrived in a town after a heavy raid. Many of the provincial theatres used to print requests in their programmes for townspeople to come forward with offers of accommodation for artists if a large company and orchestra was expected, but the supply of rooms was seldom adequate. Train journeys were slow, crowded and uncomfortable, and food in provincial (and London) restaurants and hotels got steadily worse. The peaceful days when Sunday trains carried only fish and actors were a thing of the past; during the war they carried troops and supplies, and hundreds of civilians who were working away from home and seized this one opportunity of the week to visit their families. On the night of Sunday, 26th April, for instance, the Sadler's Wells Ballet arrived in Bath just in time for the second Baedeker raid on that city. Unable to find lodgings, Constant Lambert, Henry Robinson and some others decided to camp in the theatre. During the raid the back of the building and the scene dock were damaged and but for the energetic fire-fighting of the ballet company the old theatre would have been gutted. Fortunately, the Ballet's own scenery was still at the railway station and thus escaped. The only losses sustained were two trumpets.

During the spring tour in 1942 several young dancers made important progress and began to develop as personalities. Beryl Grey, at the age of fourteen and a half, danced *The Gods go a' Begging* in Oxford and, when illness depleted the company, took over leading rôles in *Les Sylphides, Comus, Façade* (the Polka) and the second act of *Le Lac des Cygnes.* Alexis Rassine danced *Gods* with her and appeared in the *pas de trois* in *Le Lac des Cygnes.* He had joined the company in March after making a considerable reputation with the Anglo-Polish Ballet and was to be their leading classical dancer for several years. Ray Powell was beginning to show a marked talent for characterisation and Moyra Fraser gradually inherited many of the rôles which had been created by Pamela May (in *Dante Sonata* and *The Wanderer,* for instance) or June Brae (such as Josephine in *A Wedding Bouquet*). June Brae had temporarily retired from the stage in order to devote herself to her family and Mary Honer had been absent on account of ill-health, so the company had to bring along new talent quickly. Celia Franca, after much experience with the Ballet Club and International Ballet, had joined as a soloist, and another dancer from International Ballet, the pretty, red-headed Moira Shearer, was showing exceptional promise.

"Hamlet"

The 1942 summer season at the New Theatre ran from 5th May to 18th July, with evening performances at 7.15 and heavy advance bookings. Helpmann's second ballet, *Hamlet,* which had been rehearsed on tour, was presented for the first time on 19th May, the entire proceeds being donated to Mrs. Churchill's Red Cross Aid-to-Russia Fund. The Russian Ambassador and Madame Maisky were in the audience, as well as Mrs. Churchill and her daughter Sarah. It was an important and triumphant first night.

Once again Helpmann had turned to a great poet dramatist for his subject, and once again the emphasis was on drama rather than on dancing. *Hamlet* was a considerable advance on *Comus,* being vastly more imaginative, individual and daring. Almost anyone with Helpmann's background and intelligence might have produced *Comus,* but *Hamlet* was a strongly personal creation. Helpmann tried to show not the straight action of the play, but the main events as they might have flashed through the brain of the dying Hamlet, a wild accumulated pageant of the past. The music

(Tchaikovsky's "Hamlet fantasie-overture"), with its turgid emotional content and strong theatrical atmosphere, suited his subject admirably, and the different episodes merged swiftly and easily, one character giving way to another in the fashion of a dream. They were not purely pictorial, however, for sudden, disturbing comments on character were suggested by the hot embrace of Laertes by the mad Ophelia, and the continual confusion in Hamlet's mind of the images of his mother and Ophelia.

Helpmann had invited a young artist named Leslie Hurry to design the ballet, having admired his paintings at the Redfern Gallery. Hurry was at first doubtful about working for such a completely unfamiliar medium as the theatre, but Helpmann encouraged him, played him the music and described the sort of setting he wanted—"a decadent palace invested with the brooding sense of its imminent destruction" which would loom over the tiny figures of the dancers. Hurry fulfilled these requirements with remarkable success. The great architectural mass of his setting was surmounted by an enormous avenging figure with a drawn and flaming sword and the hot colours produced, on the small stage of the New Theatre, an effect of almost overpowering concentration and intensity.

The ballet was short, admirably planned and superbly interpreted. It was the high-water mark of Helpmann's contribution to the ballet theatre, and is the work for which he will be remembered as a choreographer. Excellent performances were given by Paltenghi (Claudius), Gordon Hamilton (a wizened old Polonius), Leo Kersley (the grotesque little Gravedigger), John Hart (Laertes) and Margot Fonteyn (Ophelia), but the entire ballet was dominated by Helpmann's own performance as Hamlet. White-faced and tortured with grief, despair and hate, he was on stage throughout, subduing by sheer force of personality the other characters until they became mere figments of his imagination. It was an extraordinary achievement that electrified the audience and positively terrified some of the dancers who were on stage with him. Nevertheless, *Hamlet* was a ballet (and a performance) for a small theatre. At Covent Garden, on a larger stage, too much fresh air was let in and the terrible nightmare quality was lost.

Hamlet epitomised Helpmann's beliefs about choreography. He felt strongly that there were more things in heaven and earth than

were dreamed on by the choreographers of the old classical school
or the majority of his contemporaries, and he thought Mime was
as legitimate and as important an element of Ballet as Dancing.
In explaining his view of "The Function of Ballet" to the annual
general meeting of the Royal Academy of Dancing that year,
Helpmann said: "I . . . tried to adjust the conventional mime of
the Classical School and combine it with the movement, thereby
evolving a type of mimetic-movement which should be more
understandable to a modern audience." His allegiance was essentially to the theatre, and perhaps his own deep love of Ballet was
due to the fact that it is so completely an art of the theatre: "Its
function is in the theatre, so that its appeal must be theatrical, and
therefore to me, and I am quite sure to many other choreographers,
the first and foremost thing is to appeal to the theatregoing public
and not to a specialised few. No artist likes to imagine that his art
appeals only to a specialised few."

The appeal of Helpmann's own ballets proved to be anything
but specialised. *Hamlet* was performed thirty-one times during the
next two months, a remarkable figure even for a new production.
It was the only new production of the season, however, and the
other excitements were mostly provided by the progress of the
young dancers. Early in May, Moira Shearer appeared as the
Peasant Girl in *Orpheus and Eurydice,* and on Saturday, 11th June,
Beryl Grey celebrated her fifteenth birthday by dancing the complete
four-act version of *Le Lac des Cygnes,* partnered with much sympathy and encouragement by Robert Helpmann. Ninette de Valois
was genuinely moved by the performance, and ran round the
theatre explaining the talent and promise of this "exceptionally
wonderful child" to anyone who would listen.

Another dancer who was to play a big part in the future history
of the Sadler's Wells organisation, although as a teacher and
administrator rather than as a dancer, was Peggy van Praagh. A
pupil of Margaret Craske, she had joined the Sadler's Wells Ballet
in 1941 after the London Ballet ceased operation and was put in
charge of "academic tuition." She danced Swanilda in *Coppélia*
for the first time in London on 4th June, 1942, and subsequently
took over nearly all Mary Honer's important rôles.

At the end of the season the company suffered a serious loss
when John Hart, at the age of twenty-one, was called up and

entered the Royal Air Force. He had joined Sadler's Wells in 1938, and in 1939 had won the R.A.D. Adeline Genée Gold Medal for Male Dancers, showing "conspicuous merit." This merit had been of invaluable service to the company, particularly when the call-up made its first disastrous effect and he had to take over nearly all the leading male rôles at once. At the end of the performance on 18th July, Ninette de Valois brought him forward in his Laertes costume, and the great burst of applause from the audience was a warm expression of admiration for the way he had worked during the last few years. His departure meant that Helpmann was the only man from the pre-war company who was still with them.

Ballet was introduced to a new kind of audience in August 1942 when the Sadler's Wells company appeared for a week on an open-air concert stage at Victoria Park, Bethnal Green, in support of the Government's holidays-at-home campaign. They danced *Les Sylphides, The Gods go a'Begging* and *Façade,* and were presented by the L.C.C., by arrangement with Mr. Bronson Albery (who was managing the Ballet on behalf of the Board of Governors of the Old Vic and Sadler's Wells). Audiences varied between 1,500 and 2,200, and the Bank Holiday *matinée* was completely sold out. The audience consisted almost entirely of East Enders, who were delighted with the programme and brought hundreds of their children to "watch the ladies dance." Prices ranged from 6d. to 2s. 6d., programmes price 2d., and at the first performance the 2s. 6d. seats were honoured by the presence of the Chairman of the London County Council, Mr. J. P. Blake, the Russian Ambassador and Madame Maisky, Mr. Herbert Morrison, Sir Ernest and Lady Gowers and Lord Latham, Leader of the L.C.C.

After a record tour which attracted larger audiences than ever before, the company returned to the New Theatre for a nine-week season from 20th October. A revival of *The Rake's Progress* and a light ballet by Robert Helpmann were announced. Beryl Grey and David Paltenghi were now dancing *Le Lac des Cygnes* regularly, Moira Shearer had made a success of several solo parts and Pauline Clayden was among the new recruits. John Field, who had first attracted interest as the Strange Player in the Liverpool Ballet Club's production of *The Haunted Ballroom* in 1939, and had made steady progress since joining the Wells, inherited many of John Hart's rôles and was a particularly good Laertes. But by the following

February he too had been called up and made his last appearance as Wilfrid in *Giselle*, afterwards receiving a laurel wreath and much applause.

The Rake's Progress was restored to the repertoire on 27th October, the lost scenery and costumes having been replaced with the help of Rex Whistler, as not all the original designs had survived. Helpmann repeated his magnificent performance as the Rake and Mary Honer was the Betrayed Girl while Mavis Jackson danced occasional performances. Later Fonteyn appeared in the ballet, but it was never one of her real successes. Joy Newton repeated her original success as the bedraggled ballad singer (who dismisses any pretensions to respectability when she sends her attendant musicians packing), but almost every other member of the cast was new to the ballet. Nevertheless, they succeeded in bringing it vividly to life again, and Gordon Hamilton gave a horrifying study of insanity as the Man with a Rope. Alexis Rassine, least English of all the dancers in the company, was surprisingly good as the Rake's friend.

Towards the end of November Mary Honer resigned to accept a pantomime engagement, leaving behind her a whole gallery of delightful soubrette performances—as Swanilda, as the Bride in *A Wedding Bouquet*, the Betrayed Girl in *The Rake's Progress*, the Street Dancer in *The Prospect Before Us*, and the *fouetté* girl in *Les Patineurs*. During her nine years with Sadler's Wells she had progressed from a rather flamboyant dancer to an artist of charm and lively humour, and in some of her parts she is missed to this day.

"*The Birds*"

The Birds, Helpmann's first comedy ballet, was presented on 24th November. It was arranged for the younger dancers in the company and, like nearly all other ballets deliberately designed to exclude the leading dancers, it had only a short life. *The Birds* was a piece of nonsense about the unrequited love of a comic Hen and a dreary Cuckoo for, respectively, a romantic Dove and a beautiful Nightingale. It was set in an enchanting Chinese fairy-tale garden by Chiang Yee, but the bird costumes were only partially successful. The music was Respighi's "The Birds." Moyra Fraser managed to

wring some humour from the Hen's pathetic efforts to be a nightingale, and Beryl Grey and Alexis Rassine danced their formal *pas
de deux* well enough, but the choreography was never very distinguished, and the liveliest moments were provided by Margaret
Dale and Joan Sheldon (Phillips) as a pair of perky sparrows. The
ballet may have been intended to demonstrate that Helpmann
could create light ballets with a large content of dancing, but it
only reinforced the opinion that his *forte* was for dramatic production. Constant Lambert's overture, *The Bird Actors*, which was
played as an overture to the ballet, gave as much delight as anything
that followed.

The company spent a happy Christmas in York and then visited
Bradford before taking a short holiday and returning to London.
Margot Fonteyn danced her first Swanilda on this tour and it was
with *Coppélia* that the London season opened on 25th January 1943.
Fonteyn was partnered by Alexis Rassine, and Helpmann continued
to steal the show as Dr. Coppelius, although Fonteyn gave him a
run for his money in the second act. Throughout she gave a performance of great vitality, but the gaiety seemed sometimes a little
forced and she always seemed to be acting—with all the talent she
could muster—a rôle in which she could find little real conviction.
Peggy van Praagh, temperamentally and physically far better suited
to Swanilda, shared the ballet with Fonteyn, but Sadler's Wells
never made much use of her talents as a dancer-artist. Perhaps de
Valois was already beginning to think of her primarily as a teacher,
and as an admirable person to take charge of a second company,
if and when it could be launched.

The increased number of performances being given was proving
too arduous for Constant Lambert by this time, and so Julian Clifford
was appointed associate conductor to relieve him of part of the
burden of conducting.

Ashton's "The Quest"

Towards the end of the season Frederick Ashton was given
special leave from the R.A.F. to create a new ballet, and he worked
on this during the spring tour which followed. The ballet was to
be based on an episode from Spenser's *Faery Queen*, and was to
have music specially composed by William Walton. The *décor*
and costumes were by John Piper, his first work for the theatre.

The story had been suggested to Ashton by Doris Langley Moore, and it concerned the search of a Red Cross Knight, Saint George, for Una who symbolises Truth. After many obstacles have been put in his way by Archimago the Magician—three Saracen Knights, Falsehood and all seven Deadly Sins—he is eventually united with Una and takes her to the House of Holiness, where he leaves her with Faith, Hope and Charity, pledges himself to England and sets out on his quest.

Ashton provided Walton with a very detailed scenario and tentative suggestions about the sort of music he had in mind, but time was limited and Walton had to send the music to the choreographer sheet by sheet as it was finished. Thus Ashton was forced to create his ballet piecemeal as the music arrived without ever having an opportunity to hear it as a complete score. It was finished in time for the advertised gala *première* at the New Theatre on 6th April (the proceeds on this occasion going to Lady Cripps' Aid to China Fund), but it was not surprising that *The Quest* proved to be a rather incoherent ballet.

There were some charming passages for Fonteyn as Una, some vigorous fights for the Saracens, one or two good variations for the Deadly Sins, and a final scene of utter quietness and beauty, but the ballet demonstrated all too clearly that masterpieces are not created to order within a given time limit. William Walton's score was interesting and often beautiful, and in easier circumstances might have inspired Ashton to create a fine ballet. John Piper's settings were attractive, but his costumes, particularly for the Palace of Pride scene, were far less successful. Helpmann walked about with an air of patient resignation, possibly due to the uninspiring nature of his costume, a white tunic emblazoned with the cross of Saint George. At early performances he wore a wig of golden curls but soon abandoned this and appeared with his own contemporary hair-cut which, as always, looked absurd in conjunction with a fantastic costume. Moira Shearer had her first important creation in this ballet as Pride, while Beryl Grey appeared as the false Duessa in an unpleasantly shiny magenta costume. Leslie Edwards, recently invalided out of the Forces, was outstandingly good as the magician Archimago. While it remained a patriotic novelty, *The Quest* had a certain success, but it did not enjoy, and did not deserve, a long life.

M

Despite the uneven quality of these last two productions, the popularity of the Sadler's Wells Ballet had reached such dimensions by the spring of 1943 that seat rationing had to be introduced at the New Theatre box office. Four seats for any one performance was the maximum allowed to each patron, and not more than a total of twelve seats over the season in any one application. The back stalls, priced at 4s. and 5s., were put on sale on the day of the performance only, so that members of the Forces on leave might find some seats available at short notice.

Another London season was given in May-June with a revival of *A Wedding Bouquet* as the special attraction. There was now a full orchestra, but Constant Lambert continued his unmatchable performance as orator. Installed in one of the lower boxes at the New Theatre he provided a link between stage and audience, and was close enough to the dancers to become at times part of the action. The careful deliberation with which he explained, "What is a clever saucer?"—"It is very likely practised and even has toes. It has tiny little things to shake, and were it not for its delicate blue colour would there be any reason for anyone to perceive a difference?"—was as much part of the ballet as the rapt attention with which Helpmann listened or his bow of acknowledgment for such a completely satisfying explanation. Margaret Dale took over Mary Honer's part as the Bride, and contributed an idiotic simper that was all her own.

An interesting experiment in the summer of 1943 was the appointment of Andrée Howard as choreographer to the Sadler's Wells Ballet School in order that she might create ballets for the students. "Choreographic Production" was now listed in the curriculum, and this work, together with tuition in the classical and modern repertoire, was all part of the School's special service as a training ground for a repertory ballet. Some examples of Andrée Howard's work with the students were shown at a *matinée* arranged that July by the R.A.D. Production Club when students from the Sadler's Wells School performed a *Suite of Dances* she had arranged to Handel's "Water Music." The dances were charming and the students an exceptionally talented group. They were Rosemary Scott-Giles (now Lindsay), Joan Valerie, Pauline Wadsworth, Avril Navarre, Philip Chatfield and Brian Earnshaw (now Shaw).

When the season ended on 26th June the company had a badly

needed two-week holiday before reassembling to start work on the autumn season. During the year which had just ended they had given 185 performances in London, compared with 205 during a roughly similar period in 1941–42. The proportion of classical ballets in the repertoire had dropped to about one-quarter instead of one-third as formerly. *Façade* was again at the head of the list of modern ballets, having been danced some forty times in London and a great many more times on tour, but it had a temporary rival in *The Birds*, which also achieved forty London performances.

The ballet was back at the New Theatre before the end of August with a new production of *Le Lac des Cygnes*, promised for 7th September. Julian Clifford had left and Alec Sherman replaced him as associate conductor. The season opened quietly and Fonteyn was absent for a short time on sick leave. Her part in *The Quest* was danced with touching sincerity by Pauline Clayden, and Beryl Grey made a success of Ophelia in *Hamlet*.

The first performance of *Le Lac des Cygnes* was planned as a benefit for Nicolai Sergueeff who had done such valuable work in reconstructing the classical productions for Sadler's Wells, and who had resigned from his teaching post at the school at the end of the summer. (He was replaced by Vera Volkova.) The ballet was given in a slightly compressed form, the first and second acts being played straight through without an interval and the *pas de trois* being danced in the third act, together with the Spanish Dance, Czardas and Mazurka. The entire production was designed by Leslie Hurry, and it was the most expensive and ambitious that the company had mounted. Hurry had made a close study of the ballet and the music before starting work, but it was a formidable undertaking and, in addition he had to contend with war-time shortages of fabrics and materials for building scenery. His designs were in most respects exciting and beautiful, and he had been able to give the ballet a touch of grandeur and opulence which it had never attained before at Sadler's Wells. Criticism was, however, directed against the painter's personal conception of romanticism which produced a strange, almost subterranean grotto for the "lakeside" set and introduced a swan motif into the *décor* throughout that was rather an illustration of the ballet than a setting for it. His design for a drop curtain (which, on the advice of Ninette de Valois, was never used) contains all of *Le Lac des Cygnes*—swans, castle, ruins, crown and baleful owl: indeed, there would have been little need for music, choreography or dancing. Many of the costumes were completely successful, particularly those for Benno, the Prince Siegfried, Odette and Odile, the magician Rothbart and the dancers of the *pas de trois*. The prospective brides no longer looked like poor relations but wore simple diaphanous dresses, trimmed in silver and with underskirts of shimmering rainbow tulle.

The ballet was well received and was the chief attraction throughout the season. Fonteyn and Helpmann danced the first performance with their customary skill, and Margaret Dale, Joan Sheldon and Alexis Rassine performed an excellent *pas de trois*. Later Beryl Grey and David Paltenghi were seen in the principal rôles, and Beryl Grey continued to astonish with the easy fluency and assurance of her dancing. Paltenghi was, and continued to be for several years, a good and reliable partner and an adequate mime. He had started too late ever to acquire much technique, but he rapidly learned a few tricks of the trade from Helpmann, and performed the few fragments of classical dancing that come the way of the cardboard princes with a most convincing assurance.

The London season ended on 16th October and was followed by a tour during which the first performance of a new de Valois ballet, *Promenade*, was given at the King's Theatre, Edinburgh, on 25th October.

While the Ballet was away on tour Pamela May made her return to the stage, dancing with Sasha Machov in the Sadler's Wells Opera production of *The Bartered Bride*. She rejoined the ballet company during their winter season, which began on 30th November, and made a great comeback in her original part in *Dante Sonata* on 18th December. During the early weeks of this season several changes of programme had to be made on account of ill health in the company, and there were last-minute substitutions in the cast of *Promenade* before its London *première*. Beryl Grey, who had the principal part, fell ill shortly before the opening and with typical generosity Margot Fonteyn offered to go on for her young colleague. In the final "Danse des Paysannes" Margaret Dale took over from Peggy van Praagh, also at the last minute, but despite these hurried alterations the ballet was admirably performed.

De Valois' "Promenade"

Promenade was a very slight suite of dances, linked by the person of a quavery old lepidopterist who continued his singleminded pursuit of butterflies no matter what was going on around him. The music had been selected from the works of Haydn (mostly from symphonies or piano sonatas, orchestrated by Gordon Jacob), by Edwin Evans, and he described the resulting score as "a short stroll through the works of Haydn." It was entirely delightful and, in fact, so good that it rather overwhelmed the flimsy choreography. When well danced, however, *Promenade* was an attractive opening ballet, and in its early days it was exceptionally well cast. Gordon Hamilton was the Lepidopterist, Pauline Clayden danced the gawky "Promenade" solo, Beryl Grey (and later Pamela May) with David Paltenghi gave a nice melancholy to the "Rendezvous" *pas de deux*, and the gay little *pas de trois* for two classical and one character dancer was brilliantly performed by Moira Shearer, Alexis Rassine and Ray Powell. Shearer never looked prettier than in the crisp pink and white costume she wore in this ballet, and the choreography exactly suited her dainty elegance. Her successors had an impossible task in following her, and none of them ever made anything of the part.

The ballet ended with a very fast and gay "Danse des Paysannes" and Finale, based on steps and figurations of Breton folk dances, with which de Valois was assisted by Lieutenant J. de Cadenet, of the Fighting French Air Force. The ending had a vitality that recalled *Le Beau Danube*, and was so good that it tended to leave the audience with the impression that it had seen a better ballet than was really the case; but, though slight, *Promenade* was not unattractive, and its very slightness did not become so apparent until it suffered the usual fate of alternative and inferior casts and too frequent performance.

Job was revived on 22nd December with slightly smaller numbers (eight Children of God and four Sons of the Morning, compared with ten and six at the Wells) but it did not lose in impressiveness, and Helpmann was still there to dance Satan. David Paltenghi appeared as Elihu, and Julia Farron, Palma Nye and Celia Franca were particularly handsome as the three daughters of Job in Gwendolen Raverat's richly coloured costumes. It was a welcome addition to the repertoire, a calm and ordered composition of lasting beauty.

Le Spectre de la Rose was revived on 1st February for Margot Fonteyn and Alexis Rassine, with considerable help from Tamara Karsavina who had created the ballet with Nijinsky for Diaghileff in 1911. The little work was envisaged very much as a ballet and not just a romantic *pas de deux*, and Rex Whistler was invited to design not only the setting and costumes but also a drop curtain. Once again, however, Sadler's Wells were to come to grief in a Fokine ballet. The setting was far too colourful and elegant, and the drop curtain, showing a nude male figure curled up asleep at the very heart of an enormous cabbage rose, was both unattractive and redundant. Fonteyn's costume was altogether too pretty and her curls and make-up were nearer Hollywood than ballet. The costume for Alexis Rassine resembled a pink one-piece bathing costume of the cut favoured by local authorities at public swimming baths. There was a vague pattern of rose petals which looked as if it had run in the wash and no amount of good dancing on Rassine's part could have overcome this unfortunate appearance. The utter simplicity and rapt dream quality of the ballet was completely lost, although there were signs in Fonteyn's performance that she might have given a lovely interpretation had the general production been better.

Helpmann did not go on tour with the ballet after this season as he was to act in *Hamlet* with the Old Vic. In his absence there was some reshuffling of casts, and during this tour Alexis Rassine gave his first performance as Albrecht in *Giselle*. Paltenghi appeared in *Comus* (omitting the speeches) and *Hamlet*, and Leslie Edwards as the Rake. In Derby, Beryl Grey danced her first Giselle, and another auspicious début was made at the King's Theatre, Hammersmith, later in the spring, when Moira Shearer danced Odile in *Le Lac des Cygnes* to the Odette of Pamela May. Among promising new recruits were Gillian Lynne, Avril Navarre, Anne Negus and Henry Danton.

When the company returned to London, Fonteyn was temporarily disabled by a foot injury, so the opening night performance of *Le Lac des Cygnes* on 30th May was danced by Beryl Grey and David Paltenghi, who received an enthusiastic Press.

The only new production of this season was by Andrée Howard, *Le Festin de l'Araignée*, later called *The Spider's Banquet*. The music by Albert Roussel had been composed in 1912 for a ballet scenario by Gilbert de Voisins, a descendant of Marie Taglioni, and the ballet had been produced with choreography by Leo Staats at the Théâtre des Arts in Paris in April 1913. The music had made Roussel's name as a composer and it has been used by several choreographers since Staats.

Michael Ayrton, a pupil of Eugene Berman and a close friend of Constant Lambert, who had designed a fine *Macbeth* for Gielgud in 1940, was invited to decorate the ballet. The setting was a sub-tropical garden in the South of France with all the vegetation magnified to the proportions of an insect point of view, so that the dancers were correspondingly dwarfed. A spider builds her web and ensnares several insects, but before she can enjoy her banquet she is stabbed by a praying mantis who has escaped from the web. The other creatures make their escape and night falls on the deserted garden.

Settings, costumes and choreography were all realistic, and showed considerable awareness of the cruelty of the insect world and its brief span of life. It was a grim little ballet, but too detached in its documentary style to be moving or continuously interesting in the theatre. It was as if the choreographer had felt little inspiration and had simply performed an honest job of work. The only appealing figure was the Mayfly, whose few hours of happiness were well suggested by Pauline Clayden. Moira Shearer could make nothing of the Butterfly, poorly costumed and conventionally presented, and although Celia Franca gave plenty of venom to the Spider, she had little to do but climb about her web or move grotesquely about the stage on full *pointe* with bent knees.

The ballet received its first performance at the height of the flying bomb attacks on London, and during these hot summer months performances were frequently interrupted by aid-raid warnings and ominous crashes in the distance. One night during a performance of *The Gods go a'Begging,* a flying bomb came down in Long Acre, only a few hundred yards from the New Theatre. The blast blew open the doors at the back of the Dress Circle, but the dancers never faltered and the audience remained quietly in their seats.

On account of this new danger, however, the Sadler's Wells Ballet School closed for the summer holidays at an early date, and a scheme to give a special *matinée* performance of some of the standard works in the repertoire by students of the School was abandoned. It had been intended that *Promenade, The Birds* and *Les Patineurs* should be presented as an experiment, although there was a hope in Ninette de Valois' mind that it might be the beginning of a Children's Theatre Movement of the future which could contain performances of ballet by children for children.

The year 1943–44 had been one of the most exhausting the Sadler's Wells Ballet had ever lived through. They had danced for forty-eight weeks out of fifty-two, and had given no less than 245 performances in London. The new production of *Le Lac des Cygnes* had been performed fifty-four times, *Promenade* had suffered sixty-eight performances and *Les Sylphides* fifty-four. With such a schedule of performances it was not surprising that individual programmes should sometimes be rather thin, but there was sometimes resentment in the audience on those occasions when they were offered nothing more than *Promenade, Le Spectre de la Rose* and *Le Festin de l'Araignée,* a bare two hours' entertainment containing two long intervals.

After a much-needed holiday, the company came back to London in good spirits but to a new home. This time they danced at the Princes Theatre in Shaftesbury Avenue, which had on occasions housed the Diaghileff company, although the Russians had found the stage somewhat small. The auditorium was considerably larger than the New Theatre, seating some 1,850, and the stage was larger in total area, but steeply raked and shallower in depth. The company had no difficulty in filling the theatre for every performance from their opening on 27th September until the end of the season on 2nd December. For the first time they adopted the practice of advertising the names of the principal dancers in such ballets as *Le Lac des Cygnes, Coppélia* and *Giselle.*

The season opened with *Coppélia,* the same ballet that had closed the previous London season. On 10th October *Carnaval* was revived in the Bakst *décor* and costumes, an improved rendering, although not entirely satisfactory. There were some excellent individual performances, chief among them being Pamela May's Chiarina and Julia Farron's Estrella, but the majority of the dancers still seemed unaware of the true nature of the ballet. Margot Fonteyn was inclined to smile too much as Columbine, and she had a very fussy hair style, a tangle of curls and cherries. Rassine, the new Harlequin, danced quite well, although he never came anywhere near the bone and sinew of the part. Jean Cocteau's description of Nijinsky's Harlequin gives so many clues to the dancer—"Half Hermes, half harlequin, cat and acrobat by turns, now frankly lascivious, now slyly indifferent . . ."—but Rassine seemed content just to dance it and contribute an occasional wag of the head for character. Helpmann's Pierrot moved some spectators a great deal, but others were always conscious of an underlying streak of sophistication which robbed the performance of pathos.

"Miracle in the Gorbals"

This sophistication, a detached awareness of theatrical effects and what would "get" the public, also marred for some people Helpmann's next ballet, Miracle in the Gorbals. This work began as a detailed scenario written by Michael Benthall, who had first thought of the idea while working on a gun-site in Glasgow. He was as much a man of the theatre as Helpmann and was thoroughly familiar with the world of ballet, so that the story was envisaged and described from the beginning as a work for the ballet stage. Helpmann and Benthall invited Edward Burra to design the ballet and Arthur Bliss to compose the music. It was a close and genuine collaboration. Bliss worked from the scenario and the designs and himself suggested to Helpmann the use of poses and gestures from El Greco's paintings.

The theme to which these distinguished people devoted their talents was a modern morality which sought to show that if Christ came again on earth he would meet a similar reception, although in this case death was to be by broken bottles and razor slashing instead of crucifixion. The setting was a sordid street between tenement buildings in the Gorbals district of Glasgow. A bar and a fish and chip shop formed part of the settings and in the background by the dockside a beggar crouched beside an overflowing garbage can. In the midst of much rowdy Saturday night gaiety a Suicide is brought in from the river. A Stranger appears and restores her to life. The simple people are at first overawed by the miracle and eager to become his disciples, but a brown-coated Official, resenting this challenge to his authority, incites the people against the Stranger with the help of a Prostitute, and the toughs of the district murder him most brutally. The Beggar, the would-be Suicide and the reformed Prostitute are left to mourn over his body.

The costumes were virtually realistic mass-produced cheap clothing and the setting a realistic street painting. The most distinguished piece of design was the drop curtain, the great hull of a ship at its moorings. The dancing was slight in content, and the ballet depended much more on dramatic movement and mime for its progression. The most interesting dance episode occurred after the miracle. This began as a simple barefoot reel for the girl, watched by the kneeling crowd, but gradually the entire company were drawn into the dance and the mounting frenzy of mob excitement was brilliantly conveyed. The score was intensely dramatic and just the right length, driving home the points of the story, and at the end excruciatingly realistic in its suggestion of slashing and beating.

Miracle in the Gorbals made a very strong impact in the theatre and audiences reacted to it strongly. It was variously described as a magnificent piece of contemporary drama, an extension of the frontiers of ballet, or else a piece of slap-up melodrama created with more than one eye on the box office. The religious Press was almost wholly favourable: "A powerful indictment of sin and a terrible picture of tenement society," said the *Catholic Herald*. Herbert Farjeon, a great admirer of Helpmann's work and an old friend of the Ballet, was disturbed by the treatment: "I will even go so far as to say that it is people who enjoy art of the type of *No Orchids for Miss Blandish* who will most enjoy the slices of low life and thuggism that dominate the action." [1] Haskell called it a "masterly dance drama" and was sufficiently enthusiastic to write a small book about it. Cyril Beaumont, on the other hand, after giving careful consideration to the virtues and weaknesses of the production, came to the conclusion: "Interesting as this production is in many ways, it is questionable whether such themes are suited to translation in terms of ballet, and whether this is not one of those occasions when the desire to achieve a sensational work has not overruled a proper sense of the fitness of things."

There were few dancing opportunities in the ballet, but all

[1] A programme note at one time advised patrons "not to bring young children to performances of this ballet."

thirty-five members of the cast had to give first-rate acting performances. Pauline Clayden's Suicide had much nervous tension
and pathos, Leslie Edwards gave a wonderfully sympathetic picture
of the Beggar, and David Paltenghi finely suggested the conflicting
fears and temptations of the Official. (Later, John Hart gave an
even better performance in this difficult part.) Helpmann allowed
himself little variety as the Stranger, being content to walk through
the ballet with an air of sanctity that might well have antagonised
any hard-boiled community. Without question, however, the
company brought the ballet magnificently to life, and once again
Helpmann captured the interest of the public, for *Miracle in the
Gorbals* attracted very large audiences.[1]

The last important event of the season was a revival of *Nocturne*
on 28th November. Frederick Ashton took advantage of a week's
leave to conduct final rehearsals and appear in his original rôle of
the Spectator.

At the end of the first performance he received a great ovation
from the audience and made one of his rare speeches from the
stage. "I want to thank you for the affection with which you have
remembered my ballet," he said, "and to tell you how pleased I
am to discover that, after three and a half years' absence, I can still
raise my arms."

When the season ended Ninette de Valois thanked the audience
for its continued support at the larger theatre, but was unable to
give any precise details of future plans. A provincial tour, with
Christmas in York, would be followed by a continental tour for
ENSA and the British Council, but after that plans were still
uncertain. The British Council had been anxious to send the company to South America on a goodwill mission from about May to
September 1945, and negotiations for this tour reached a fairly
advanced stage before the plan was eventually abandoned. Transport demands were then at peak level, both in the European and
Pacific theatres of war, and shortage of shipping space was the
reason given for the cancellation of the tour. When the war ended
the visit ceased to be diplomatically necessary, but in any case it

---

[1] Stanley Holden first attracted attention as an urchin in this ballet. He was
required to roll a motor tyre across the front of the stage, and on at least one
happy evening managed to send it over the footlights into the orchestra. The
comments of the Musicians' Union are not recorded.

is doubtful whether the company was really in shape to undertake such a mission in 1945. The rather tired Sadler's Wells company, with war scars still showing in many of its productions and the personnel depleted by the call-up and after-effects of military service, was in no state to take British culture to the wealthy cities and vast opera houses of South America, where shortages and rationing were unknown and where brilliant audiences would have utterly eclipsed the brave but inevitably tarnished splendour of most of the productions.

The less ambitious visit to Belgium and France, however, was highly successful. The company, numbering over eighty and including an orchestra of thirty, set off at the end of January in the midst of a bitterly cold spell. Fitted out in ENSA khaki uniforms and bundled up in fur gloves, boots and thick scarves, they never-theless were extremely cold during the journey and not much warmer when they arrived in Brussels. There was thick snow on the ground, no electric light in the city from 7 a.m. to 6 p.m., no heating and no hot water at any time. This continued for four days, and the theatre staff had to work late into the night to get every-thing ready for the next evening's performance as it was impossible to work in the theatre without electric light during the day. After four days the thaw set in and conditions improved, and the only difficulty then was an epidemic of 'flu which "laid the company out in a strict but quite orderly rotation." Consequently when John Hart turned up to watch a performance he was greeted with joy and sent on stage at once in *Les Patineurs*.

The first performance was given at the Théâtre des Variétés for ENSA and during the three weeks' stay in Brussels three public gala performances were also given at the Théâtre Royal de la Monnaie under the auspices of the British Council. These per-formances were all sold out within a few hours of the box office opening, and the company had a great reception.

On 19th February the first contingent left for Paris. No train between Brussels and Paris could, at that time, take the full com-pany and orchestra, and they had to travel in two parties. The rail journey, which in peacetime lasts for some four hours, took between thirteen and fifteen hours. Nevertheless, they opened at the Marigny Theatre in Paris on the 21st and played for a week and a half to ENSA audiences that consisted of 85 per cent. American troops.

They were sold out for every performance, Sundays included, and the success continued when the British Council presented them at the Théâtre des Champs-Élysées for a further eight performances. A single programme was given at the theatre in Versailles, where the company danced *Les Sylphides, The Rake's Progress* and *Façade* against black curtains.

The excitement of being back in Paris was intense. The dancers took classes with the great Russian teachers, visited the Paris Opéra and were warmly entertained everywhere. After six years' artistic isolation they were eager to talk with French designers, musicians and dancers again, and they were introduced to Roland Petit, Renée Jeanmaire, Ludmilla Tcherina and others who were then just on the verge of careers that were radically to affect the future course of French ballet. It was at an ENSA performance in France that Captain Michael Benthall saw his ballet *Miracle in the Gorbals* for the first time.

After a month in Paris the Ballet returned to Belgium to play five performances in the old opera house of Ghent, to an audience of troops who would have cheerfully packed the theatre for a fortnight. Accommodation was so difficult in Ghent, which was swarming with Allied troops, that all male members of the company had to sleep in the theatre, a big rehearsal room being converted into a dormitory. One civilian performance was given there, and afterwards single performances at Bruges and Ostend. The repertoire for this tour consisted of *Les Sylphides, Carnaval, Les Patineurs, Promenade, The Rake's Progress, Hamlet, Miracle in the Gorbals, Façade* and *Dante Sonata,* all presented with full orchestra, costumes and scenery. The Sadler's Wells Ballet had the proud distinction of being the largest company to have been sent out by ENSA and the first British company to entertain European civilian audiences since the declaration of war.

As the South American trip had not materialised the company returned to the New Theatre on 17th April, and remained there for a ten-week season. Alec Sherman left and his place was taken by Geoffrey Corbett, who had been chorus master and assistant conductor at Sadler's Wells before the war and had been serving with the R.N.V.R. Two of the company's best male dancers returned to them in April, Michael Somes and Harold Turner, both of whom had been discharged from the Forces for medical reasons, and Frederick Ashton was back before the end of the season. Michael Somes appeared on the opening night as Pierrot in *Carnaval* and discharged the job honourably if unspectacularly. (He had been badly injured in a lorry accident while in the Army and had to undergo a serious operation. He made a remarkable recovery, but was to feel the effects of the injury on occasions for many years to come.) Harold Turner made his come-back in his most famous rôle, the blue skater in *Les Patineurs,* which had never been quite the same without him. He gave the part a sturdiness, a wit and a speed that no other dancer quite captured, although Leo Kersley came near to it and Michael Boulton has since captured the tongue-in-cheek perky humour.

On Saturday afternoon, 21st April, Pamela May gave her first London performance as Swanilda in *Coppélia,* a portrait of delightful gaiety and wit. Her performance was a surprise to many people who had thought of her as coldly classical, yet curiously enough she was not equalled in this part at Sadler's Wells until another purely classical dancer, Svetlana Beriosova, came to play it. Michael Somes was soon dancing the four acts of *Le Lac des Cygnes* with Beryl Grey, and Pamela May also danced the full ballet, with David Paltenghi. The company was beginning to get back to something like a proper complement of male and female dancers, and in some respects was stronger than it had ever been. On V.E. night they were dancing *Coppélia,* and Helpmann could not be restrained from improvising his own celebrations on stage. Coppélia's balcony was decked with flags and the last act got completely out of hand.

On 7th June, after nearly five years of darkness, Sadler's Wells Theatre reopened, and on 24th July the ballet company went back to its original home for an eight-week season. There was a certain sentimental interest in the occasion, but it was very apparent that the company had outgrown both the facilities and the requirements of Sadler's Wells. They had a successful season and revived *The Haunted Ballroom, Job* and *The Wanderer,* in which Gillian Lynne gave a performance of great power and plastic beauty in the second movement. It was to be the last occasion on which *Job* would be seen in its original Raverat designs and *The Wanderer* has not since been revived. Sixty-three performances of ballet were given at the Wells, and with the previous seasons at the New and

Princes Theatre this brought the total of London performances during the year to 227. *Miracle in the Gorbals* had moved to the head of the list as the most frequently performed ballet, having had forty-five performances in London, but *The Birds* had been dropped.

In mid-November the company was to go to Germany for some ten weeks for ENSA (without Fonteyn and led by Pamela May), and at the end of the Sadler's Wells season Ninette de Valois made a cautious announcement that they hoped "to be back in London early in the New Year." It was not then possible to make an official announcement, but most people had a fairly shrewd idea where the company would be dancing in London in future. A clue was provided by the promoters of Mecca Dancing, who announced that ballroom dancing at the Royal Opera House, Covent Garden, would come to an end on Saturday, 20th October. Under the Mecca management the Opera House had flourished as a dance hall throughout the war, and it was estimated that some six million people—the Servicemen of all nationalities as well as civilians— had danced there. Mecca Dancing relinquished the Opera House with regret, for they would have liked to continue there as well as at the Lyceum Theatre, which was being converted to a dance hall. It was stated that Covent Garden would in future be devoted to Opera and Ballet.

PART V

THE ROYAL OPERA HOUSE, COVENT GARDEN

CHAPTER X

THE FIRST SEASON

IN the autumn of 1945 an official announcement was made about the future activities of the Sadler's Wells Ballet. The Governors of Sadler's Wells and the Covent Garden Committee had agreed that after 1st January 1946 the ballet company should operate under the management of the Covent Garden Committee for an initial period of four years. The Sadler's Wells School of Ballet would continue under the direction of the Governors of Sadler's Wells and a second ballet company was to be formed at Sadler's Wells Theatre. Ninette de Valois was to be Director of the Sadler's Wells Ballet, the Sadler's Wells School and the new company. Both the Governors of Sadler's Wells and the Covent Garden Committee were to work in close association with the Arts Council of Great Britain.

From this time forward the Arts Council was to play an increasingly important part in the life of the Sadler's Wells Ballet, and some brief account of the Council's own development is necessary. At the end of 1939 it had been suggested to the Pilgrim Trust that it might be desirable to set up a Committee to provide financial assistance for the arts in wartime. The Secretary of the Trust was then Dr. Thomas Jones, and he took up the idea with enthusiasm. The Pilgrim Trust, which had been in existence since 1930, was a charitable body which administered a fund originally provided by the American business magnate Stephen Harkness for the promotion of culture. Aid for the arts in wartime was a cause likely to appeal to the Trustees, and they voted a sum of £25,000 for this purpose. A committee of six people, under the Chairmanship of Lord Macmillan, then Chairman of the Pilgrim Trust, was set up to administer the fund, and the Board of Education immediately provided offices and a secretary, Miss Mary Glasgow. It was decided to call the committee the Council for the Encouragement of Music and the Arts, a name quickly abbreviated to CEMA.

In April 1940 the Treasury came into the picture and agreed to double the initial contribution of £25,000, and to do the same with all future donations, pound for pound, up to £50,000, in recognition of the value and importance of the work that was being done. Aid was given to certain large orchestras, to amateur and professional drama, to the Old Vic Drama and the Sadler's Wells Opera companies. The principle having been established, the Council successfully launched and official support obtained, the Pilgrim Trust felt that its work was accomplished, and after about two years withdrew from CEMA. Lord Macmillan retired and Lord Keynes became the new Chairman on 31st March 1942.

Keynes took up the idea with his customary enthusiasm, and was very largely responsible for the subsequent extension of the now accepted principle of the need for Government support for the arts in a community where private patronage is becoming increasingly rare. The duty of CEMA during the war was "to maintain the opportunities of artistic performance for the hard-pressed and often exiled civilians," and it was concerned only with high art: popular entertainment for Servicemen and war workers was left to ENSA. From the first Keynes laid particular emphasis on the importance of maintaining standards, and he also contended that the various projects should be, in the main, self-supporting and economically well managed at least so far as their daily working was concerned. He favoured guarantees and grants for the purpose of establishing a theatrical project, for instance, but did not expect it to run thereafter at a heavy and continual loss. His interest in the Sadler's Wells Ballet was, of course, of long standing, but the work it accomplished throughout the war, both before and during its association with CEMA, increased his admiration continually.

Towards the end of the war, when his mind was much occupied with future plans and "economic possibilities for our grand-children," Keynes came to the conclusion that CEMA must not be allowed to disappear from the scene, and he was instrumental in persuading the Treasury and the Ministry of Education to put it on a permanent basis with the title of the Arts Council of Great Britain. He introduced the new body in a broadcast talk in July 1945: "At the start our aim was to replace what war had taken away; but we soon found that we were providing what had never existed even in peacetime. That is why one of the last acts of the Coalition Government was to decide that CEMA with a new name and wider opportunities should be continued into time of peace. Henceforward we are to be a permanent body, independent in constitution, free from red tape, but financed by the Treasury and ultimately responsible to Parliament, which will have to be satisfied with what we are doing when from time to time it votes us money. . . . Our name is to be the Arts Council of Great Britain. I hope you will call us the Arts Council for short, and not try to turn our initials into a false, invented word. We have carefully selected initials which we hope are unpronounceable."

Throughout his association with CEMA, Keynes had come increasingly to believe that in the post-war future London must set a standard which should be an example to the rest of the country and he was naturally interested in the future of Covent Garden. When negotiations about the use of the Opera House began in 1944 he threw himself into them with enthusiasm. The well-known firm of music publishers, Messrs. Boosey & Hawkes, had taken a five years' lease of the Royal Opera House, and the result of their discussions with CEMA was that a Covent Garden Opera Trust[1] was set up to provide a new kind of direction which would not only revive Covent Garden as an opera house but ensure that it gave more scope to native talent. Lord Keynes became the first Chairman of the Trust, although he continued also to be Chairman of CEMA and subsequently of the Arts Council. The administration of the theatre was placed in the hands of David Webster, who had managed the Liverpool Philharmonic Society very successfully during the war. (He had come into contact with the Vic-Wells Ballet during the 'thirties when he had been associated with the Liverpool Ballet Club, an active organisation which used to mount classical and modern ballets, assisted by guest artists from the Wells.)

The Covent Garden Opera Trust was faced with a formidable task. Its immediate purpose was to establish a resident opera company and a resident ballet company, of the highest standard and consisting mainly of British artists, which together would make Covent Garden the centre of the capital's musical life throughout the year. There was every intention of inviting foreign companies to appear there as well, but the old pre-war system of occasional

[1] In 1950 the Trust was reorganised as "The Royal Opera House, Covent Garden Limited."

spectacular seasons of Grand Opera or Russian Ballet followed by months of inactivity were at an end. The building of a national opera company of the quality worthy of a great opera house was to take many years of trial and error, but a truly national ballet company was already in existence, and the first action of the Trust was to invite the Governors of Sadler's Wells to lease them the Sadler's Wells Ballet *en masse* for an initial period of four years.

The Governors of Sadler's Wells, with a generosity and an unselfish concern for the best interests of the ballet company that has never been sufficiently appreciated, agreed to the transfer, although they lost their biggest money-maker, received no adequate compensation and were to feel the effects of the loss financially for years to come. As they remarked a little wistfully in the Annual Report for 1945–46: "The Ballet has now gone to Covent Garden. . . . We are left with the Ballet School and the task of building up a second ballet company under the direction of Ninette de Valois." During the period July–December 1945 the Ballet had shown a profit of almost nine thousand pounds (including as much as £729. 16s. 3d. on the sale of photographs). When it was transferred to the management of the Covent Garden Opera Trust at 31st December 1945, Sadler's Wells was faced with heavy capital expenditure in assembling and launching a new company, and, despite a guarantee against loss from the Arts Council for £5,000, the results of the first year's working of this company showed a loss of over £3,000. But no word of complaint was made, and it was not until the reserves of Sadler's Wells were almost exhausted in 1950 that the matter of respective grants, expenses and commitments was called in question.

The acquisition of the Sadler's Wells Ballet was of very great value to the Covent Garden Opera Trust, and of prime importance in its efforts to establish a National Lyric Theatre. It was also to be of service to the art of ballet, in that it helped to keep the opera house open throughout the year and thus to make it available to other ballet companies of the world. The Arts Council was prepared to make handsome contributions towards the work of the Trust, and the Ballet would have the benefit of this increased financial security. All profits, however, would be ploughed back into the work of the opera house, and although the salaries of the principal artists might be considerably higher than in the old days at Sadler's Wells, no one connected with the Ballet stood to make a fortune from the change in situation and in status. The time had come, however, when such a move was not only desirable but imperative for the further development of the company.

To mark time must eventually mean to slip back, and by 1945 the Sadler's Wells Ballet had reached a stage in its artistic progress beyond which, under existing conditions, it could not advance any farther. The Governors of Sadler's Wells had been the first to admit that to base such a company once again out in Islington and limit its performances to two or three a week would have been a retrograde step and would have kept it perpetually in low water financially. This would have restricted the scope of the productions and kept salaries low. By 1945 the leading dancers were no longer potential stars, but stars with very great reputations. Many of them had been with the company for ten years or more, and were entitled to see some reward for such devoted service. Geographically, Sadler's Wells on its bleak corner in Islington, remote from the West End, was not the place for a national company which had by now a genuinely national public.

Covent Garden, on the other hand, offered the ballet a home in the heart of the capital, the fashionable centre of London's musical life. There would be room for more dancers and a larger *corps de ballet,* for productions of the size and grandeur required for the proper presentation of the big classical ballets, and for an orchestra of opera house dimensions. Dancers were steadily rejoining after release from the Services, and once they were back and in form again, and with the resources of the School to draw upon and the probable recruitment of occasional outstanding dancers from else-where (*the Sadler's Wells Ballet never has been and never will be a "closed shop" reserved for graduates of its own school*), it was hoped to build the company into a unit comparable with the greatest companies of both the present and the past.

There were to be regular London seasons and freedom to tour abroad when opportunity offered. The few visits which the company had already made to the Continent had indicated how much interest there would be in longer peacetime tours, and in due course visits to America were also envisaged. Ninette de Valois had known ever since she produced *The Sleeping Princess* in 1939 that if her company was to become a truly national organisation, capable of playing in the great national opera houses of the world such as Paris and New York, it must be based at Covent Garden and have sufficient financial security to live up to its new surroundings. The nation's opera house must, in fact, be the goal of the nation's ballet.

The offer from the Covent Garden Opera Trust in 1945 opened the way to exciting new developments. For the dancers there was the lure of the great stage, for designers the money and the technical equipment to implement their most ambitious schemes, and for Constant Lambert and his musicians the promise of a great orchestra. At the same time it presented a challenge bigger than anything the company had faced before, and this was calculated to appeal to the Irish in de Valois. Lord Keynes, as was his wont, envisaged a big spectacular opening, and instead of starting the easy way by presenting three established favourites from the modern repertoire, de Valois undertook to put on an entirely new production of *The Sleeping Beauty*, decorated by Oliver Messel and costing more than £10,000. The opening night was to be 20th February 1946.

Meanwhile a second company was in process of formation at Sadler's Wells under the direction of Ursula Moreton, with Peggy van Praagh as ballet mistress. During the winter of 1945–46 the little group of dancers rehearsed a repertoire of their own and danced with the opera company, making their first appearance in *The Bartered Bride* on 26th January 1946. The School was also on the verge of great new developments, for plans were going ahead to acquire new premises and establish a fully educational institution. A beginning was made with the introduction of a modicum of general education into the Senior School (fifteen years of age and over) for pupils who were devoting most of their time to ballet classes.

The amount of work that went on that winter in all three departments of the Sadler's Wells Ballet organisation was breathtaking. Ninette de Valois managed to keep an eye on everything and seemed to draw new energy from the very immensity of the task. The war was only just over, and virtually all the materials which were needed for the reopening of the Royal Opera House were in short supply. Fabrics for costumes, wood and canvas for building scenery, labour to carry out all the multifarious jobs, even equipment for the offices, presented daily problems. The company had just six weeks in which to rehearse the new production, and as there is no large rehearsal room at Covent Garden the work had to be done in nearby halls or studios.

Inside the opera house the work of restoration and re-equipment was going on at the same time. Everyone worked in makeshift quarters that were moved or altered every day, and every different department—production manager, stage director, painters and carpenters, as well as dancers—seemed to want to use the stage at the same time. Ninette de Valois held a conference of the heads of departments in her office every Saturday (and every Saturday the office was located in a different part of the opera house), and they all reported their difficulties and insoluble problems. Joy Newton, who was ballet mistress at the time, has described how calmly de Valois dealt with every setback and how she seemed to thrive on difficulties. It was only if someone said everything was going "according to plan" that she became worried and anxious.

The Awakening of the Sleeping Beauty

Nevertheless by 20th February everything was in order behind the scenes and the front of the house had been restored to something like its pre-war splendour; someone had even succeeded in procuring real silk of the appropriate pink colour for the little shades which decorate so charmingly the various tiers of the auditorium.

The opening night was a great occasion historically, and sociologically a strange compromise between the splendours of pre-war premières at Covent Garden and the austerity standards that had prevailed during the war. The curtain went up at 7 p.m., by which time the audience had assembled. The King and Queen and the two Princesses, Queen Mary, the Prime Minister and Mrs. Attlee, Mr. Ernest Bevin, members of the Diplomatic Corps, representatives of all musical and artistic London and those ladies to whom Keynes referred habitually as "the ancient hens of glory," were all in their seats. Lord Keynes, as Chairman of the Covent Garden Opera Trust, with his wife Lydia Lopokova, was to receive the Royal guests, but before they arrived he became unwell and had to retire. Lydia Lopokova took his place, and thus one of London's most beloved ballerinas from the Diaghileff epoch brought the King and Queen to their box to see an English ballerina, Margot Fonteyn, dance *The Sleeping Beauty*.[1]

Lord Keynes recovered in time to watch and enjoy the performance, and both he and Ninette de Valois must have reflected on all that had been accomplished since they worked together for the Camargo Society and Lydia Lopokova danced with the modest little Vic-Wells Ballet in *Cephalus and Procris*. Constant Lambert also, as he went into the orchestra pit to conduct the national anthem, with which all seasons at Covent Garden traditionally begin and end, must have remembered that very first evening of ballet at the Old Vic Theatre, fifteen years before, when he performed the same service for Lilian Baylis and Ninette de Valois at "a greatly reduced fee."

It was an emotional evening and it was difficult for anyone who knew and loved the company to view the performance coldly and objectively. The arrival of these artists, still so young, at such a goal was something to touch the heart and the imagination. The settings of Oliver Messel, with their airy grandeur, their vistas of formal gardens and architecture that brought to mind the splendours of the Teatro Olimpico of Vicenza, were delightful in themselves and cleverly designed so that they did not submerge the company with heavy grandeur. The colours of the costumes *en masse* were so lovely that it was not until subsequent visits that people began to notice that not all the designs were equally felicitous and that some of the more fantastic costumes—such as those for the fairies' cavaliers with their exotic headdresses—were less attractive in realisation than on paper (partly, perhaps, because the dancers never adopted sufficiently fantastic make-up). Some costumes also suffered from being executed in fabrics which were too insubstantial and did not hang or move well.

Choreographically the new production followed fairly closely the former Wells version, staged by Sergueeff. A change was to

[1] The title of the ballet had been altered to *The Sleeping Beauty*, as it was a more exact rendering of the original fairy-tale name, *La Belle au Bois Dormant*, and Diaghileff's objection (that not all his Auroras were beauties) could not be levelled against the Sadler's Wells ballerinas. The name also had a sentimental interest for de Valois. At the age of five she had been taken from her home in the foothills of the Wicklow Mountains to Dublin for her first visit to a theatre, and she had seen the pantomime *The Sleeping Beauty*.

use the Panorama music as an overture to the last act, and to show only the last stages of the Prince's journey into the castle. The Awakening led straight into the last act and the Gold, Silver, Sapphire and Diamond fairies were replaced by a *pas de trois* for Florestan and his Sisters (as in the Diaghileff 1921 production), with new choreography by Frederick Ashton (and some of Messel's best costumes). Ninette de Valois herself arranged a Russian character dance for the Three Ivans to the music which had formerly been used for the Prince's last act solo (it was not until 1953 that the Prince was given a solo at Covent Garden). Frederick Ashton arranged the Garland Waltz quite attractively, but its patterns were rather obscured by fussy costumes. The company was enlarged, as formerly, by students from the school and by some "supers"; for example, the four big Negroes who attended the King were students from Morley College.

The dancers, on the opening night, must have been in an anxious frame of mind. They were not only dancing in a very large theatre very soon after the years of enforced confinement in the tiny New Theatre, but they were invading a stage that was held by many people to be sacred to the Russian Ballet. They knew that there would be complaints in some quarters simply because they were not Russian, and this attitude did in fact persist for a considerable time among certain members of the audience—although it disappeared with surprising suddenness after the 1947 season by the Original Ballet Russe.

The success of that opening performance was due to the company as a whole rather than to individual triumphs. Princess Aurora Fonteyn was dancing magnificently, but it was apparent that she had yet to take the measure of the great auditorium and project her performance to its outermost areas. Always an artist of restraint, despising flamboyant tricks of presentation, she had to learn gradually how to adapt her performance, but when she did at last establish full mastery of her new surroundings her interpretation was all the richer for having been felt from within and not built up by a series of superficial additions.

Helpmann, both as Carabosse and Prince Florimund, seemed not at all troubled by the enlarged frame he had to fill, and in fact the only rôles in which he ever failed at Covent Garden were ones which were totally unsuited in themselves to the large theatre, such as the Rake and Hamlet. Among the other dancers, Beryl Grey as the Lilac Fairy and Julia Farron as the Queen "came over" with immediate warmth, and successes were scored by Moira Shearer, Margaret Dale, Pamela May and Alexis Rassine. It was apparent that most of the dancers had much to learn, and that both mime and dancing would have to be gradually acclimatised to the new surroundings. Large groups of courtiers or fairies were not making their presence felt sufficiently, and although the performance was beautifully rehearsed and well executed it did not have any great strength of impact. These very shortcomings, however, lent interest to the future. Here was room for growth indeed.

On the following evening Pamela May danced Aurora, partnered by David Paltenghi, and a newcomer from Moscow, Violetta Prokhorova (Elvin), appeared in the Blue Bird *pas de deux* and took command of the stage with impressive ease. The difference in style was immediately apparent; the Russian girl had a beautifully developed back, highly arched feet and great grandeur in adagio movements. The introduction of such a strong and completely different personality gave the Blue Bird *pas de deux* an excitement it had not achieved for many years at Sadler's Wells. Pamela May that night gave the first of many beautiful performances as Aurora at Covent Garden. It is the most purely classical of all the great ballerina rôles, and Pamela May was the most purely classical of English dancers. Later performances sometimes varied in quality when she was suffering from a troublesome knee, but at her best she was a fine Aurora and deserves a place among the most honoured exponents of the part.

The Sleeping Beauty naturally attracted a great deal of publicity, coupled with that which was accorded to the Opera House itself, and it was an immediate success with the public. It played successfully for the next month, and early in March Moira Shearer danced her first Aurora. It was a performance that was a little superficial from the dancing point of view, but extraordinarily mature as a piece of stagecraft. She looked exquisitely lovely, but the very delicacy and fragility of her style robbed it of effectiveness when seen from a great distance, and throughout her career at Covent Garden she remained a dancer for the stalls rather than for the amphitheatre or gallery.

On 18th March the first programme of English ballet, as distinct from ballet by English dancers, was given at Covent Garden. The programme consisted of *The Rake's Progress, Nocturne* and *Miracle in the Gorbals,* thus representing the three principal choreographers of the company. *The Rake's Progress* was given in the Rex Whistler settings made for the small New Theatre, masked in by a special proscenium designed by Oliver Messel as a tribute to Whistler, and employing architectural arabesques and fantasies in which he would have delighted. Masking down can sometimes be satisfactory in a large theatre, but in the case of *The Rake's Progress* it seemed to make lighting difficult and to reduce the dancers to the size of puppets. The effect of the ballet was sadly impaired, and although it received much applause from people who had never seen it else-where its life was seriously imperilled. Ninette de Valois was so unhappy about its appearance at Covent Garden that she used to take refuge in the bar when it was being given, and did not enjoy seeing it until it was restored to Sadler's Wells Theatre in 1951 and came back to lusty life in its proper home.

A new ballet by Frederick Ashton to César Franck's "Symphonic Variations" had been scheduled for 20th March, but Michael Somes, who was to have a leading part, slipped a cartilege in his knee early in the season, and on account of his absence the ballet had to be postponed. *Dante Sonata* was performed instead, and on the same evening *Les Patineurs* arrived at Covent Garden. The stage was enlivened with a mass of Japanese lanterns, and the pretty set and Meyerbeer music were perfectly at home in the Victorian opera house. Turner danced his original rôle, Shearer and Paltenghi were the couple in white, and Avril Navarre astonished a new audience with the speed and brilliance of her *fouettés.*

As *Symphonic Variations* had been postponed, Robert Helpmann had the distinction of creating the first new ballet which the company presented at Covent Garden, and by strange coincidence it proved to be the last he was to make for them. *Adam Zero* had its first performance on 10th April, and its chief interest was that it provided the audience with a fascinating introduction to the technical resources of the Opera House. The scenario was by Michael Benthall, and was a highly involved allegory of the Life and Death of Man, conveyed "in terms of a company creating a new ballet." Fundamentally such a theme had possibilities, but in realisation it became sadly over-complicated and overloaded with symbolism.

The characters were named after personages in a ballet company and each symbolised in turn various figures in the life of the Principal Dancer ("Adam Zero"), played by Helpmann himself. As the cycle of man's life moves on, these people assume different functions, so that many of the dancers had to impersonate several characters. June Brae, in particular, in her rôle as The Choreographer, was required to be both Creator and Destroyer, and as Ballerina "his first love, wife, and mistress." The specific intention of the author was that the ballet should call on all the resources of the theatre: "Lighting, stage mechanism, dance conventions, musical forms and costumes and scenery of all periods are used to symbolise the world of 'Adam Zero'," wrote Michael Benthall in his programme note. The intention was admirable and *Adam Zero* was unquestionably the work of a man in love with the theatre, but unfortunately it never managed to become a ballet. The canvas was so crowded and so packed with incident that no single point could emerge clearly, and one was inclined to reflect on the audience's bemused attention in the light of Logan Pearsall Smith's remark that it is possible for boredom to be carried to such lengths that it becomes, in itself, a mystical experience. (For some people, it must in fairness be reported, *Adam Zero* was something very near to a mystical experience.) A strong and theatrical score by Arthur Bliss and settings by Roger Furse, on similar lines to those he designed for Laurence Olivier's production of *The Skin of our Teeth*, helped to maintain interest, and there was a moment of pure, wonderful theatre at the end when all the crowds had gone and June Brae, the Destroyer, circled the vast empty stage in a scarlet cloak.

June Brae had been "loaned" to Covent Garden by the Sadler's Wells Opera Ballet, and her performance, in all her rôles, was masterly. Her warm, vibrant personality reached effortlessly throughout the big theatre and she achieved her effects with the utmost simplicity. David Paltenghi as the Stage Director in the ballet stalked about in horn-rimmed spectacles with great determination and almost terrifying omnipotence, but there were few opportunities for the dancers. Henry Robinson, the actual Stage Manager of the Sadler's Wells Ballet, probably had the most fun displaying all the Covent Garden stage equipment and was responsible for the breath-taking moment when the great cyclorama began to move.

On 24th April came Ashton's *Symphonic Variations,* pure ballet for just six dancers, and it came like a shaft of sunshine, illumining the whole repertoire. *Symphonic Variations* was perhaps the most completely beautiful dance composition Sadler's Wells had ever presented and it was also the most masterly. Ashton chose the most difficult choreographic approach of all, that of creating pure dancing which grows out of the music yet establishes its own validity and does not merely echo the thoughts of the composer, and the success of the ballet was as much due to his unfaltering musical response as to his choreographic inventiveness. There was nothing virtuoso about the dancing; it was unceasingly lovely and created an impression of effortless lyricism and almost godlike serenity which at moments quickened under the urgent tempo of the music to blaze "like splendour out of heaven."

Sophie Fedorovitch designed a simple backcloth of clear green with black lines as the only decoration, and white costumes, with occasional adornments of black or silver, which were as great an inspiration as Ashton's own. The six original dancers were Margot Fonteyn, Pamela May, Moira Shearer, Michael Somes, Brian Shaw and Henry Danton. They gave perfect realisation to the choreographer's intentions, all appreciating the design of the ballet as a whole and none trying to obtrude their own personalities. The ballet tried their endurance to the utmost, allowing no absence from the stage, permitting no suspicion of strain, and coming towards the end of a season that had been (particularly for the three Auroras) singularly tiring. At first it was feared that this perfect cast might prove irreplaceable, but this has not been the case. *Symphonic Variations* seems to have some inspiring quality that infects every dancer who appears in it, and it may well prove to be Sadler's Wells' contribution to the classical repertoire of the future.

A classic from the Diaghileff-Fokine period was added to the Covent Garden repertoire on 15th May when *Les Sylphides* was revived. Margot Fonteyn, Moira Shearer, Anne Negus and Alexis Rassine were the principal dancers. The ballet was well danced from the academic point of view, but still lacked feeling and romantic atmosphere. The harsh lighting did not help in establishing a mood of reverie, but one noticeable improvement was that the bodices of the girls' costumes were at last made of a dull fabric and not

the shiny satin which had formerly caused displeasure. Norman
Thomson, a young Canadian dancer who had made himself very
useful in *The Sleeping Beauty* (he was a notable Florestan), appeared
in some later performances of *Les Sylphides*, and gave an exceptionally good performance of a part that is now one of the most difficult
assignments for a male dancer.

On 12th June *Giselle* made its reappearance in new *décor* and
costumes by James Bailey, a young designer discovered by Ashton,
whose first important work for the theatre this was. It was a first
taste of the "bigger and better" philosophy which was to disfigure
so many of the early productions. Bailey's designs were attractive
and very much on the right lines, but they were carried out with
rather too much splendour. The habiliments of the nobles, in
particular, were so ridiculously ornate that they completely swamped
the simple style of the old ballet. It was not until several years had
passed that Bailey was given an opportunity to modify his designs
and improve the general balance of the production. His present
version is infinitely better and a real evocation of the Romantic
period.

Nevertheless this first fussy version was a popular success and,
as is usually the case with the rarely performed *Giselle*, it filled the
house. Fonteyn danced faultlessly, but seemed to have lost the
pathos of her earlier performances, and Alexis Rassine never
managed to make a complete character of Albrecht. He had some
sympathetic moments but seemed to find it difficult to maintain a
performance, and would occasionally lose contact with the audience
and slouch or stroll about the stage as if at a rehearsal. It was this
lack of continuity in his performances that prevented him from
ever quite attaining the position that his gifts as a dancer and mime
should have earned for him.

Some experiments in production effects were introduced into
this *Giselle* with no very marked success. The Queen of the Wilis
(Beryl Grey) was required to come up from the bowels of the
earth through a cavernous opening and some Flying Wilis on
wires skimmed about at the beginning of the second act. They
were "produced" with rather less imagination than is usually
expended on the Rhine Maidens, and simply floated about from
one side of the stage to the other. One memorable evening a Flying
Wili came too close to the earth and collided in very human fashion

G. B. L. Wilson

THE SLEEPING BEAUTY

Above: The scene of chaos at the dress rehearsal. Ninette de Valois (in dark suit, centre) arguing with Robert Helpmann (back to camera, in dark dressing gown) about costumes. *Below:* The performance. Violetta Elvin and Alexis Rassine dancing the Blue Bird *pas de deux*

Action photograph by Frank Sharman

Action photographs by Roger Wood

with Albrecht as he prayed by the tomb of Giselle. After that the phantoms were not seen again at the Royal Opera House.

Just before the end of the season Beryl Grey danced her first Aurora, a performance of amazing ease and confidence, which won her a great reception. Gillian Lynne took over the part of the Lilac Fairy and by this time Frederick Ashton was enjoying himself hugely as the Fairy Carabosse. Robert Helpmann had to leave the company temporarily at the end of May to undergo an operation, so when the triumphant season came to an end on 29th June it was David Paltenghi who partnered Fonteyn in *The Sleeping Beauty*. Beryl Grey was the Lilac Fairy and Prokhorova and Rassine danced the Blue Bird *pas de deux*.

The success of this first Covent Garden season had exceeded the most optimistic expectations. It had been extended several times and lasted in all for some eighteen and a half weeks, breaking the previous record for ballet at Covent Garden by four and a half weeks. During the 131 performances there had been hardly an empty seat in the house, and it was estimated that over a quarter of a million people had been to the theatre. *The Sleeping Beauty* had been performed seventy-eight times, and four different ballerinas had been seen as Aurora. The company went off for a well-earned holiday, and afterwards made a provincial tour which started on 5th August and took them to Newcastle, Aberdeen, Edinburgh and Glasgow.

What an exciting summer was 1946 for the London ballet-goer! Sadler's Wells had provided a whole host of wonderful performances and one new masterpiece of choreography. Les Ballets des Champs-Élysées were the first visitors to arrive in post-war London, and they brought reminders of the importance of the French designer in the creation of ballets, while Jean Babilée was a revelation to that part of the audience which had grown up during the war virtually unaware of what male dancing could and should be. During July and August the American Ballet Theatre at Covent Garden was a trans-Atlantic tonic and stimulus, shaking the London audience out of the complacency bred of wartime isolation and emphasising again the pathetic state of English male dancing. These Americans were no lilies of the field, said one writer: "Boy, did they toil and spin!"

That English male dancing should be in a sorry state was not

o

surprising. It was more surprising that any male dancers remained. They had all been through a long period of overwork, lack of sleep from raids, or from inadequate accommodation when on tour, lack of proper food (they never received extra rations), and shortage of ballet shoes—a positive danger at times as a worn-out shoe can cause many accidents. These conditions applied to the girls as well as to the men, but most of the men had in addition spent several years in the Forces and would need months of hard work to find their real form again. The young graduates from the School had grown up in a period when really first-rate male dancing had practically disappeared from the English stage, and unfortunately there were few good male teachers resident in England. Babilée, Eglevsky and the other French and American dancers showed these boys for the first time the real standard at which they had to aim, and the public, too, was quick to see the difference. It was perhaps no bad thing that the lesson was brought home so suddenly and sharply. The problem was very widely discussed in the dance periodicals, and various remedies were gratuitously suggested by well-meaning critics.

The situation could not be remedied overnight, however, and de Valois was confident that she had sufficient talent growing up in the School to restore the status of the male dancer in due course. The vast widening of the popularity of ballet during the war was gradually overcoming the prejudice of parents against their sons taking up dancing as a career, while the scholarships offered by the School were attracting promising pupils. With the end of war came renewed contact with the Dominions, and there began a steady migration of young Dominion dancers to London, with a first ambition of studying at the Wells school, and an ultimate goal of being accepted for one of the companies. (As long ago as 1938 Arnold Haskell had reported from Australia that Sadler's Wells was the goal of every young dancer, and the progress of Australian artists such as Robert Helpmann and Laurel Martyn was being eagerly followed.) These new sources of talent, coupled with the ever-growing scope of the School and the better teaching facilities for boys which it could offer, were the best guarantee of a supply of male dancers in the future. But ballet is an art that is best learned slowly, and no changes in style or personnel, if they are to have long-term value, can be made overnight.

After their provincial tour the company paid a visit to Vienna, under the auspices of the British Council. It was for this expedition that Herbert Hughes and Louis Yudkin worked out their famous code and numbering system for all the company's belongings. This proved so efficient and was so enthusiastically welcomed by Customs officials everywhere that it has since been adopted by most other touring ballet companies. Every article down to the last pair of ear-rings and property dagger was listed, numbered and packed under the code of its particular ballet, and Hughes and Yudkin brought the whole system to such a point of perfection that when the Sadler's Wells Ballet arrived in America in 1949, over 6,000 separate articles of equipment were cleared through the New York Customs in one hour.

The performances in Vienna were given at the Volksoper—the Vienna equivalent of Sadler's Wells Theatre in London—as the Vienna Opera House had been burnt out during the war. Children from the State Opera Ballet crammed the wings of the theatre every night to watch the performance, and the English dancers were greatly impressed by the magnificent staffing and equipment of the Viennese state theatres. The first few performances drew only moderate attendances, but as soon as the notices began to appear and people discovered or heard how good the English ballet was, the demand for seats increased to such an extent that the State Administration asked the company to prolong their visit for three days, a request which they reluctantly had to decline as they had only ten days in which to return to London and stage their new production of *Coppélia*.

CHAPTER XI

GROWING PAINS AND THE ARRIVAL OF MASSINE

THE winter ballet season 1946–47, opened at Covent Garden on 25th October with *Coppélia,* newly decorated for the opera house by William Chappell, who had been responsible for the gay 1940 production. Had he been content to leave matters much as they were he might also have been successful at Covent Garden, but, alas, everything was made bigger and brighter and the general effect was of an over-coloured picture postcard. The principle seemed to be that everything had to be doubled for the larger stage; there were twice as many flags in Act I, and the tartan sash for Swanilda in Act II was twice as large. Helpmann as Dr. Coppelius wore a wig that would not have disgraced the clown Whimsical Walker; whether inspired or depressed by this he played for laughs all the way—and, it must be recorded, he won them. Leslie Edwards, who followed him, subdued the wig and subdued the clowning and was more successful in suggesting the old man's dabblings in necromancy. Margot Fonteyn danced Swanilda at the first performance and Moira Shearer at the second. Shearer was well suited to this ballet and had a sparkling prettiness that matched the music. Rassine, Turner and John Hart all appeared as Franz, although none of them could quite overcome the absurdity of the last act costume with its floppy tunic and wide sleeves.

On 12th November the first performance was given of a new Ashton ballet, *Les Sirènes,* for which Lord Berners composed the music and Cecil Beaton designed the scenery and costumes. Ashton had long wanted to do a ballet with an Edwardian setting vaguely based on the novels of Ouida and the plot of *Les Sirènes* owed something to *Moths.* The setting was the *plage* at Trouville at the height of the season in 1904. Children, Nannies, the Smart Set, a Spanish dancer La Bolero, an Oriental Potentate and an Australian Tenor all disported themselves on the beach to the amusement of the mermaids and the seagulls.

Beaton has described the original intention of the collaborators as being "to create an atmosphere that was mysterious and vaguely sinister; it was to be a foggy day on the beach and there should be a sense of desolation behind all the *mondaine* high-jinks," but unhappily the original idea got lost on the way and too many "amusing" incidents and stage properties crept in. A display of Edwardian bathing costumes convinced the audience that it was all meant to be a rollicking farce and they received the early motor-car and the lovely balloon in which the Potentate descended in a similar spirit. The music was very light, a charming echo of popular melodies of the period, but it did not create the atmosphere of nostalgia that might have saved the ballet.

The dancers did all they could to make their flimsy material interesting and contributed an amazing galaxy of characterisations. Fonteyn flashed her teeth and her red heels as La Bolero, Helpmann stood on his head and even broke into song as Adelino Canberra (of the Adelaide Opera), Ashton was a delightfully pudgy King Hihat of Agpar, Beryl Grey pretty and silly as Countess Kitty, and Michael Somes twirled his moustachios with terrible heartiness as Captain Bay Vavaseur. It was not their fault that the ballet brought to mind a fragment of dialogue from Thomas Peacock's *Headlong Hall*. Mr. Gall, a very profound critic, is talking about landscape gardening:

> "I distinguish the picturesque and the beautiful, and I add to them, in the laying out of grounds, a third and distinct character, which I call unexpectedness."
>
> "Pray, sir," said Mr. Milestone, "by what name do you distinguish this character when a person walks round the grounds for a second time?"

Ashton's failure to provide any real dance interest for the second and any subsequent viewings meant that *Les Sirènes* had but a poor expectation of life. It was withdrawn after only eighteen performances and has not been given since.

Unfortunately *Les Sirènes* was not only an unsatisfactory but a highly expensive production, and coming immediately after the tasteless refulgence of the new *Coppélia,* it aroused much misgiving about the new-found riches of the company. Everyone began to point out that it was often more difficult to decorate a ballet on

£5,000 than on £500, and that the flummery of excessive decoration was beginning to swamp the personalities of the dancers. When *Le Lac des Cygnes* was brought into the repertoire on 19th December it was shown in its former Hurry settings and costumes, and although these were not ideal for the ballet there was a welcome absence of "dazzle" about them and the production in general looked well on the large stage. Fonteyn's Odette-Odile now began to acquire a new depth of emotion and Helpmann partnered her admirably. Gillian Lynne gave much pleasure by her fine elevation and quality of movement as one of the leading swans and the *corps de ballet* showed to special advantage in the lakeside scenes.

Christmas brought a realisation of one of Constant Lambert's long-cherished ambitions. Purcell's *The Fairy Queen* was staged at Covent Garden, at his suggestion, with the Sadler's Wells Ballet, soloists and chorus of the Covent Garden Opera and an acting cast. The production acted as a bridge from the seasons of ballet to the subsequent seasons of opera by the newly formed Covent Garden company. Lambert, who was working in close association with Karl Rankl, the Musical Director of the opera company, was himself responsible for the adaptation and Frederick Ashton (Production Consultant to the opera company) arranged the choreography. Michael Ayrton designed scenery and costumes in the Inigo Jones manner, which, despite certain last-minute disappointments caused by technical limitations and shortage of certain materials, were among the best early designs shown at Covent Garden. The settings in particular showed an understanding of the requirements of an opera house stage which is rare in English designers. The production was by Frederick Ashton and Malcolm Baker Smith and maintained a judicious balance between the various elements of acting, singing and dancing, but so specialised have the tastes of audiences become that few people were able to appreciate the entertainment as a unity. The ballet audience was bored by the singing, the opera audience resented the dancers, and the Shakespeare enthusiasts who had been reared at the Old Vic were horrified by the whole proceeding.

Some of Ashton's choreography had perforce to be conventional, but he also arranged some very original and beautiful dances, notably the Echo Dance in which the movements of a tall dancer in the foreground (Beryl Grey) were echoed in turn by a medium-sized dancer behind her and then by a small dancer in the background, thus creating a remarkable illusion of perspective. In the *Masque of Love* in the second scene of Act II, a *pas de deux* for the Spirits of the Air was performed by Margot Fonteyn and Michael Somes with such exquisite, effortless grace that they seemed hardly to touch the ground. Some of the movements and floating lifts were so lovely that Ashton decided to preserve them and was able to incorporate them into the choreography of *Symphonic Variations* by making some slight revisions. Others appeared years later in the choreography for the Queen of Air in *Homage to the Queen*.

Robert Helpmann appeared as Oberon (an acting rôle) in this production, and early in 1947 he received leave of absence from Covent Garden to act in *The White Devil* and *He Who Gets Slapped* in a repertory season at the Duchess Theatre, which he and Michael Benthall directed. From this date Helpmann's interest in acting began to increase, and although he remained with the Sadler's Wells Ballet until 1951, he did not attempt any more choreography and his influence on the repertoire began to decline.

The achievements of the first year's work at Covent Garden and the successful establishment of the Sadler's Wells Ballet as a national company were recognised in the New Year Honours List by the conferment on Ninette de Valois of the decoration Commander of the British Empire (C.B.E.). While no one was more fitted to receive the distinction, one suspects that had she had her own way de Valois would have put the letters after the title of her company, and when congratulations were showered upon her she always pointed out how much was owed to the loyal support of her colleagues. "It is because of their work that I am here as your guest to-day," she told the Executive Committee of the Royal Academy of Dancing when they entertained her at luncheon.

Nineteen forty-seven was the beginning of the "Massine period" in the history of the Sadler's Wells Ballet. Before the war Ninette de Valois had been anxious to invite a great choreographer to come and work with her company over a lengthy period, to create new ballets for them and to leave the mark of his genius on the repertoire, but the war had prevented such a plan being implemented. As a result of the postponement she was now able to offer a larger company, a more handsome theatre and richer resources to her guest. Massine undertook in the first instance to rehearse and revive two of his most celebrated ballets, *The Three Cornered Hat* and *La Boutique Fantasque*, both of which had first been produced in London (for Diaghileff, in 1919). He also agreed to appear as guest artist in his original rôles of the Miller and the Can-Can dancer.

The first performance of *The Three Cornered Hat* by the Sadler's Wells Ballet, on Thursday, 6th February 1947, was a great night at Covent Garden. The audience included all the old die-hard supporters of the Russian Ballet, some of whom had never bothered about Sadler's Wells before and looked up to Massine as the one professional in a group of hopeful amateurs. From the first pulsing drum beats in the orchestra expectation was at fever pitch, and when the curtain rose to show Massine standing on the stage, taut and slim as ever, the audience broke into spontaneous cheering. The Picasso setting was there, a little faded-looking and a little underlit, and the audience seemed to sense immediately that everything was going to be "all right."

The performance was of a remarkably high standard throughout. Fonteyn as the Miller's wife had a new sort of rôle—feminine in a passionate and earthy way—and she responded to it with surprising fire. John Hart as the Corregidor gave a masterly characterisation of senile lechery and Alexander Grant, newly recruited from the second company, gave a neat, swift and happy study of Idzikowski's old part of the Dandy. The rest of the company danced with a zest and conviction that compensated for some uncertainty about Spanish style, and Lambert's superb sense of rhythm made him an ideal conductor for the de Falla music—which must be one of the most exciting ballet scores in existence.

The ovation at the end of the performance was such as impresarios dream about. It reflected all kinds of different emotions—delight in the ballet itself, delight that Sadler's Wells should succeed within the preserves of Russian Ballet, and delight that Massine was once again dancing in London. Massine was the Miller and the Miller was Massine, and Time itself seemed to have respected the fact. The years might have taken some toll in speed and sharpness, but the total effect of his performance was still superlative. It was one of those rare occasions in the ballet theatre when delight is universal; no one looked elderly and sad and muttered, "but you should have seen it ten years ago."

La Boutique Fantasque followed on 27th February and was an anti-climax. It was all there in outline but never achieved homogeneity as a complete ballet. There was too much self-conscious "acting," and the make-up of the dancers was too naturalistic. The Derain setting and costumes were used and the toyshop was still flooded with golden Riviera sunshine, while the Rossini music tinkled and charmed its way throughout the theatre. But the atmosphere was no longer *fantasque,* and Time had had less respect for the Can-Can dancer than for the Miller. Massine at fifty-one inevitably lacked the agility of twenty-one, thirty-one or even forty-one (which had been his age when he last danced *Boutique* in London), and on the first night his companion Can-Can dancer, Moira Shearer, was almost paralysed with fright. She came quite bravely through the ordeal and was the most satisfactory Can-Can dancer the Wells ever produced, but she never managed to be "champagne on the stage" as Danilova was and before her Lydia Lopokova. This sort of temperament is rare in the English theatre (among actresses only the name of Gertrude Lawrence comes to mind) and it is possible that *La Boutique Fantasque* failed simply because it was not a suitable work for English dancers to perform. They made a brave try (and probably did better than the Russians would have done in, say, *Job* or *The Rake's Progress*), and there were some nice individual performances—from Farron and Turner in the Tarantella, Henry Legerton as the Assistant (the only dancer, as Madame Rambert once remarked, who gave a performance that was truly *fantasque*), and John Hart as the portly shopkeeper. Alexis Rassine was a first-rate Snob and Michael Somes led the Cossacks with a flourish.

The early performances of *La Boutique Fantasque* may also have been affected by the English weather, because they took place during the Fuel Crisis which struck the country early in 1947 The first-night programme was printed on a single folded sheet of thin paper with an apologetic note, "The Management regret the curtailment of the Programme, which is due to the power cut." However, in warmer weather, with changes of cast and even, in 1954, after rehearsals with Grigorieff and with Ansermet to conduct, the ballet was never altogether satisfactory with the Sadler's Wells company.

The opera company had by now started performances at Covent

Garden and was sharing the Opera House with the ballet. For the first production, Bizet's *Carmen*, Beryl Grey was loaned by the ballet to dance a solo and she made such a success of it that she received more applause than anything else in the opera. "That's the last opera of mine you ever appear in," said Leonard Boosey, when he went round to congratulate her.

Performances of ballet continued until 21st June, by which time the season had lasted for thirty-four weeks, although towards the end the dancers had not been appearing every night. After a holiday the company rehearsed *The Sleeping Beauty* again and took it to Manchester for two weeks before going on to the first Edinburgh Festival of Music and Drama, where they danced the same ballet for two weeks from 25th August. On 9th September they set off on an extensive European tour, arranged by the British Council. Helpmann and Shearer, who were working on the *Red Shoes* film, remained behind, and so did Frederick Ashton, who was to produce his *Valses Nobles et Sentimentales* for the second company, now called the Sadler's Wells Theatre Ballet.

The tour took the Sadler's Wells Ballet to Brussels, Prague, Warsaw, Poznan, Oslo and Malmo, and almost everywhere they were greeted by old friends. As the train steamed into the station in Warsaw, Leon Woizikowski,[1] one of the greatest of all Polish character dancers, was seen standing on the platform to greet them, and for Ninette de Valois in particular it was a wonderful experience to meet again her old colleague of Diaghileff days and to find him safe and well after the years of war. Once again, the English company were impressed by the important place occupied by theatres in the national life of the Eastern European countries; much of Warsaw was still in ruins, but a first task had been to rebuild and re-equip the theatres. An interesting experience for the dancers was the "Trade Union *Matinées*," which were given at 3.30 p.m. The majority of the workers finished their day at 3 p.m. (they started at 7 or 8 in the morning) and would go straight to the theatre, where they received the ballet with great enthusiasm.

Symphonic Variations was the most successful ballet in Warsaw, but Prague seemed to prefer the Helpmann ballets and *Dante Sonata*. The company were greeted on arrival in Prague by Sasha Machov, ballet master of the Prague National Theatre, who had

[1] Now ballet master at the State Opera House in Warsaw.

produced dances for the Sadler's Wells Opera Company during the war. They danced at the Velka Theatre and had a considerable success, notwithstanding the fact that classical dancers from Leningrad and Moscow and the Moiseyev folk dance group from Moscow had visited Prague earlier in the year. The *Lidova Demokracie* summed up the season by saying that not only were they not disappointed by the English dancers "but they surpassed by far our highest expectations."

In Oslo the Ballet was honoured by a visit from King Haakon, and they were delighted to meet Louise Browne, the musical comedy actress and dancer, who had been living in Oslo since her marriage and had opened a ballet school there. Fonteyn, Pamela May, Beryl Grey, Michael Somes, John Hart and Harold Turner gave a special exhibition demonstration for Norwegian teachers and students at her school under the guidance of Frederick Ashton. (He had joined the company for the Scandinavian finish of the tour, de Valois having returned to London to start work on the arrangements for the new season.) *Symphonic Variations* had another triumph in Oslo and one critic was moved to describe it as "one of the greatest ballets the world has ever seen." The last night of the tour was celebrated with an all-night party in Malmo attended by Danish, Swedish and English dancers, which is still remembered, in spirit if not in any precise detail, by all who attended it.

The tour had been a rapid one—no stop in any town exceeding six days—but it had been highly successful. The British Council had at last learned how to handle advance publicity (and how to get the necessary material out of the company in good time), and news of the Sadler's Wells Ballet's visit to Vienna the previous year had circulated throughout Europe to an amazing extent. ·

CHAPTER XII

PROGRESS

O N 12th November 1947, the Sadler's Wells Ballet returned to Covent Garden with one very great change in its personnel. After an association of sixteen years Constant Lambert had decided to resign from his position as Musical Director in order to devote more time to composition. His departure was a very great blow, but the claims of his other interests had to be recognised. No one who has worked for a ballet company has ever found time to do much outside creative work at the same time, and the recent production of *The Fairy Queen* alone had occupied his entire artistic life for a period of over six months. No new appointment as Musical Director was made at the time of his resignation. The conducting was shared by Geoffrey Corbett and Hugo Rignold.

The season opened with *Giselle* and *La Boutique Fantasque*. The most notable performance was that given by Michael Somes, who appeared as Albrecht in *Giselle* with Fonteyn. He had no easy task in following Robert Helpmann in the classical rôles which had for so long been associated with him, and some of the audience were inclined to resent the appearance of a new partner for Fonteyn. Nevertheless his performance that evening was a genuine and personal interpretation and an indication that he would develop into a true *premier danseur noble*.

On 18th November, *Checkmate* was revived for the first time since the Holland disaster of 1940. Costumes and *décor* were redesigned by E. McKnight Kauffer and followed the originals fairly closely. The choreography was very much as it had been in the earlier production and the only increase in numbers was in the Black Pawns, of whom there were now eight instead of six. The movements seemed to have been somewhat stylised, perhaps on the assumption that naturalistic movement and mime was unsuited to the large theatre, but the general effect of the ballet was unchanged. Much of it was still impressive, there were still *longueurs* and the ending was a magnificent piece of theatre. Pamela

May and Harold Turner had the leading rôles of Black Queen and Red Knight, and Gordon Hamilton did his best as the Red King but failed to establish him as a sympathetic character. Other dancers who tried the part—among them Leslie Edwards and Ray Powell—had no more success and unfortunately Robert Helpmann never appeared in the part at Covent Garden. Had he failed as well it would have proved conclusively that the big theatre had killed the character. Beryl Grey and Michael Somes later danced the ballet with success and another excellent team were Gillian Lynne and John Field.

There were some fears when *Checkmate* was revived that it had become dated and belonged only to the nineteen-thirties, but it soon became a staple item in the repertoire and is the de Valois ballet most frequently performed by the company to-day. (It is often included in the programme when the Press is invited to see a new ballet and has probably through the years had more good reviews in *The Times* than any other ballet on record.)

The grim tragedy of *Checkmate* was followed, a week later, by Massine's new ballet for the company, *Mam'zelle Angot*, and the first-night was an infectiously happy evening in the theatre, despite much pre-opening gloom and foreboding on the part of the dancers (notoriously the worst judges of a new ballet's worth or prospects). The ballet was based on the operetta by Lecocq, *La Fille de Madame Angot*, and had first been staged by Massine in 1943 for the American Ballet Theatre with a cast that included Nora Kaye, André Eglevsky and Rosella Hightower. It had been successful outside New York, but had not remained for very long in that company's repertoire. For Sadler's Wells Massine revised the choreography considerably and entirely new settings and costumes were commissioned from André Derain, while Gordon Jacob orchestrated the music. The ballet was danced on the opening night by Margot Fonteyn as Mam'zelle Angot, Alexander Grant as the Barber, Moira Shearer as the Aristocrat, and Michael Somes as the Caricaturist. It was a ballet very much to Massine's usual formula for a lively *ballet bouffe*, but it had tremendous vitality, and the music kept the atmosphere gay and the pace swift. The first-night audience loved it, but the Press on the whole was grudging. Obviously *Mam'zelle Angot* was not a great or an important ballet and every critic seemed at pains to point this out, quite ignoring the fact that it was all tremendous fun and an excellent tonic for both dancers and audience.

The Derain setting for the Market Place was in his most felicitous manner and the drop curtains were delightful. Both *décor* and costumes were gay in that lighthearted fashion which English designers seem to find so difficult (this was before *Pineapple Poll*) and the gaiety infected the dancers. Fonteyn's Mam'zelle Angot had precisely the champagne quality that used to be associated with Danilova, and it was a great disappointment when she gave up the part after a few performances. Alexander Grant had his first big opportunity as a character dancer as the Barber, a whimsical, endearing little person in a tow-coloured wig, the Abel Drugger of the ballet. He bounced about the stage like a rubber ball when happy and in moments of adversity collapsed, "a little, boneless monument of despair." The more formal style of Shearer and Somes was contrasted with these two character parts, and they performed the inelegant *pas de deux* in the second scene with great ease and tact.

The rest of the company showed their usual flair for creating tiny parts successfully and established a whole population of characters. John Hart as a Government Official was a gouty old roué, half-way between Rowlandson and Peter Arno; Franklin White an absurd Chief of Police; Leslie Edwards, Henry Legerton and John Field (later John Cranko), as the bucolic Butcher, Tailor and Bootmaker stood stalwartly by the little Barber and comforted him with many a manly handshake; and Richard Ellis was the Officer with a solemn sense of duty, who was melted by one flicker of a woman's false eyelash. In addition, there were neat little *entr'acte* sketches of pirates, savages and minstrels, and some beautifully, balletically rustic market women in the first scene.

The third new production of the season, following one ballet by de Valois and one by Massine, was by Frederick Ashton, and was in great contrast to the other productions. *Scènes de Ballet*, which received its first performance on 11th February 1948, was like *Symphonic Variations* in that it had no "plot"; it was a restatement of Ashton's creed that *ballet is dancing*. Ashton took his cue from Stravinsky's description of the music as "patterned after the forms of the classical dance, free of any given literary or dramatic argument," and he seemed to be allowing his mind to play over classical choreography as he had known it in all its manifestations from Petipa right down to Balanchine and even Ashton himself. The ballet was Ashton's homage to the classic dance.

The ballet began with enormous grandeur with the *premier danseur* and four boys on the stage; the movements were sharply defined and austere. Twelve girls entered in fours and there was a passage for this whole *corps de ballet* of great staccato complexity. The ballerina entered at the end of a long line of girls, travelled rapidly forward and performed an introductory *pas* of great speed and brilliance. Although the choreography was not formally divided into variations, the ballerina and *danseur* would occasionally be detached from the rest to perform *pas seuls* or *pas de deux,* and there was a beautiful adagio passage for the ballerina and the five men. The whole ballet was composed with expert technical skill that resembled a passage of brilliant orchestration. Movement stated in one corner of the stage would be echoed in another, repeated elsewhere with a slight variation, and then caught up into a mass of beautifully correlated dancing. Ashton had never before used a *corps de ballet* with such complexity.

The first-night audience was unenthusiastic, however, and the next day's Press was cool. This may have been partly due to the rather astringent intellectual quality of both music and choreography, which had no literary associations or romantic undertones. The *décor* by the young French designer André Beaurepaire was not entirely satisfactory and the costumes were not particularly becoming, either in colour or design. Both Margot Fonteyn and Michael Somes seemed a little ill at ease. Fonteyn, to begin with, adopted a mocking Parisian glitter and was inclined to smile too broadly and too often, while Somes, after a good start, lapsed into an uncomfortable rigidity of movement. At the second performance Moira Shearer appeared in the ballerina rôle, which suited her natural speed and rather icy brilliance. In due course Fonteyn, too, began to dance it without affectation and with her own natural elegance. The ballet gradually overcame the prejudices of the audience and was eventually recognised to be a choreographic composition of exceptional quality.

Scènes de Ballet was included in the repertoire which the company took to Holland in March when they danced in Amsterdam, The Hague and Rotterdam under the patronage of the Wagner Society and the British Council. Their 1940 visit was of course vividly remembered and their progress had been followed in Holland, but it was obvious after the first performance that the achievements were far beyond the expectations of the Dutch public, dancers and critics. There was a general feeling that the English dancers had developed a style of their own and that the ideal of ballet being a unity of dancing, music and painting was taken seriously. Although Holland is usually considered a stronghold of the Central European school of dancing, much addicted to the work of Jooss, Trudi Schoop and Harald Kreutzberg, it was *Symphonic Variations* which was the greatest success. One critic said that with this ballet Ashton had made "*de la musique visible*" and had placed himself in the first rank of contemporary choreographers.

The visit to Holland lasted only for one week, from 12th to 19th March, and on their return home the company started rehearsing *Le Lac des Cygnes,* which was being thoroughly overhauled before being put back into the repertoire on 13th April. The emendations were mostly suggested by Harijs Plucis, the company's new ballet master, who had come to them from Latvia, and although they were quite small in themselves, the sum effect was to inject new life into the production and into the performances of Fonteyn and Somes. The unearthly pallor of Fonteyn's new make-up for the Swan Queen symbolised the greater depth of tragedy which she now found in Odette. Her technical accomplishment seemed to allow her infinities of time in which to develop the finest shades of meaning from every gesture, every movement, and the alliance, indeed the *absorption,* of this expressiveness into the lovely classicism of her dancing made her an ideal interpreter of this most romantic of classical ballets. Her Odile gained in flash and pace from the alterations in the choreography, and if she lacked real diamond brilliance she found other ways of pointing the contrast between the two characters. Michael Somes as Prince Siegfried gave a performance of remarkable completeness in which mime, dancing and partnering were all part of a real characterisation. The *pas de trois* was now put back into the first act of the ballet and costumed gaily in red and green. It looked vastly better in this setting and was nicely danced by Clayden, Elvin and Rassine.

Job was to be presented for the first time at Covent Garden on 20th May and was made the occasion for a Gala Performance in

LE LAC DES CYGNES

Margot Fonteyn and Michael Somes

GUEST ARTISTS

Above: Leonide Massine acknowledging applause after *The Three Cornered Hat.*
Below: Alexandra Danilova in *La Boutique Fantasque*

Action photographs by G. B. L. Wilson

aid of the Sadler's Wells Ballet Benevolent Fund, through the courtesy of the Covent Garden Opera Trust. Sir Adrian Boult conducted the first performance and Michael Benthall lent his expert advice on lighting. For the Covent Garden production Ninette de Valois decided to replace the original settings and costumes by new ones designed by John Piper, for she wanted a change and also feared the originals would look old-fashioned, and not be suitable for the larger theatre. Geoffrey Keynes was called in to lend books and to advise, and de Valois gave the matter much careful thought.

John Piper also studied the Blake drawings very thoroughly and for him the assignment was full of difficulties. He had particular trouble with the Pastoral design—anxious to preserve "a sense of Blake-ness and rusticity" but anxious also to preserve his own style as an artist. The resulting designs were consequently a "Piperised" view of Blake rather than Blake's designs transferred almost exactly to the stage as in Mrs. Raverat's version. Ninette de Valois was delighted with the result (and got very cross with Richard Buckle when he did not show the same enthusiasm).

Dr. Vaughan Williams was also consulted about the new production, but the only observation he had to make was that the music for the episode of Satan on God's throne ought to be an organ solo (it is so played at concert performances), and he remembered that Covent Garden used once to own a large and powerful organ. This had disappeared during the war, however, and so the passage had to be faked for orchestra as at Sadler's Wells. He welcomed the idea of new settings and costumes and hoped something would be done about what he described as "Elihu's 'you simply can't wear them out' pants."

There were some differences of opinion about the new *décor* and costumes (the warm colours were particularly missed), but the production as a whole was full of beauty and quiet reverence and Benthall's lighting for the first time imparted a rarefied atmosphere to the heavenly scenes. The beauty of the orchestral playing under Sir Adrian Boult will not soon be forgotten. Helpmann's Satan was a performance of devilish, darting venom, and Alexis Rassine was an excellent Elihu.

A special attraction at the Gala Performance was the appearance of Alicia Markova and Anton Dolin in the *Don Quixote pas de deux*.

P

They had been invited by Ninette de Valois and David Webster to appear with the Sadler's Wells Ballet as guest artists for some special performances and had accepted with delight. It was their first appearance in London for some nine years. In the interim they had been dancing mostly in North and South America and had been instrumental in the foundation of the American Ballet Theatre. They came back to perform some of their most famous rôles with the company they had assisted generously in its early days and they came back to an audience which was largely unacquainted with their work. (In the Sadler's Wells Ballet itself they were strangers to the younger dancers; neither Beryl Grey nor Moira Shearer had ever seen them dance.)

Dolin had been in England for two days before the Gala, but Markova came almost straight off the boat and had scarcely forgotten the roll of the ship before she was dancing at Covent Garden. It was unfortunate that they chose to appear in a classical *pas de deux* which is, above all things, a display of virtuosity and not ideally suited to their particular talents. They were received politely but not with adulation. The evening, which had opened with *Hamlet,* ended with a good performance of *Symphonic Variations,* but the choice of ballets did not induce a particularly festive atmosphere, and it seemed strange to have a Gala Performance without Margot Fonteyn. She was in Paris that spring, creating the part of Agathe in *Les Demoiselles de la Nuit* for Roland Petit.

Markova and Dolin had their proper triumph on 7th June when they appeared in *Giselle.* Markova set the seal of her mature and final interpretation upon the whole series of fine performances which London had witnessed during the past few years. Fonteyn, Chauviré and Sally Gilmour had all contributed much, but Markova seemed to contain in her fragile body the very spirit of Giselle. It is difficult to analyse the special magic of her performance, because it is so much a matter of pure intuition. Technically she is no virtuoso—in 1948 there was an obvious loss of speed and elevation in her dancing—but her *échappés, soubresauts* and *petits ronds de jambe en l'air* remain exquisite. Her reading of the part gives due prominence to her most individual qualities of lightness and delicacy, the first act having a pathetic fragility and the second a quality of intangibility that no other dancer has equalled. Dolin's

Albrecht, far more restrained than formerly, was a warm and living character and at the same time a *danseur noble* in the great classical tradition.

The pure classicism of *The Sleeping Beauty* was a great contrast to the romanticism of *Giselle* and the leading rôles in this full-length version were new to both dancers. They learned the ballet in two weeks and gave performances of great style and understanding. Markova's Aurora was built on her beautiful stage presence, precise, almost fastidious, execution and great aristocracy of bearing. It was not perhaps an ideal part for her at that stage of her career, and yet it was a great Aurora nonetheless. Dolin as Prince Florimund demonstrated admirably that it is possible to look royal on the stage without being wooden or just supercilious. His first entrance was magnificent and his mime throughout the essence of clarity. (His secret is that he *enjoys* these parts and does not dismiss them as mere cardboard princes.) His Prince Siegfried was also a fine characterisation but Markova was less successful in *Le Lac des Cygnes* than in the other two ballets. She danced exquisitely in *Les Sylphides,* however, and Dolin enjoyed a personal triumph in *Job* when he appeared again in his original part of Satan.

The visit of these two great artists was an invaluable experience for both the young dancers in the company and for the younger members of the audience. They had seen the stagecraft that comes from long experience and they had (or one hopes they had) realised that there could be more than one way of performing a particular rôle or dancing a particular variation. Certain little points of production which the visitors introduced in *Giselle* were retained by the company and when one critic had the poor taste to complain that they were dancing "simplified" versions of the classics, Ninette de Valois wrote a stern rebuke in reply.

Towards the end of the season, on 25th June, came Massine's first entirely original ballet for Sadler's Wells. Alas, *The Clock Symphony* added nothing to the reputations of either choreographer or company. Expensively, tastefully but heartlessly decorated by the incomparable French designer Christian Bérard, it was danced to Haydn's Clock Symphony and was a rather fussy fairy story about a Princess wooed by three suitors. She chooses a poor young clock-maker whose gift is an elaborate Chinese clock. The rival suitors damage the mechanism but the clock-maker soon repairs it and everyone lives happily ever after. Moira Shearer was enchantingly pretty as the Princess and Alexander Grant had a few seconds of effective dancing as the clock-maker (in the usual glamorous rags which make poverty, in the world of ballet, so enticing). But everyone else was kept on the hop the entire time to very little purpose and the overwhelming effect was one of rather childish silliness. Anne Heaton, newly promoted from the Sadler's Wells Theatre Ballet, had a tiny effective rôle among the porcelain clock figures as the Wife of the Mandarin. There was nothing of enduring interest in the ballet, however, and it received only ten performances.

The season ended on 17th July with *The Sleeping Beauty*, having lasted (in conjunction with the opera) almost continuously since the previous October. After a holiday, the company went to Edinburgh for the last weeks of the Festival and afterwards they danced at the Davis Theatre, Croydon, filling the giant cinema without difficulty. On 21st September they opened at the Théâtre des Champs-Élysées in Paris and once again found Paris initially difficult, for prices of seats were very high and the theatre was not full. The first performance was well received, however, and Fonteyn was rewarded by a multitude of flowers for her dancing in *Scènes de Ballet* and *Symphonic Variations*. Business soon improved and the company won much warm appreciation, but chiefly for their dancing, because the decoration of the ballets did not astonish Paris. *Le Lac des Cygnes* was probably the greatest success of the two-week season and was danced by an all-star cast, headed by Fonteyn and Helpmann and with Moira Shearer and Pamela May as the two leading swans. *Miracle in the Gorbals* was also much admired: "The English Ballet has taught me something new," said Boris Kochno to Ninette de Valois after the first performance of this ballet.

After leaving Paris the company went to Germany, where they found all performances had been sold out well in advance. They opened in Dusseldorf on 6th October and during the visit gave the following ballets: *Les Sylphides, Checkmate, Scènes de Ballet, The Rake's Progress, Dante Sonata, Les Patineurs,* and *Symphonic Variations.* The two outstanding successes were *Les Patineurs* and *Symphonic Variations.*

CHAPTER XIII

CINDERELLA

THE 1948–49 season opened at Covent Garden on 25th November with a new ballet by Frederick Ashton, *Don Juan*. This was danced to the Richard Strauss tone poem and had a setting and costumes by Edward Burra. The ballet was prefaced by a quotation from *La Morte Amoureuse* by Gautier, translated by Swinburne: "The love that caught strange light from Death's own eyes." The ballet took no account of the version of the story by the German poet Lenau on which Strauss based his music.

It was a strange phantasmagoria in which Don Juan pursued his various *amours* and was finally subjugated by "La Morte Amoureuse." *Don Juan* was a slick and highly professional piece of ballet-making with no real heart or drive to it. This may have been because there was no strong central character to hold it together and Helpmann was completely ineffective in the rôle that was devised for him as Don Juan, despite an attention-compelling costume of violent colour. Fonteyn (and later Elvin) danced with great strength and intensity as "La Morte Amoureuse" and Shearer showed a new warmth and grace as a Young Wife. The music is so concentrated and brief in duration, however, that it can hardly sustain a complete ballet and the introduction of carnival figures, in gaily striped costumes, used up a lot of precious music and forced the ballet to a rather abrupt conclusion. It was quite effective at first viewing, but was rather in the superficially elegant style of Ashton's earlier work.

At the first performance Margot Fonteyn had the misfortune to strain a ligament while dancing and this prevented her from appearing with the company for some three months. Inevitably this accident cast a gloom over the opening weeks of the season and there were some rather dispirited performances. On the other hand, Constant Lambert (who had been to Paris to conduct for the company) returned on a part-time basis to share the artistic direction with Ninette de Valois and Frederick Ashton, and, of course, Robert Helpmann was back as a permanent member of the company. Beryl Grey danced a particularly fine Odette-Odile early in the season, and with Pamela May, Moira Shearer and Violetta Elvin all dancing well, the company was not without ballerinas. Nevertheless the spirit of the company always seems to be affected by Fonteyn's absence, and on this occasion it must have been a particular disappointment to Frederick Ashton, who was already working on his first three-act ballet, *Cinderella,* and wanted her for the title rôle. The ballet was scheduled for production on 23rd December and was so obviously a Christmas entertainment that postponement was impossible, so the part of Cinderella was instead entrusted to Moira Shearer, then at the height of her *Red Shoes* film fame.

Ashton had envisaged the production of English ballets which would occupy an entire programme as early as 1939, when the revival of *The Sleeping Princess* at Sadler's Wells had directed attention to the three-act ballet. Now that the opportunity had come for him to create the first full-length English ballet, he was faced with a considerable responsibility, but he was ready for the task. It was vitally important that *Cinderella* should succeed, for a failure in three acts could not be hidden in the repertoire among established favourites. In the event, *Cinderella* was an immediate popular success and became one of the biggest "hits" of the theatrical season, drawing excellent houses and being featured extensively as a news story in papers and magazines.

Ashton's choice of subject and music both imposed difficulties and provided opportunities. The action of the ballet was prescribed in advance by Prokofiev's music, but the subject was bound to conjure up memories of the traditional treatment of the story in the form of an English pantomime. Ashton steered a middle course, creating choreography that was entirely individual and as contemporary in style as the music and following Petipa only in a love of the classical school in all its aristocratic beauty. There was no inexplicable mime, no formal *pas de deux* (of the *adage, variation* 1, *variation* 2, *coda,* type) and no last-act Wedding Celebrations. The pantomime element was allowed to intrude only insofar as the Ugly Sisters, played by men, were concerned.

The first act introduced the family, saw the sisters off to the Ball and then brought on the Fairy Godmother to show Cinderella a vision of the four seasons before granting her wish to go to the Ball. The second act was the Ball itself, Cinderella's conquest of Prince Charming and her flight as the clock struck twelve. In the last act the Ugly Sisters returned home, the herald arrived with the missing slipper, which established Cinderella as the lost princess (an episode perfectly suited to ballet), and there was a final apotheosis in which Cinderella and her Prince sailed away in a magic boat while the starry lights of the fairies' wands waved them godspeed.

The French designer Jean-Denis Malclès was responsible for the decoration of the ballet and he created some enchantingly pretty costumes and fairy-tale settings which lent themselves well to the transformation scenes. The departure of Cinderella to the Ball in her fairy coach, at great speed across a vast open stage, was one of the most magical moments of the ballet. Choreographically the best episodes were Cinderella's solo with her broom, the variations for the fairies of the seasons, the *pas de deux* for Cinderella and the Prince, and their brief, final *adage*. Throughout, the ballet was conveyed in terms of dancing and even the broad humour of the Ugly Sisters was given balletic expression—as in their valiant attempts to learn a gavotte and their equally valiant performances at the Ball.

Ashton used his dancers admirably with such complete understanding of their individual abilities that re-casting the ballet removed much of its original quality. The fairy variations, in particular, depended on Nadia Nerina's ebullience and fresh, young charm for Spring; on Violetta Elvin's indolent, undulating arms for Summer; on Pauline Clayden's speed and agitation for Autumn; and Beryl Grey's large, sweeping movements as Winter. The Ugly Sisters were "naturals" for Helpmann and Ashton, but have come less easily to their successors. Helpmann's portrait of the extrovert, rapacious younger sister, continually hogging the largest men and the largest oranges, was uproariously funny. Ashton's cowering and timorous elder sister, defeated always in the battle for men and finery, and death at a party, was such a perfect study of insecurity that it became touching as well as funny. Pamela May was a beautiful Fairy Godmother, and Alexander Grant, whimsical and musical, made something positive and endearing of the Jester. There was some good dancing from the *corps de ballet* and particularly from the four boys who appeared as friends of the Prince, but unfortunately the *enchaînements* devised for them were weak in character and, coupled with the pastel shades of their costumes, this prevented their dancing from making any strong, masculine impact.

The rôle of Cinderella gave Moira Shearer a great opportunity and she rose to it without betraying any sign of nervousness. Looking lovely and elegant as any film star among the cinders, she danced with a new-found freedom and swiftness, and in the beautiful ballroom *pas de deux* she showed feeling as well. Violetta Elvin later gave a different and more moving performance. She emphasised tenderness in the first act and in the second had the wide-eyed excitement of a young girl at her first ball. It was not until Fonteyn returned on 25th February to dance Cinderella, however, that every aspect of the character came truly to life. She was not afraid to look a drab and frightened waif at the beginning and this lent her transformation an additional radiance. It was one of her richest, deepest characterisations and has developed in beauty ever since. Unfortunately the general presentation of the ballet has not been afforded equal attention and it has suffered from under-rehearsal, bad stage-setting and miscasting to a quite exceptional degree. The music did not find favour in all quarters to begin with and has worn no better than the other elements, although it, too, has suffered from indifferent performance.

In March 1949, the Sadler's Wells Ballet extended a welcome to two great artists, Alexandra Danilova and Frederic Franklin, who came to dance with them as guests. Unhappily, the success of the previous year's experience with Markova and Dolin was not repeated. Danilova, a legendary character, came of an entirely different background from that of the Wells dancers. Nationality, temperament, training and experience separated her from the English company and the English repertoire and her performances remained always those of a guest and never part of the overall production. Franklin, an English dancer, had made his name with the Markova-Dolin Ballet, and in 1938 joined the Ballet Russe de Monte Carlo. (It was always a disappointment to Ninette de Valois that she failed to secure him for Sadler's Wells.) In America with the Ballet Russe de Monte Carlo he had won a great reputation as a character dancer of brilliance in ballets as diverse as *Rodeo* and *Schéhérazade,* but in London he had no opportunity to show his prowess and was seen only in the classical ballets as partner to Danilova.

They appeared for the first time with the Sadler's Wells Ballet on 14th March in *Coppélia* and later in *Le Lac des Cygnes* (Act II) and *Giselle*. Danilova danced the Can-Can in *La Boutique Fantasque* with Massine, unremarkably at the first performance (she was hampered by a slight injury), but on the occasion of her last appearance with the company, on 9th April, she gave a performance in this ballet of such gaiety and vitality that time not only stood still— it rolled back.

A Wedding Bouquet was staged at Covent Garden on 17th February with the original chorus restored and the original unintelligibility restored as well. The ballet in 1937 had been almost first in the field to find the Edwardian period "amusing," but during the following ten years the subject had been rather overworked in the English theatre. This may have been one of the reasons why *A Wedding Bouquet* seemed a little out-moded. More than one spectator walked out of the Opera House that night muttering, "I am older than a boat." The dancers seemed conscious that the ballet was not getting over on the first night and by trying too hard to be funny destroyed the style of the ballet. Only June Brae, back in her original rôle of Josephine, was relaxed and consequently delightful. Moira Shearer had a big success as the demented Julia, one of the few character parts she was ever allowed to play during her years with Sadler's Wells.

This season also saw the first London performance of Violetta Elvin in the second act of *Le Lac des Cygnes*. She gave a genuinely personal interpretation that owed nothing to the performances of her fellow ballerinas at Sadler's Wells and everything to her Russian training and careful coaching by the fine Russian teacher, Vera Volkova. She made her first entrance with a high, thrusting *pas de chat* into the centre of the stage and at once suggested the powerful conflict of a woman's soul imprisoned in the body of a swan. The strong beat of her arms on the final exit, the proud arch of her back and the carriage of her head and shoulders, all contributed to the conception of the part, and much of her dancing, particularly in the *adagio* passages, was already assured and beautiful. It was a performance of great potentialities and aroused intense interest and admiration.

On 24th March *Apparitions* was seen for the first time at Covent Garden, with scenery and costumes newly designed by Cecil Beaton to meet the needs of the new production. Constant Lambert conducted the first performance, and the abiding memory of that evening is of the great ovation which was accorded to him, quite spontaneously, by the audience which had missed him sadly during the period of his absence from the company. It was louder and longer than the applause which greeted the ballet itself when the curtain fell, and this was not unsuitable, for Lambert's arrangement of the Liszt music proved to be the most enduring element in the ballet.

In May the British Council arranged for the Sadler's Wells Ballet to appear at the Teatro Communale in Florence in connection with the May Festival. At the special request of the Festival authorities *Cinderella* was included in the repertory, together with *The Rake's Progress, Symphonic Variations, Hamlet* and *Checkmate*. The conductors were Warwick Braithwaite and Robert Irving, who had been appointed conductor to the Sadler's Wells Ballet early in the year. The theatre, which seats some 3,500, was sold out for every performance, and *Cinderella* was surprisingly successful with this non-English audience. *Symphonic Variations* was also greatly admired—"Here choreography and execution soar to the highest emotional plane," said the *Nazione*—and Margot Fonteyn and Moira Shearer enjoyed personal triumphs.

At the end of the Italian season four of the dancers, Moira Shearer, Anne Heaton, Michael Somes and Alexander Grant, went on to Turkey to give some performances at the Opera House, Istanbul, and at the theatre in Ankara, in order to promote interest in the work that was being done there to establish a national ballet under the guidance of Ninette de Valois and by teachers sent out from the Sadler's Wells School.

July was a holiday month, and in August there was a month's season at Covent Garden, during which the company tried out the repertoire and the casts that were to be taken to the United States of America and Canada when the Sadler's Wells Ballet made its biggest overseas venture in the autumn. Constant Lambert was going with them to New York, and he appeared at the conductor's desk at Covent Garden on many occasions during this season, always being greeted with affection by the audience. London had a lively month speculating about the respective chances of the different ballets in New York, appraising Leslie Hurry's modified settings for *Le Lac des Cygnes*, and being rather bored and sceptical about the revival of *Façade*. When the London season ended the American repertoire was packed up and nearly fifty tons of scenery and costumes were shipped across the Atlantic on the *Fort Spokane*. The dancers meanwhile went off to dance in three suburban cinemas in ballets which were not going to be shown in America.

CHAPTER XIV

TRANSATLANTIC TRIUMPHS

The First American Tour

THE visit to America was the result of some years of discussion and negotiation.

The American impresario Sol Hurok had broken with Ballet Theatre early in 1946, and had been left without a ballet company but with commitments to present one throughout the following season. Sadler's Wells was suggested to him but he had not then seen them at Covent Garden, and instead he concocted a company which was called the Original Ballet Russe. It consisted of the remnants of the de Basil company and repertoire, plus four ballets from the repertoire of the Marquis de Cuevas' Ballet International, and Markova and Dolin as guest artists.

Hurok's experiences with this company were disastrous—financially, artistically, emotionally—and he thought the time had come to end his lifelong association with ballet; he even contemplated calling his autobiography *To Hell with Ballet*.

Then Hurok saw *The Sleeping Beauty* at Covent Garden and realised that ballet still had power to excite him. He longed to present the company in America, but he remembered the rougher passages in his associations with ballet companies in the past and took no immediate action. Then he discovered that an American ballet company was discussing plans to present the Sadler's Wells Ballet at the Metropolitan Opera House, and this at once moved him to action. At about the same time he was commissioned by Governor Grover Whalen to organise an International Dance Festival as part of the celebrations for the Golden Jubilee of Greater New York and immediately he got into touch with David Webster.

Webster spent parts of January and February 1948 in New York and had many conversations with Hurok, who made a definite offer that the Sadler's Wells Ballet should participate in the Festival and afterwards make a tour of America. Unfortunately, however, the Festival ballet performances could not be given at the Metropolitan Opera House, and would have to be given in the far smaller City Center Theater. The stage at this theatre was too small to accommodate the Sadler's Wells productions of either *The Sleeping Beauty* or *Giselle*, and Webster felt that the company should not be asked to make its New York début without either of these two major works. Reluctantly he had to decline Governor Whalen's invitation, and with the failure of the New York arrangements the remainder of the proposed American tour was cancelled.

Nevertheless Hurok and Webster had agreed in principle that an American season by the Sadler's Wells Ballet was both possible and desirable, and Hurok continued to work towards that end. The New York Golden Jubilee Festival took place in October 1948 (the Paris Opéra Ballet participating), and by the following January Hurok had signed the Sadler's Wells Ballet for its first American tour, to open on 9th October 1949, at the Metropolitan Opera House, New York.

Ninette de Valois, as well as David Webster, was anxious to show the Sadler's Wells Ballet in America, and believed that they were ready for the expedition. Many discussions took place about the particular ballets which should be shown, and there were many arguments and differences of opinion. Hurok was insistent that the opening night programme should consist of *The Sleeping Beauty*, and he was also responsible for the inclusion of *Façade* in the repertoire. London ballet people tried to tell themselves that this was on account of the tremendous publicity and *réclame* which had resulted from Dr. Edith Sitwell's recent appearances in New York, where she had recited her poems in a presentation of the original *Façade* entertainment, but the reason for Hurok's insistence was probably far less high-minded. *Façade* had been infallible ballet box office in England for nearly twenty years, and he knew that in America the appeal with the general theatre public would be just as great. As usual, he was perfectly right.

For the first time in American theatrical history, tickets for the Sadler's Wells season were put on sale at the end of June, four months before the season was due to commence, and this proved to be a completely accurate assessment of the public demand that resulted. The Hurok publicity machine is a very wonderful organisation but even so the amount of interest shown in the company's visit, not only in New York but throughout the United States, was extraordinary. For several weeks before the opening the New York dance world talked about nothing else, and even outside the dance world to be introduced as "from England" meant that one was immediately bombarded with questions about the company (which Americans persist in calling "the Sadler Wells") and about the beautiful Moira Shearer—for *The Red Shoes* had enjoyed great popularity in America.

The company flew in to New York on 4th October, the girls handsomely fitted out by all the leading *couturiers,* so that they might act as ambassadors for British fashion. (The boys, who received not so much as a pair of socks apiece, took a rather jaundiced view of their colleagues' splendour.) Press photographers thronged the airport, all clamouring for "cheesecake" pictures, and the girls put a brave face on it, hitched up their skirts and showed a leg. In New York the company were lodged in a variety of hotels; the administration at the sober Gotham, the leading dancers at the St. Moritz overlooking Central Park, and the remainder of the company at the Bryant on a noisy corner of Broadway and 56th Street. For nearly all of them it was the first sight they had had of New York, and the excitement engendered by that fabulous city, then enjoying a spell of brilliant Fall sunshine, did much to make them forget their nervousness about the opening night. All over the town were examples of the widespread interest in their visit, and at the theatre every dancer found waiting for him or her a copy of *Dance News,* a special issue devoted to welcoming them to New York. Ninette de Valois, touched and impressed by this gesture, telephoned her thanks to the editor of *Dance News,* Anatole Chujoy, and he invited her to lunch at the Russian Tea Room on 7th October, two days before the opening.

Ninette de Valois arrived for this luncheon in an anxious frame of mind. She was still quite convinced that Hurok was wrong in opening with *The Sleeping Beauty.* She felt this was the wrong choice, because firstly New York was not used to full-length ballets, and, secondly, the ballerina (Fonteyn) did not appear on the stage until the second act. She thought the audience would not respond to the pantomime and the variations in the Prologue, that the curtain would come down without applause and the house would be cold for Fonteyn's entrance. Chujoy did his best to allay her apprehensions, and expressed the opinion that Lambert would be greeted with applause, that there would be applause after the overture, on the rise of the curtain, after each variation and particularly for the Lilac Fairy, stop-the-show applause for Ashton after the Carabosse *pas d'action* and an ovation for everybody when the curtain fell. De Valois did not entirely believe him but went back to rehearsal slightly reassured.

The Metropolitan Opera House in New York, or "the Met" as it is always called, is a large, drab mass of brickwork which stands between 39th and 40th Streets on Broadway, just south of Times Square. It is in the heart of the garment-makers' district, and instead of the barrowloads of vegetables which obstruct the streets around Covent Garden, there are trolleys full of dresses, suits, overcoats—every conceivable off-the-peg garment—which are trundled round from factory to wholesaler to retailer by hand and seem miraculously to emerge safely from the tangle of traffic through which they pass. The auditorium of the Met is considerably larger than Covent Garden and seats about 3,600 people. It is similarly shaped but is wider, deeper and higher. There are five great circles and behind them all are wide promenades carpeted in crimson. The woodwork is dark and the upholstery crimson, and the atmosphere one of old-fashioned opulence, but lacking the period charm and elegance of Covent Garden. Nevertheless the decoration was an immediate source of pleasure to Margot Fonteyn, who was shown round by Nora Kaye as soon as she arrived in America and was both relieved and delighted to find that it had age and atmosphere and was not "all steel and chromium." The great glory of the Met is its curtain of gold brocade, which looks magical when lit by footlights and forms a perfect background when artists, and particularly dancers, take calls in front of it.

The Gala Opening of the Sadler's Wells season was timed for 8 p.m. instead of the usual 8.30, so that the critics could see the whole of *The Sleeping Beauty* and still meet their deadlines. By 6 p.m. a knot of people were waiting to be let in to fight for the best places in the Standing Room (in a position roughly equivalent to the back of the Stalls Circle at Covent Garden), and by 7.45 the whole pavement outside the Met was seething with people; some trying to enter, some still hoping to buy tickets, sharpers trying to sell tickets for fabulous sums, and curious sightseers. It was very hot (the temperature had shot up to 85°), and by 8 p.m. the Met was packed full. Every seat was occupied, the standees were four deep on the main floor and there were enough people wedged into the first tier boxes (the famous Golden Horseshoe) to have given the New York Fire Department heart failure. Below the Mayor's box were draped the Union Jack, the Stars and Stripes and the flag of the City of New York. All Society and all the dance world were there in full feather, and the atmosphere of excited anticipation was intense.

Alexander Woolcott once remarked that the English have an extraordinary ability for flying into a great calm. Despite all the worries and preparations of the months preceding their American début, the Sadler's Wells dancers by the actual opening night had worked themselves into an appearance of perfect *sangfroid*. The performance of *The Sleeping Beauty* which they gave excelled anything they had done in Europe, and the dancers were conscious of (and almost astonished by) the ease and confidence with which they danced once they were actually out on the famous stage.

The evening progressed as Mr. Chujoy had foretold. There was a great outbreak of applause when Constant Lambert appeared at the conductor's desk, and this was an immediate expression of friendly interest as if the Americans appreciated the part he had played in the building of Sadler's Wells. He conducted the national anthems, and before he was half-way through *God Save the King* every English person in the audience was conscious of sudden national pride, so that the success of the company became a matter of almost personal anxiety. Of success there could be no doubt after the rise of the curtain. There was warm applause for Oliver Messel's setting, incomparably more magnificent than anything offered at that time by the American ballet companies, and little bursts and spurts of applause as the different personages made their entry, culminating in a real welcome for Beryl Grey as she came on as the Lilac Fairy. The fairy variations were danced by Violetta Elvin, Pamela May, Anne Negus, Pauline Clayden and Avril Navarre, and all were well received, Beryl Grey's variation arousing particular enthusiasm. By the end of the Prologue there was a feeling of well-being throughout the audience, and Mayor O'Dwyer leaned over from his box to say to Ninette de Valois, "You're in,

CINDERELLA

Above: Frederick Ashton and Robert Helpmann as the Ugly Sisters, with Margot Fonteyn

Right: Moira Shearer

Photographs by Roger Wood

Walter E. Owen

ARRIVING IN NEW YORK

David Webster, Leslie Edwards, Robert Helpmann, Nora Kaye, Frederick
Ashton, Margot Fonteyn, Sol Hurok

TWENTY-FIRST BIRTHDAY GROUP

Baron

lady." Completely mystified, she had to hurry off and ask the first American she could find if this was "good or bad."

The curtain rose on Act I, the Spell, and by now the company were really enjoying themselves. The Waltz ended and the orchestra began the exciting build-up that heralds the first appearance of the Princess Aurora. A ripple of expectation seemed to run through the audience and they began to applaud long before Fonteyn actually appeared on the stage. She consequently made her entrance to applause that swelled into a tremendous ovation and from then on it was more than success—it was triumph. The great moments of the evening were, of course, the *Rose Adagio* and the superb last act *pas de deux*. Both were danced with complete confidence, ease and beauty, and Harold Turner, who was appearing as the First Prince, said afterwards that he had never known Fonteyn so relaxed, so completely without strain in the Rose Adagio. It was the performance of her career to that date, and Helpmann excelled himself as Prince Florimund. Each of them seemed to have added an extra inch to their stature as artists, to have taken the final step from the top of the ladder of national celebrity into the company of internationally supreme artists of the theatre.

At the end of the performance the great gold curtain rose and fell again and again as the audience cheered and cheered their approval. It was a mass triumph and at the same time an individual triumph; "a great company" and "a great ballerina" were the words on everyone's lips. The stage was banked in flowers and at last into the midst of all this colour and pageantry came the slight, elegant figure of Ninette de Valois to express her thanks to the audience and to win their hearts with the simple admission, "Frankly, we were *terrified* of you."

After the performance a giant party was given for the company by Mayor William O'Dwyer at the Gracie Mansion, the official residence of the Mayor of New York, with its lawns overlooking the East River. Buses conveyed the dancers from the theatre to the party and they were accorded a police escort (usually reserved for the President and visiting rulers), which led them with sirens screaming across the city and through all the traffic lights—an experience which the younger dancers enjoyed as much as anything on the entire trip. Soon after midnight the newspapers were on sale in Times Square and the reviews were excellent. Both sober dance critics and hardened columnists were unanimous and lavish with their praise. Only one bored gossip writer complained that it was all "as dignified and as unexciting as one of Queen Mary's hats."

(A tremendous amount of extra publicity accrued to the company on account of the Mayor having as his guest Miss Sloan Simpson, a former model, whom he subsequently married. Their picture was sent out by all news services and appeared in hundreds of papers throughout the United States with a note to the effect that it had been taken at the opening of the Sadler's Wells Ballet. Everyone who subscribed to a press cuttings service for notices of the ballet was inundated with clippings of this picture from newspapers in every state of the Union.)

The great question after the opening performance was, of course, could they keep it up? Over the season it became obvious that they could, although it also became quite clear that all the repertoire was not going to find equal favour and that a different opening night programme could have put a very different complexion on the company's reception in America.

The modern ballets came in for a considerable amount of criticism and were treated with some reserve by the critics. They were all willing to admit that America could offer nothing comparable to the big classical productions, but in the field of short modern works they felt (and rightly) that they could hold their own. *The Rake's Progress* was greatly admired and *Symphonic Variations* won some very warm supporters, although the Press was inclined to misunderstand it and dismiss it as "watered Balanchine." *Façade*, to the stupefaction of everyone but Mr. Hurok, was a smash hit. It came over extraordinarily well in the vast theatre, audiences doted on it and called it "cute" and the critics loved it. *Hamlet* had a rather mixed reception and notices, and *Miracle in the Gorbals* "got by," but only just: ballet people tended to think it "bad Tudor" and the Modern Dance people thought it wasn't dancing at all. "It is done in dramatic rather than choreographic terms, and there can be no doubt that the stageful of people is skilfully handled," wrote John Martin in the *New York Times*. "But there is surely not a cliché missed or a platitude avoided." *Apparitions* was another failure. The audience found it old-fashioned and dreadfully slow. On the other hand, *A Wedding Bouquet*, with Lambert as orator, was perfect fare for sophisticated New Yorkers, and they liked

Checkmate as well. *Job,* however, was a total loss. As de Valois had foreseen, no one understood its particular style or the sources of its inspiration, and it was dismissed as being dreadfully boring. *Cinderella* had a rather sticky first performance, but was later highly successful and earned some wonderful press notices for the Ugly Sisters. No modern ballets came anywhere near the popularity of *The Sleeping Beauty* and *Le Lac des Cygnes,* and critics who had used up nearly all their superlatives about *The Sleeping Beauty* became even more eloquent about *Le Lac des Cygnes* (although one critic complained, "Four acts of swans is a lot of swans," and another thought Fonteyn's *fouettés* were a dismal failure when compared to the dazzling display of pyrotechnics given by the Rockettes at Radio City Music Hall.)

The reason for the great popularity of the classical ballets was that the full-length versions were entirely new to New York, and they were the ballets which best displayed the qualities in which Sadler's Wells excelled and in which most American companies were deficient. American dancers were the first to remark and applaud the superiority of the Sadler's Wells *corps de ballet,* the *ensemble* work and the general standard of production. There was a strong feeling, however, that dancer for dancer the Americans could hold their own, and given sufficient security in which to carry out long-term policies, they could do as well.

Fonteyn was recognised everywhere as a unique artist. The way in which she identified herself with a rôle and refrained from any obvious appeal to the sensibilities of the audience was a revelation to the Americans. Moira Shearer's picture filled the gossip columns and her name filled the theatres throughout the tour. From the beginning the American public loved her. Beryl Grey also had an immediate success, both on account of her clean, strong dancing and her warm personality. For the rest there was admiration but not amazement, and the male dancing was emphatically found unsatisfactory on this first visit. The boys were not considered strong dancers, but on the other hand their style and bearing in the classical ballets was greatly admired.

Criticism was genuine and honest, and in every case the company was judged by the highest standards. Reviewers naturally differed in their individual approach according to their respective knowledge and experience, and some American slang and curious

phrasing in the more popular papers gave continual shocks to the
English dancers. Robert Helpmann must have been particularly
astonished to read in one paper the critic's opinion that "Robert
Helpmann appears to be England's equivalent of Anton Dolin."

The public welcome and the overwhelming hospitality lavished
upon the dancers by the whole of New York's ballet society was heart-
warming in its generosity. The School of American Ballet and Ballet
Arts both threw open their classes to the company, who thus had
opportunities to work with such teachers as Balanchine, Doubrovska,
Muriel Stuart, Oboukhoff, Lazovsky, Nemchinova and Craske.

The Sadler's Wells Ballet in New York was more than a smash
hit. It was the greatest ballet success ever known in that city, and
rivalled the musical *South Pacific* in popularity and box-office
takings (the Press, in fact, called the ballet *North Atlantic*). During
the four-week season of thirty-four performances in New York
the company grossed $256,000 exclusive of tax, and *Variety* gave
them its front-page banner headline, the first time ballet had
achieved this distinction since the foundation of the paper in 1905.
Under inch-high letters proclaiming "Ballet Bowls over Broadway," *Variety* reported the financial successes of the Sadler's Wells
Ballet and the Ballets de Paris of Roland Petit, which was also
appearing in New York, and came to the following conclusion:
"That a dancing troupe from Paris would prove to be exhilarating
and sexy was somewhat to be expected. But that a ballet company
from stolid Britain, the land of mutton and ale, of tweeds and
Scotch whisky, would prove to be exotic and glamorous, was a
complete surprise. It's given a fairy-like quality to Broadway."

The New York season ended on 6th November with a great
ovation from the audience and a speech of thanks from Ninette de
Valois. Constant Lambert returned to London at the end of the
New York engagement, and his place was filled on the tour by
Robert Zeller. The ballets *Cinderella, Job* and *Apparitions* were
shipped home at once, as they were not thought suitable for touring.
The company set off in a special train of six baggage cars, a diner
and seven Pullmans, the first stop being Washington. There
President Truman attended the opening performance at Constitution Hall, but as there were no facilities for hanging scenery the
ballets had to be presented with only costumes, props and limited
lighting effects. The highly polished surface of the stage caused

many mishaps among the dancers, and the fact that Fonteyn herself slipped over at one point was thought sufficiently newsworthy to be reported in the next day's English newspapers.[1]

After Washington the Sadler's Wells Ballet visited Richmond, Philadelphia, Chicago, East Lansing and Detroit. *The Sleeping Beauty* was shipped home after the Chicago engagement, and eight members of the company, who were not required in the smaller repertoire that was to be shown on the remainder of the tour, also returned to London. Ninette de Valois also took leave of the company after Chicago in order to attend to business in London. She travelled quietly under her own name of Mrs. A. P. Connell, and was not recognised until she reached London Airport. Even there she might have slipped through unnoticed, but a reporter recognised the smart travel coat she was wearing as one of the "Sadler's Wells fashions" and then identified the wearer. The Press was held at bay that evening by Dr. Connell while his wife rested after her journey, but early the next morning she was back at work at Covent Garden and calmly announcing her intention to produce a new ballet, *Don Quixote,* the following February.

From Detroit the ballet company crossed to Canada, where they danced in Toronto, Ottawa and Montreal. In Toronto they were greeted by a heavy snowstorm, by free Coca-Cola, presented by the makers, and a rival attraction in the form of the Calgary Stampeders, who had invaded Toronto for the yearly football game. Stampeders and dancers were introduced to each other at a City Hall reception, and each patronised the other's entertainment when free time allowed. In Montreal the box-office success was so remarkable that one newspaper published a cartoon of a hold-up with the gunman saying, "Never mind the money—give me those Sadler's Wells Ballet tickets." The tour ended in Montreal on 11th December, so the dancers were home in good time for Christmas.

The dancers had only a few days' holiday and opened their winter season at Covent Garden on 26th December. The obvious choice for a "welcome home" programme would have been *The Sleeping Beauty,* but the scenery had been damaged in transit from

---

[1] When the dancers returned to London they were comforted by Sir Stafford Cripps. "Speaking as a member of the Treasury," he said, "I can tell you that you are not the only persons who have slipped up in Washington."

America and was not sufficiently repaired for the ballet to be given, so *Cinderella* was chosen instead. It was, however, a completely unsuitable ballet for such a gala occasion. The theatre had been completely sold out for weeks in advance and the company had never before had so much publicity throughout the national Press, yet the warmth and excitement that should have characterised the evening was curiously absent.

Cinderella is not an applause-catching ballet. It does not have great climaxes in the dancing or big "entrances" when an English audience can let itself go, and on this occasion the audience let the curtain rise in silence and greeted the whole of the first act with no more than polite applause—as if they wanted to show that they were not barbarians like the Americans and would not dream of applauding while the ballet was in progress. By the end of the evening things had improved a little, and at the very end there was a tremendous ovation, but by then the damage had been done. The dancers had had a thoroughly miserable evening, were depressed and discouraged, and probably longing to catch the next boat back to America, where friendly applause and the warm response of audiences had continually stimulated them to fine, tingling performances.

De Valois and Balanchine Ballets

Audience and dancers soon recovered from the anti-climax of this opening performance, however, and the early weeks of the London season progressed smoothly, the repertoire consisting mainly of the classical ballets, with many varieties of cast. On 20th February, as planned, the first performance was given of *Don Quixote*, Ninette de Valois' first creation at Covent Garden.

The music by Roberto Gerhard had originally been commissioned by Mr. Harold Rubin at the time he was director of the Arts Theatre Ballet, with the intention that it should be produced at the Arts with Sara Luzita as Dulcinea. The Arts Theatre Ballet disbanded, however, and the ballet was never produced. The music was put on one side, although parts of it were broadcast from time to time. The challenge of a canvas as large as the Cervantes novel, with its endless possibilities for character drawing, was a subject to attract de Valois, and she decided to do the ballet. An adaptation was made of some celebrated passages from the novel, each forming a virtually self-contained scene but linked by the figure of the Knight himself into one long adventure in the dream world of his own making.

The ballet as a whole was a work of impressive intellectual understanding rather than of imagination, a style imposed, perhaps, by the music, which lacked big climaxes and romantic melodies. Throughout the ballet emotion was curiously lacking, and the only really moving moment was Sancho Panza's pathetic fright and sorrow when he realised his master was dying. Decoratively, *Don Quixote* was more satisfactory. Edward Burra, the designer, had already worked for the opera company at Covent Garden, and he designed sets of a grandeur and bareness that matched the arid Spanish landscape. The drop curtain of the lean knight on his lean horse, with Sancho Panza perched behind, was one of the best things in the ballet, but the costumes were less interesting.

The choreography as a whole resembled the more pedestrian parts of *Checkmate* (the windmills of *Don Quixote* at once recalled the castles in the chess ballet), but there were some very original movements for Fonteyn as the peasant Aldonza Lorenzo, an earthy maiden whose gestures were rough, turned in, mocking, seductive and magnificently alive. As Dulcinea she performed simple classical *enchaînements* which displayed her gifts as a classical dancer rather than her interpretative abilities. The Knight himself was afforded only the slightest thread of choreography, however, and only a superhuman artist could have created a sufficiently strong character to unite the various episodes of the ballet. Helpmann, in a superb make-up, tried valiantly but was defeated by the choreographer before he began. Many of the small parts were played with skill and insight, and Alexander Grant was particularly successful in establishing the greasy peasant Sancho Panza as a real person.

Don Quixote was received with respect—respect such as the status of the choreographer might inspire—and it had some genuine admirers, who thought it a serious work worthy to stand alongside *Job*, *The Rake's Progress* and *Checkmate* as an example of de Valois' work on an heroic scale. To others, it was less satisfactory. One critic headlined his review with a quotation from Belloc, "Remote and Ineffectual Don," and the chief complaint was of a lack of theatrical vigour, action and interest. For the first time in her life, Ninette de Valois was facing a charge of being clever but boring.

Frederick Ashton had spent most of February in New York producing *Illuminations* for the New York City Ballet, but he flew back immediately after the first performance and was in London in time for the Command Performance which was given at Covent Garden on 9th March. The Sadler's Wells Ballet had been invited to provide a programme in honour of the visit of the President of the French Republic and Madame Auriol, who were the guests of the King and Queen. The Royal Opera House was specially decorated by Oliver Messel for the occasion, and for the first time since the war the auditorium was able to match the spectacle in beauty and magnificence. The gala programme consisted of *Symphonic Variations*, *Façade* and the last act of *The Sleeping Beauty*. In addition, Constant Lambert conducted a performance of his "Aubade Héroique." The artists were presented during an intermission and Ninette de Valois was decorated with the Legion of Honour by President Auriol.

Early in March George Balanchine arrived in London to start rehearsals for his *Ballet Imperial*, which he was to produce for Sadler's Wells in return for Ashton's *Illuminations*. The first performance had been announced for 5th April, which did not allow very much time for rehearsals, but the company learned the intricate choreography in three weeks and won the sincere admiration of Balanchine. New *décor* and costumes were designed for the production by Eugene Berman, his first work for Sadler's Wells, although he had collaborated with Ashton in 1939 on *Devil's Holiday* for the Ballet Russe de Monte Carlo.

Ballet Imperial was the first Balanchine ballet the English dancers had performed, and they discovered at once that it was truly a dancers' ballet of pure dancing, but containing none of the emotional undertones that Ashton usually suggested in his most abstract compositions. The dancers proved their ability, as a well-trained and efficient company, to interpret the work of a strange choreographer, and Sadler's Wells gained a masterpiece of choreography.

"Choreographic movement is an end in itself, and its only purpose is to create the impression of intensity and beauty," wrote Balanchine in some informal "Notes on Choreography," and

Ballet Imperial was a perfect illustration of this thesis. The curtain rose on two diagonal lines of dancers—eight girls facing eight boys—and it seemed a statement of the resources the choreographer would use: a stage for dancing on, dancers to dance, Tchaikovsky's second piano concerto to set the pulse, and the handsome Berman set of gold curtains, blue ermine-wreathed pillars and a surmounting Imperial eagle to pay homage to the Russian tradition to which the movement would owe its inspiration. Throughout the ballet there was an exultance in movement, movement for its own beautiful sake, that was immediately communicated to the audience. How fresh, how joyous were the *sissonnes* in which Beryl Grey traversed the stage with upraised arms! How simple, yet how beautiful, was the end of the *pas de deux* when Fonteyn gently lowered her heel to the ground and her head to her partner's shoulder. *Ballet Imperial* admitted no subservience to the other arts. It was an end in itself, and that end was ballet.

The first performance was well danced, but the company improved further as they became more familiar with the ballet. Three ballerinas were launched in the leading rôle before Balanchine returned to America. Fonteyn (who danced two performances before going to Milan for some guest appearances at La Scala) was musical, beautifully placed and composed, but not naturally suited to the style of the choreography. She would better have graced one of Balanchine's lyrical ballets such as *Serenade* or *Apollo* or his romantic *Night Shadow*, for she is above all a dancer who excels in choreography which has a heart.

Moira Shearer, on the other hand, had the right flash and brilliance and also the speed. Violetta Elvin had the Russian grandeur of style and excelled in the *adagio,* but at early performances she tended to bluff her way through the more intricate passages (and much of the choreography for the ballerina is of exceptional difficulty). The real "Balanchine dancer" in the company, however, was unquestionably Beryl Grey, who danced the secondary rôle. From the beginning she seemed confident and happy; a dancer pure and simple, a wonderful, magnificent dancer, she seemed to glory in the performance, and she has never had a better rôle.

The men in the ballet are subsidiary to the women—as in the Imperial Russian Ballet and as in most of Balanchine's works—but Michael Somes gave a performance of great style and quality which won a fine tribute from Lincoln Kirstein. The company as a whole rose to the demands of the ballet, and each dancer gave a performance of soloist standard without ever intruding upon the design of the ballet. It was a wonderful experience to see the large company all *dancing* together as if their hearts would burst with the joy of it, and to see them rise in the air simultaneously beating *entrechats,* and then drop to one knee with arms extended in a gesture of exultation.

The ballet seemed to act as a tonic for the company as well as for the audience. The spring of 1950 was a period of invigorating performances and the success of the new production, coupled with the great triumphs of the American tour, seemed to give the dancers new assurance and attack. By now the dancers all knew that they would be returning to America in the autumn for a return engagement at the Metropolitan Opera House in New York and a more extensive tour of the continent. At the end of April it was announced that $141,000 had been taken in advance bookings, five months before the season was due to open, and it was confidently expected that all tickets would have been sold by the end of May.[1] These reports were continually encouraging for the company, and all the dancers looked forward to another American tour, but in the meantime there were excitements at home.

Ballabile

On 5th May at Covent Garden there was a Gala Performance, in aid of the Sadler's Wells Ballet Benevolent Fund. The occasion saw the first performance of a new ballet by the young French choreographer Roland Petit. It also introduced to the Covent Garden repertoire *décor* and costumes by Antoni Clavé, who had made such a sensation with his work for Petit's *Carmen* the previous year. For Sadler's Wells Petit arranged a light-

---

[1] Advance publicity hand-outs from the Metropolitan included a description of *Le Lac des Cygnes* that is now a classic: "The Sadler's Wells Ballet is the only company here performing the full and magical four acts of Tchaikovsky's celebrated work with original excruciating vignettes of great eighteenth-century dancers and theatre managers. . . ." The explanation was that *The Prospect Before Us* had at one time been scheduled for the American repertoire, and although the ballet was subsequently dropped, one line of descriptive matter got left in the hand-out.

hearted little ballet which he called simply *Ballabile*. He had discussed the idea with Constant Lambert when they met in New York the previous year, and Lambert suggested the music should be his beloved Chabrier. He arranged the score, choosing some gay compositions and some nostalgic ones, and conducted a number of performances. Clavé's contribution was brilliant and matched the music in beauty and charm.

The choreography was not particularly distinguished, and subsequently the ballet fell into a decline and was almost killed by alternative, inadequate casts, but the early performances had an enchantment of their own. Petit has—or had then—a happy gift of avoiding the obvious. He could invent nonsensical situations and pay his audience the compliment of never quite explaining them. There is something provocative in this uncertainty, and it is a quality that is becoming increasingly rare in ballet to-day. One of the loveliest episodes in *Ballabile* was "Sunday on the River," when Alexander Grant, with his special gift of appearing solitary in the midst of a crowd, walked across the stage, climbed a ladder and sat quite still, fishing. There was no explanation, no reason; he just fished. In the "Street in the Rain" section there was a funeral which was ghoulishly funny and equally unexplained. Roland Petit, in fact, could throw rings round the moon as gaily as Jean Anouilh, but unfortunately *Ballabile* lacked any real backbone of choreography to support the fantasies. The choreography seemed to have been tossed off casually once the general *mise-en-scène* had been arrived at and it had no real affinity with any other element of the production.

Music, *décor* and actual dancing were all, however, of the first order and succeeded in carrying the flimsy choreography. Unconventional in his casting, as in all things, Petit chose his dancers with scant regard for official promptings, and gave Anne Negus her first real opportunity as a comedienne—an opportunity which brought her immediate success, although it came too late to compensate for the years of disappointment which had preceded it or to affect her decision to leave the company. Margaret Dale, in a tiny passage as an equestrienne, displayed a vitality and a lovely strong jump that won her spontaneous applause at every performance. Violetta Elvin was the most romantic figure and had a warm beauty that suggested she might have been an excellent Carmen.

Alexander Grant was the central character, linking the episodes; he was very good and yet he might have been better. There was less heart to the character than to his Jester, his Barber, or his Sancho Panza, and perhaps a more artificial make-up would have helped.

Coming of Age

An event of special significance for everyone who had ever worked with or watched the Sadler's Wells Ballet took place on 15th May 1950. On that evening, in the presence of H.R.H. Princess Margaret, the company celebrated their twenty-first anniversary[1] with a coming-of-age performance at Sadler's Wells Theatre in Islington, in which past and present members of the company participated. It was an occasion of purely private delight, fun and memories, and would have meant very little to a stranger who knew nothing of the company's history. The ballets performed were *The Haunted Ballroom, A Wedding Bouquet,* the orgy scene from *The Rake's Progress* and *Façade.* In as many cases as possible the different parts were performed by the artists who created them, and in the casting of other rôles precedence was given to length of service. Rehearsals had been going on for some time and there had been many happy reunions. Most of the girls who had danced at the early performances were by now married and mothers of substantial families, and they compared their respective waistlines and lack of turn-out with glee.

The performance was not an occasion for individual triumphs, because the whole point of the evening was to honour the company as a company, over its whole twenty-one years. Nevertheless there must have been lumps in many throats at the spectacle of Margot Fonteyn, looking tiny and wan, playing her early part of the Young Treginnis. Walter Gore came back to play the Rake—and to play him vastly better than in 1935—and Sheila McCarthy was there to serenade a bottle with her corsets. Ursula Moreton hitched up her skirts as the Street Dancer and Molly Brown (the mother of five boys) was once again the little servant. William Chappell

---

[1] It was really, of course, only twenty years since the first full evening of ballet had been given at Sadler's Wells, but nobody noticed the mistake until the anniversary had been celebrated. The twenty-fifth anniversary, consequently, had to be scheduled for six years after the "twenty-first"—in the spring of 1956!

was unhappily prevented from dancing Popular Song in *Façade* as he had sprained an ankle rehearsing the day before, but it was danced with awe-inspiring gravity by Harold Turner and Walter Gore. Perhaps *A Wedding Bouquet* was the most fun of all, with the inimitable Helpmann, with Mary Honer looking radiant and unchanged as the Bride, with Constant Lambert reciting the words from a table on the stage (fortified by real champagne), and all the "original cast" getting in a delightful and hopeless muddle— not least Ninette de Valois, who undertook her old part of Webster and gave the audience that night some glimpse of her true gaiety and complete lack of pomposity as she collapsed exhausted at one point and, with a helpless giggle, just gave up.

At the end dancers and audience sang "Auld Lang Syne" together, and Ninette de Valois, acknowledging a tremendous personal ovation, once again turned the credit away from herself with a deep-felt tribute to "those artists whose discipline, comradeship and the putting of art before self has enabled English Ballet to win through."

For the audience it had been a wonderful evening, but for the company, past and present, it had probably been even better. When the curtain fell on the orgy scene from *The Rake's Progress* the group of mothers were rewarded by hearing the choreographer declare, "Well, I shall *always* have that danced by married women in future," and when the final curtain came down the dancers themselves had an opportunity of expressing their admiration for their Director. The cheering could be heard long after the audience had reluctantly left the theatre and the attendants had tidied away the last empty ice-cream carton.

The season that ended on 8th July had lasted without a break for twenty-eight weeks in London, following immediately after the American tour, but when Ninette de Valois came on to the stage to make her customary speech it was to say good-bye to the London audience for a long spell of about six months. One solitary week of performances would be given at Covent Garden in August and then the company would be away on a much longer second tour of the United States and Canada. They would be back early in 1951 but without two artists who were that night giving their farewell performances. Palma Nye and Harold Turner, who for many years had been invaluable members of the company, danced the leading rôles in *The Three Cornered Hat* and received a special tribute from the audience.

The season had been an interesting and successful one, and the introduction of two guest choreographers had been welcomed by both dancers and audience. The three new ballets had all received a large number of performances, and *Ballet Imperial* headed the list of all ballets with twenty-nine performances (even *Les Patineurs* could boast only twenty-five). Choreographically the palm went to Balanchine for *Ballet Imperial* and decoratively to Clavé for *Ballabile,* but the standard of *décor* in the other two new ballets, by Berman and Burra, was exceptionally high. Ashton's only new ballet of the year, *Illuminations,* had been for another company, but his important work for English ballet had been recognised in the Birthday Honours by the decoration, C.B.E.

The dancers had had a hard season, but an invigorating one, and they prepared for the next American visit with confidence. The farewell week in London contained nothing of special interest, as only ballets not being shown in America could be given, and it was probably the only season in the company's history when no ballets by either de Valois or Ashton were given. The audience gave the company an enthusiastic send-off, and there were many friends and well-wishers assembled in Floral Street the following week when they all boarded the buses that were to take them on the first stage of their trans-Atlantic expedition.

The Second American Tour

The tour this time was to be considerably more ambitious. The company were to travel some 15,000 miles through America and Canada, visiting thirty-two towns in the space of nineteen weeks. The task of planning and organising this expedition in advance was gigantic, particularly as the firm policy of the company was to tour the ballets in their proper condition, with no cutting down of scenery or personnel. It was felt that the company had a charge to show every side of English ballet and not just a few works that might be particularly popular at the box office.

This meant that a repertoire of considerable size had to be packed up and shipped across the Atlantic, and, even more nerve-wracking, it had to be moved over the length and breadth of the American continent. Difficulties of space and time in some of the theatres which were visited meant that not all the ballets could be shown. *The Sleeping Beauty*, for example, takes fourteen hours to hang and must have a theatre with counterweights and a huge fly gallery, so it was arranged that this ballet should sometimes be sent on ahead to the next large town while the rest of the repertoire and the company itself made short stops in smaller auditoriums. *Le Lac des Cygnes* was the full-length ballet which travelled most easily and this was to be performed forty-nine times during the tour, more than any other work in the repertoire. *Façade* (forty-six) and *Les Patineurs* were the others most frequently given.

The Sadler's Wells Ballet left by Stratocruiser on Tuesday, 5th September, for New York, stopping only at Iceland. Radio communications with Idlewild Airport were interrupted and they consequently arrived at New York unheralded. There were some valiant Press photographers waiting for them nonetheless (they had camped out at the airport and waited for the plane to arrive), and the dancers were bombarded with the usual questions about what they thought of American steaks, were they glad to be back, and had they any dollars?—which, as a matter of fact, they hadn't, until David Webster arrived in a great hurry to give them their first supply.

The day after their arrival in New York the whole company were hard at work. Classes and rehearsals were held in the beautiful rehearsal room high up in the Metropolitan Opera House, and many were the expressions of regret that Covent Garden did not contain similar facilities.

The opening night was Sunday, 10th September, an evening of greyness and drizzle and sultry, humid heat. The ballet was *Le Lac des Cygnes* and the reception as joyful as ever, although this time it did not have the special impact of unexpected, overwhelming triumph. The ovation for Fonteyn and Somes at the conclusion of the third act *pas de deux*, however, was prolonged and tumultuous.

The classical ballets were once again the great successes in New York and the modern works fared less well. The production of *Giselle* was subjected to serious criticism, and Fonteyn's performance did not receive the unreserved praise that was accorded to her Aurora and Odette-Odile. Moira Shearer, on the other hand, received handsome tributes for her performance as Giselle, and this reaction confirmed the impression the two ballerinas had made in

London during the summer. Fonteyn at that period had lost the pathos of her first act and not yet achieved a really ghostly quality in the second. Fine dancing seemed to overshadow the characterisation and one admired without being moved. Shearer, on the other hand, was giving a very lovely and gentle interpretation, and although her appearance was a little too sophisticated and glamorous, she had a lightness and grace that must have resembled in some ways the qualities Carlotta Grisi first brought to the unhappy peasant girl.

More "alternative casts" were offered this time. The Americans were interested to see younger dancers attempt major rôles, and considered their respective merits seriously. Of the modern works, *Don Quixote* was not a success and neither was *Dante Sonata*. *Façade* was as popular as ever.

Official entertaining was slightly less arduous than it had been the previous year, but private hospitality flowed as generously as ever. A party which gave the company special pleasure was that given by the staff at the Met in the foyer of the opera house. Charles Chaplin came to watch performances in New York and kept a friendly eye on the company thereafter, arranging for them to see *City Lights* at the M.G.M. try-out theatre in Philadelphia (the whole company came out crying), and later, in Los Angeles, arranging a ballroom dancing contest at the big opening-night party. (Typically, it was won by the non-dancing manager of the company, Herbert Hughes.)

At the end of the New York season Ninette de Valois went off to Canada to lecture to women's clubs and the company went south via Philadelphia, Richmond and Pittsburgh to Atlanta. There they had their first taste of the American South and were enchanted alike by the soft, southern drawl of their new friends, the warm hospitality and the romantic appearance of the country-side. After Atlanta, Birmingham, New Orleans (which they adored), and then Houston, Texas, where the dancers made full use of the large swimming pool in the hotel grounds. The long trek across the desert via El Paso to Los Angeles was made in the company train ("the Ballet Special"), which consisted of six Pullman sleeping-cars with double-decker berths and four scenery wagons. There was also a lounge coach with an ever-open bar which did good business. Two days of this close confinement passed happily enough;

MARGOT FONTEYN

in her costume for the last scene of Ashton's *Daphnis and Chloë*

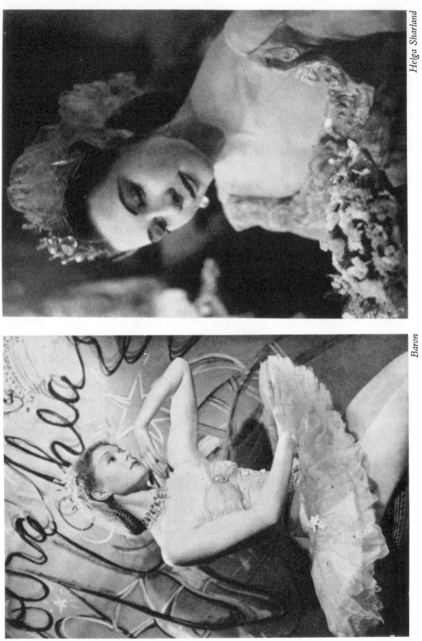

BERYL GREY

MOIRA SHEARER

and it was during this period that Canasta established a hold on the company. As they travelled along beside the Rio Grande they all thought of Constant Lambert, who had returned home to London, and when they came across brilliant tropical flowers near the Californian border, Frederick Ashton became quite homesick for his childhood home in South America.

At Los Angeles they were met by Mr. Hurok and Miss de Valois, who had returned from her lecturing in Canada. This was to be the first performance on the West Coast and there was a little nervousness, for much of the success of the remainder of the tour would depend on the reception in Los Angeles and San Francisco.

The Los Angeles opening, however, was an almost overwhelming success. It was a great artistic and social occasion and the audience which came to see the dancers was so star-studded that the dancers spent no little time peeking through the curtain at the audience. Throughout their stay the company were made much of by the film colony: there was continual hospitality, visits to the film studios and always the wonderful, appreciative, exciting audience. Danny Kaye visited every dressing-room after a performance of *Giselle*. Sir Laurence and Lady Olivier were frequently present, and when Greer Garson met some of the dancers at Universal Studios she put her arms round two of them and said, "We cockneys are really proud of you all." A special pleasure for some of the older members of the company was to meet Pearl Argyle's husband, Kurt Bernhardt, once again and to see her two children, for her untimely death in 1947 had been a great sorrow to all who had known and loved her.

The first-night audience in San Francisco was a society one which received the company with polite applause that reminded them of the more difficult kind of gala performance in London. The Press was restrained in its enthusiasm and sometimes very critical. The season was successful, but it was not the "push-over" that the company had enjoyed in most other cities.

By this time the strain of touring was beginning to show. There were many minor strains and skinned toes and Pamela May and Gerd Larsen had to return home for medical treatment. At the end of the two-week San Francisco engagement Ninette de Valois also returned to England (to start work on a revival of *The Prospect Before Us* for the Sadler's Wells Theatre Ballet), and the company

R

remained in the charge of Frederick Ashton, Herbert Hughes and Mary Skeaping, the ballet mistress.

These were but temporary absences, however. The departure which saddened the company was that of Robert Helpmann, who resigned after nearly twenty years' service with Sadler's Wells. He gave his last performance in San Francisco on 11th November 1950, in the *pas de deux* from the third act of *The Sleeping Beauty*, dancing, as so often before, with Margot Fonteyn. As they watched from the wings many of the company remembered the part he had played in the building of Sadler's Wells and regretted that circumstances had not allowed a special performance at which his own affectionate London audience, as well as his colleagues, might have taken leave of him and paid the tribute that was his due.

After San Francisco came the really hard part of the tour, when stops were brief and to stay more than one night in a city and enjoy the luxury of sleeping at an hotel was an event of the first magnitude. Three days were spent in Denver and as this marked the half-way point on the tour the opportunity was seized for a company party. A collection was taken and invitations went out for a fancy dress party—company only, no outside guests, no need to behave as artistic ambassadors from Great Britain. Strange and wonderful were the costumes that were devised and, not surprisingly, it was one of the best parties of the tour.

Christmas in Chicago was a great success. The company launched their season with *The Sleeping Beauty*, and the opening performance was followed by a wonderful party given by Mr. and Mrs. Thomas Hart Fisher. Mrs. Fisher being herself a dancer (Ruth Page), the golden rule was observed of feeding the dancers the moment they arrived, starving, from the theatre and then letting them join the other guests after hunger had been appeased. The British Consul kept an eye on the dancers and made sure that no one was left at a loose end on Christmas Day, and in the evening David Webster gave them a party which they arranged for themselves, as he was not able to be present. Alfred Rodrigues organised a cabaret and the hit of the evening was "The Swans that Stayed Behind in Kansas City," sung to the Kansas City tune from *Oklahoma!* and performed by Kenneth Macmillan, Ray Powell and Leslie Edwards in jeans, check shirts and the swan head-dresses from *Le Lac des Cygnes*.

Afterwards came Winnipeg, Boston, Westchester, Toronto, Ottawa, Montreal and Quebec. There was snow in Quebec and tobogganing and the real end of the tour in sight. The orchestra queued up to collect signed photographs from Margot Fonteyn and nearly drove the orchestra manager insane by doggedly waiting for their pictures long after the interval bell had rung. After the last performance a farewell dinner was given by Mr. Hurok at the Château Frontenac, at which his farewell speech of appreciation was acknowledged by Herbert Hughes. Then there was a completely spontaneous and unrehearsed gesture. As Hughes sat down, one of the dancers rose and proposed a toast to their ballerina, Margot Fonteyn. The cheering which followed rivalled anything that had been achieved by any audience on the tour, and one wonders if, perhaps, it meant more than all the public clamour to Fonteyn herself.

The company flew home from Montreal, arriving at London Airport at 3.15 in the morning, tired, now that all the excitement was at an end, and longing only for a rest. They had travelled some 21,000 miles and the American and Canadian publics had paid over two million dollars to see them dance. Throughout the tour there had been hardly an empty seat in any theatre (three empty seats and the company would say it was a poor house) and they had brought back with them over half a million dollars. Lord Keynes would have been proud of them.

CHAPTER XV

REACTION AND REGRESSION

THE "welcome home" performance was better organised this time. Princess Elizabeth was in the audience and the ballet was *The Sleeping Beauty*. Tired the dancers must have been, but they gave a fine performance and were rewarded with an ovation and a multitude of flowers in London's best manner. Acknowledging the tributes, Dame Ninette de Valois explained that in London the company were really more nervous than when facing a new audience abroad, because "abroad we are a novelty, but here we are a habit."

The New Year Honours List had been published while the company was away and the dancers had learned with delight—delight that was shared by the entire dancing world—that their Director had been created a Dame Commander of the Most Excellent Order of the British Empire. The dancers had indicated their pleasure, as soon as they were reunited with "Madam," by singing all together, "There is Nothing Like a Dame" (a tribute which made de Valois laugh and cry at once), and now the London audience had an opportunity to show its appreciation in a more formal, but nonetheless sincere, fashion. The happy opening night was not, however, the prelude to a notable season.

The company returned home to a very heavy schedule of work. The Festival of Britain was being held during the summer of 1951 and there was an obvious duty for the ballet at Covent Garden both to produce new works and to revive and include in the repertoire certain British ballets of historic importance which had not been given for some time. This meant an exhausting period of rehearsals in addition to actual performances, and the company were in poor condition after the long American tour, which had allowed no proper opportunities for regular classes or for rest.

Casualties began early. Moira Shearer fell ill after one performance, Beryl Grey soon after, and there was a general epidemic of influenza. Pamela May was unable to dance throughout the spring and summer. The settings had suffered from all the travelling, packing and unpacking, and many backcloths were creased and shabby. One of the pillars in *The Sleeping Beauty* snapped off at the bottom quite early in the season and hung like a stalactite for several months.

Nevertheless, Frederick Ashton worked away at his new ballet *Daphnis and Chloë,* and on 5th April the company called up all their reserves of strength to give it a magnificent first performance. The ballet was received calmly by the audience, however, and very coolly by an ungrateful Press.

Daphnis and Chloë was first produced by the Diaghileff *Ballets Russes* at the Théâtre du Châtelet in Paris in 1912. Maurice Ravel had been so enthusiastic about the first Diaghileff season in 1909, that he offered to compose a ballet for the company, and *Daphnis and Chloë* was the subject chosen. Ravel spent a long time on the score, however, and by the time the ballet was ready for production Diaghileff seemed to have lost interest in it. It was put on at the end of a Paris season, immediately after all the controversy that had attended the first performances of Nijinsky's *L'Après-midi d'un Faune* and after Diaghileff had quarrelled with his first choreographer, Fokine. The ballet had beautiful settings and costumes by Léon Bakst, Nijinsky and Karsavina as principal dancers, and choreography devised with great feeling by Fokine (who always had a particular affection for the ballet), but it had a short and unlucky life. Although well received in London in 1914, *Daphnis and Chloë* was dropped during the war and not revived until 1924, when it was produced in Monte Carlo with Anton Dolin as Daphnis. A few weeks later it was given in Barcelona and then dropped by Diaghileff for good.

Musically, the ballet was without question a masterpiece, and Ashton had long cherished a desire to use Ravel's score for a ballet. He was convinced that it would no longer be right to approach the work in the same spirit as Bakst and Fokine had done, for the eyes of 1951 are not the same as those of 1912, and Ashton wanted his ballet to be a contemporary restatement of an old story, not a resuscitation of an earlier presentation of that story. A recent holiday among the Greek islands had convinced him that the myths and legends and even the gods of ancient Greece were still very much present in the atmosphere and in the lives of the people, and he wanted, above all, to suggest this timeless quality.

He invited John Craxton to design the settings and costumes, knowing that this young painter shared his feeling about Greece and knew the country well. The settings were entirely successful— clear symbols of a hot classical landscape—but the costumes were not quite right. The basic idea had been to dress the young men and women in costumes which would be contemporary in style but have echoes of antiquity about them, and the soft folds of the girls' costumes succeeded both in looking beautiful and suggesting the draperies of Greek sculpture. But the trousers and shirts of the boys were too like modern painters' overalls and the problem of dressing the nymphs and fauns imaginatively was not solved.

These defects of costume and various small weaknesses in the actual staging and narration of the story were reported at length by the critics, but the beauty of the choreography, the really important factor, was overlooked. The opening pastoral scene had, of necessity, to be simple in style, and Ashton asked only for simple *enchaînements* from the good-looking dancers he had selected. Throughout the ballet he used a soft lyric style of his own, eschewing any attempt at reconstructing "Greek dance" and building into the framework some magnificently expressive *soli* and *pas de deux*. Outstanding were the solo for Fonteyn, as with bound hands she danced Chloë's mute appeal to the pirate Bryaxis, and the radiant *pas de deux* at the end when she was reunited with Daphnis. The ballet ended with a mass dance of rejoicing, which was built closely on Greek folk-dance figures and was exhilarating in its fast rhythms and great leaps of exultance.

Fonteyn's performance, and the rôle which Ashton had created for her, received unanimous praise from all critics. Michael Somes had a difficult part as Daphnis but discharged it musically and well. Violetta Elvin as the seductive Lynkanion and Alexander Grant as the Pirate Chief were also excellent. *Daphnis and Chloë* was essentially a company ballet, however, and depended for good performances on fine dancing and sincere feeling throughout. The dancers were required to dance with their hearts as well as their bodies, and this they admirably succeeded in doing.

Ashton must have been disappointed with the reception accorded to the ballet, but he never wavered in his conviction that his treatment of the subject was the right one. In time the ballet won its audience and he could listen with satisfaction to the cheers which became customary at the end. On the third American tour of the Sadler's Wells Ballet, *Daphnis and Chloë* at last received the public recognition it deserved; the American critics hailed it as a masterpiece and in New York it did much to establish Ashton's position as one of the foremost choreographers of the century.

The absence of Shearer and Grey brought Nadia Nerina into ballerina rôles that season, rather sooner than might otherwise have been the case. She responded well to the demands of Cinderella and Odette and it became clear that her range was wider than had at first been suspected. A strong, clean dancer, with a gay little personality, she had achieved her early successes as a soubrette, but she now began to show command of purely classical rôles as well.

The season, in general, was not an inspiring one, and the company were impatient for it to end so that they might take a badly needed holiday. The final casualty was the setting for *Les Patineurs,* which had suffered badly on its North American travels. It stood up bravely to the early weeks of the London season but eventually went down fighting in the course of a performance, section after section of the trellis collapsing on the stage until there was no room for dancing and the performance had to be abandoned. *The Times,* with its usual nice feeling for the right headline, reported the occurrence gravely under the title "Fallen Arches."

The company reassembled at Covent Garden and opened a month's season on 3rd July. In the course of this season they were to present *Tiresias,* a new ballet commissioned by the Arts Council for the Festival of Britain. The music had been composed by Constant Lambert, who was also responsible for the scenario (he had wanted to use it for a ballet ever since Camargo days). Frederick Ashton was to create the choreography, and Isabel Lambert (the composer's wife) was to design the scenery and costumes. The first performance, on 9th July, was made the occasion of a Gala Performance in aid of the Sadler's Wells Ballet Benevolent Fund and was attended by Her Majesty the Queen. The leading parts were danced by Margot Fonteyn (who had just received a C.B.E. in the Birthday Honours List) and Michael Somes.

The theme of the ballet did not appear promising, for Lambert had confined it to the events which led up to the transformation of Tiresias into a blind soothsayer. He is first seen as a manly youth, but after killing two copulating snakes is changed into a woman. As woman, Tiresias enjoys a crowded love life and then kills the two snakes again, this time being changed back into a man. In the final scene the gods Hera and Zeus are arguing as to whether men or women derive most pleasure from love. They send for Tiresias to settle the dispute, and he says the woman has the most enjoyment. Hera in fury strikes him blind, but Zeus grants him the gift of prophecy as compensation and it was as an old white-headed man telling fortunes that Tiresias tapped his way with the aid of a stick off the stage.

Lambert's score was dry, brittle and brilliantly suggestive of the action it was to support, but it was almost an hour long. Ashton dutifully created an hour of choreography to go with it, but inspiration seemed to flag and most of the ballet was no more than honest craftsmanship; adequate, tasteful, and completely un-interesting. The only passage that suggested the real abilities of Ashton was the long *pas d'action* for the female Tiresias, which culminated in a passionate *pas de deux*. The ballet was handsomely decorated in bold fierce colours and it was conscientiously per-formed by a well-drilled company.

Tiresias was received with the polite applause that characterises most gala performances, but during the intermission it was obvious that there was strong feeling about the quality of the ballet. A large body of critical and well-informed people were of the opinion that the ballet needed drastic cutting, and even then was unlikely to make a first-class work. It was compared to the more stereo-typed productions of moribund national theatres. The story was quite unintelligible from the stage action and there were many who blamed Ashton for having undertaken the commission in the first place. On the other hand, Sophie Fedorovitch was stating repeatedly and doggedly her opinion that it was "a great ballet," and the late Lionel Bradley thought it was a masterpiece. An experienced American critic called it "stunning"—and she meant it appreciatively, not literally.

The next day's Press was mixed but not particularly enthusiastic and by the time the weeklies and Sunday papers appeared, criticism was growing more trenchant: Richard Buckle in *The Observer* took the opportunity to question the whole artistic direction at Covent Garden for ever having allowed the ballet to reach the stage, and he followed up this initial article with two more in which he developed his argument. The storm was aroused not on account of the failure of a single work to come up to expectations (although failure on such an expensive and spectacular scale could not be overlooked), but because *Tiresias* came after a thoroughly depressing spring season when a series of poor performances had forced people to inquire into the policies which had brought the company to such a situation. All the mistakes that had been made during the previous five years were remembered and there was more criticism voiced about Sadler's Wells than ever before in its history.

Chastened, worried and depressed, the company travelled up to Edinburgh in August to dance at the Festival and there they received the news of Constant Lambert's death. To all the company who had known and loved him it was a great sorrow, but for Frederick Ashton it was a particularly heavy loss. Since Lambert conducted for Ashton's *Leda and the Swan* at a Sunshine *Matinée* in 1928, he had been an ever-present friend and counsellor, and most of Ashton's ballets had been created in close collaboration with him.

The company danced *Tiresias* in Edinburgh with heavy hearts and loyal devotion to its composer. From that time they seemed to identify it with Lambert's memory and have since made great efforts to keep it alive, almost by the will-power exerted in its performance. Fonteyn, in particular, danced as one possessed; she had a passionate intensity in this ballet which she has not equalled in any other rôle.

When the September season opened at Covent Garden, several valuable soloists who had been with the company for a long time had left and there were many new faces in the *corps de ballet*. Illness and indisposition were again rife and Fonteyn had strained a foot and was unable to appear. The season clashed directly with the farewell season being given at Sadler's Wells Theatre by the ballet company there, which was about to set off on a tour of Canada and America and which had by this time built up an excellent and exciting repertory.

For all kinds of reasons, therefore, the September season was a sorry affair. There were many empty seats at Covent Garden and some extraordinary casting policies—some forced on the management by necessity, others quite inexplicable. It was a season in which it seemed that anybody could try anything; any girl who could learn a part quickly seemed to step into ballerina rôles. The resulting performances were never less than competent, but seldom anything more, and mere competence in the theatre is one of the dullest things imaginable.

A few good things emerged, however, notably Nerina's first Swanilda, Elvin's Giselle and Pauline Clayden's Chloë. Revivals of *Ballabile* and *Scènes de Ballet* were disappointing, but *Giselle* was considerably improved. Whether on account of fault-finding by American critics or the example of an excellent new production by Dolin's Festival Ballet at home, the production had been thoroughly overhauled and many faults remedied. The peasant *pas de deux* was reintroduced in the first act as an entertainment for the Duke and Bathilde and proved popular, although it was performed in a virtuoso style ill-suited to the romantic nature of the ballet.

At the conclusion of this most unfestive Festival summer, the Ballet went on a short provincial tour, returning to Covent Garden on 21st November for the customary long winter-spring season.

On 12th December an entirely new ballet by Leonide Massine was produced. This was *Donald of the Burthens,* in which the choreographer attempted to do for Scotland what he had previously done for Spain in *The Three Cornered Hat.* The music was commissioned from Ian Whyte and *décor* and costumes (the most distinguished part of the proceedings) were designed by Robert MacBryde and Robert Colquhoun.

The story was about a young woodcutter who makes a pact with Death and dramatically the ballet was doomed from the start: there is no way of indicating a bargain in mime. Death was to give the young woodcutter magical powers of healing, but he was always to obey her instructions. When he tricks her and restores the sick king to health she is determined to be revenged and soon claims him.

The individual figures were hardly developed at all, although Alexander Grant made a brave attempt to bring Donald to life and Beryl Grey moved about menacingly in red body tights as Death. The beauties of *Donald of the Burthens,* and they were considerable, were in the ensemble dancing; in the gentle Waulking Song, the lament for the sick king, and the Country Dance which was an old Scottish lilt danced by six girls. The entry for the sword dance was magnificent, but the actual dance suffered from being performed in a completely un-Highland style, although traditional steps were used almost unaltered. There was one very lovely little episode right at the end when a group of children forget the words of a prayer and are reminded of them by Donald. Had Massine only chosen a story which could have been easily conveyed in this fashion, or had he been content to make a *divertissement*-style ballet on Scottish themes, all might have been well. But the ballet was so weak dramatically that it was almost nonsensical and the music was lamentably thin. *Donald* had a bad Press and a short life, and was generally considered a final disaster in a thoroughly unsatisfactory year. (The fact that Massine had at one time wanted to produce *Le Sacre du Printemps* for Sadler's Wells with the original Roerich *décor* and costumes did not make people feel any happier about the Scottish *mélange* offered instead.)

Dame Ninette that winter set to work with painstaking thoroughness to get the repertoire back into shape again. She conducted the majority of rehearsals herself and soon had the company dancing well together in both the classics and the modern ballets, but there was a time lag in the effect on the box office of these improved performances, and it was some time before the confidence of the audience was recaptured. A lot of prominent people who knew nothing whatever about the subject were eagerly rushing into print to proclaim that ballet was "finished" and opera was ousting it as the fashionable art of the day. There were persistent rumours that Dame Ninette was retiring or relinquishing control of the Covent Garden company—rumours which possibly originated in the fact that a board of advisers to the ballet had been set up at Covent Garden and no public announcement had been made about it. Dame Ninette wasted little time in answering these rumours but went steadily on with her work and was rewarded with a fine revival of *The Sleeping Beauty* on 9th January 1952.

The scenery had been freshly painted and the costumes refurbished and the many new dancers in the *corps de ballet* were easily assimilated into the production. Some slight revisions were made in the choreography. A new solo for Aurora was inserted in the Vision

Scene, using yet another unfamiliar fragment from Tchaikovsky's gigantic score. The programme said "after Petipa," but apart from one or two uncharacteristic movements the solo seemed remarkably like Ashton at his lyrical best. A solo was also inserted for Prince Florimund in Act III, this by Ninette de Valois "after Petipa." It was built chiefly on *entrechats* and *doubles tours* and varied slightly in arrangement according to which dancer was performing.

Fonteyn was still absent, so this revival became known as the season of the four Auroras—Grey, Elvin, Nerina and Rosemary Lindsay all appearing as the Princess. Of the four, Grey was the most assured and most at ease; she had strength and fluency and gave a performance that was consistently good, although it seemed to lack the final touch of grandeur. Elvin's movement was all grandeur; poses and extensions had a magnificent isolation, but she had yet to knit every passage into a complete unity and give the flow of inevitability. Nerina's Aurora was enchanting in its joyous youth. A born dancer, she soared happily on to the stage and communicated her love of dancing to the audience. At that time she was eager and unself-conscious and it was not until later that too serious and obvious a concentration on "interpretation" marred the effect of her natural feeling for movement.

Rosemary Lindsay's Aurora, like all her work, was sincerely felt and admirably mastered. A sound dancer of great musical sensibility and gentle orthodoxy, she typifies the qualities of the English school. The qualities her Aurora lacked were strength of personality, real freedom of movement, and originality.

Things were rapidly improving by this time, and when Fonteyn came back on 9th February, in *Daphnis and Chloë,* the company began to look like itself again. On that evening the audience was given the rare opportunity of seeing, during a single performance, almost every leading dancer in the company. It was an impressive showing and a reminder that the Sadler's Wells Ballet *at full strength* was still a very wonderful organisation.

On 4th March another new ballet was presented, this one by Andrée Howard and called *A Mirror for Witches.* Had it been more successful, this might have provided a strongly dramatic work which could have filled the place once occupied by the Helpmann ballets and given the overworked *Checkmate* an occasional rest.

Based on a novel by Esther Forbes, it was a grim story of witch-hunting and burning in Brittany and New England. A similar subject was brilliantly treated in the Danish film *Day of Wrath,* which captured all the horror and terror of a witch hunt, and it was inevitable that *A Mirror for Witches* should be compared to this film.

The subject, unfortunately, proved to be more suited to film than to ballet. The period costumes were such exact copies of Puritan dress that they prevented any vigorous or interesting dance movement. The whole conception and staging of the ballet, which lasted about fifty minutes, was that of a realistic theatrical production, and consequently the supernatural happenings—such as the encounter between the young witch-child Doll and the unexplained Stranger—were so divorced from the rest of the action as to be unconvincing.

Certain episodes were handled cleverly, in particular the trial of Doll at the end of the ballet, and the lighting and general presentation were excellent. The ballet had moments of dramatic fire and conviction and must be counted a sincere and honourable attempt. Denis ApIvor's score was strongly theatrical in places, and the settings by Norman Adams were good if gloomy. The dancers served their choreographer well. Anne Heaton, who had danced another doom-haunted girl in Andrée Howard's *Mardi-Gras* at Sadler's Wells some years before, made a valiant attempt to create sympathy for the strange Doll. April Olrich later gave a fine performance of this part, but it was never clear whether Doll was responsible for the disasters that overtook the village. Leslie Edwards as a kindly sea captain gave one of his fine character portraits, and John Hart, Philip Chatfield, Margaret Dale and Joan Benesh were all excellent in smaller parts. The ballet was dominated, however, by Julia Farron's performance as Hannah, the captain's wife, who is bitterly jealous and suspicious of Doll from the beginning, and finally succeeds in having her convicted and burnt. It was a performance of concentrated emotion, strong Puritanical convictions and feminine hatred, and a climax to all the smaller portraits previously created by this outstanding actress-dancer.

In April the Sadler's Wells Ballet paid their first visit to Portugal, under the auspices of the British Council. They flew out to Lisbon, sixty-eight strong, with a repertoire that included *Le Lac des Cygnes, Symphonic Variations, Checkmate, The Rake's Progress, Ballet Imperial,*

Les Patineurs and *Les Sylphides*. From 15th to 23rd April they danced at the San Carlos Theatre in Lisbon and from the 25th to the 28th at the Rivoli Theatre, Oporto—where the opportunities for sampling the native port have, alas, left a stronger impression with most of the company than any more serious activities!

They arrived in Lisbon on Easter Sunday in brilliant sunshine and began rehearsing next day on the stage of the San Carlos Theatre, which is so severely raked that there is a notice which says, "Dancers are reminded not to touch or even breathe on the scenery owing to the difficulties presented by the steep stage." There was great public interest, and the opening gala performance was attended by the President of the Republic and a distinguished audience. Prices of seats were very high and there was a flourishing black market, but there was invariably a sign "Esgotado" (sold out) in front of the theatre.

The last performance in Lisbon was attended by many of the former crowned heads of Europe and many diplomats. Flowers almost covered the stage and congratulations poured in from all sides. *Le Lac des Cygnes* was the most popular ballet—with a special personal success for Fonteyn. *Checkmate*, *Les Patineurs*, *Ballet Imperial* and *The Rake's Progress* were also much admired, but *Façade* was a complete flop. The Portuguese simply did not think that it was funny, and some of the intelligentsia protested that it was beneath the dignity of their famous opera house.

The company returned to London invigorated by their success and the sunshine and none the worse for the lack of sleep caused by the very late starting times in Portugal and the nightly parties. On 4th April, at Covent Garden, another new ballet was produced, thus making a total of five new works in just over a year by four different choreographers. *Bonne-Bouche* was by the young South African choreographer John Cranko, who had been carefully nursed with the Sadler's Wells Theatre Ballet for some years and had proved himself the previous season with the popular *Pineapple Poll* and the poetic *Harlequin in April*.

Bonne-Bouche was very different from its predecessor at Covent Garden, being unashamedly lighthearted and with no more serious purpose than to amuse and delight. It was a cautionary tale, in the Evelyn Waugh *Black Mischief* manner, about the fate that may overtake a pretty young flapper whose only ambition is

O TEATRO NACIONAL DE S. CARLOS

em colaboração com
THE BRITISH COUNCIL
e
THE ARTS COUNCIL OF GREAT BRITAIN

apresenta
DE 15 a 23 DE ABRIL DE 1952

a grande companhia

(DA ROYAL OPERA HOUSE COVENT GARDEN)

SOB A DIRECÇÃO DE
NINETTE DE VALOIS

COREÓGRAFO PRINCIPAL
FREDERICK ASHTON
DIRECTOR MUSICAL
ROBERT IRVING

MAESTROS
JOHN HOLLINGSWORTH E ROBERT IRVING

ORQUESTRA SINFÓNICA NACIONAL

COM OS ARTISTAS
MARGOT FONTEYN

VIOLETTA ELVIN   **BERYL GREY**   **NADIA NERINA**

MICHAEL SOMES

JOHN FIELD   **ALEXANDER GRANT**   **JOHN HART**
ALEXIS RASSINE   **BRIAN SHAW**

SOLISTAS E CORPO DE BAILE

REPERTÓRIO
**BALLET IMPERIAL • CHECKMATE • FAÇADE • LE LAC DES CYGNES • LES PATINEURS
THE RAKE'S PROGRESS • SYMPHONIC VARIATIONS • LES SYLPHIDES**

TIP. RUA DO FERREGIAL, 13 — LISBOA — IMP. EG. — 30-3-952

for bigger and better diamonds. It proved a tasty morsel, if not a sustaining diet.

The settings by Osbert Lancaster—of a Kensington square and an African jungle—were great fun, and the ballet was packed full of amusing incidents, amusing costumes, amusing "props." Arthur Oldham's music was full of funny allusions, and the dancers were given full scope to indulge their natural gifts for caricature and dressing up. The first two-thirds were pleasant enough, but the last scene went on much too long and killed the good effect of the opening for in comedy, more than in any other realm of the theatre, it is imperative to stop immediately you have said all there is to say.

The dancing was patchy, sometimes witty and well contrived— as in the perfect little cameo entrance for the Officer at the beginning —sometimes rather conventional and relying too much on the multitude of comic stage properties. Choreographically *Bonne-Bouche* was vastly inferior to Cranko's previous winner, *Pineapple Poll,* and it shared with Ashton's *Les Sirènes* an inability to sustain interest at subsequent performances once the surprise value had worn off. Nevertheless when the company are fooling to the top of their bent and when the audience is in a mellow and appreciative mood the ballet can certainly "go."

Brian Shaw, as the unfortunate hero of strong moral fibre, astonished by a performance of genuine (and never over-stated) comedy as well as some fine dancing. Pauline Clayden was a delightfully silly, gangling flapper, and Pamela May was her formidable mother, melted by the very sparkle of a diamond. Margaret Dale, leading the League of Light with devastating brightness, Gilbert Vernon as the Officer with a Past, Philip Chatfield and Rosemary Lindsay as a couple of Sporting Neighbours, and John Hart as a gouty old roué with a weak heart more fatal than Giselle's, were all quite wonderful. It was a rather smart and amusing joke for a season, but the sort of ballet that needs impeccable performance if it is to survive for many years.

The summer season ended on 5th July with a performance of *The Sleeping Beauty.* Most of the dancers from the New York City Ballet were in the audience that night, and in her curtain speech Dame Ninette welcomed them back to London, describing them as "a great American company." She also gave news of her own company's future plans, and was able to announce that when they returned in September they would present a new three-act ballet by Frederick Ashton, *Sylvia*. This event duly took place on 3rd September, and it was immediately apparent that Sadler's Wells were back on top of the world again.

CHAPTER XVI

A COMPANY OF ROYAL DIMENSIONS

SYLVIA was the largest and most ambitious new ballet Sadler's Wells had ever presented, and was throughout conceived on a scale and presented with a magnificence that rivalled the productions of the great national companies of earlier generations. Dame Ninette had always said it would take five years for the company to establish itself at the opera house on a truly national standing, and this was the production with which maturity was reached.

Sylvia had been first produced at the Paris Opéra in 1876 with choreography by Louis Mérante, but it had not been seen in its entirety in England before. Ashton had wanted to use the honeyed Delibes music for some years and had seriously contemplated such a production in 1947. Inevitably the ballet echoed the production conventions of the Paris Opéra in the 1870s, but it was presented with taste and affection as a charming *pastiche* rather than an exact evocation of the period. The choreography was lyrical, as befitting so sweet and pastoral an atmosphere, and there were no spectacular set pieces in the Petipa style, although the construction of the *soli* for the principals and the last-act *pas de deux* would have done the Russian master credit.

As a production, a work of stagecraft for a great theatre, *Sylvia* was a remarkable achievement. Robin and Christopher Ironside, the designers, devised settings in the realistic nineteenth-century manner that were artistically alive and not just old-fashioned. Their costumes were less uniformly successful, but all those for the principals were good, and the design of ballet costumes is something which will never be learned overnight by painters, howsoever distinguished. There were complaints from some people about excessive use of "props" and trimmings, but these are so inevitably part of the period as to be well justified. The artificial *cortège* of the peasants in Act I, for instance, was an enchanting piece of Second Empire nonsense.

Criticism was again carping and there was a great deal of petty fault-finding. Ashton had by this time reached the sort of eminence at which critics take delight in shooting; *Sylvia* did not receive the appreciation it deserved until it arrived in New York a year later.

On the opening night in London, Fonteyn's performance shared honours with Ashton's choreography, for she carried the ballet on her slim shoulders with disarming ease, disguising the fact that much of the dancing is extremely difficult. Other ballerinas have been less successful in the entire ballet, although all of them have succeeded in various passages. Beryl Grey's strong and beautiful style was best seen in Act I, but the costume for the huntress Sylvia did not become Violetta Elvin or Nadia Nerina. Elvin's triumph was the seductive second act, and Nerina had a crisp precision in the last-act *pizzicato*. A year later Svetlana Beriosova was to be a memorable Sylvia, but the rôle has remained Fonteyn's by creation and continued excellence in performance.

Michael Somes (returning from an intensive period of study in Paris) danced particularly well as the Shepherd Aminta, and Philip Chatfield, a tall and strong dancer, was outstandingly good in the two *soli* when he followed Somes in the part. John Hart as the dastardly villain Orion gave a brilliant performance in a part that could easily have degenerated into mere "ham," and Alexander Grant as the lively and helpful Cupid was first-rate.

Without doubt *Sylvia* was a popular success and a completely enjoyable spectacle. It took its place among the three-act ballets as a new "classic," but from the beginning its most sincere admirers recognised that it must be only an isolated excursion into the realm of forgotten nineteenth-century ballet spectacles. A single experiment might be enchanting, but a series could be disastrous for the creative health and well-being of the English ballet. The danger is great: the nineteenth-century ballets offer many good stories and dramatic situations suitable for presentation in magnificent settings on an opera-house stage and they are just far enough away to be "period" and fashionably amusing. The missing element, however, is enough good music to sustain such spectacles for a modern audience, and there is a good chance that this consideration may prevent a flood of revivals—at Covent Garden at least.

The month's season at Covent Garden was mostly devoted to *Sylvia,* but on the last night Svetlana Beriosova appropriated most of the applause by making her début at the Opera House in *Coppélia*, a ballet she had danced with great success formerly at Sadler's Wells Theatre.

On 29th September the company went to Berlin to dance *Les Patineurs, Daphnis and Chloë, Checkmate, Scènes de Ballet, Donald of the Burthens* and *Giselle* during five performances at the Stadtische Oper as part of the International Festival. The great success of the visit was *Giselle,* and after the last performance the audience was still calling for Fonteyn and Somes long after the stage had been stripped. Mary Wigman, high priestess of the modern dance in Germany, was in tears, and at a party afterwards she told Franklin White: "It does not matter what type of dancing I see, when I see sincere work, produced in good taste, as I saw to-night in *Giselle,* then I am greatly moved."

The Berlin visit was followed by a provincial tour in England, and during this tour, at Southampton, Margot Fonteyn contracted diphtheria. It was a slight attack, but rest and great care were pre-scribed by her doctor and she was unable to appear during the first part of the Covent Garden season, which began on 15th November (with a *matinée*).

On 17th November *Apparitions* was revived—with Michael Somes and Anne Heaton—and also *Job* in honour of the eightieth birthday of Vaughan Williams. At the end of November, Violetta Elvin was given leave of absence to dance at La Scala, Milan, as guest artist for some ten weeks. A new production of *Le Lac des Cygnes* was in preparation and was expected to be ready just before Christmas. Fonteyn was not strong enough to dance by then, so the honour of the first performance went to Beryl Grey and John Field.

The first performance of this revised production was given on 18th December in the presence of Her Majesty the Queen Mother and H.R.H. Princess Margaret. It was a Gala Performance of great beauty and excitement, although it was disturbing to see Fonteyn in the audience, looking pale and tired, instead of on the stage.

The production had been carefully revised and thoroughly rehearsed. A *pas de six* to the familiar waltz was inserted in the first act with choreography (for three girls and three boys) by Frederick Ashton and an interval was placed after the first act. The Neapolitan dance was included in the Act III *divertissement* for the first time in a Sadler's Wells production, arranged as a *pas de deux* by Ashton in the style of the marvellous Bournonville tarantellas of *Napoli*.

This tarantella, danced by Julia Farron and Alexander Grant with great speed, sureness and vivacity, stopped the show on the opening night and at all subsequent performances, but the *pas de six* aroused less enthusiasm. The style of the choreography blended less well with the work of Petipa and Ivanov, as it was modern and contrapuntal in style. It was beautifully danced but had no dramatic significance, and extended by a little too much the preliminaries which have to be worked through before the arrival of the ballerina.

Both Beryl Grey and John Field gave excellent performances, and were rewarded with warm applause from an audience that held both in great affection. The real star of the evening, however, was Leslie Hurry. His designs were the all-important factor in transforming the former good version of *Le Lac des Cygnes* into a first-class production of great beauty, traditional style and rich colouring. He had achieved that rare feat of re-working his original designs and improving on the weak elements without sacrificing the good things. He admitted afterwards that when he first designed the ballet in 1944 he had found great difficulty in subordinating his personal vision as a painter to the traditions attached to the ballet and had seen it all then "through the eyes of Rothbart." He gave credit to Dame Ninette for his eventual understanding of the problem; she had never ceased to insist on the need for all separate parts of the ballet—*décor*, costumes, dancers, even audience—to be subordinated to the requirements of the ballet as a whole so that none should dominate at the other's expense.

The new production had one of the most unanimously enthusiastic Press receptions of any Sadler's Wells ballet. The public appeal was tremendous and the ballet drew full houses, although for several weeks there were no famous "stars" appearing in it.

In the absence of Fonteyn, Elvin and then Grey, Nadia Nerina and Rowena Jackson danced a number of performances, and both young dancers justified the trust that had been placed in them. For Nerina it was a logical extension of her repertoire in the ballerina parts, but for Rowena Jackson it was rather a surprise promotion. Her first performance in this most difficult and important double rôle was given on a Saturday afternoon, and was quite astonishing in its calm assurance and unforced, easy style. It was indeed a triumph for the teaching methods of the Sadler's Wells organisation, for it was the first major classical rôle she had undertaken and she acquitted herself with real merit. Later that season she was to dance Aurora in *The Sleeping Beauty*—a more difficult task in some respects, because Aurora has no character and is purely a ballerina. It was a sound performance, but a copy-book one: all the rules had been carefully learned, but there was no warmth of feeling to bring the ballet to life.

Svetlana Beriosova danced her first Odette in Act II of *Le Lac des Cygnes* at Covent Garden at the end of January, and gave a performance of beautiful style and eloquence and rare promise.

At the beginning of February the ballet company took part in a revival of Gluck's *Orpheus,* which Frederick Ashton was to produce and Sophie Fedorovitch to decorate. It was to prove a tragic opera. Kathleen Ferrier, whose noble and unforgettable Orpheus was the centre of the whole production, was unable to sing more than two performances before succumbing to the illness from which she subsequently died. A week before the first performance Sophie Fedorovitch died in her London studio, the result of leakage from a faulty gas main.

In these circumstances the opera was listened to with full hearts and eyes dimmed with tears, and the beautiful young dancers, laying their flowers at the tomb of Eurydice, seemed to be paying tribute to a great artist who had played a quiet but vital part in the whole development of English ballet. Through Marie Rambert, Sophie Fedorovitch had met Frederick Ashton as long ago as 1926, when she designed *A Tragedy of Fashion* for him. Since then she had been a devoted friend, wise counsellor and valued colleague, collaborating with Ashton on many ballets, and understanding better than almost any other designer the special needs of a dancer. *Horoscope, Dante Sonata, Nocturne, Symphonic Variations* and *La Fête Étrange* were only some of the ballets she designed, and her care and influence were not confined to her own works, for she served for some time before her death on the Board of Advisers to the ballet at Covent Garden. Her loyalty to any individual or organisation, once given, was steadfast, and although a shy person she would stand her ground and state her case doggedly when she felt called upon to defend someone or something that she loved.

It was a sad time for the company, and there was also much anxiety about Margot Fonteyn, who had started working again but became so quickly exhausted that her doctors advised a further postponement of her return to the stage.

Moira Shearer, however, rejoined the company for a short time as guest artist, appearing first in *Symphonic Variations* and later as Giselle, Aurora and Odette-Odile. Her performances were marked by a new warmth and gentleness, a softness in style and a greater communication of feeling. Her Giselle and Aurora in particular were performances of great beauty, but she was unable to sustain the exhausting third act of *Le Lac des Cygnes* and seemed, in general, to be somewhat lacking in stamina. Unhappily many critics pounced on this lack of strength and made ungenerous comments on her performances, ignoring the new qualities which had enriched her dancing. Before the end of the season she strained a tendon and did not dance with the company again after May 1953.

On 3rd March John Cranko's second ballet for the Covent Garden company was presented. *The Shadow* took the winds of March with beauty and gave Svetlana Beriosova a rôle which admirably exploited her romanticism. The theme was very simple: a young man is continually thwarted in his desire for a Romantic Love by a menacing black-cloaked figure. When eventually he takes courage and opposes the Shadow, however, it crumbles into nothingness and the road to happiness is open to him. Cranko had been going through a phase of cloudy over-symbolism in some of his work for the Sadler's Wells Theatre Ballet, but in the case of *The Shadow* he seemed to have decided on what he wanted to say and then set to work quite straightforwardly to say it.

His facility and zest for lively dance invention was given good scope in the dances for the young boys and girls and the merry amoral prancings of the extrovert young woman (Rosemary Lindsay), who sought to console the youth. In contrast, were the beautiful *adages* devised for Beriosova and the simple, soaring *pas de deux* in which the lovers were finally united. John Piper decorated the ballet in fresh pink, green and tangerine colours. The strongly flavoured Dohnanyi music was an interesting choice, the different movements of the suite serving the different characters well.

In the spring Alicia Markova, who had recently severed her

connection with Festival Ballet, appeared at Covent Garden as guest artist, dancing her incomparable Giselle on 16th March and later *Les Sylphides* and the second act of *Le Lac des Cygnes*. Fonteyn was in the audience to watch her Giselle and also Anton Dolin. He later paid a handsome tribute to her Albrecht, Michael Somes, who, "though never effacing himself, never obtruded too much, but nevertheless gave a great performance."

Two days later Markova was in the front of the house watching Fonteyn make her reappearance after an absence of five months. She came back in *Apparitions* in the part she had created and always loved. As the Woman in Balldress she had a rôle that was not technically exacting, although emotionally it made considerable demands on the artist. She gave a quite simple performance, probably not up to her own exacting standards, and obviously she felt that the ovation which greeted her at the conclusion was overgenerous. The applause, however, had nothing to do with her actual dancing, but was an attempt on the part of the audience to indicate to her their pleasure and happiness in her recovery and return to the stage. It was a demonstration of warm personal affection and was not confined to the public alone. Many of her colleagues had slipped through to the front of the house to cheer, and commissionaires and cloakroom attendants suddenly appeared at the back of the circles and added their applause and shouts of "Margot!" to those of the rest of the audience. More than fifty bouquets were laid at her feet, in a line which stretched from one side of the great stage to the other, and she stood there alone among her flowers receiving the homage of London.

Fonteyn danced her way back carefully, appearing only in one-act ballets at first, but she was soon ready for the exhausting second scene of *Tiresias,* and on 7th May she set the seal of her performance on the new production of *Le Lac des Cygnes,* dancing it with such depth of feeling and understanding that all technical considerations were made irrelevant by the overall beauty of the performance.

Easter-time was chosen for the *première* of Andrée Howard's new ballet *Veneziana,* danced for the first time on 9th April. The ballet aimed to be no more than a *divertissement* with a Venetian setting and was decorated by Sophie Fedorovitch, her last work for the stage. (She did not live to supervise the actual making of

the costumes, however, and would probably have made considerable modifications in the workroom as had always been her custom.)

The music had been arranged by Denis ApIvor from the operas
of Donizetti, mostly from *La Favorita* and *Dom Sebastien*, and was
danceable and gay. Unfortunately the first performance was not a
great success, partly because it was not a very good performance.
Both dancers and orchestra seemed under-rehearsed and faulty
timing gave undue prominence to a false climax before the end of
the ballet. Subsequently *Veneziana* was slightly revised and much
better performed and it became a gentle, slightly under-stated, but
very charming opening ballet. There were no spectacular parts (it
was not meant to be a virtuoso show-piece), but Ray Powell
made an endearing figure of a solitary Punchinello and Violetta
Elvin (later Svetlana Beriosova) danced with beautiful grave dignity
as La Favorita.

The Sadler's Wells Ballet suffered a severe loss in April when
their stage director, Louis Yudkin, was killed in an air crash while
on his way to supervise stage arrangements for the visit of the
Covent Garden opera company to Bulawayo. He had been with
the organisation for some fifteen years and his loyal and quietly
efficient service had been of inestimable value to the ballet company.

The early summer of 1953 was entirely given over in London
to celebrations in connection with the Coronation of Her Majesty
Queen Elizabeth II, and the Sadler's Wells Ballet paid their tribute
with a new ballet, specially commissioned for the occasion. Frederick
Ashton undertook the responsibility of acting as a sort of choreographer laureate and arranging a ballet in which virtually the
whole Sadler's Wells Ballet would appear. A young musician
named Malcolm Arnold, who had studied composition in Italy
and for a while had been principal trumpet player in the London
Philharmonic Orchestra, was invited to compose the music. Oliver
Messel designed the setting and costumes for the ballet and the
title chosen was *Homage to the Queen*.

The first performance was given on Coronation Night, 2nd
June. The proceedings started at 8 p.m. with the second act of
Le Lac des Cygnes, in which Fonteyn was partnered by Robert
Helpmann, who returned as guest artist for the occasion. At 9 p.m.
the Queen's Speech was broadcast throughout the Opera House, and
at the conclusion the new ballet was given.

The simple theme of the ballet was that the elements of Earth, Water, Fire and Air should all come to pay homage to the new Queen. A formal entry was arranged, in the manner of the old court masques, for each group of dancers, led by a ballerina and her cavalier. Each group in turn then danced its homage, and at the end all the dancers returned to the stage, while in the misty background was seen the figure of Gloriana, the first Elizabeth, handing her branch of freedom to the young Queen, who rose before her in all the splendour of her coronation robes.

The nature of the ballet meant that it had to be episodic, and the great number of detached *soli* and *pas de deux*—always further isolated by applause—prevented it from achieving any homogeneous pattern as a whole. The formal promenades were unusual and pleasing and the whole episode for the Queen of the Waters (Elvin, partnered by John Hart) was of outstanding choreographic beauty. For Fonteyn and Somes as Spirits of the Air, Ashton devised one of his most breathtaking and spectacular *pas de deux,* in which Fonteyn was more often lifted into the air than dancing on the ground. There was so much dancing in the ballet and so much of it was good that with cutting and editing it might have been a masterpiece. Nevertheless it was received with enthusiasm, and audiences have since taken particular pleasure in seeing all the leading dancers of the company in a single ballet—an opportunity not often vouchsafed them.

The music was soaring, melodious and ideal for dancing, if not very profound, and the general stage picture was as expensively pretty as one of Messel's gala programme cover designs. Most of the costumes for the girls were lovely, but those for the men (particularly in the Fire episode) were unattractive in both colour and design.

The Coronation season ended on 27th June. It had been a far more satisfactory year than the previous one, and the company went off on holiday in good spirits. They assembled again early in August and gave a two-week season at Covent Garden prior to their third American tour. David Blair joined them (from the Sadler's Wells Theatre Ballet) for this season and appeared as one of the Prince's friends in *Cinderella*. This ballet was the mainstay of the two-week season, as the other full-length ballets were on their way across the Atlantic, and it showed rather shocking evidence of having been brought out in a hurry. It was badly under-rehearsed, the stage-setting was disgraceful and the scenery in grave danger of falling to pieces. The orchestra seemed to have forgotten the score completely and more than one member of the audience threatened to parade in front of the theatre with a banner saying, "Unfair to Cinderella."

The Third Visit to North America

The Sadler's Wells Ballet left England in a Stratocruiser on 6th September for their third visit to America in a rather nervous frame of mind. They had been absent from New York for three years and they had a fabulous reputation to live up to—it was, in fact, Mr. Hurok's custom to bill them throughout the length and breadth of the United States as "the fabulous." They were without Moira Shearer, Beryl Grey and Robert Helpmann, all big names in America, and they were not at all sure that the Americans would like the new ballets in their repertoire.

The opening performance of *Le Lac des Cygnes* took place in an overpowering heat-wave on 13th September, and afterwards the dancers were depressed and convinced the season was going to be a "flop," although every seat had been sold in advance. The new production was not so successful in New York as in London, although the Neapolitan dance stopped the show and the applause for Fonteyn and Somes was tremendous. Both the dancers and critics in the audience felt that it had not been an outstandingly good performance. They attributed this variously to heat, nerves and the unlucky date on which they opened, but all feared that on this third occasion the magic was not going to work.

Three days later, however, on 16th September, they danced *The Sleeping Beauty*, and with this ballet the season suddenly came to life. The company was in fine fettle and Fonteyn was at her joyous, beautiful best. The audience went wild for them and from then on the New York engagement became increasingly successful.

The full-length ballets retained their popularity and the revised version of *Giselle* was warmly approved, as was Fonteyn's performance. *Les Patineurs* and *Checkmate* were established favourites, but the rest of the repertoire was new to American audiences. *The Shadow* had only a mild success in New York, but it fared better on the tour and was particularly well liked in Chicago. *Don Juan* was coolly received, but the other three Ashton ballets, *Homage to the Queen, Daphnis and Chloë* and *Sylvia* received more enthusiastic notices than had ever before been accorded to the company's modern ballets. The leading critics could not speak too highly of Ashton and they acclaimed him as a great choreographer. The Hurok office was not slow to make the most of this triumph and programmes would be announced in the newspapers in the following terms: "To-night, 8.30—Sold Out! FREDERICK ASHTON NIGHT. Three Ballets by the Noted English Choreographer."

The show-business paper *Variety* reported the return of Sadler's Wells in its own jargon: "Sadler's Picks Up Where it Left Off at Top Terp, B.O. Level; 23G SRO Bow." [1]

The tremendous success of the New York season, more complete than on either of the previous visits, seemed to follow the company throughout the United States and Canada. In Toronto they gave *The Sleeping Beauty* for the first time, and danced it at the Maple Leaf Gardens to an audience of 9,332, of whom 500 were standing. When Violetta Elvin danced *Le Lac des Cygnes* at the third and last performance, attendance went up to 9,475, the largest crowd the company had ever drawn.

Everywhere they were welcomed back, and everywhere they made new friends. Margaret Lloyd, the distinguished critic of the *Christian Science Monitor,* wrote of them in Boston, "It is not the size but the quality, not the fame but the proof, that gives the Sadler's Wells Ballet its prestige." "London Ballet Troupe Lives Up to Ballyhoo" was a less graceful headline in Minneapolis, but it meant very much the same thing.

In San Francisco and Chicago the Press was less enthusiastic. Claudia Cassidy, the critic of the *Chicago Tribune,* paid her customary homage to Fonteyn but dismissed *Homage* as a "monumental bore" and *Sylvia* as an "overstuffed bore." Other critics and some distinguished teachers in Chicago agreed with her on these points, but nevertheless 60,000 people watched the company dance at the Civic Opera House and all sixteen performances were sold out.

[1] Roughly translated, this means that the company was still at the top of the tree by both terpsichorean and box-office standards. The opening night had taken some $23,000 at the box-office with standing room only available.

Throughout America *Le Lac des Cygnes* was the most frequently performed and most popular of the classical ballets, and Fonteyn's Odette-Odile was her most praised performance. Down in Atlanta, Georgia, the critic of the *Constitution* wrote, typically, "her dancing reflects that extra 'something' which must be genius. As the frightened swan in the first act, she wasn't a dancer. She was a swan, with frightened eyes."

At the end of this record-breaking tour the English dancers said good-bye to America on television, and the programme was impressive. They appeared on "Toast of the Town," a variety show run by the newspaper columnist Ed Sullivan, which included every kind of music-hall act and visiting celebrity. The appearance of ballet in the programme earned Sullivan a newspaper headline, "Longhair Breaking Out All Over on TV," but the experiment was an unqualified success with viewers from coast to coast of the United States.

An abbreviated version of *Les Patineurs* was followed by Fonteyn and Somes in their *pas de deux* from *Homage,* impeccably danced. Fonteyn, Somes and Ashton were then introduced to the television audience, godspeed was wished the whole company, and finally the orchestra played *God Save the Queen* and all the studio audience rose to their feet. There had never been anything quite like it on American television before.

The nineteen-week tour of 12,000 miles had included twenty cities in the United States and four in Canada. One hundred and thirty-six performances had resulted in estimated gross profits of $2,023,000, tax-exempt in the United States (although not in Canada) as a non-profit-making concern. Sadler's Wells brought home over $600,000 (£232,000) of this total, $100,000 more than they had earned in 1950. From this figure heavy travelling expenses had to be deducted and also a balance of salaries (only part had been paid in dollars), but the remainder, which went into the coffers of the Royal Opera House, was still a goodly sum.

A New Coppélia

The ballet returned to Covent Garden on 23rd February, the eighth anniversary of their arrival there, and gave *The Sleeping*

Beauty, fast becoming their trade-mark but unquestionably the best vehicle in the repertoire for showing the company at full strength and Fonteyn in her most famous rôle. Svetlana Beriosova, who had had much success in America, was ill on the opening night, so the Lilac Fairy was danced by pretty Mary Drage instead. Casualties from the American tour had not been serious, with the exception of Violetta Elvin, who had strained a ligament badly in Vancouver when dancing *Homage,* and Dame Ninette was stoutly determined that this time her dancers should not be overworked after their return home. She was herself preparing a new production of *Coppélia, Homage to the Queen* had been danced only a few times in London and there was a large and varied repertoire in a good state of rehearsal. She was prepared to offer as much novelty as she could in the way of new casting, but she put her foot down firmly about new ballets, or numerous revivals.

The new *Coppélia* was shown on 3rd March, a week after the opening of the season. It had been redecorated by Osbert Lancaster, and some revisions (only slight) had been made in the production to give the story more credence. Osbert Lancaster's settings were a vast improvement on the previous ones and the sensible Danish device was adopted of ending the ballet where it began, in the town square, rather than in some amorphous glade. The toyshop scene was the best and the assortment of dolls that Lancaster assembled there was enchanting. (Particularly attractive was the Scottish dancer, a complete little Staffordshire figure. This strongly native quality crept out in several places in Lancaster's designs, and it would have been interesting to see the ballet presented in a completely English setting.) The costumes were very gay, but there was an excess of red in the first act and an excess of ribbons and stage jewellery in the last act. Nevertheless, the general effect was one of bright, spandy newness, and if some people said it looked like *White Horse Inn*, the Director was well satisfied ("At last I've got it right, haven't I?" she was heard to say cheerfully in an interval), and the public doted on it.

Nadia Nerina danced the first Swanilda, with David Blair as Franz and Frederick Ashton a slightly music-hall Dr. Coppelius. An excellent interpretation of the difficult Dawn solo was given by Anya Linden, a young soloist of promise, who had attracted much attention during the previous season.

Nerina's natural gaiety and vitality were well displayed in *Coppélia* and she deserved the distinction of dancing the first performance. There is a joke in the London ballet world that every new production at Sadler's Wells is cast in triplicate (and a favourite pastime is to imagine a fifteenth cast of the utmost horror), but this *Coppélia* had five Swanildas, five interpreters of Franz and four old toymakers before it was more than a month old. Avril Navarre, merry and vivacious, Svetlana Beriosova, witty and charming, Rosemary Lindsay and Margaret Dale all gave good performances as Swanilda, and among the boys Alexander Grant was particularly good as Franz. Leslie Edwards and Franklin White had both played Dr. Coppelius before, but the revelation of this production was the Dr. Coppelius of John Hart, a rich, crusty old character of great personality.

Two other dancers made important début performances during the later weeks of this season. Pauline Clayden and Anne Heaton were both allowed to dance Giselle in London for the first time. Pauline Clayden's was a sad little waif, with occasional flashes of nervous gaiety in the first act, and a gentle melancholy in the second. It was an interpretation of taste and feeling, very much what one would have expected from the experience of her Chloë, Ophelia and Flower Girl in *Nocturne*. On the other hand Anne Heaton, a less experienced artist who had danced fewer leading rôles, astonished by the remarkable maturity of her performance. It was both felt and understood and danced with a beauty of placing and control that were a great tribute to her training. It was not a first sketch at Giselle, but a complete and moving performance. She was partnered by John Field, a good mime and fine dancer, who created considerable sympathy for Albrecht, particularly in the first act.

Early in June the company crossed to Holland to appear at the Holland Festival, but the visit was not altogether satisfactory. Much of the repertoire was now too unwieldy to fit easily into theatres of less than opera-house dimensions, and the travelling between the different towns in Holland had been awkwardly arranged, so that there was little time for setting stages or rehearsing. A little shamefaced, and more convinced than ever that opera-house companies needed to be seen in opera houses, the company returned across a rough North Sea to finish their London season.

The last excitement of this season was Svetlana Beriosova's first Aurora in *The Sleeping Beauty*, a performance of present beauty and infinite promise which caused much excitement and won her a fantastically good Press.

Fonteyn and Somes paid a brief visit to Yugoslavia early in June to dance *Le Lac des Cygnes* with the Yugoslav National Ballet. During the week they were in Belgrade they enjoyed a great triumph, were fêted everywhere, and endeared themselves to the Yugoslavs both by their dancing and their personalities. When the Covent Garden season finished on 26th June these two dancers, with a small group of their colleagues and with Frederick Ashton in charge of choreography, went to Granada to appear at the Festival there—again with remarkable success. Ashton arranged a new solo "The Entrance of Madam Butterfly" for Fonteyn and she danced it exquisitely in a costume designed by Christian Dior—a *tutu* surmounted by a little Japanese wrap. Violetta Elvin, meanwhile, took a small company of dancers to Wales to appear in both large towns and small mining villages, and in a different *milieu* enjoyed a comparable success.

When the four-week holiday period was over, towards the end of July, the company reassembled to complete rehearsals with Serge Grigorieff and Lubov Tchernicheva of Stravinsky's *The Firebird*, which they were to dance for the first time at the Edinburgh Festival as part of the Homage to Diaghileff celebrations. The experience of working with these two great Russians, who had been respectively *régisseur* and *maîtresse de ballet* to the Diaghileff company, was both stimulating and rewarding for the Sadler's Wells dancers. For the first time they began to understand the qualities which Fokine asked for in his ballets, and there could be no better person to instruct them than M. Grigorieff, who had felt, from the very beginning in 1909, the deepest sympathy and admiration for Fokine's ideals.

The first performance of *The Firebird* was given in Edinburgh on 23rd August, and for the occasion one of Diaghileff's greatest conductors, Ernest Ansermet, came to conduct. The *décor* and costumes were those designed by Natalia Gontcharova for Diaghileff's 1926 revival of the ballet, and they were carried out with as much care and devotion as were expended on rehearsals of the ballet. On the stage of the Empire Theatre in Edinburgh,

a music-hall stage of great width, no depth and little height, the
ballet was sadly cramped (it was such a squash that one boy somer-
saulted backwards over the footlights at a rehearsal), but anyone
could see that at last Sadler's Wells had got a Fokine ballet "right,"
and all the important things were there for a completely successful
performance once they were back at the Royal Opera House.

The homage paid by Sadler's Wells to Diaghileff was robbed of
its full effect in Edinburgh by the inadequacy of the theatre facilities and Dame Ninette told the Press roundly that if the city
wished to have good ballet at its Festival it must provide a better
theatre. Another tribute paid to Diaghileff in Edinburgh was the
Exhibition organised by Richard Buckle, which was later brought
to London by *The Observer* and enjoyed such remarkable success.
After the first performance of *The Firebird* in Edinburgh all the
Sadler's Wells company were entertained at the Exhibition and for
several hours, in the dim lighting and fantastic settings of Leonard
Rosoman, the young dancers wandered among the fabulous
exhibits, illustrating every phase of Diaghileff's career. For many
of them it was a voyage of discovery (for few dancers are interested
in epochs other than their own); they inspected designs and photographs with awe and chortled happily over a caricature of "Madam"
by Nicholas Legat.

For Dame Ninette herself, however, the evening was robbed of
enchantment by grave worries about the Sadler's Wells Theatre
Ballet in London. This young company had returned from a
highly successful South African tour and had made a formal
demand, through Equity, for increases in salaries. The Governors
of Sadler's Wells were perfectly prepared to grant increases but
stood doggedly by their conviction that increases must be in
accordance with the merit of individual dancers and not a flat-rate
increase all round as Equity demanded. Equity was equally determined not to give way, and the dispute made the front pages of
all the national papers. The principle of increases by merit and
merit only was felt by the Governors and Dame Ninette herself
to be so important that they would have disbanded the company
rather than yield the point, and for several anxious days at the
end of August it seemed as if this might indeed happen. Eventually,
however, agreement was reached. The dancers accepted increases
which averaged about 30s. each but varied from dancer to dancer.

T

Many people were astonished to learn how little the young ballet dancers earned and all sorts of rather misleading comparisons were made. The point that fundamentally governs salaries in an organisation such as Sadler's Wells is that the artists have chosen to work in a profession which does not, in its long-term operations, make large sums of money. Their position is comparable to that of a financial expert who chooses to remain in academic life rather than to accept a highly remunerative post with an industrial organisation.

The aspect of the dispute which most disturbed Dame Ninette, however, was the way in which the negotiations were handled. The official procedure of Equity prevented her from discussing the matter with her dancers in a frank and friendly way, and she felt that her company was growing into a sort of industrial organisation operating under trade-union principles, and was no longer a devoted band of artists. It was perhaps the price of success and of the great expansion in the organisation which was continually widening the gap between the Director and her younger dancers. Nevertheless it hurt her deeply.

The Sadler's Wells Ballet took part in only the first week of the Edinburgh Festival in 1954, and then returned to London on the Saturday night train, opening at Covent Garden the following Monday. The first performance of *The Firebird* in London was also conducted by Ansermet, who shared the ovation with Grigorieff, Tchernicheva and the dancers. It was one of the great occasions in the company's history. The revival was applauded unreservedly by many people who had known the Diaghileff production, and several dancers who had then appeared in the ballet went backstage with tears in their eyes to congratulate the new interpreters.

Fonteyn's Firebird immediately took a place among her greatest achievements. She had been considerably helped at rehearsals by Tamara Karsavina, who created the rôle for Diaghileff in 1910, and in her strange and fantastic make-up she bore an uncanny resemblance to her great predecessor. She might not have spectacular elevation (no dancer was ever blessed with supremacy in every movement of her art), but she had an ability to cover the stage very rapidly with swift, darting *jetés* that gave the illusion of flight. Whether trembling in the Prince's grasp, exultantly lifting the golden apples in her mouth, or mesmerising Kostchei and his followers into a deep sleep, she captured the very spirit of the Firebird.

Michael Somes as Prince Ivan learned and performed a rôle that was quite different from anything he had attempted before, because this was the first entirely *Russian* ballet that Sadler's Wells had attempted. He adopted a curious and typically Russian gait, a quizzical half-mocking, half-anxious expression, and at the end, standing motionless on the stage while the vast company assembled round the Prince and Princess, his gift of handsome nobility matched that of Beriosova, a true Tsarevna of exquisite gentleness and beauty. Frederick Ashton, in a grotesque make-up and in Gontcharova's inspired costume, was a remarkable Kostchei. The huge company of dancers responded magnificently to the demands of the unfamiliar Fokine choreography.

This revival of *The Firebird* marked a new achievement for the Sadler's Wells Ballet. From the very beginning Ninette de Valois had refused to rely on the productions of the Russian Ballet, but had built up a modern repertoire of ballets created specially for her company, establishing over the years the beginning of an English tradition in ballet-making. At the time *The Firebird* was produced, however, the company was strong enough in artistic and financial resources to do justice to this masterpiece from another epoch. Sadler's Wells was also strong enough in personality to undertake such a revival without fear of being accused of succumbing to the Russian school. The dancers were not only capable of withstanding comparison with the Ballets Russes companies of the 'thirties, but they gave a performance that was judged by many people to be superior to anything seen in London since Diaghileff's own 1926 presentation of the ballet. In fact, Sadler's Wells was, in its homage to Diaghileff, doing Russian Ballet an inestimable service by preserving, in this faithful re-creation, a ballet that might otherwise have disappeared from the international repertoire.

CHAPTER XVII

THE END IS THE BEGINNING

IN September 1954 there was an exchange of ballet companies between the Théâtre National de l'Opéra de Paris and the Royal Opera House, Covent Garden. The Corps de Ballet de l'Opéra[1] came to London for two weeks from 28th September, and the Sadler's Wells Ballet danced at the Paris Opéra for two weeks from 27th September.

It was an historic occasion and one which meant a great deal to Ninette de Valois. She announced it in terms of obvious excitement and pride to the London audience (which responded rather phlegmatically to her news). She was taking her company, not yet twenty-five years old, to the great national theatre of France as an exchange, on a footing of equality, for the Corps de Ballet de l'Opéra which had been in existence for 275 years. It was unquestionably an important occasion and was heralded as such by the Press of both countries, but, in so far as the ballet public in each capital was concerned, neither visit was an unqualified success. The Paris Opéra Ballet in London was applauded rather for its dancers than for its ballets. It was compared not only with the Sadler's Wells Ballet but with other visiting French companies and with the best ballet that London had seen over the years, and although there was much to applaud there was also much to criticise.

In Paris the Sadler's Wells Ballet received sharper criticism than it was accustomed to. The French critics, also, were judging the visitors against the highest standards (not necessarily the performances of the Paris Opéra Ballet). French taste was not expected to be ravished or influenced by the standard of *décor,* since even its warmest admirers would not claim that the Sadler's Wells repertoire is as *chic* or as revolutionary as Paris continually demands. However, it was something new for the work of Oliver Messel, held in such

[1] In France this means the entire company and not just a section as in the English use of *corps de ballet.*

Edward Mandinian

SCÈNES DE BALLET

Margot Fonteyn and Michael Somes

Roger Wood

SYLVIA

Violetta Elvin and John Field in the Act III *pas de deux*

NADIA NERINA

SVETLANA BERIOSOVA

unquestioned reverence at home ever since James Agate hailed his work for *La Belle Hélène,* to be described in the Press in such terms as the following: "L'aveuglante laideur des décors et des costumes . . . écrase un spectacle dont on voudrait cependant retenir quelques-uns des incontestables mérites" (*Figaro*), or, "Le décor . . . est laid, horriblement conventionnel" (*Franc Tireur*), or the summing up in *Paris Presse,* "Notre public de balletomanes . . . n'a pas été moins surpris par l'abîme qui existe entre le goût anglais et le goût français en matière de décors et de costumes . . . [décors] que nos metteurs en scène ont oubliés depuis plus d'un demi-siècle."

The season opened with *The Sleeping Beauty,* and Paris was not particularly impressed. A distinguished audience received it quietly, the general impression seeming to be that it was "une soirée . . . avec des moments réussis" but that Paris could quite happily live without full-length ballets. Fonteyn's triumph was rather at the expense of the whole than an integral part of it, as was customary in England and America. "En somme" said one woman as she emerged from the Opéra, "le Sadler's Wells Ballet, c'est Margot Fonteyn." The lack of enthusiasm for *The Sleeping Beauty* in Paris may have been partly due to the fact that the production was nearly ten years old and that the ballet was ripe for revision and re-dressing. The Sadler's Wells people were, of course, perfectly aware of this fact, and were already making plans for a transformation of the ballet to be effected at a suitable and opportune time.

Le Lac des Cygnes, a more recent and elegant production, was preferred in Paris to *The Sleeping Beauty*, and Violetta Elvin had a particular triumph in this ballet. One critic described her as "Plus femme, plus charnelle que la transparente Margot," and after the Act II adagio she was recalled five times—"C'est rarissime à l'Opéra!" commented *Le Monde.*

The critics spoke their minds about the whole repertoire, applauding the things they liked, and stating quite clearly their objections to the things they did not like. *Mam'zelle Angot* went over well (thanks to Derain's setting and Nadia Nerina), and, not surprisingly, *Tiresias* (danced by Somes and Elvin) was liked and respected.

"Ce style étranger pourtant n'est pas le nôtre," said Olivier Merlin when he summed up the season in *Le Monde.* "Plus discipliné et plus composé, il est moins spontané et moins artiste."

But, like the Americans, he was quick to pay tribute to the dancers' lovely feet and "leurs chaussons sans 'pointes' de bois. Divin silence!"

The Paris audience throughout the visit was large and warm in its applause. The company might not have created a fashionable sensation but it was much admired and enjoyed by the general public, and the youthful English national ballet fared quite as well in Paris as the venerable French national ballet fared in London.

From Paris the Sadler's Wells Ballet went on to Italy to dance in Milan at the Scala, in Rome, Naples, Genoa and Venice. Everywhere they enjoyed their customary triumphs. The Italian critics and public alike hailed the visit as one of the greatest artistic importance. The dancers took full advantage of the kindness and hospitality of friends who arranged for them to see as much of the art treasures of Italy as possible, and it was a visit of happiness and enthusiasm on both sides. The repertoire shown in Italy consisted of the two full-length Tchaikovsky ballets and three modern ballets, *Mam'zelle Angot* and *Tiresias* having been sent home after Paris. The titles displayed outside the Scala looked particularly attractive and enticing in Italian, and when the company arrived they felt a new interest in dancing *Le Bella Addormentata nel Bosco, Il Lago dei Cigni, I Pattinatori* and *Omaggio alla Regina*. Even *Checkmate* seemed a novelty when described as *Scacco Matto*.

From the sunshine and pleasures of Italy to an English provincial tour in November and December was a rude contrast, but the visits to Oxford, Bristol and Manchester were considered important, for Dame Ninette wished the company to be seen, in those theatres large enough to accommodate it, throughout the country for several weeks every year. They had not visited Manchester for a number of years, however, and perhaps they had been away a little too long. The theatre was not sold out every night, but reviews were good and audiences enthusiastic.

Back in London, the company opened their long winter-spring season at Covent Garden on 16th December with *Mam'zelle Angot, Ballet Imperial* and *The Firebird,* all by Russian choreographers. *Mam'zelle Angot* was back in excellent shape again, and received a lively performance from Nadia Nerina, Alexander Grant and David Blair (as the Caricaturist). *The Firebird* seemed, if anything, to be increasing in magnificence, but *Ballet Imperial* had once again dropped into the "competent" category of performance. On 1st

January 1955, Beryl Grey, who had been absent for some eighteen months on maternity leave, returned to the company and received a tumultuous welcome from a faithful audience for her performance in *Le Lac des Cygnes*.

On 6th January two new ballets by Frederick Ashton, dedicated to the memory of Sophie Fedorovitch, were given a joint *première*. Both were "minor" works; short one-act ballets which might have complemented each other to make an attractive double bill. Neither, unfortunately, was an unqualified success, although *Rinaldo and Armida* could be counted a very honourable near-miss.

Rinaldo and Armida owed only its title to the allegorical poem by Tasso. Armida, an enchanted maiden, attracts lovers to her sinister garden where, against a white snowscape, black leaves drift down continually from the gaunt black trees. She is doomed to die, however, if she falls in love with a man and returns his kiss. If she withholds her affection, the man who loves her must die. The ballet was virtually a dramatic *pas de deux* for Svetlana Beriosova and Michael Somes, and for them it contained some beautiful and expressive dancing. Beriosova suggested most movingly the gradual transformation of a cold-hearted beauty into a woman who is roused to such passion that she forfeits her life to enjoy the forbidden kiss. Somes conveyed with equal intensity the ardour and then the terror of Rinaldo, who only escaped from the garden by the death of his beloved. Two non-dancing figures were introduced, but they contributed little to the story. The choreography was entirely concentrated on the lovers, and might have made a more powerful impression had the extraneous trappings been removed. At times the ballet recalled the beauty and economy of Andrée Howard's little masterpiece, *Death and the Maiden*. Peter Rice's setting was entirely in black and white; it was atmospheric and very elegant but perhaps a little too *chic* for such an emotional theme. The turgid music by Malcolm Arnold was melodious and theatrical but rather reminiscent of a high-class film score. The ballet, in fact, failed to be satisfying as a whole, although the two leading dancers were given a great reception and won excellent notices. Perhaps the most important merit of *Rinaldo and Armida* was that it showed Beriosova might be capable of inspiring Ashton to create lyrical and emotional choreography, and in this respect it roused hopes for the future.

The other new ballet was *Variations on a Theme of Purcell*, danced to Benjamin Britten's "Young Person's Guide to the Orchestra." Individual dancers were identified with individual instruments, and the ballet was a work of "pure dancing" with a formal seventeenth-century opening and close, in the manner of Purcell, and a more contemporary central section in the style of Britten. The setting was a very uninteresting walled garden with a bust of Purcell placed dead centre. (At the dress rehearsal this bust was turned round towards the close of the ballet to show, on the reverse, a bust of Britten; but this device was abandoned before the first performance.)

Alexander Grant appeared as a fantastic creature in many different costumes and served as some kind of connecting figure between the different variations. Unfortunately the variety of costumes simply drew attention to the fact that much of the choreography allotted to him was exceedingly feeble. The principal female dancers were Nadia Nerina, Rowena Jackson and Elaine Fifield, who did their utmost with the choreography but were unable to impose much meaning on a formless ballet. They were further hampered at the first performance by being almost unable to hear on the stage the individual instruments they were supposed to follow, and the setting was placed so far downstage that they were cramped in addition. At later performances the music was relayed to the stage and the garden wall of the setting pushed farther back, but the ballet was still a muddle. This was the more the pity as it did give some indication of the number of good male dancers in the company, and had the choreography been less fussy their prowess would have showed the more clearly.

Elaine Fifield's appearance in this new ballet was her first important assignment at Covent Garden. She had joined the company in the autumn of 1954, after being absent from the Sadler's Wells Theatre Ballet for some time on maternity leave. She danced what was required of her in *Variations on a Theme of Purcell* with a nice precision and control, but she had little opportunity to impose a personality. That opportunity came on 22nd January when she danced Swanilda for the first time at Covent Garden. She had danced it many times at Sadler's Wells, and her performance transferred happily to the larger stage. Natural gaiety and vitality were allied to a remarkably strong technique, and it was wonderful to see again a dancer with such an easy gift of speed—a quality that is not common among English dancers.

Four weeks afterwards another young dancer took over another important rôle. On 19th February Svetlana Beriosova danced Odette-Odile in *Le Lac des Cygnes* for the first time in London (she had danced it the previous December in Belgrade as guest artist with the Yugoslav State Ballet). She was not quite ready for such an arduous rôle and nervousness robbed even her second act of its previous emotional quality, but it was nonetheless an auspicious début. Beauties of line and phrasing, beauties of musical responsiveness and of dramatic understanding, placed her performance among those rare events which, in future, everyone present would boast of having witnessed. She was admirably partnered and assisted through the ordeal by John Field. In the first act a delightfully young, fresh and charming *pas de trois* was danced by Anya Linden, Cynthia Mayan and David Blair, three dancers of a new generation who inspire great confidence for the future of Sadler's Wells.

The early days of February were enlivened for all the dancers and staff of the Royal Opera House, as well as for ballet lovers throughout the world, by the announcement of Margot Fonteyn's impending marriage. From the moment the story broke until she was married to Dr. Roberto Arias in Paris on 6th February, Fonteyn was front-page news in all the national papers. The occasion caused universal delight and happiness but there was a little tearfulness in the company, for the dancers had to admit that in future she would belong less exclusively to them. Aided by an excited audience, they gave her a wonderful send-off during the performance the night before her wedding. She was dancing in *Daphnis and Chloë*, and when she made her last entry, carried on stage by Michael Somes, a shower of rose petals fell on to the stage and the dancers pelted her with streamers and confetti while the audience cheered its own good wishes. Fonteyn was absent only two weeks and her return (in *The Firebird*) was another great evening at Covent Garden. Her popularity and her artistry had never been greater and it became almost impossible that spring to obtain seats for any performance when she was dancing, although at other times there were frequently empty seats in all parts of the Royal Opera House.

On the occasion of Frederick Ashton's next new ballet, *Madame Chrysanthème*, Margot Fonteyn was in the audience with her husband and Elaine Fifield created the leading rôle. The ballet was adapted from the novel by Pierre Loti, which also served as the inspiration for *Madame Butterfly*. Two French sailors, Pierre and Yves, land in Nagasaki. Pierre desires a temporary wife but is not attracted by any of the beauties offered to him. Suddenly he sees a young girl seated apart and will have none other. A price is agreed with her parents, the silver dollars are handed over and Pierre and Chrysanthème are united before a Dignitary. After festivities and dancing, night falls and Pierre and Chrysanthème retire. Chrysanthème is anxious to please her sailor. Next morning, however, Pierre has to rejoin his ship. Chrysanthème sadly gives him a bouquet of her name flowers and begs him to return for a last farewell. He believes that she loves him and presently returns. She does not hear him come in and quietly continues to count her silver dollars, the fruits of her marriage. Without making his presence known, Pierre leaves for ever.

The music for the ballet was composed by Alan Rawsthorne and the scenery and costumes designed by Isabel Lambert. With Ashton, they succeeded in creating a lovely and delicate work of art. The simple little story was free of all sentiment; the settings and costumes an exquisite adaptation of Japanese art to the ballet stage. The music was clear and beautiful, with melodies warm enough to carry the emotional scenes but, again, no trace of sentiment. It was the most distinguished score that had been composed for the company for a great many years.

Elaine Fifield, white and tiny, justified Ashton's confidence with a performance of real understanding. The choreography was designed largely to show the remarkable flexibility of her feet and she performed the movements with a neatness and control that prevented them from ever becoming grotesque. She was infinitely touching at the end of the *pas de deux* when, all fears overcome, she knelt at her sailor's side and pattered gently towards him on her hands. Yet there was never a suggestion that the liaison was of lasting consequence to her. She counted her blessings with a calm, untroubled acceptance.

Alexander Grant danced Pierre with a merry opening flourish and then more than a touch of real compassion. His solo at the marriage celebrations, based on traditional hornpipe steps, was executed with magnificent flourish. Desmond Doyle, as brother

Yves, established a likeable rogue, Ray Powell was the obnoxious marriage broker and Leslie Edwards made a brief, but remarkable, appearance as an aged Dignitary. Pauline Clayden and Anne Heaton as Mlle. Pluie d'Avril and Mlle. Wisteria, two courtesans, were entirely delightful. Indeed all the girls looked enchanting in their Japanese costumes and the contrast between male and female dancing was strongly pointed.

Unfortunately the ballet was produced during the strike which prevented the publication of any London newspapers and it could not thus enjoy the acclaim and publicity it deserved. It was not a ballet on an heroic scale; but within the limits of what it set out to do it was a very nearly perfect collaboration.

The ballet launched, Ashton went off to Copenhagen to produce *Romeo and Juliet* for the Royal Danish Ballet. At home the company continued its season with a revival of *Sylvia*, with a revised production of *Les Sylphides* (restored by Serge Grigorieff and Lubov Tchernicheva to its original form), with some magnificent performances of *The Firebird* and *Daphnis and Chloë*, and the seasonal revival of *Job* in which Anton Dolin had expressed a wish to make his last guest appearance with the company.

Meanwhile, in the background, preparations went ahead for the company's fourth tour of North America, scheduled to open in New York early in September 1955, and plans were being laid for the administration of White Lodge, in Richmond Park, the new residential premises of the Sadler's Wells School. With the acquisition of White Lodge it became possible to move the entire Junior School to Richmond, thus freeing 45 Colet Gardens for the Senior School. The house next door, 46 Colet Gardens, was also acquired at this time and the company was able to give up the rehearsal room at the Old Hammersmith Town Hall and transfer its headquarters to Colet Gardens. The integration of Senior School and company was thereby further strengthened. Throughout the School, increased teaching responsibility is being given to former dancers of the company, such as Pamela May and Harold Turner, while present members (for example, John Field) are also encouraged to give classes.

Thus the wheel comes full cycle. Dancers who made the Sadler's Wells Ballet what it is to-day are gradually beginning to take up new duties and to pass on their knowledge and experience to younger generations. And once again it is all working out according to plan. "Members of a permanent repertory ballet company must form the teaching staff of the future," wrote Ninette de Valois in 1938. "They alone will eventually know the theatre's complete requirements for the future generation of dancers." At Covent Garden Ailne Phillips, who danced in the earliest ballets and then taught so many of the present young dancers while they were at the School, keeps an eye on her former pupils and teaches them theatrecraft as well as technique. John Hart has taken over the duties of Ballet Master to the company and Michael Somes is showing a gift for administration. The continued service of these dancers, together with that of all their colleagues who play different, but vital, parts in the organisation that is the Sadler's Wells Ballet, is the best assurance of a continuing tradition of ballet within this country. For, as Ninette de Valois wrote long ago, "the work has not been thought out just for the present, but for those days, months and years that go to make up the future. In brief . . . there has been planted for you in the middle of London a true heritage. It is your duty to protect this gift—and see that it lives and expands."

Houston Rogers

Margot Fonteyn as The Firebird

THE FIREBIRD

Svetlana Beriosova and Michael Somes

CURTAIN CALL

APPENDICES

APPENDIX A

THE SADLER'S WELLS SCHOOL

History

THE present Sadler's Wells School is a logical development of the small school that was established within the walls of Sadler's Wells Theatre by Ninette de Valois in 1931. The first advertisements appeared beneath a photograph of the theatre (in pouring rain) captioned "England's Home of Ballet." Emphasis was entirely on training for a repertory ballet company and the nucleus of the company has from the beginning consisted of finished students from the School. The training was technically sound and highly professional. Many celebrated teachers of various nationalities worked there at different periods, but the entire curriculum was supervised by Ninette de Valois, with Ursula Moreton as her chief assistant. Later Ailne Phillips was also to play a very important part.

Technical training was all that could be provided in the early years, but the wider curriculum offered at the Academy of Choreographic Art had shown that Ninette de Valois was aware of the importance of a general artistic education for a dancer. She hoped one day to have a fully educational establishment such as existed in those countries which possessed state-endowed ballet companies. At the time the first Sadler's Wells School was founded an enthusiastic young man named Arnold Haskell was advocating in *The Dancing Times* the need for lectures on art and music as part of the day-to-day training of English dancers.

To-day, Ninette de Valois has the school she dreamed about; Ursula Moreton is in charge of the Ballet School and Arnold Haskell is Director and Principal.

The School achieved its present status as a fully educational establishment in 1947, the war having postponed this development by six or seven years. In September 1947 the old Froebel Institute in Colet Gardens, Barons Court, was opened as the new premises of the School, and all classes were transferred there from Sadler's Wells Theatre. The building was not altogether ideal, but it had been adapted to meet the main needs of a ballet school and had exceptionally large and well-ventilated halls for dancing. Moreover, it is within easy reach of Covent Garden by underground railway.

The School began cautiously and rather experimentally. At first full education was offered for girls only, but after a year de Valois decided that the same facilities must also be offered to boys. Some fifteen or twenty boys were accepted and taught separately by their own tutor.

Progress was gradual, but so steady that by 1951 the School was recognised by the Ministry of Education as an efficient primary and secondary school. The curriculum is much the same as in other schools, except that a daily ballet class takes the place of all other forms of physical activity.

Another extension of the School's facilities occurred in 1955, when White Lodge in Richmond Park was acquired for the Junior School and opened in September as a boarding as well as a day school. The removal of the Junior School to Richmond freed more space at Colet Gardens for post-educational and professional classes, and in addition No. 46 Colet Gardens was purchased to become the company rehearsal room and headquarters of the company.

The need for residential premises became increasingly obvious during the early years of full education at Colet Gardens. Children were attracted from all over the world as well as from all over the British Isles, and the problem of boarding them with foster parents or in hostels was a source of continual worry. Dancing is a very special vocation and education towards that end needs to continue, in some respects, throughout the twenty-four hours. Proper food, fresh air and proper amounts of sleep are as important to the young dancer as exercises at the *barre*. The students come from every kind of home and while many parents and foster parents co-operate admirably with the School authorities, there are frequent cases of over-pampering at one end of the scale and inadequate home diets of baked beans and fried fish and chips at the other. At White Lodge the child's physical well-being can be guarded as carefully as its prowess in the classroom.

Methods of Selection

The Junior School of Sadler's Wells can at present take about 175 students. The Senior School is more elastic, but the process of selection is a serious responsibility. Every effort is made at the auditions to pick children who are likely to complete the course successfully, but so many unforeseeable factors enter the picture as a child grows up that it is impossible to guarantee in advance that a child will develop into a suitable dancer for one of the ballet companies.

The age of entry is roughly between nine and eleven, because this age is the best at which to try to judge if a child is likely to be of the right type. English children mature slowly, and Dame Ninette shares Cecchetti's belief that they can start training two years later than, say, Italians. The children may have attended associate classes at the School once or twice a week from an earlier age, but they are nevertheless required to go to the public audition before they are accepted as full-time students of the School.

Auditions are held at intervals during the School year and are attended by Dame Ninette, Arnold Haskell, the Head Mistress, Miss McCutcheon, the ballet staff and the School's physiotherapist, Miss Celia Sparger. The children are seldom asked to perform more than a few simple exercises at the *barre* (much to the disappointment of those who come prepared to dance *La Mort du Cygne*), but they do these exercises in bathing dresses and the staff are able to assess the physique of the individual children. Anything radically wrong can be detected at once, but all children who seem suitable and promising are afterwards given a detailed physical examination by the physiotherapist.

Miss Sparger has a unique combination of knowledge of physical education, physiotherapy and ballet technique. She first came into contact with ballet in the days of the Academy of Choreographic Art, when she treated one of the dancers for a strained back. Ninette de Valois made her acquaintance and began to send other dancers to her for remedial treatment and also children from the School for correct placing. Miss Sparger studied ballet herself with Margaret Craske in order to understand the dancers' problems and to appreciate the fervour that inspired their work, and she was consulted frequently by Sadler's Wells dancers from 1931 onwards. (She says she always knew when Frederick Ashton was rehearsing a new ballet by the number of aches and pains among the dancers; he was always trying new movements that brought new muscles into play and caused moans and groans from the dancers he was working with. Nevertheless, all of them would sooner have died than miss a rehearsal or give up a part in an Ashton ballet.) When the School was enlarged in 1947, Ninette de Valois was quick to secure the services of Celia Sparger as consulting physiotherapist, and her experience and special knowledge have ever since been of the greatest value.

The physical examination which Miss Sparger conducts takes account of such things as the child's possible height (impossible to predict accurately, but the child of an exceptionally tall family is usually discouraged), faults of posture, length of back, high shoulders, structure of the limbs, and the all-important structure of the foot.

Physical suitability is not the only factor considered, however. School records are investigated and intelligence, evidence of temperament or personality, and an interest in the arts may often help a borderline case into the school. Book-learning alone is no recommendation; if a child shows promise but has a poor academic record, Miss McCutcheon may sigh, but Dame Ninette will probably take her and quote, in support of her contention that talent is very possible without intellect, an experience of her Dublin days. (She was producing at the Abbey Theatre once and a young Irish girl gave an extraordinary and moving performance. When she came off, the girl said, "Ah, sure, an' I don't know what that was all about.")

The children are always asked *why* they want to dance, and this produces some strange replies. One small boy from the North said immediately, "They tell me there's mooney in it." (He was accepted.) Another boy of exceptional promise, who seemed to all the examiners to have the makings of the ideal male dancer, replied very crossly, "*I* don't want to dance; I want to go in the Navy. All this is just *mother*." (With real regret, the examiners turned him down and wished him luck in the Senior Service.)

Between 300 and 400 children are seen each year and perhaps 10 per cent of them are accepted. Their training at the School lasts for nine years and only about one quarter of those accepted stay the entire course. (These figures compare favourably with national academies which have been established for several hundred years. Violetta Elvin, for instance, studied in a class of twenty-five students at the ballet school in Moscow. Of these twenty-five, only six finished the course and only three were accepted for the theatre.) Being a ballet dancer is a very specialised career. Children are required to give up many things if they wish to become dancers; they need to have a vocation. Some never acquire this single-minded dedication and these are the ones who usually leave the ballet after a few years. Others accept the demands of their chosen career very young. A short while ago a beautiful and promising child from the School was offered an important film contract. She not only refused the offer; she felt deeply insulted.

Training

Children are accepted for a year in the first instance and their progress is very carefully watched. They are given a physical examination each term and the resulting reports are scrutinised together with reports on their prowess in the classroom. Usually the physical ailments are minor; fatigue, which the children will not admit but which reveals itself in posture, or sudden increases in weight. Enforced rest and the dropping of a class or so a week soon correct these ailments, and many foot troubles

U

are traced not to ballet classes but unsuitable or down-at-heel shoes, in the case of the youngsters, or the lure of high heels with the sixteen-year-olds. Injuries are rare and the few which do occur are usually among older students doing more advanced work. Anything more serious than a minor strain or sprain is sent to hospital and treated there.

Although a child may be physically strong, however, there may be manifestations of other obstacles to her success as a dancer. Each year there are spines which cannot be mobilised sufficiently, hips which resist all efforts towards turning out, feet which present unexpected difficulties. If these are obviously going to militate against the child's progress as a dancer the parents are urged at once to concentrate on a career other than ballet. The disappointment will be great at twelve years old or fourteen, but the frustration and the heartbreak at twenty-one could be disastrous. The Sadler's Wells Ballet School gives no mixed (*i.e.* musical comedy or dramatic) theatre training and "rejects" from the School are frequently urged to take up this kind of training else-where. A child who might never be suitable for the *corps de ballet* of a repertory ballet company may nevertheless later become a star of the first order in some other branch of the theatre.

For the children who remain in the School, the course of training is as follows. In the Junior School, dancing forms only a part of the child's general education and is limited to a daily class of one-and-a-quarter hours, usually first thing in the morning. All the children have a regular lesson in Dalcroze eurhythmics until they are fourteen, and this is now recognised as part of the academic syllabus. Between thirteen and four-teen the children all take the elementary R.A.D. examination, because if they are going to teach later, certificates will be important. All other R.A.D. examinations are voluntary, however, and not compulsory, and it is left entirely to the student to decide whether she wants to continue with them. Between fourteen and fifteen the children concentrate on work for their General Certificate of Education (and no child is ever advised to leave at this crucial stage of the academic syllabus), but once this hurdle is passed they are at last able to concentrate on dancing. They then move into the post-education class and the amount of dance study is greatly increased. Character, *pas de deux*, and mime classes occupy an important part of the syllabus. It is only at this stage that mime is taught, for the gestures soon become automatic and meaning-less if taught to very young children. In addition, the students receive about eight hours' tuition each week in such subjects as French, English, Art, Music Appreciation and History, including a series of lectures by Arnold Haskell on History of the Theatre and Dancing.

Students from outside who join the School come into the post-educational class, and it is at this stage that most of the Dominions dancers arrive. (The R.A.D. has given invaluable help in the form of grants to young dancers in the Dominions to enable them to pay their fares to England.) Students who join at this stage have an equal chance of being accepted for one of the companies'as those dancers who have attended the Wells School from the age of ten. Fundamentally, quality is the all-important consideration, but account has also to be taken of adaptability. If a dancer comes late with a strongly ingrained style that differs markedly from that taught at Sadler's Wells, the chances of successful absorption into the company are not very great. Schools are therefore advised not to hold on to promising pupils for too long; if they wish to make a career in the Sadler's Wells Ballet, they are best advised to join the School immediately they have taken their school certificate.

Dame Ninette is aiming at a definite English style of dancing and believes that it is now emerging (*emerging* is an important word) as a mixture of the best of the French, Russian and Italian methods. A class which is unique to the Sadler's Wells School is the Plastique Class, which is essentially a personal idea of Dame Ninette and a development of the old Composition Class of Academy of Choreographic Art days. It is based on classical principles of weight and balance and is in no sense "modern" dance. Pupils are, for example, asked to stand in fourth position *straight*—neither turned out nor turned in—and with the knee straight above the foot. Easy transference of weight and good balance are acquired in this basic position and it is then developed into curves and other patterns. Some such movements occur in Fokine ballets (Harlequin in *Carnaval,* for instance) and de Valois has used them a lot in *Job* for the Angels, Elihu and the Messengers. It was partly because she found it so difficult to get classically trained dancers to do any movement *straight* (if told not to turn out, they invariably turn in) that Dame Ninette introduced the plastique class at the School. It enables dancers to tackle freer movements outside the strict classical syllabus and enables them to run on the stage and also to walk naturally—which is a difficult assignment for a classically trained dancer. Many of the exercises are performed within imaginary limitations; for instance, the dancer either imagines herself as standing against a flat wall, or with her hands and arms spread across a flat table, or else the whole movement is performed as if within a hoop, to impress a sense of pattern and the "drawing" of the movement on the dancer's mind.

Importance is attached to the necessity of having many teachers so that no child becomes completely dependent on a single teacher. The children pass each year from one teacher to another, who knows precisely the point they will have reached in their dance studies. Each year's course is planned as a whole and a routine has to be followed, but towards the end of the year when the syllabus has been completed the teacher has freedom to try ideas of her own. Normal school holidays were soon found to be too long for dancers, so now the children are encouraged to come back, for dancing lessons only, for the last weeks of the academic holiday. They do an ordinary class and then learn a few dances afterwards. Dances from the ballets in the Sadler's Wells repertoires are taught throughout the School, graded according to difficulty for the different years.

The composition of the different classes is the same for dancing as for academic work in the Junior School and all the children are treated exactly the same. At the school desk and at the *barre* they are all equal, and this is by no means the general rule in dance studios. One Swedish dancer who worked for several years at the School put it this way: "I have never seen a school before without that 'popular pupil' system. They treat all the pupils the same, no matter who they are or where they come from."

Boy Pupils

The attitude towards boys taking up dancing as a career is gradually changing in England, although it is always difficult to attract the right sort of boy. The proportion of boys accepted at auditions is naturally very much higher than the proportion of girls. (Many of the most promising come from Lancashire, where a local tradition of tap and clog dancing has possibly counteracted the notion that dancing is an unsuitable occupation for boys.) In the School the boys are taught separately and they maintain an attitude of rugged independence which is strongly encouraged by the staff. It is illustrated by the following story. During a recent summer-school session, at the end of the School year, problems of accommodation were more than usually complicated and, as a makeshift measure, a few very young boys and girls were given a class together in one of the rehearsal rooms. While they were at work Margot Fonteyn, Robert Helpmann and Michael Somes happened to pass the door and stayed to watch. The children saw them in a mirror and the boys became very embarrassed and agitated. Afterwards one small boy went up to the teacher to express his displeasure and to say, "Will you kindly explain to Mr. Helpmann that it is not at all *usual* for us to have a lesson with the girls."

The gradually changing attitude towards male dancing in England has penetrated even into the armed forces. The boys all do their national service and, *providing they have had four or five years' good training before they do their national service,* it does them no harm as dancers. The army authorities are prepared to co-operate and occasionally ask if certain jobs are harmful to dancers. Dame Ninette often receives letters from boys doing their military service on the lines of the following: "Dear Madam, If you will write to my C.O. and say that I should not go for long tramps in boots but in my own shoes, he will let me."

The Making of a Dancer

The three stages of a dancer's career are studentship, apprenticeship and specialisation. Studentship at the School provides the sound technical foundation, the complete classical education in dancing. At the end of the course the students reach the Theatre Class and during their year in this class they walk on in the larger ballets at Covent Garden and sometimes dance in the *corps de ballet*. From the Theatre Class they are accepted into either the company at Covent Garden or the one at Sadler's Wells, depending on the vacancies and the types of dancers required in each company at that particular moment.

With dancers as with wine, the vintage varies from year to year. In a bad year a group of unremarkable graduates may be taken on for the *corps de ballet* at Covent Garden, because there happen to be several vacancies, whereas in a good year there may be fewer vacancies and dancers of greater ability will be rejected. No "rejection" is final and absolute, however. The dancer may keep in touch and may be successful later when a vacancy occurs. (Most of the "rejects," of course, accept jobs in other ballet companies or in musicals, television or films. People then say "another talent overlooked by Sadler's Wells." What they never think of saying is "another example of excellent Sadler's Wells training.")

Apprenticeship continues during the first two or three years that a dancer is in a company. Her studies continue and she gradually learns the repertoire and begins to show, on the stage, an aptitude for rôles of a particular kind. It is during this period that a dancer comes to know herself as an artist and to develop her personality until she is ready to specialise in the type of rôles that best suit her style and character. It is impossible to assess a dancer's precise style and stage personality in the classroom, for so many of them do not "come alive" until they reach the stage and are seen in performance. Many a shy little mouse will then blossom into a beauty of assurance and many an extrovert character from the classroom will fail completely to "come across."

The Place of the School in the Organisation

The work that is done in the Sadler's Wells School is of vital importance but it must always be a background activity. Publicity is discouraged and while there is a great desire to attract dancers of quality, the quantity must always be limited. The School was first established to supply the ballet company with dancers, and even to-day it still has a main function of training dancers for the Sadler's Wells Ballet and the Sadler's Wells Theatre Ballet.

At the same time, there is a large and growing demand from abroad for teachers and choreographers from Sadler's Wells, and the organisation recognises this as a responsibility to be met. There is no wish to hoard at home the products of the School or to close the doors against dancers from overseas. Since 1947 Dame Ninette has personally conducted an annual course in "The Constructive Teaching of Ballet" for teachers of dancing from all over the world. Every class, demonstration and lecture is held in an informal atmosphere and questions and expressions of opinion are welcomed. The Ballet Staff of the School and the company participate and certain dancers give up much time to demonstrate during the course.

The Sadler's Wells School is still very young in experience and has much to learn. Much has been achieved but the desire of the Director is for a continual seeking after knowledge and a willingness to share the fruits of experience and practice with other schools and theatres throughout the British Isles and throughout the world.

APPENDIX B

THE SADLER'S WELLS THEATRE BALLET

THE second Sadler's Wells ballet company began life in a modest way as a small group of dancers, assembled in order to appear in the opera ballets at Sadler's Wells Theatre and to give occasional performances on their own. The company was originally envisaged as something in the nature of a stepping stone to Covent Garden; a stage where dancers and choreographers could gain practical experience before moving on to the more august precincts of the Royal Opera House. After a few years of experiment, mistakes and gradual progress, however, the company established itself as an complementary organisation of first-class creative importance.

The present Director of Sadler's Wells is Norman Tucker, whose responsibilities correspond closely to those of David Webster at Covent Garden. The ballet company is directed by Ninette de Valois, who makes all policy decisions, but the daily rehearsing and organisation of the company is left to her Assistant Director, Peggy van Praagh.

The ballet company has an obligation to provide good ballet at very low prices in a people's theatre (thus continuing the work of Lilian Baylis). At the same time it does valuable work in touring the provinces to show some achievements of the Sadler's Wells organisation in small towns and theatres which could not accommodate the company from Covent Garden.

During the first nine years of its life the company danced in opera ballets at Sadler's Wells and played concurrently with the opera company in London, but by 1955 it became obvious that this policy was uneconomic and that concentrated seasons of all-opera or all-ballet would free the companies for more touring outside London, without cutting appreciably the sum total of London performances. This change of policy necessitated the formation of a small group of dancers to be attached to the opera company and to appear only in the opera ballets.

The repertoire consists mostly of contemporary ballets by young artists, for the grant which the Arts Council makes to Sadler's Wells each year is specifically intended for the encouragement of young painters and musicians as well as young choreographers. The large-scale classics can be better presented at Covent Garden and they remain the province of that company. *Coppélia,* however, is well suited to a smaller

311

theatre, and the second act of *Le Lac des Cygnes* is included in the repertory if there is a classical ballerina in the company whose performance
can justify its revival. *Les Sylphides* has become a part of every dancer's
education and is almost essential in a touring repertory, and Fokine is
also represented by *Carnaval*. Certain ballets from the English repertoire
which are not suitable for presentation at Covent Garden (for example,
The Rake's Progress) are preserved at Sadler's Wells.

Young choreographers are encouraged to a marked degree and
during the nine years of its existence no less than fifteen different choreographers have produced ballets for the company. When particular
promise is shown—for instance in the cases of John Cranko, Alfred
Rodrigues and Kenneth Macmillan—further opportunities are given
very quickly. "A young choreographer," says Ninette de Valois, needs
to produce not one isolated work but "at least two productions per
annum in the same environment and with the same artists for a considerable period of time."

Valuable first experiments in choreography were also made by an
organisation known as the Sunday Choreographic Group, which was
run by the dancers (of both companies) themselves. Ninette de Valois
welcomed this idea of trying out new ideas in choreography before a
private audience and stepped in to introduce the first programme herself from the stage.

One stipulation was made to the Sunday choreographers; there must
be no expenditure on *décor* or fancy costumes. The choreography was
to stand or fall on its own merits, and not be smuggled through shrouded
in elaborate stage dressing. The wisdom of this stipulation was immediately apparent and the two most promising early creations, by Kenneth
Macmillan and David Poole, were in no way hampered by the restric-
tion. The belief of Ninette de Valois in this respect is the same as that
once put forward by Tamara Karsavina: "It is interesting to note," said
the great ballerina, "that material restrictions in stage matters tend to
stimulate ingenuity. I won't deny that material security is essential to
the proper *development* of the theatre, but in some of its initial stages
poverty may be a blessing if it leads to relying on art's own means and
not on outside help."

Dancers, as well as choreographers, are encouraged to spread their
wings in the Sadler's Wells Theatre Ballet, which is essentially a company of soloists or potential soloists. A *corps de ballet* of the dimensions
needed at Covent Garden is not required at Sadler's Wells and nearly
every dancer has opportunities to appear in solo parts at one time or
another. When vacancies occur, Ninette de Valois, Ailne Phillips, Ursula
Moreton and Peggy van Praagh discuss the talent available in the School

and decide which dancers are best suited to go to Sadler's Wells and which will be most useful at Covent Garden. Size, style and personality all affect the decision, but once made it is not irrevocable. There is great flexibility in the personnel of both companies and the interchange is now in both directions. Some dancers are unhappy in the large company and prefer to be bigger fish in the smaller pond at Sadler's Wells. When this happens they are allowed to return, providing there is a vacancy. On the other hand, some dancers (David Blair, for example) soon feel cramped on the smaller stage at Islington and long for the wide spaces of Covent Garden. If they have ability and are needed at the Opera House they are encouraged to make the change.

The Sadler's Wells Theatre Ballet gave its first performance on 8th April 1946, at Sadler's Wells, dancing in *Promenade*, *Assembly Ball* (created for them by Andrée Howard) and the third act of *Casse Noisette*, in which Margaret Dale and Norman Thomson appeared as guest artists. The faithful Sadler's Wells audience cheered the young dancers loudly, but the general atmosphere was too boisterous and unprofessional to be pleasing. Three dancers stood out: June Brae and Leo Kersley, who had returned to lead the company, and an exceptionally promising sixteen-year-old named Anne Heaton. Later a new ballet by Celia Franca, *Khadra*, was staged in striking *décor* by Honor Frost, and this brought forward another talented youngster, Sheilah O'Reilly. *Façade* and *The Gods go a'Begging* were revived that season and also *Les Sylphides* and *Le Spectre de la Rose* (the last for the economical sum of £19, 12s. 2d.).

Revivals from the old repertoire were an economic necessity, but they imposed a hard task on the young dancers. As long as they appeared mainly in works handed down from an older sister they were regarded as "children" and their performances were more like school dancing displays than professional programmes. Well-trained and attractive, with much vivacity and talent, they could not overcome memories of their predecessors in the old ballets, and in these circumstances the experience given to the dancers was of doubtful value. The older members of the audience sighed for the good old days and the new audience was so indulgent that at times it seemed to consist entirely of fond mothers, aunts or cousins of the dancers.

The first year's work showed a loss, but was not too unsatisfactory when account was taken of all the expenses of formation and rehearsal. In 1946–47 the Arts Council increased its guarantee against loss to £5,000 and the following productions, by six different choreographers, were added to the repertory: *The Vagabonds*, *The Catch*, *Mardi Gras*, *Bailemos*, *The Haunted Ballroom*, *La Fête Étrange* and *Adieu*. *La Fête Étrange* (made originally for the London Ballet in 1940 by Andrée Howard) was particularly important as it demonstrated for the first time that the dancers were artists of quality and sensitivity, capable of interpreting adult choreography. Nadia Nerina and Donald Britton made their names that season.

The financial results were not good, however, and drastic changes in policy were made during 1947–48. London performances by the ballet company were cut down to Saturday *matinées* only (except for first performances of new ballets to which the Press was invited) and frequent short winter tours were undertaken with two pianos. The new ballets produced were *Parures, Children's Corner, Valses Nobles et Sentimentales, Les Rendezvous, Tritsch-Tratsch* and some small *divertissements*. Elaine Fifield arrived from Australia to join the company and from South Africa came Patricia Miller, Maryon Lane and David Poole. The new policy reduced the net deficiency on the season at Sadler's Wells Theatre to £1, 2s. 9d., and in view of these improved results, and also the improvement in performances, more ballet programmes were given in London during 1948–49. The company was beginning to dance together as a unit and to acquire a real personality of its own. Three of the new productions that year found immediate popular favour, namely a revival of *Capriol Suite*, Andrée Howard's *Selina*, and a Spanish *divertissement* called *Jota Toledana*, which Pirmin Trecu and Sheilah O'Reilly danced to thunderous applause.

Disaster overtook the company on tour that summer, when in the early hours of Thursday, 2nd June, the Theatre Royal at Hanley, where they were dancing, was destroyed by fire. All the scenery and most of the costumes of the entire touring repertory of nine ballets was destroyed and the dancers lost most of their personal belongings as well, but that same afternoon they began rehearsing a "post-fire" repertory in the Tabernacle Rooms in Hanley and the following Monday night the curtain went up punctually at the New Theatre in Hull. The little group of apprentice dancers was learning to be a professional company.

The process of growing up continued during the 1949–50 season. John Cranko had proved himself to be the most promising of the young choreographers tried out at Sadler's Wells and he was given full opportunity to develop his craft. During 1949–50 he produced *Sea Change* and *Beauty and the Beast* and the following season *Pastorale, Pineapple Poll* and the strangely poetic *Harlequin in April*. With these three ballets the company seemed to find itself, and during the 1951 Festival of Britain season they had the satisfaction of hearing their new ballets praised more highly than the new productions being offered at Covent Garden. They had proved themselves as an independent creative organisation; as in the case of the original company, the process had taken just five years.

The American tour in 1951–52 completed the process of turning the Sadler's Wells Theatre Ballet into a completely professional company with a distinct personality and assurance. It also gave them a temporary false size and magnificence for American audiences expected a twin and not a younger sister, so that a full-length *Coppélia* and part of *Casse Noisette*, decorated refulgently by Cecil Beaton, were thought essential for box-office purposes. Both productions remained in the repertoire after the American tour and earned their place, for they suited the young dancers well. It was in *Coppélia* that Svetlana Beriosova established herself securely in the affections of the general London ballet audience. Patricia Miller and Elaine Fifield were also delightful Swanildas and Stanley Holden and David Poole gave performances of Dr. Coppelius which their seniors at Covent Garden could not surpass.

Since 1952 the company has continued its true work of encouraging and developing young artists. Cranko out-reached his grasp in *Reflection* but followed it with an utterly theatrical, moving and beautiful ballet, *The Lady and the Fool*, which became the first work created for this company to be taken into the Covent Garden repertoire. Alfred Rodrigues has contributed an interesting and successful dramatic ballet, *Blood Wedding*, and Kenneth Macmillan shows choreographic talent of exceptional promise and sensitivity.

Lively and able young dancers come to the fore continually and exhibit characteristics which differ from but are complementary to those of the dancers at Covent Garden. In general the dancers of the Sadler's Wells Theatre Ballet seem more robust and more carefree than their seniors but the actual style of dancing is the same. As dancers move on to Covent Garden fresh opportunities are given all the time to those who remain. There is thus an atmosphere of continual change, of work in progress rather than the perfection of an end-product. Inevitably some people look upon this situation as unsettling, but the strength of the company and its place in the organisation depends upon a state of fluidity—providing that it can, at the same time, hold the interest and confidence of the public. If the Sadler's Wells Theatre Ballet remained unchanged in personnel for five years it might blossom into a magnificent ballet company, but the state of affairs thereafter, both at Covent Garden and at Sadler's Wells, might well be artistic bankruptcy or stalemate.

APPENDIX C

THE WORK OF SADLER'S WELLS OVERSEAS

THE Sadler's Wells Ballet, through its dancers, teachers and choreographers, has contributed to the art of ballet in many countries, and the demand for advice and assistance grows all the time. Olive Deacon in South Africa and Laurel Martyn in Australia were among the first Wells-trained dancers to do pioneer teaching work overseas. More recently Richard Ellis and Christine du Boulay have settled in Chicago; Lorna Mossford is working in the same city; Leo Kersley is in Rotterdam; and Stanley Holden and Stella Farrance are in South Africa. The old advertising slogan of the ballet teacher "late Imperial Russian Ballet" is fast giving way to a new credit line: "former soloist in the Sadler's Wells Ballet."

Two dancers who have appointments of particular importance are Alan Carter and Gordon Hamilton. Alan Carter was appointed *Ballettmeister* at the Munich Staatsoper on 1st September 1954, with complete control over all artistic and administrative policies relating to the internal running of the ballet company. His title represents the Continental use of the term "ballet master," for he is responsible for choreography as well as the rehearsal of ballets. Gordon Hamilton went to the Vienna State Opera Ballet in 1955 as classical ballet instructor to the entire Vienna Ballet (75 dancers) and principal teacher in the ballet school (80 children). He was also engaged specifically to revive the great classical ballets and readily acknowledges that it was his six years' work under Ninette de Valois with the Sadler's Wells Ballet which gave him his knowledge of the classics and equipped him for the job.

It was during the first Canadian tour of the Sadler's Wells Ballet in 1949 that plans were laid for the establishment of a Canadian National Ballet. Ninette de Valois was consulted and gave her opinion that a Canadian ballet could certainly succeed, provided that it was well run and genuinely national in character, with dancers drawn from throughout the Dominion. At her suggestion, Celia Franca was invited to Canada for an exploratory visit and she was sufficiently encouraged by the talent she discovered to take on the task of organising and running the company.

The general policy of the National Ballet of Canada is to employy

Canadian artists and through them to provide first-class cultural entertainment for audiences at home and abroad. There are many fine young
dancers available, trained by Canadian teachers and eager to work in
their own country instead of having to look for employment in one of
the British or American ballet companies. The repertoire has been built
on similar lines to that of the Sadler's Wells Ballet. To a firm foundation
of classical ballets have been added some examples of Fokine's choreography, some contemporary works of importance (such as Tudor's
Jardin aux Lilas), and original ballets created specially for the company.
By the beginning of 1955 the National Ballet was strong enough to
undertake a full-length production of *Le Lac des Cygnes* and could show
in Vancouver-born Lois Smith an Odette-Odile worthy of the title
ballerina.

Turkey

Perhaps the most interesting and important missionary work by the
Sadler's Wells organisation, however, is that which is being done in
Turkey. During the war years the distinguished opera producer Carl
Ebert spent much time in Turkey and was almost solely responsible for
the establishment there of a National Opera Company. The early performances of opera were given in halls in the "Halkevi," centres of
education and culture established by the People's Party under Kemal
Ataturk, as there was no theatre suitable for productions of Western
opera. After the war, however, plans were laid for the conversion of a
large modern exhibition building in Ankara into a national theatre and
concert hall, and the Turkish Government began to consider the need
for the formation of a ballet company. Through the intermediary of the
British Council the Turkish Government approached Sadler's Wells
and the R.A.D. for advice and in the summer of 1947, Ninette de Valois
went out to Turkey to make a tour of inspection. She visited primary
and secondary schools, colleges, physical training and folk-lore institutes
and other educational centres, and conferred with the head of the Fine
Arts Administration and the Minister of Education. Any idea of setting
up a company at once was out of the question, but the Turkish Government was prepared to wait ten years until the right sort of material
could be discovered and trained and agreed to establish a school of ballet.
De Valois recommended Joy Newton as Director and she was later
joined by Audrey Knight and afterwards Margaret Graham (who has
now returned to teach at the Sadler's Wells School).

The first school of ballet in Turkey opened at Yesilkoy, 24 kilometres
outside Istanbul, on 6th January 1948 (on Twelfth Night, exactly seventeen years after the reopening of Sadler's Wells Theatre). Seventeen

girls and eleven boys, between the ages of seven and ten, were accepted and provided with a general education as well as ballet classes. For three years the ballet school remained at Yesilkoy but in March 1950, it was made a branch of the State Conservatoire with the same status as the existing sections for Opera, Music and Drama, and moved to Ankara. Free tuition is given and subsequently the dancers are under an obligation of service to the State, with graded salary scales as they obtain their diplomas.

The children are taught Dalcroze eurhythmics, as it helps them to understand Western music, which both melodically and rhythmically is totally new to them. Although the teaching is British, however, the aim is that the eventual ballet company shall be Turkish, drawing on the great wealth of native folk dance and performing ballets created by Turkish composers, artists and dancers.

As yet only annual recitals are attempted, for the course takes nine years and there will be no graduates until 1957. In May 1951 Ninette de Valois flew out to Turkey to arrange for the students a little ballet called *The Leaf of Happiness,* which was based on a Turkish legend concerning Keloglan, a character familiar to all Turkish children. Other ballets have been arranged by Joy Newton and by Beatrice Appleyard, who succeeded her as Director in November 1951. In the autumn of 1954 Molly Lake and her husband Travis Kemp arrived in Ankara and took over the Directorship from Beatrice Appleyard. The number of students is now about fifty and the initial prejudice against girls working in the theatre is gradually being overcome. From the beginning many talented boys were attracted to the School and each year the quality of the material seems to improve. The larger number of students is among the lower age groups, and the years 1958, 1959 and 1960 are expected to be interesting and valuable ones from the point of view of graduation. In these years ballet in Turkey should begin to develop and it is hoped that creative ability will also emerge. One nineteen-year-old boy already shows potentialities for becoming a major figure in Turkish Ballet, both as a dancer and as a choreographer.

The progress that has been made in Turkey is the more remarkable when it is remembered that ballet is virtually unknown in that country. The walls of the ballet studios in the School are hung with photographs of great dancers, but the children have never seen them dance. Films are used for instructional purposes and in 1949 four Sadler's Wells dancers, Moira Shearer, Michael Somes, Anne Heaton and Alexander Grant, went out to Turkey to give some demonstration performances and appear with some of the children at the annual recital. Nevertheless, many of the young Turkish students show a natural talent for ballet and a real love and appreciation of its possibilities. The eventual union of the Western style of dancing with the native culture is something that is bound to be of interest and importance, and it will have historic significance as the first national ballet ever to have been founded *from* England.

APPENDIX D

THE SADLER'S WELLS BALLET BENEVOLENT FUND

THE Sadler's Wells Ballet Benevolent Fund, founded by Arnold Haskell in 1936, exists to help members and ex-members of the Sadler's Wells Ballet companies, whether dancers or otherwise, when through sickness or other cause they are in need of assistance. It also assists members of the companies and students of the School by means of grants for special tuition, medical expenses, or maintenance, and provides pensions for members of the companies who, on retiring from their service, may need the help of the Fund. From time to time in the past it has also done valuable work in assisting with the expenses of productions, guaranteeing seasons which seemed financially precarious and making good losses (such as those sustained in Holland in 1940).

The "national" status of the Sadler's Wells Ballet does not carry with it as yet any state pension such as is provided for dancers at the Paris Opéra, the Royal Theatre in Copenhagen, or the Soviet state theatres. Dancers at the Bolshoi Theatre in Moscow, for example, are entitled to retire from the stage after twenty years' service at a pension equal to 50 per cent of their last salary. This pension is added to their salary if they continue to work in the theatre either as character dancers or teachers.

English ballet is scarcely old enough to have met the problem in an acute form as yet, but the needs of retiring dancers will one day have to be provided for. The Benevolent Fund depends on voluntary contributions and draws its largest income from gala benefit performances given by the dancers themselves and warmly supported by their regular audience in London. The Trustees of the Fund are Arnold L. Haskell, Dame Ninette de Valois, and Donald Albery. The Honorary Secretary and Treasurer is The Hon. Eveleigh Leith, 15 Walton Street, London, S.W.3.

APPENDIX E

LIST OF BALLETS PRODUCED BY THE SADLER'S WELLS BALLET

Titles in bold type indicate ballets which are still performed by either the Sadler's Wells Ballet or the Sadler's Wells Theatre Ballet. This does not mean, however, that none of the others will ever be revived.

Date	Theatre	Ballet	Choreographer	Composer	Designer
13.12.28	Old Vic	Les Petits Riens	de Valois	Mozart	O. P. Smyth
9.5.29	Old Vic	The Picnic (The Faun)	de Valois	Vaughan Williams	Hedley Briggs
19.12.29	Old Vic	Hommage aux Belles Viennoises	de Valois	Schubert	O. P. Smyth
18.12.30	Old Vic	Suite de Danses	de Valois	Bach, *arr.* Goossens	O. P. Smyth
5.5.31	Old Vic	Danse Sacrée et Danse Profane	de Valois	Debussy	Hedley Briggs
(First produced by the Camargo Society, 19.10.30.)					
5.5.31	Old Vic	The Jackdaw and the Pigeons	de Valois	Hugh Bradford	William Chappell
21.5.31	Sadler's Wells	Cephalus and Procris	de Valois	Grétry	William Chappell
(First produced by the Camargo Society, 25.1.31.)					
22.9.31	Old Vic	**Job**	de Valois	Vaughan Williams	Gwendolen Raverat
(First produced by the Camargo Society, 5.7.31. Revived at Covent Garden with *décor* by John Piper, 20.5.48.)					
22.9.31	Old Vic	Regatta	Ashton	Gavin Gordon	William Chappell
23.11.31	Sadler's Wells	Fête Polonaise	de Valois and Judson	Glinka	O. P. Smyth
(Camargo *décor* by Edmond Dulac first used at Sadler's Wells, 11.6.32.)					
16.12.31	Old Vic	The Jew in the Bush	de Valois	Gordon Jacob	Bertrand Guest
30.1.32 (*Matinée*)	Sadler's Wells	Narcissus and Echo	de Valois	Arthur Bliss	William Chappell

Date	Theatre	Ballet	Choreographer	Composer	Designer
30.1.32 (Matinée)	Sadler's Wells	Rout	de Valois	Arthur Bliss	
(Produced by the Academy of Choreographic Art, 22.1.28. Revived at the Abbey Theatre, Dublin, and for Camargo Society, 25.1.31.)					
4.3.32	Old Vic	**Le Spectre de la Rose**	Fokine, rev. Dolin	Weber	Costumes after Bakst
(Revived by Karsavina with *décor* by Rex Whistler, New Theatre, 1.2.44. Produced by Sadler's Wells Theatre Ballet, 6.5.46.)					
4.3.32	Old Vic	Italian Suite	de Valois and Dolin	Lalo and Cottrau	Phyllis Dolton
8.3.32	Sadler's Wells	**Les Sylphides**	Fokine, rev. Markova	Chopin	
(Revived with *décor* by Hugh Stevenson during season 1935–36. Original Benois setting acquired 1937.)					
11.3.32	Sadler's Wells	The Enchanted Grove	Rupert Doone	Ravel and Debussy	Duncan Grant
19.3.32	Sadler's Wells	Nursery Suite	de Valois	Elgar	Nancy Allen
(Revived for scholarship pupils, with *décor* by William Chappell, 14.12.36.)					
5.10.32	Sadler's Wells	Le Lac des Cygnes, Act II	Petipa-Ivanov, rev. Markova and Dolin	Tchaikovsky	
11.10.32	Sadler's Wells	Douanes	de Valois	Geoffrey Toye	Hedley Briggs
(Revived with *décor* by Sophie Fedorovitch, 29.10.35.)					
17.10.32	Old Vic	The Lord of Burleigh	Ashton	Mendelssohn, *arr.* Edwin Evans	George Sheringham
(First produced by Camargo Society, 15.12.31 Revived with *décor* by Derek Hill, 7.12.37.)					
1.11.32	Sadler's Wells	The Origin of Design	de Valois	Handel, arr. Beecham	William Chappell
(First produced by the Camargo Society, 11.6.32.)					
15.11.32	Sadler's Wells	The Scorpions of Ysit	de Valois	Gavin Gordon	Sophie Fedorovitch
(First produced in a different version by the Academy of Choreographic Art, 26.11.28.)					

Date	Theatre	Ballet	Choreographer	Composer	Designer
17.1.33	Sadler's Wells	Pomona	Ashton	Constant Lambert	Vanessa Bell
		(First produced by the Camargo Society, 19.10.30. Revived with *décor* by John Banting, 23.9.37.)			
7.2.33	Sadler's Wells	The Birthday of Oberon	de Valois	Purcell, *arr.* Lambert	John Armstrong
21.3.33	Sadler's Wells	**Coppélia,** (Acts I and II)	Ivanov, rev. Sergueeff	Delibes	Edwin Calligan
		(Revived with addition of third act and some new choreography by Sergueeff and *décor* by William Chappell, 15.4.40. Revived with new *décor* by William Chappell at Covent Garden, 25.10.46. New production by Ninette de Valois with *décor* by Osbert Lancaster, 2.3.54. Produced by Sadler's Wells Theatre Ballet with *décor* by Loudon Sainthill, 4.9.51.)			
26.9.33	Sadler's Wells	The Wise and Foolish Virgins	de Valois	Kurt Atterberg	William Chappell
24.10.33	Sadler's Wells	**Carnaval**	Fokine, rev. Evina	Schumann	Elizabeth and Marsh Williams
		(Revived with *décor* and costumes after Bakst, 27.9.35, and again at Princes Theatre, 10.10.44. Produced by Sadler's Wells Theatre Ballet, 21.5.47.)			
30.10.33	Old Vic	La Création du Monde	de Valois	Milhaud	Edward Wolfe
		(First produced for the Camargo Society, 26.4.31. Revived, with white faces, 12.3.35.)			
5.12.33	Sadler's Wells	**Les Rendezvous**	Ashton	Auber, arr. Lambert	William Chappell
		(Revived with new *décor* by William Chappell, 16.11.37. Produced by Sadler's Wells Theatre Ballet, 26.12.47.)			
1.1.34	Old Vic	**Giselle**	Coralli-Perrot, rev. Sergueeff	Adam	Barbara Allen
		(Revived with new *décor* by William Chappell, 27.5.35. Again, with new *décor* by James Bailey, at Covent Garden, 12.6.46, and again, 13.9.51.)			
30.1.34	Sadler's Wells	**Casse Noisette**	Ivanov, rev. Sergueeff	Tchaikovsky	Hedley Briggs
		(Revived with new *décor* by Mstislav Dobujinsky, 8.1.37. Produced by Ashton for Sadler's Wells Theatre Ballet with *décor* by Cecil Beaton, 11.9.51.)			

Date	Theatre	Ballet	Choreographer	Composer	Designer
3.4.34	Sadler's Wells	**The Haunted Ballroom**	de Valois	Geoffrey Toye	Motley
(Produced by Sadler's Wells Theatre Ballet, 7.1.47.)					
9.10.34	Sadler's Wells	The Jar	de Valois	Casella	William Chappell
20.11.34	Sadler's Wells	**Le Lac des Cygnes (in four acts)**	Petipa-Ivanov, rev. Sergueeff	Tchaikovsky	Hugh Stevenson
(Revived with some new designs by Stevenson, 21.12.37. New production with *décor* by Leslie Hurry, New Theatre, 7.9.43. New production, also with *décor* by Hurry, Covent Garden, 18.12.52.)					
19.12.34	Old Vic	Uncle Remus	Sara Patrick	Gordon Jacob	Hugh Stevenson
26.3.35	Sadler's Wells	Rio Grande	Ashton	Constant Lambert (words by Sacheverell Sitwell)	Edward Burra
(First produced by the Camargo Society, 29.11.31, in a slightly different version under the name *A Day in a Southern Port*.)					
20.5.35	Sadler's Wells	**The Rake's Progress**	de Valois	Gavin Gordon	Rex Whistler, after Hogarth
(Revived with *décor* re-designed by Rex Whistler, 27.10.42. Presented at Covent Garden, 18.3.46, inside a frame designed by Oliver Messel. Produced by Sadler's Wells Theatre Ballet, 18.6.52.)					
8.10.35	Sadler's Wells	**Façade**	Ashton	Walton	John Armstrong
(First produced by the Camargo Society, 26.4.31. New *décor* and costumes by John Armstrong, 23.7.40. Produced by Sadler's Wells Theatre Ballet, 29.4.46.)					
26.11.35	Sadler's Wells	Le Baiser de la Fée	Ashton	Stravinsky	Sophie Fedorovitch
10.1.36	Sadler's Wells	The Gods go a'Begging	de Valois	Handel, *arr.* Beecham	Hugh Stevenson
(Produced by the Sadler's Wells Theatre Ballet, 6.6.46.)					
24.1.36	Sadler's Wells	Siesta	Ashton	Walton	Argyle's costume by Matilda Etches
11.2.36	Sadler's Wells	**Apparitions**	Ashton	Liszt, *arr.* Lambert	Cecil Beaton
(Revived with some new designs by Beaton at Covent Garden, 24.3.49.)					

Date	Theatre	Ballet	Choreographer	Composer	Designer
17.4.36	Sadler's Wells	Barabau	de Valois	Rieti	Edward Burra
13.10.36	Sadler's Wells	Prometheus	de Valois	Beethoven, *arr.* Lambert	John Banting
10.11.36	Sadler's Wells	Nocturne	Ashton	Delius	Sophie Fedorovitch
16.2.37	Sadler's Wells	**Les Patineurs**	Ashton	Meyerbeer, *arr.* Lambert	William Chappell
27.4.37	Sadler's Wells	**A Wedding Bouquet**	Ashton	Lord Berners (words by Gertrude Stein)	Lord Berners
15.6.37	Théâtre des Champs Élysées	**Checkmate**	de Valois	Arthur Bliss	E. McKnight Kauffer

(Revived, re-designed by McKnight Kauffer, Covent Garden, 18.11.47.)

Date	Theatre	Ballet	Choreographer	Composer	Designer
27.1.38	Sadler's Wells	Horoscope	Ashton	Constant Lambert	Sophie Fedorovitch
7.4.38	Sadler's Wells	Le Roi Nu	de Valois	Jean Françaix	Hedley Briggs
10.5.38	Sadler's Wells	The Judgment of Paris	Ashton	Lennox Berkeley	William Chappell
10.11.38	Sadler's Wells	Harlequin in the Street	Ashton	Couperin	Derain

(Enlarged version of ballet first presented at the Arts Theatre, Cambridge, 28.2.37.)

Date	Theatre	Ballet	Choreographer	Composer	Designer
2.2.39	Sadler's Wells	**The Sleeping Princess**	Petipa, rev. Sergueeff	Tchaikovsky	Nádia Benois

(Revived in a new production with *décor* by Oliver Messel under the title **The Sleeping Beauty,** for reopening of Covent Garden, 20.2.46.)

Date	Theatre	Ballet	Choreographer	Composer	Designer
27.4.39	Sadler's Wells	Cupid and Psyche	Ashton	Lord Berners	Sir Francis Rose
23.1.40	Sadler's Wells	Dante Sonata	Ashton	Liszt	Sophie Fedorovitch, after Flaxman
24.4.40	Sadler's Wells	The Wise Virgins	Ashton	Bach, *arr.* Walton	Rex Whistler
4.7.40	Sadler's Wells	**The Prospect Before Us**	de Valois	Boyce, *arr.* Lambert	Roger Furse

(Produced by Sadler's Wells Theatre Ballet, 13.2.51.)

Date	Theatre	Ballet	Choreographer	Composer	Designer
27.1.41	New Theatre	The Wanderer	Ashton	Schubert-Liszt	Graham Sutherland
28.5.41	New Theatre	Orpheus and Eurydice	de Valois	Gluck	Sophie Fedorovitch

Date	Theatre	Ballet	Choreographer	Composer	Designer
14.1.42	New Theatre	Comus	Helpmann	Purcell, *arr.* Lambert	Oliver Messel
19.5.42	New Theatre	Hamlet	Helpmann	Tchaikovsky	Leslie Hurry
24.11.42	New Theatre	The Birds	Helpmann	Respighi	Chiang Yee
6.4.43	New Theatre	The Quest	Ashton	Walton	John Piper
25.10.43	King's, Edinburgh	Promenade	de Valois	Haydn, *arr.* Edwin Evans	Hugh Stevenson
	(Produced by Sadler's Wells Theatre Ballet, 8.4.46.)				
20.6.44	New Theatre	Le Festin de l'Araignée	Andrée Howard	Roussel	Michael Ayrton
26.10.44	Princes	Miracle in the Gorbals	Helpmann	Arthur Bliss	Edward Burra
10.4.46	Covent Garden	Adam Zero	Helpmann	Arthur Bliss	Roger Furse
24.4.46	Covent Garden	**Symphonic Variations**	Ashton	César Franck	Sophie Fedorovitch
12.11.46	Covent Garden	Les Sirènes	Ashton	Lord Berners	Cecil Beaton
6.2.47	Covent Garden	**The Three Cornered Hat**	Massine (revival)	Manuel da Falla	Picasso
27.2.47	Covent Garden	**La Boutique Fantasque**	Massine (revival)	Rossini, *arr.* Respighi	Derain
26.11.47	Covent Garden	**Mam'zelle Angot**	Massine (revival)	Lecocq	Derain
11.2.48	Covent Garden	**Scènes de Ballet**	Ashton	Stravinsky	Beaurepaire
25.6.48	Covent Garden	Clock Symphony	Massine	Haydn	Bérard
25.11.48	Covent Garden	**Don Juan**	Ashton	R. Strauss	Edward Burra
23.12.48	Covent Garden	**Cinderella**	Ashton	Prokofiev	Jean-Denis Malclès
20.2.50	Covent Garden	**Don Quixote**	de Valois	Roberto Gerhard	Edward Burra
5.4.50	Covent Garden	**Ballet Imperial**	Balanchine (rev.)	Tchaikovsky	Eugene Berman
5.5.50	Covent Garden	**Ballabile**	Petit	Chabrier, *arr.* Lambert	Antoni Clavé
5.4.51	Covent Garden	**Daphnis and Chloë**	Ashton	Ravel	John Craxton
9.7.51	Covent Garden	**Tiresias**	Ashton	Constant Lambert	Isabel Lambert
12.12.51	Covent Garden	Donald of the Burthens	Massine	Ian Whyte	MacBryde and Colquhoun
4.3.52	Covent Garden	A Mirror for Witches	Howard	Denis Aplvor	Howard and Norman Adams

Date	Theatre	Ballet	Choreographer	Composer	Designer
4.4.52	Covent Garden	**Bonne-Bouche**	Cranko	Arthur Oldham	Osbert Lancaster
3.9.52	Covent Garden	**Sylvia**	Ashton	Delibes	Robin and Christopher Ironside
3.3.53	Covent Garden	**The Shadow**	Cranko	Dohnanyi	Piper
9.4.53	Covent Garden	**Veneziana**	Howard	Donizetti, *arr.* ApIvor	Sophie Fedorovitch
2.6.53	Covent Garden	**Homage to the Queen**	Ashton	Malcolm Arnold	Oliver Messel
23.8.54	Empire, Edinburgh	**The Firebird**	Fokine, rev. Grigorieff, Tchernicheva and Karsavina	Stravinsky	Gontcharova
6.1.55	Covent Garden	**Rinaldo and Armida**	Ashton	Malcolm Arnold	Peter Rice
6.1.55	Covent Garden	**Variations on a Theme of Purcell**	Ashton	Britten	Peter Snow
1.4.55	Covent Garden	**Madame Chrysan-thème**	Ashton	Rawsthorne	Isabel Lambert
9.6.55	Covent Garden	**The Lady and the Fool**	Cranko (revised version)	Verdi, *arr.* Mackerras	Richard Beer

BIBLIOGRAPHY OF SOURCES

ANTHONY, GORDON. *Markova.* (With a Foreword by Ninette de Valois.) Chatto & Windus, London, 1935.

The Vic-Wells Ballet. (With an Introduction by Ninette de Valois.) Routledge, London, 1938.

The Sleeping Princess. With articles by Constant Lambert, Nadia Benois and Arnold L. Haskell. London, dated 1940, issued 1942.

Robert Helpmann. (With an Introduction by Ninette de Valois.) Home & van Thal, London, 1946.

Margot Fonteyn. (With an Introduction by Ninette de Valois.) Phœnix House, London, 1951.

Alicia Markova. (With an appreciation by Dame Adeline Genée-Isitt.) Phœnix House, London, 1951.

BEATON, CECIL. *Ballet.* Allan Wingate, London, 1951.

BEAUMONT, C. W. *The Vic-Wells Ballet.* Beaumont, London, 1935.

Alicia Markova. Beaumont, London, 1935.

Complete Book of Ballets. Putnam, London, 1937.

Supplement to Complete Book of Ballets. Beaumont, London, 1942.

Ballets of To-day (being a second supplement to the *Complete Book of Ballets*). Putnam, London, 1954.

The Sadler's Wells Ballet. Beaumont, London, 1946.

Leslie Hurry. Faber & Faber, London, 1946.

Margot Fonteyn. Beaumont, London, 1948.

Dancers Under My Lens. Beaumont, London, 1949.

BEDELLS, PHYLLIS. *My Dancing Days.* Phœnix House, London, 1954.

BUCKLE, RICHARD. *The Adventures of a Ballet Critic.* Cresset Press, London, 1953.

CHAPPELL, WILLIAM. *Studies in Ballet.* John Lehmann, London, 1948.

Fonteyn, Impressions of a Ballerina. Rockliff, London, 1951.

CHUJOY, ANATOLE. *The Dance Encyclopedia.* A. S. Barnes & Co., New York, 1949.

COTON, A. V. *A Prejudice for Ballet.* Methuen, London, 1938.

DENT, EDWARD J. *A Theatre for Everybody.* T. V. Boardman, London and New York, 1945.

DE VALOIS, NINETTE. *Invitation to the Ballet.* John Lane, The Bodley Head, London, 1937.

DE ZOETE, BERYL. "Frederick Ashton, Background of a Choreographer." *Horizon,* Volume vi. No. 31, July 1942.

DOLIN, ANTON. *Divertissement*. Sampson Low, Marston & Co., London, undated (1931).

Ballet Go Round. Michael Joseph, London, 1938.

Markova—Her Life and Art. W. H. Allen, London, 1953.

GRAY, TERENCE. *Dance-Drama: Experiments in the Art of the Theatre*. W. Heffer & Sons, Cambridge, 1926.

GUEST, IVOR. *The Romantic Ballet in England*. Phœnix House, London, 1954.

HARROD, R. F. *The Life of John Maynard Keynes*. Macmillan & Co., London, 1951.

HASKELL, ARNOLD and RICHARDSON, P. J. S. (Editors). *Who's Who in Dancing, 1932*. The Dancing Times, London, 1932.

HASKELL, ARNOLD L. *Ballet: A Complete Guide to Appreciation*. Penguin Books, Harmondsworth, Middlesex, 1938.

Balletomane's Album. A. & C. Black, London, 1939.

Ballet to Poland (Editor). A. & C. Black, London, 1940.

The National Ballet. A History and a Manifesto. A. & C. Black, London, 1943.

Miracle in the Gorbals. The Albyn Press, Edinburgh, 1946.

Sadler's Wells Ballet Books (Editor): 1. *The Sleeping Beauty*. 2. *Job* and *The Rake's Progress*. 3. *Hamlet* and *Miracle in the Gorbals*. 4. *Carnaval, Le Spectre de la Rose*, and *Les Sylphides*. The Bodley Head, London (for the Governors of the Sadler's Wells Foundation). 1949.

In His True Centre: An Interim Autobiography. A. & C. Black, London, 1951.

The Ballet Annual (Editor). A Record and Year Book of the Ballet, Nos. 1–9. A. & C. Black, London, 1947–1954.

HOWLETT, JASPER. *Talking of Ballet*. Philip Allan, London, undated (1935).

HUROK, S. *S. Hurok Presents: A Memoir of the Dance World*. Hermitage House, New York, 1953.

LAMBERT, CONSTANT. *Music Ho!* Faber & Faber, London, 1934.

LANDSTONE, CHARLES. *Off-Stage*. Elek Books, London, 1953.

LEEPER, JANET. *English Ballet*. Penguin Books, London, 1944.

LYNHAM, DERYCK. *Ballet Then and Now*. Sylvan Press, London, 1947.

MANCHESTER, P.W. *Vic-Wells: a Ballet Progress*. Victor Gollancz, London, 1942.

MANDINIAN, EDWARD. *The Fairy Queen*. With a preface by Professor E. J. Dent, and articles by Constant Lambert and Michael Ayrton. John Lehmann, London, 1948.

MARSHALL, NORMAN. *The Other Theatre*. John Lehmann, London, 1947.

NEATBY, KATE. *Ninette de Valois and the Vic-Wells Ballet*. British-Continental Press, London, 1934.

PERUGINI, MARK EDWARD. *A Pageant of the Dance and Ballet*. Jarrolds, London, 1935.

SHAWE-TAYLOR, DESMOND. *Covent Garden*. Max Parrish, London, 1948.

SITWELL, OSBERT. *Laughter in the Next Room*. Macmillan & Co., London, 1949.

Noble Essences. Macmillan & Co., London, 1951.

SPARGER, CELIA. "Physiotherapy at the Sadler's Wells School of Ballet." *Physiotherapy*, January, 1952.

STEIN, GERTRUDE. *Everybody's Autobiography*. Heinemann, London, 1938.

STOREY, ALAN. *Arabesques*. Newman Wolsey, London, 1948.

VAN DAMM, VIVIAN. *To-night and Every Night*. Stanley Paul & Co., London, 1952.

VAN PRAAGH, PEGGY. *How I Became a Ballet Dancer*. Nelson, London, 1954.

WHITE, FRANKLIN. *Sadler's Wells Ballet Goes Abroad*. Faber & Faber, London, 1951.

WILLIAMS, HARCOURT (Editor). *Vic-Wells: The Work of Lilian Baylis*. Cobden-Sanderson, London, 1938.

PERIODICALS

The Dancing Times, edited by Philip J. S. Richardson, from 1926 to date

Ballet, edited by Richard Buckle, 1939–1952.

Ballet To-day, edited by P. W. Manchester, 1946–1952.

Covent Garden Books, edited by Anthony Gishford or Michael Wood, Nos. 1, 2, 3, 5, 6, 8.

The Old Vic-Sadler's Wells Magazine, 1931–39.

Dance News of New York, edited by Anatole Chujoy, 1942 to date.

Souvenir Books of the Sadler's Wells Ballet's American tours, 1949, 1950–51, 1953.